Modern Internet Regulations and Laws in Educational Technology

Bruce L. Mann
Memorial University, Canada

IGI Global
Scientific Publishing
Publishing Tomorrow's Research Today

Vice President of Editorial	Melissa Wagner
Director of Acquisitions	Mikaela Felty
Director of Book Development	Jocelynn Hessler
Production Manager	Mike Brehm
Cover Design	Jose Rosado

Published in the United States of America by
IGI Global Scientific Publishing
701 East Chocolate Avenue
Hershey, PA, 17033, USA
Tel: 717-533-8845
Fax: 717-533-7115
Website: https://www.igi-global.com E-mail: cust@igi-global.com

Library of Congress Cataloging-in-Publication Data

Names: Mann, Bruce Leslie, 1950- author
http://id.loc.gov/authorities/names/no2001012204
http://id.loc.gov/rwo/agents/no2001012204
Title: Modern Internet regulations and laws in educational technology / authored by Bruce L. Mann.
Description: Hershey : IGI Global Scientific Publishing, 2026. | Includes bibliographical references and index. | Summary: "This book focuses on legal issues that arise from the information society supported by computers, wireless communications and the Internet, including killfies, social media suicides, on-campus shootings, and the surveillance culture in schools and universities. It also explores the domain name system and the tension between a course author's right to be recognized and remunerated for their original intellectual expression and the public's right to freely use the material for learning"-- Provided by publisher.
Identifiers: LCCN 2025009773 (print) | LCCN 2025009774 (ebook) | ISBN 9798337331263 hardcover | ISBN 9798337331270 paperback | ISBN 9798337331287 ebook
Subjects: LCSH: Educational technology--Law and legislation http://id.loc.gov/authorities/subjects/sh2001006306 | Internet in education--Law and legislation http://id.loc.gov/authorities/subjects/sh00001083 | Information technology--Law and legislation http://id.loc.gov/authorities/subjects/sh2011004309 | Intellectual property http://id.loc.gov/authorities/subjects/sh85067167
Classification: LCC K3740 .M365 2025 (print) | LCC K3740 (ebook) | DDC 344/.07--dc23/eng/20250307
LC record available at https://lccn.loc.gov/2025009773
LC ebook record available at https://lccn.loc.gov/2025009774

British Cataloguing in Publication Data
A Cataloguing in Publication record for this book is available from the British Library.

For my parents, Leslie and Jeanne Mann, who never discouraged my writing.
Bruce Mann
June 2, 2025

Table of Contents

Preface vi

Section 1
Information Technology Law in Educational Technology

Chapter 1
Lawful Trojan Horse 1

Chapter 2
Hacking Then and Now 23

Chapter 3
Surveillance and Moral Panic 57

Chapter 4
Delete, Delete, Hang Up on Social Media 83

Chapter 5
Legal Initiatives: The U.K., the U.S., and Europe 113

Chapter 6
Legal Initiatives: Canada 129

Chapter 7
Adverse Effects Discrimination 159

Chapter 8
Online Dispute Resolution: Structured Argument and Technology 175

Chapter 9
Online Dispute Resolution: The Presentation Design and Evaluation 197

Section 2
Intellectual Property Law in Educational Technology

Chapter 10
Copyright Distinctions: The Lone Ranger and The Posse 221

Chapter 11
Trademarks: The Badges of Origin 253

Chapter 12
Academic Domain Names 277

Chapter 13
Patent Law and the Entrepreneurial University 299

Compilation of References 329

About the Author 381

Index 383

Preface

The title of the book describes the intersection of two related disciplines, "Educational Technology" and "Information Technology Law". "Educational Technology" is the study and ethical practice of facilitating learning and improving performance through the creation, use, and management of technological processes. "Information Technology Law", also known as "IT Law", "Internet Law, "Cyberlaw" and "Technology Law", is the study of wrongful acts over the Internet. "Educational Technology Law" is a new and emerging sub-discipline in Education. Who should read Educational Technology Law? The primary readership are non-lawyers - School Administrators, Computing Educators, Instructional Designers, Teachers, Librarians, and graduate students with an interest in Educational Technology Law.

INFORMATION TECHNOLOGY LAW IN EDUCATIONAL TECHNOLOGY

Chapter One provides an overview of Trojan Horse attacks and the legal framework in the U.K., the U.S., and other jurisdictions used to address them, including federal statutes, executive directives, and regulatory measures. In Europe, each country relies on its own legal framework for counterterrorism. Veeam's *Cyber-Resilient Data Recovery Strategy Report (*Veeam Software, *2024)* has recommended that organizations invest in education and training programs to empower their workforce to become active participants in the cybersecurity risk management process. The *CrowdStrike Global Threat Report (Kurtz, 2025)* also recommended educating users in security awareness training. A recent U.S. study on the *Global Cost of Ransomware (2025)* recommended that training programs focus on how users can make better decisions about their email content, social media replies, and web browsing habits.

Chapter Two defines "hacking" as the act of exploiting weaknesses in a computer system or network to gain unauthorized access to personal or organizational data. Hackers employ various techniques to conceal their tracks by routing their attacks through the machines of unsuspecting individuals, sometimes involving thousands of devices. A *Certified Ethical Hacker* is a qualification earned by demonstrating the skills needed to access a computer system and assess its vulnerabilities using the same methods and tools as a malicious hacker, but lawfully and legitimately. Several universities offer short-term intensive training in cybersecurity, known as "boot camps," as well as Associate's, Bachelor's, Master's, and even Ph.D. programs in Cybersecurity.

Chapter Three explores the recent surveillance culture in schools, highlighting the tension between data collection and monitoring and students' privacy. Proponents contend that surveillance tools safeguard students by detecting bullying, violence, or mental health concerns like depression and suicidal thoughts. Critics argue that ongoing surveillance damages student trust and conditions them to see intrusion as normal. The chapter reviews a recent report by the *American Civil Liberties Union* (Marlow, Greytak, Duarte & Sun, 2023), which shows that, despite claims from technology companies, surveillance in American schools has not improved student safety.

Chapter Four opens by describing recent lawsuits alleging that social media companies have deliberately designed their platforms to be addictive, worsening a mental health crisis among youth. An associated concern is screen time that excludes time needed for schoolwork. Other issues concern doxing and swatting. "Doxing" is a cyber-attack that publicly reveals someone's private or personally identifiable information online without their consent. "Swatting" is a false report that alerts authorities. Although swatting reports have decreased, the trend over time indicates that violent incidents in schools continue to increase year over year.

Chapter Five is an introduction to the Paisley Snail case in the U.K., and the law of negligence without a contract, which, in the U.S., mandates that school administrators take reasonable steps to protect students from foreseeable harm despite potential breaches of privacy and freedom of speech, hence the controversy over the *Kids Online Safety Act (KOSA).* Critics say KOSA is essentially a disguised censorship that would suppress lawful, important speech online, especially for young people

In ***Chapter Six.*** In Canada, courts have long recognized that schools owe a duty of care to students, with the standard being that of a reasonably prudent parent. The legal framework for ensuring safe schools includes the *Criminal Code of Canada (1985), the Young Offenders Act (1985), the Canadian Charter of Rights and Freedoms (1982),* provincial school acts, and the common law. The Department of Justice in Canada has compiled a list of twelve Criminal Code offences that may apply to instances of cyberbullying. One or more criminal cases are associated with each of the twelve Criminal Code offences.

Chapter Seven explores a landmark case of adverse effects discrimination, which describes a situation where a government policy that seems to treat everyone equally actually harms a protected group. The policy in question aimed to get recipients under 30 into training programs and work while they developed valuable technological skills to secure permanent jobs. Unfortunately, the government only allowed 30,000 training placements for the 85,000 welfare recipients under 30.

Chapter Eight. Online Dispute Resolution has evolved from an experimental concept to a widely adopted system in e-commerce, courts, and international dispute resolution. The future of ODR will likely involve greater AI automation, smart contracts, and global legal frameworks to handle digital disputes more efficiently. This chapter briefly describes the short history of ODR technology platforms like *Modria* that use AI to assist in dispute resolution, and some of the more prevalent systems for classifying online dispute resolution, such as WIPO's "Expedited Arbitration," a time-sensitive form of arbitration.

Chapter Nine. Conflict is the raison d'être of online disputes, especially when the dispute is difficult, emotional, or there's a large amount of money in dispute, there are many parties, or when there is a perception of judicial bias or prejudice (Katsh & Rule, 2016). Substandard presentations made by inarticulate and lesser dispute-wise disputants can make the bargaining conditions uneven (American Arbitration Association, 2006) compared to professionally presented cases by more dispute-wise respondents (Hörnle, 2002). During an online dispute, sound cues can be used to resolve a conflict and balance the conditions (Mann, 2009).

INTELLECTUAL PROPERTY LAW IN EDUCATIONAL TECHNOLOGY

Part B of the book is an exploration into the tension between a course author's right to be recognized and remunerated for their original intellectual expression and the public's right to use their material for learning. This tension became the incentive for the first copyright law of 1710, called the "Statute of Anne", which was passed for the encouragement of learning by vesting the copies of printed books in the authors or purchasers of such copies. Understanding the different types of intellectual property is important information that Educational Technologists would do well to acquire. Readers will encounter questions such as, "Why are there different types of legal protection for various parts of an online course?"

Chapter Ten concerns copyright law, which stands as the world's most recognizable form of intellectual property and yet is perhaps the most misunderstood in educational technology. What isn't always clear is that *copyright* constitutes an economic right, distinct from *les droits d'auteur* or the moral rights of the author, which is the right to be acknowledged for one's expression. The chapter makes a brief review of relevant copyright institutions and goes on to describe ownership of online course materials and methods developed either by a solo faculty member or "Lone Ranger" who does everything or by several committee members, or by a "Posse," who contribute variously, each contribution providing a different measure of lawful protection (Mann, 2020).

Chapter Eleven describes trademark law. In the U.S., trademarks are used to identify and distinguish one source of goods from another, making it easier for a consumer to discern who has produced a particular product or service. Unregistered trademarks in common law countries such as the U.S., the UK, Australia, Canada, and New Zealand all rely on the law of Passing Off, wherein one party's goods or services are presented in a way that, whether intentionally or not, misrepresents their goods or services with those of another party.

Chapter Twelve describes academic domain names as text-based Internet addresses used in a Web browser to denote the physical location of a particular host server. Academic domain names are unregistered trademarks that aim to distinguish the programs and services of one university from those of another. A student organization can request to have its domain name hosted by the University. The UDRP is responsible for resolving disputes between domain name owners and trademark holders.

Chapter Thirteen investigates the use of patent law in educational technology, focusing on faculty and student innovations within the entrepreneurial university and the potential rewards of protecting intellectual property. In the United States, a patent grants exclusive rights to a person or organization to develop and use an original invention or method for a limited time. Whereas copyrights are registered at the *Library of Congress* with the *U.S. Copyright Office,* patents and trademarks are registered at the *United States Patent and Trademark Office* (USPTO, 2007). For one to be granted a patent, an invention must be useful, novel, and not obvious. Universities are incentivized to establish start-ups when they hold the patent rights to an invention.

RECURRING THEMES

Jurisdictional Differences

One of the four recurring themes in the book concerns the jurisdictional differences in regulations, laws, and legal systems across different geographical areas and legal authorities. These differences can impact governance, law enforcement, and individual rights. For example, jurisdictional differences exist between countries that follow common law (e.g., the U.S. and the U.K.) and those that follow civil law (e.g., Quebec and France), which shape how laws are created, interpreted, and enforced.

A second jurisdictional difference in the book concerns criminal law and the varying penalties for identity theft and school shootings, which impact law enforcement and legal proceedings. A third jurisdictional difference arises in the protection of intellectual property rights, such as patents and copyrights, which can vary in scope and duration between jurisdictions, as well as the enforceability of mashups under copyright, patent, and trademark law. A fourth jurisdictional difference in the book concerns breaches of contract law, terms of liability, and remedies for violations, which vary by jurisdiction.

Educational Technology

A second recurring theme in the book is Educational Technology, a generic descriptor intended to include other terms such as instructional technology, educational media, learning technology and other variants (Reiser & Ely, 1997). Educational Technology fills multiple roles in higher education (Shurville, Browne & Whitaker, 2009) and school systems (Murphy, Allred & Brescia, 2017). Ritzhaupt, Martin, Pastore, and Kang's (2018) survey of Educational Technology professionals showed key competencies in instructional design, project management, learning theories, and working in teams. The focus of this book concerns modern Internet regulations and laws in Educational Technology.

There have been many classifications of the Educational Technologist over the years. Luppicini (2005) described the Educational Technologist as someone who uses a goal-oriented, systems approach to problem-solving educational performance that utilizes tools, techniques, theories, and methods to design, develop, and evaluate human and mechanical resources to facilitate and guide changes in educational systems and practices. Others have labelled Educational Technologists according to their contributions to industry (Woo, 2015), higher education (Shurville, Browne & Whitaker, 2009), or public education (Lorenz, Kikkas, & Laapere, 2014).

Still others (Bardone, Tonni & Chounta, 2020) theorized the role of the Educational Technologist as a "variety-handler" using Stafford Beer's Viable System Model and Ross Ashby's Law of Requisite Variety to attenuate variety in the school environment. I prefer Professor Mitchell's original classification of the Educational Technologist as working in any one of five roles, depending on their occupation and training (Mitchell, 1975), that is, as: *Learning Consultant, Learning Resources Manager, Educational Materials Producer, Educational Systems Developer,* or *Educational Planner.*

Learning Consultant

A Learning Consultant, whether onsite or itinerant, conducts needs assessments of administrators and academic and non-academic staff for knowledge gaps, then leads the design, development, implementation, and evaluation of workshops, courses, and team-based learning both online and onsite. The Learning Consultant's job may entail developing checklists, interview schedules or surveys for the needs assessments, acquiring and organizing learning materials, analyzing data to develop instructional analyses, drawing learning hierarchies for managers or staff, writing instruction and feedback, producing animations and speech cues, and conducting formative evaluations.

Learning Resources Manager

A Learning Resources Manager, also known as the School Librarian or Media Specialist, is an onsite, work-from-home, or hybrid position. This person might administer a help desk for instructors and Media Centre Staff, manage a learning support system in a department, or purchase educational resources within a fiscal budget. The Learning Resources Manager's job may entail project coordination and marketing. The Learning Resources Manager can also deliver educational communications and services, research, communicate with external agencies, and evaluate effectiveness.

Educational Materials Producer

An Educational Materials Producer, also known as an Instructional Designer, can conduct research and upload or write expository text for online courses, workshops, or seminars, including design documents, instructional media, storyboards, and scripts for multimedia products. The Materials Producer edits video clips, adds narration, directions, hints, feedback, and reminders for hybrid and online courses, and formulates recommendations for improvement. The Materials Producer job may entail content identification and product formulation, message design, production, and evaluation, which will inevitably rely on subject matter experts and require some teaching or training.

Educational Systems Developer

An Educational Systems Developer can bring their full-stack development experience, and knowledge of TypeScript, React, Node.js, GraphQL, and PHP to work on the digital education products used in schools and distributed through Web and mobile platforms. The Educational Systems Developer collaborates with other developers to alpha and beta test, AGILE prototype with the team, and formative evaluate the products with faculty and students.

Educational Planner

The Educational Planner analyzes, plans, and manages large educational systems, including the significant components of an organization (e.g., facilities planning of a multi-campus college). The Educational Planner will develop and manage a development team that may comprise instructional developers, content writers, videographers and/or graphic designers. The job may entail *macro-system development,* comprising locations for laying cable to data closets for computer modems, hubs, routers, and printers. The Educational Planner's responsibilities may entail tracking the control system that manages, commands, directs, or regulates the behaviour of other devices or systems.

Expert-Peer Assessment and Formula

A third recurring theme in the book is the expert-peer online assessment that appears in Chapter 13 for Peer-To-Patent and Chapter 9 for resolving online disputes. Chapter 9 recommends the expert-peer assessment formula during peer-to-patent as a standard method of counting the quantitative evaluations (Mann, 2020). Claimants and respondents post their cases and arguments anonymously and independently in a secure area. Next, two or more peers review the cases independently, assign a numerical mark, and then write comments on each presentation without knowing the expert's assessment. A designated expert assigns a numerical mark and writes comments independently of the peers. The scores are tallied and compared with the comments. The validity of the method and formula was tested (Mann, 2005) and further developed, adding anonymity and accountability factors to reduce ceiling effects and friendship marking (Wadhwa, Schulz & Mann, 2006).

Attentional Networks

A fourth recurring theme in the book is the new perspective on attention. Three chapters discuss this new perspective on attentional networks: Chapter 2 on cybersecurity training, Chapter 8 on online dispute resolution, Chapter 11 on trademarks, and Chapter 12 on academic domain names. Brain-scanning technologies offer us a new perspective on attention when disputants are trying to resolve a conflict online or when ethical hackers decide to hack back. Attention is not one thing as previously thought, but three interdependent networks comprising an attentional system: *alerting attention, orienting attention* and *executive attention* (Corbetta & Shulman, 2002; Posner & Petersen, 2012). Understanding these differences can be crucial for educators, school systems, and universities that operate across borders to navigate legal challenges effectively (Mann, 2025).

Bruce L. Mann
Memorial University, Canada

REFERENCES

Audal, J., Lu, Q., & Roman, P. (2008). Computer Crimes. *The American Criminal Law Review*, *45*(2), 233–274.

Bardone, E., Tonni, T., & Chounta, I.-A. (2020). The educational technologist as a variety-handler, Videoconferencing for remote music lessons as a case in point. *Education and Information Technologies*, *25*(5), 4015–4040. DOI: 10.1007/s10639-019-10091-5

Canadian Charter of Rights and Freedoms. (1982). Justice Laws Website, https://laws-lois.justice.gc.ca/eng/const/page-15.html

Corbetta, M., & Shulman, G. L. (2002). Control of goal-directed and stimulus-driven attention in the brain. *Nature Reviews. Neuroscience*, *3*(3), 201–215. DOI: 10.1038/nrn755 PMID: 11994752

Criminal Code of Canada. (1985). https://laws-lois.justice.gc.ca/PDF/C-46.pdf

Fandom (2019). Information technology law, *The IT Law Wiki,* retrieved 12 August 2019, https://itlaw.wikia.org/wiki/Information_technology_law

Hörnle, J. (2002). Online Dispute Resolution in Business-to-Consumer E-commerce Transactions. Journal of Information, Law and Technology. (2).

illumio (2025). The global cost of ransomware: Study, https://cdn.prod.website-files.com/63e25fb5e66132e6387676dc/679bc0561e9ed06d78d5d9c0_The-Global-Cost-of-Ransomware-Study.pdf

Katsh, E., & Rule, C. (2016). What we know and need to know about online dispute resolution, South Carolina Law Review, 67(2), 329-344, https://scholarcommons.sc.edu/sclr/vol67/iss2/10 67(2)

Kids Online Safety Act (KOSA), H.R. 7891 (2023). https://www.congress.gov/bill/118th-congress/senate-bill/1409/text

Kurtz, G. (2025). *CrowdStrike global threat report.* CrowdStrike, Inc.

Lorenz, B., Kikkas, K., & Laapere, M. (2014). The role of Educational Technologist in implementing new technologies at school, *International Conference on Learning and Collaboration Technologies,* 288–296. DOI: 10.1007/978-3-319-07485-6_29

Luppicini, R. (2005). A Systems Definition of Educational Technology in Society. *Journal of Educational Technology & Society*, *8*(3), 103–109.

Mann, B. L. (2005). Making your own educational materials, part I. *International Journal of Instructional Technology & Distance Learning, 10*(2).

Mann, B. L. (2006). Conducting formative evaluations of online instructional material. In Mann, B. L. (Ed.), *Selected styles in web-based educational research* (pp. 232–242). Information Science Publishing. DOI: 10.4018/978-1-59140-732-4.ch016

Mann, B. L. (2008). The evolution of multimedia sound. *Computers & Education, 50*(4), 1157–1173. DOI: 10.1016/j.compedu.2006.11.002

Mann, B. L. (2009). Smoothing some wrinkles in online dispute resolution. *International Journal of Law and Information Technology, 17*(1), 83–112. DOI: 10.1093/ijlit/ean017

Mann, B. L. (2020). *Applying Internet Laws and Regulations to Educational Technology, Public Policy and Administration Book Series*. IGI Global.

Mann, B. L. (2025). Speech cueing curricular multimedia: Instructional design that activates the orienting attention network. *Journal of Interactive Learning Research, 36*(2), 191–214. DOI: 10.70725/115195dejbne

Marlow, C., Greytak, E., Duarte, K., & Sun, S. (October 2, 2023). Digital dystopia: The danger in buying what the edtech surveillance industry is selling, report, *American Civil Liberties Union,* https://www.aclu.org/publications/digital-dystopia-the-danger-in-buying-what-the-edtech-surveillance-industry-is-selling

Mitchell, P. D. (1975). The discernible educational technologist. *Programmed Learning and Educational Technology, 12*(5), 306–325. DOI: 10.1080/1355800750120510

Murphy, C. A., Allred, J. B., & Brescia, W. F. (2018). The role of educational technology professionals as perceived by building administrators. *Education and Information Technologies, 23*(1), 179–191. DOI: 10.1007/s10639-017-9593-2

Posner, M. I., & Petersen, S. E. (1990). The attention system of the human brain. *Annual Review of Neuroscience, 13*(1), 25–42. DOI: 10.1146/annurev.ne.13.030190.000325 PMID: 2183676

Posner, M. I., & Petersen, S. E. (2012). The attention system of the human brain: 20 years after. *Annual Review of Neuroscience, 21*(35), 73–89. PMID: 22524787

Reiser, R. A., & Ely, D. P. (1997). The field of Educational Technology as reflected through its definitions. *Educational Technology Research and Development, 45*(3), 63–72. DOI: 10.1007/BF02299730

Ritzhaupt, A., Martin, F., Pastore, R., & Kang, Y. (2018). Development and validation of the educational technologist competencies survey: Knowledge, skills, and abilities. *Journal of Computing in Higher Education, 30*(1), 1–31. DOI: 10.1007/s12528-017-9163-z

Shurville, S., Browne, T., & Whitaker, M. (2009). Accommodating the newfound strategic importance of educational technologists within higher education: A critical literature review. *Campus-Wide Information Systems, 26*(3), 201–231. DOI: 10.1108/10650740910967384

U.S. Department of Justice. (1989). *Computer Crime: Criminal Justice Resource Manual.* National Institute of Justice.

Veeam Software. (2024). Building a cyber-resilient data recovery strategy, https://webobjects2.cdw.com/is/content/CDW/cdw/on-domain-cdw/brands/veeam/veeam-nist-security-white-paper-cdw.pdf?ci=8722

Wadhwa, G., Schulz, H., & Mann, B. L. (2006). Effects of anonymity and peer-accountability during online peer assessment. In Mann, B. L. (Ed.), *Selected Styles In Web-Based Educational Research* (pp. 300–331). Information Science Publishing. DOI: 10.4018/978-1-59140-732-4.ch020

Woo, D. (2015). Reviewing and constructing categories for Educational Technology professionals. *International Journal of Education and Development Using Information and Communication Technology, 11*(1), 148–163.

Young Offenders Act. (1985). https://laws.justice.gc.ca/PDF/Y-1.pdf

Section 1
Information Technology Law in Educational Technology

Chapter 1
Lawful Trojan Horse

ABSTRACT

A Trojan horse is concealed from you and triggered when you launch your favourite computer application, like an email greeting card. School districts are especially susceptible. Unlike malicious Trojan horses, however, lawful Trojans are used under strict regulations, oversight, and judicial approval. Law enforcement, a government agency, or an authorized entity will deliberately deploy a lawful Trojan horse to conduct surveillance or gather information from specific targets within legal frameworks. The United States has developed a thorough legal framework to tackle cyberattacks, including federal statutes, executive directives, and regulatory measures. The U.S. has categorized school cyberattacks into five major types: data breach, ransomware, email compromise, distributed denial of service (DDoS), and invasion attacks. Several countries in Europe have recommended that law enforcement agencies learn to hack into computers and mobile devices to access their data. But what type of training is required: prevention or retaliation? Who requires this training?

TROJAN HORSE

A Trojan Horse is a malicious computer program disguised as legitimate or harmless software, designed to trick users into downloading and installing it. Once installed, the Trojan Horse can infect the device by stealing data, installing additional malware, or granting attackers unauthorized access. A Trojan Horse payload may either cause temporary harm or permanent damage, such as logging keystrokes to steal passwords or credit card numbers.

You can do whatever you want with a Trojan horse on a compromised computer. That computer would be as good as your own. You would own it. Now imagine you owned 100,000 such computers scattered worldwide, each running and being looked

DOI: 10.4018/979-8-3373-3126-3.ch001

after in someone's home, office, or school. Imagine that with just one command, you could tell these computers to do whatever you wanted (Solomon & Evron, 2006).

AMERICAN SCHOOLS CYBERATTACKED

Between April 2016 and November 2022, 1,600 cyberattacks targeting school districts were reported across the U.S., according to *K12 Security Information eXchange* (2023). From January 2023 to June 2024, 83 ransomware attacks on school districts were reported on K12 schools; 21 of these attacks took place in the first half of the year, according to CBS News (Quraishi, Sen, Pham, Corral & Johnston, 2024).

Figure 1. Cyberattacks on U.S. school districts

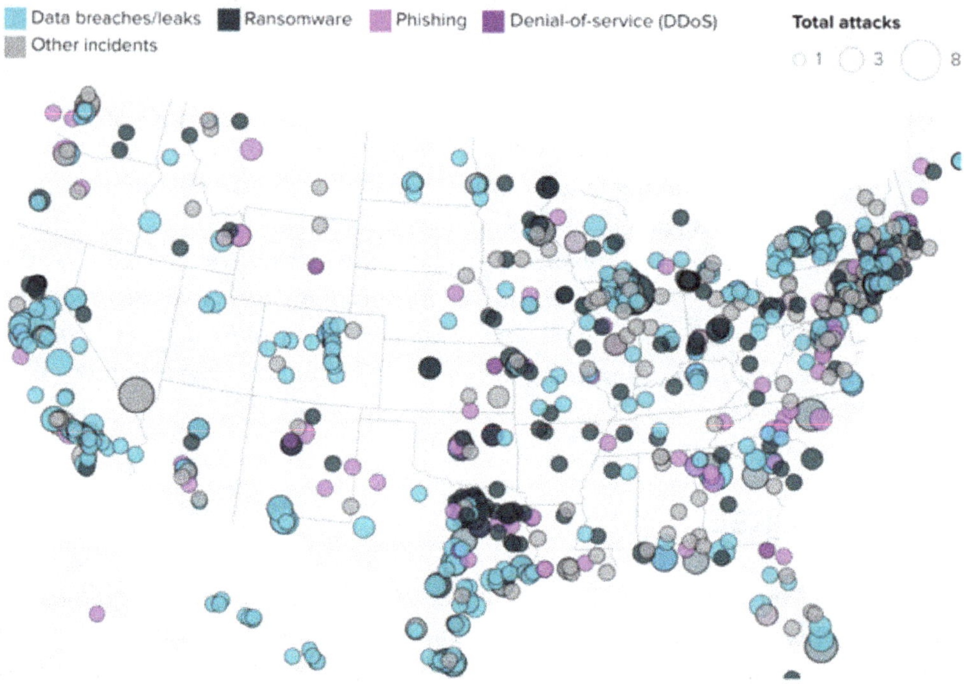

(K12 Security Information eXchange, 2023)

In May 2024, the *U.S. Department of Education* launched the *Government Coordinating Council for the Education Facilities Subsector*, an unprecedented collaboration among federal, state, local, and tribal governments to safeguard schools from cybersecurity threats.

Schools and districts are being targeted because they are resource-rich for bad actors, looking for being able to attack whole systems, try to shut down systems, try to get information, personally identify information or just prevent the district from normal functioning on all different levels (*U.S. Deputy Secretary of Education* Cindy Marten, 2024).

CYBERATTACK TYPES

The *Multi-State Information Sharing and Analysis Center (MS-ISAC)* mission in the United States is to enhance the overall cybersecurity posture of *U.S. State, Local, Tribal, and Territorial (SLTT)* government organizations through coordination, collaboration, cooperation, and improved communication. The *Cybersecurity and Infrastructure Security Agency (CISA)* is part of the *United States Department of Homeland Security.* It is responsible for cybersecurity and infrastructure protection at all levels of government, coordinating cybersecurity programs with U.S. states and strengthening the government's cybersecurity defences against private and nation-state hackers. Research from MSISAC and CISA indicates that school cyberattacks are categorized into one of five major types.

Data Breach

Although not primarily driven by financial motives, data breaches entail the exfiltration and disclosure of personally identifiable information belonging to students, faculty, staff, families, and third-party vendors. This information can subsequently be exploited to initiate further cyberattacks, such as those listed below.

Ransomware

A ransomware attack can lock users out of an entire school environment, disrupting learning until systems are restored. These attacks often lead to class cancellations, significant remediation costs, reputational harm, and ongoing concerns about an institution's ability to defend against future attacks. Furthermore, since many modern ransomware incidents involve data exfiltration as well as encryption, there is a genuine risk of personally identifiable information (PII) being leaked online, regardless of whether a ransom is paid. Additionally, following a ransomware attack, leaders of educational institutions face scrutiny from faculty, students, and public officials.

Ransomware attacks are frequently executed using a Trojan. Ransomware is a type of malware designed to restrict access of an organization or individual to their computer files. By encrypting these files and demanding a ransom payment for the decryption key, cyber-attackers place organizations in a situation where paying the ransom becomes the easiest and most economical method to regain access to their files. Some variants have introduced additional functionalities—such as data theft—to further motivate ransomware victims to pay the ransom. The increase in ransomware incidents was the focus of a White House summit, which convened law enforcement, educators, and technology providers to discuss strategies for protecting the nation's schools.

Unauthorized access to computers or networks using malware, compromised access credentials, phishing, or similar methods is a serious concern. Network intrusions are generally carried out to gain entry to systems and exfiltrate sensitive information for financial exploitation. Additionally, network intrusions can block access to computers, networks, or critical infrastructure until a ransom is paid. Ransoms are typically demanded in cryptocurrency (United States Secret Service, 2024).

Email Compromise (BEC)

In a school BEC attack, a hacker gains control of an internal email account and exploits that access for financial gain. Typically, after obtaining access, the threat actor will send out fraudulent emails soliciting the transfer of funds from within the educational organization or from various third-party vendors with which the educational institution partners.

Distributed Denial of Service (DDoS)

A DDoS attack involves multiple compromised systems overwhelming a target on a network, such as a server or website, resulting in a denial-of-service error. This prevents legitimate users from accessing the network. DDoS attacks on educational institutions can lead to significant losses in learning time, as essential systems and resources remain unavailable until IT and security teams can resolve the situation. When students and teachers cannot access their applications or data, it effectively cancels school and resembles the cyber equivalent of a snow day.

Invasion (Online Class and School Meeting)

Invasion attacks significantly disrupt educational institutions that rely on remote tools for activities like online learning and virtual PTA meetings. Hackers infiltrate these unsecured class sessions and meetings to interrupt them with various harmful content, including hate speech and pornography.

TROJANS IN THE NEWS

A few examples illustrate the activity of a Trojan Horse computer program (Munson, 2019; Webroot, 2019). For an update on Trojan Horses, visit FANDOM.

Jackpot Panda

In 2023, JACKPOT PANDA continued to use trojanized executables to deploy malicious utilities or second-stage implants. Starting in May 2023, the adversary utilized a trojanized installer for CloudChat, a China-based chat application popular among illegal, Chinese-speaking gambling communities in Mainland China. The trojanized installer, hosted on CloudChat's website, initiated a multi-step process that ultimately deployed XShade — a novel implant with code that overlaps with JACKPOT PANDA's unique CplRAT implant.

Zeus

Zeus aka Zbot, is a successful trojan horse virus with 3.6 million infections and numerous variants employed to execute various types of attacks. Even today, the Zeus trojan and its variants are a major cybersecurity threat, and many computers that run Microsoft Windows are still at risk (Baker, 2023). *Zeus* is challenging to detect when using older antivirus programs and outdated security software, as it conceals itself through powerful stealth techniques. This is often regarded as the main reason why the *Zeus* trojan has evolved into the most potent botnet on the Internet. It is perhaps best known for its successful breach of the *U.S. Department of Transportation*. Zeus shares several characteristics with *Wajam,* including encrypted code sections, dynamic library loading, and encrypted payloads.

In September 2011, the FBI launched an investigation into a modified version of the *Zeus Trojan* known as *GameOver Zeus (GOZ).* The most dangerous Zeus variant, *Gameover Zeus,* allows the user to launch a potentially devastating ransomware attack on a computer running Microsoft Windows (Baker, 2023). It is believed that *GOZ* was responsible for over one million computer infections, resulting in financial losses that exceeded $100 million.

The *United States Department of State's Transnational Organized Crime Rewards Program* is offering a reward of up to $3 million for information leading to the arrest and conviction of Evgeniy Mikhailovich Bogachev, aka "lucky12345" (FBI, 2025). In August 2012, Bogachev was indicted under the nickname "lucky12345" by a federal grand jury in the District of Nebraska on charges of conspiracy to participate in racketeering activity, bank fraud; conspiracy to violate the *Computer Fraud and Abuse Act*; conspiracy to violate the *Identity Theft and Assumption*

Deterrence Act; and aggravated identity theft (FBI, 2020). In May 2014, Bogachev was indicted using his real name by a federal grand jury in the Western District of Pennsylvania. In the same month, a criminal complaint was filed in the District of Nebraska that connected the nickname "lucky12345" to Bogachev and charged him with conspiracy to commit bank fraud.

Wamjam

Wamjam utilizes anti-analysis and evasion techniques, including the daily release of metamorphic variants, steganography, obfuscation of string and library calls, encrypted strings and files, an array of deep and diversified junk code, polymorphic resources, valid digital signatures, randomized filenames and root certificate Common Names, as well as encrypted updates (Carné de Carnavale & Mannan, 2019). Moreover, Wajam employs anti-detection measures that range from disabling the *Windows Malicious Software Removal Tool* to excluding its installation paths from Windows Defender, and in some cases, leveraging rootkit capabilities to conceal its installation folder from users.

Password-Stealing Trojan Horse

Wirenet is a password-stealing Trojan notable for being one of the first to target Linux and MacOS users, many which were migrated from Windows operating systems due to perceived security flaws. Researchers from a Russian security company, Doctor Web, discovered a backdoor Trojan that specifically targets Linux and MacOS users (Zorz, 2012). Dubbed *Wirenet*, this Trojan records passwords entered in Firefox, Chrome, Chromium, and Opera (but not Safari). The *Wirenet Trojan* also functions as a keylogger, meaning it sends the gathered keyboard input data to intruders. Additionally, the *Wirenet Trojan* steals passwords entered by users in Opera, Firefox, Chrome, and Chromium, as well as passwords stored by applications such as "Thunderbird", "SeaMonkey", and "Pidgin".

The *U.S. Justice Department* accused more than 100 individuals of purchasing and using "Blackshades," a password-stealing Trojan horse designed to spy on victims through their web cameras, steal files and account information, and log victims' keystrokes (Krebs, 2014). Blackshades was an effective and user-friendly tool for remotely compromising and surveilling targets. Early in its development, researchers at CitizenLab discovered that Blackshades was being used to spy on activists seeking to overthrow the regime in Syria. The product was sold through open hacker forums and even included an active user forum where customers could receive assistance in configuring and using this powerful surveillance tool. Although in recent years, a license for Blackshades sold for several hundred Euros, earlier versions of the product were sold on PayPal for just $40.

Mobile Banking Trojan

The Mobile Banking Trojan steals login credentials from mobile banking apps or replaces legitimate apps with malicious ones. Banking Trojans rely on impersonation. Upon launch, the Trojan displays a seemingly legitimate login page for the banking app it is masquerading as, requiring the victim to enter their banking credentials or credit card details, which are then sent to the attacker's remote server (Ying, 2019). A more advanced tactic employed by some Banking Trojans involves login pages dynamically loaded from a remote server based on the legitimate banking apps installed on the device. Thus, the attacker only needs one banking Trojan to infiltrate a victim's device, enabling them to steal credentials from multiple banks. Android banking trojans are a serious cyber threat to everyday users that, through clever trickery, steal passwords and drain bank accounts. "Android/Trojan.Bank.SharkBot" is a Malwarebytes' detection name for a family of banking Trojans and their droppers that target Android devices, including "Spy.Banker.MYT", ".Spy.Vultur", ".Dropper.Xeno", ".Agent.PWSCR", ".Spy.Brat", and ".Bankbot" (MalwareBytes, 2025).

Who Can You Trust?

Citadel is a banking Trojan that has dominated the malware scene for criminals focused on stealing online banking passwords and draining bank accounts (Constantin, 2012). U.S. prosecutors state that *Citadel* infected over 11 million computers globally, leading to financial losses of at least half a billion dollars. Like most sophisticated banking Trojans, *Citadel* was marketed and sold in hidden, underground cybercrime marketplaces. *Citadel* featured an online technical support system for clients that allowed them to report bugs, suggest and vote on new features for future malware versions, and track trouble tickets that could be addressed by both malware developers and fellow *Citadel* users. Clients could also utilize the system to chat and share insights with other malware users.

It was this very interactive nature of *Citadel's* support infrastructure that ultimately allowed FBI agents to locate and identify Russian hacker Mark Vartanyan, aka "Kolypto" (U.S. Attorney's Office, 2017). The core seller of *Citadel* was nicknamed "Aquabox," and the FBI was eager to identify Aquabox and any programmers he had hired to help develop *Citadel.* Aquabox took the bait and asked the FBI agents to upload a screenshot of the bug they had discovered. European authorities arrested the alleged key players behind the development and deployment of *Citadel.*

Norwegian press reported that a 27-year-old Russian man identified only as "Mark" was arrested in the Norwegian town of Fredrikstad at the request of the FBI (Nielson & Staalesen, 2024). FBI agents had purchased several licenses of *Citadel* from Aquabox. Soon, the agents began suggesting tweaks to the malware that they could use to their advantage. Posing as active users of the malware, FBI agents informed *Citadel* developers that they had discovered a security vulnerability in the web-based interface that *Citadel* customers were using to track or collect passwords from infected systems.

ProRat Trojan

In a lawful intervention, a Trojan horse like *ProRat can* infect a system and open a port on the suspect's computer, allowing the law enforcement agent to log keystrokes, steal passwords, control files, download and run files, format drives, take screenshots, and view system information. *ProRat* is a backdoor Trojan, more commonly known as a Remote Administration Tool. Like other Trojans, it operates using a client and server. ProRat opens a port on the computer, enabling the client to perform numerous operations on the server. *ProRat* is available in both a free and a paid version. *It* is known for having a server that is almost impossible to remove without up-to-date antivirus software (ProRat, 2008).

ProRat includes a server creator with features that enable it to evade detection by antivirus and firewall software, allowing it to run stealthily in the background. The software removes or disables system restore points and displays a fake error message to mislead victims. It is often bundled with other file types, such as image files; when the image file is viewed, the server is installed in the background, undetected if no antivirus software has been installed. *ProRat facilitate*s numerous malicious actions on the suspect's machine.

OTHER TROJAN HORSE PROGRAMS

Backdoor Trojan

A Backdoor Trojan enables hackers to remotely access and control a computer, often to upload, download, or execute files at their discretion. Backdoor malware and viruses bypass authentication procedures to access systems and prevent their presence from being detected (Firewalls.com, 2025). The designation as a Trojan indicates that this form of attack does not reproduce by spreading to additional files after infection. Once a Trojan gains a foothold in a system, it adds itself to the computer's startup routine so that rebooting the computer will not permanently end malicious processes (Sagduyu, Erpek, Ulukus & Yener, 2022).

Backdoor Trojan programs are becoming increasingly popular among malware creators due to the shift in motivation from fame and glory to money and profit (Lau, 2019). *Nivdort* is a backdoor trojan that spreads through spam emails to steal people's passwords. It can also download additional malware onto a computer and modify system settings (Bankvault, 2019). In today's black market economy, a computer with a backdoor can be exploited for various criminal activities that generate income for its controllers. Schemes such as pay-per-install, sending spam emails, and harvesting personal information and identities are all methods of generating revenue (MalwareBytes, 2025).

Exploit Trojan

An Exploit Trojan attack seeks to maintain a persistent presence on the victim's network in search of valuable information. Attackers typically employ it to execute shell commands that create new user accounts. If users refrain from opening spam emails and attachments, the risk involved is limited. However, if the Exploit Trojan installs itself on a computer containing important files, those files are likely to be copied or corrupted (Brown, 2019).

The Trojan W32/PFV-Exploit, detects files containing a Blackhole (F-Secure, 2025). BlackHole is a commercial crimeware designed to be integrated into hacked or malicious sites to exploit web browser vulnerabilities for installing malware of the customer's choice (Krebs, 2016). Russian authorities sentenced Dmitry "Paunch" Fedotov, the developer of the notorious Blackhole exploit kit that's been linked to large amounts of fraud, to seven years in prison - an unusually severe sentence for online crime in that nation. Most of Paunch's customers used the kit to enlarge botnets powered by *Zeus* and *Citadel* banking Trojans, which are typically deployed by cyberheists targeting consumers and small businesses. Dmitry "Paunch" Fedotov was arrested along with a whole team of other cybercriminals who worked to sell, develop, and profit from Blackhole.

Rootkit Trojan

A Rootkit Trojan is a type of malware that conceals itself on a user's computer to stop malicious programs from being detected, which enables malware to remain active on an infected computer for a longer period (Fortinet, 2025). The *ZeroAccess*

Rootkit Trojan, for example, is the most recent rootkit virus to achieve widespread infiltration across numerous computers.

Whereas traditional viruses try to infect and destroy as many systems as possible before being halted by anti-virus software, rootkits focus on keeping the target system functional while placing it under the control of an external party (Eldridge, 2019). They usually grant a remote user administrative privileges, enabling them to manipulate files and maintain control over the target system. Once the target system is under the administrator's control, it turns into a "botnet" or "zombie" computer, aiding the intruder in executing fraudulent activities, downloading additional malware, and opening software back doors for hackers to exploit. Because rootkits operate at the same privilege level as anti-malware software, they are more challenging to remove; the target computer cannot determine which program should possess greater authority to disable the other.

Banker Trojan

A Banker Trojan is designed to target users' banking accounts and financial information. It attempts to steal account data for credit and debit cards, e-payment systems, and online banking systems (Fortinet, 2025). A Banker Trojan can appear to be legitimate software until it is installed. It specifically targets personal information used for banking and other online financial transactions (Kenton, 2018). Its *modus operandi* involves redirecting traffic from banking and financial websites to another site, ostensibly one to which the intruder has access.

Once executed, the software replicates itself onto the host computer, creating folders and setting registry entries each time the system starts up. It searches for specific cookie files related to personal finance that have been stored on the computer by financial websites during internet visits. The Trojan can perform several actions, including running executable files, downloading and sending files remotely, stealing information from the clipboard, and logging keystrokes. It gathers cookies and passwords and may remove itself from the computer when commanded.

DDoS Trojan

The Distributed Denial of Service (DDoS) overloads a network with traffic by sending multiple requests from a computer or a group of computers from numerous different sources to overwhelm a target web address and cause a denial of service (Fortinet, 2025). The DDoS Trojan disables the network by overwhelming it with requests. A large number of machines are deceived into installing the DDoS Trojan, allowing the intruder to remotely gain control of one or all the machines via a client that communicates with a master server (Munson, 2019). By bombarding the target server with traffic, the DDoS Trojan effectively renders it unavailable to legitimate users. The DDoS Trojan is crucial for ensnaring computers into a botnet. Through this primary machine in their zombie network, hackers can direct attacks at particular companies, computers, or websites. DDoS Trojan attacks are often aimed at well-known brand-name products and services. Those behind these attacks may make financial demands to stop their actions.

Who Can You Trust?

In January 2020, Brian Krebs reported in his tech blog *KrebsonSecurity that* a man in Georgia who operated a service designed to protect companies from crippling distributed denial-of-service (DDoS) attacks had pleaded guilty to paying a DDoS-for-hire service to launch attacks against others (Krebs, 2020). Tucker Preston, 22, pleaded guilty in a New Jersey court to one count of damaging protected computers by the transmission of a program, code, or command.

Downloader Trojan

A Downloader Trojan targets a computer that has already been infected by malware, then downloads and installs more malicious programs to it. This could be additional Trojans or other types of malware like adware (Fortinet, 2025). The program is designed to download additional malware, often including more Trojans, onto a device. The *Emotet Downloader Trojan,* for instance, spreads through emails that entice victims into downloading a Word document, which contains macros that, upon execution, use PowerShell to download a malicious payload (Beek, 2017). Emotet has been noted for downloading a range of payloads, including ransomware, Dridex, Trickbot, Pinkslipbot, and various banking Trojans.

COUNTER-CYBERTERRORISM: TRAINING METHODS

U.S. Legal Framework to Address Cyberattacks

The United States has developed a thorough legal framework to tackle cyber-attacks, including federal statutes, executive directives, and regulatory measures. Key components include:

Computer Fraud and Abuse Act (CFAA)

The *Computer Fraud and Abuse Act (CFAA)* was enacted in 1986 to criminalize unauthorized access to computers and networks, covering offences such as computer espionage, fraud, and damage to protected computers. The Act has been amended several times—in 1989, 1994, 1996, and by the *USA PATRIOT Act* in 2001, then in 2002, and again in 2008 by the *Identity Theft Enforcement and Restitution Act*. With each amendment, the types of conduct it encompasses have broadened. In 2015, President Obama proposed expanding the CFAA along with the *Racketeer Influenced and Corrupt Organizations Act (RICO)*. Cloudflare researcher Marc Rogers, Senator Ron Wyden, and Representative Zoe Lofgren opposed this measure on the grounds that it would render many typical internet activities illegal. In 2021, the Supreme Court ruled in *Van Buren v. United States*, providing a narrow interpretation of the phrase "exceeds authorized access."

U.S. Electronic Communications Privacy Act

The *Electronic Communications Privacy Act (ECPA)* extends restrictions on wiretaps to electronic communications, prohibiting unauthorized interception and access to these communications during transmission. "Electronic communications" refers to any transfer of signs, signals, writing, images, sounds, data, or intelligence of any kind that is transmitted in whole or in part by a wire, radio, electromagnetic, photoelectronic, or photo optic system and affects interstate or foreign commerce, but excludes:

- Wire or oral communication
- Communication made through a tone-only paging device
- Communication from a tracking device (as defined in section 3117)
- Electronic funds transfer information stored by a financial institution in a communications system used for the electronic storage and transfer of funds

Title I of the ECPA protects wire, oral, and electronic communications while they are in transit. It establishes requirements for search warrants that are more stringent than those in other contexts. Title II of the ECPA, known as the *Stored Communications Act (SCA)*, safeguards communications held in electronic storage, particularly messages stored on computers. However, its protections are weaker than those of Title I and do not enforce heightened standards for warrants. Title III prohibits the use of pen registers or trap and trace devices to record dialling, routing, addressing, and signalling information used during the transmission of wire or electronic communications without a court order.

Signed into law in March 2022, the *Cybersecurity and Infrastructure Security Agency (CISA)* requires that covered entities in critical infrastructure sectors report significant cyber incidents and ransomware payments to the Cybersecurity and Infrastructure Security Agency (CISA).

Executive Order on Improving the Nation's Cybersecurity

Issued in May 2021, the *Executive Order on Improving the Nation's Cybersecurity* aims to enhance federal cybersecurity standards, improve information sharing between the government and private sector, and advance the adoption of secure software development practices. The United States faces persistent and increasingly sophisticated malicious cyber campaigns that threaten the public sector, the private sector, and, ultimately, the security and privacy of the American people. The federal government must bolster its efforts to identify, deter, protect against, detect, and respond to these actions and actors.

United States Cybersecurity Strategy

Released in March 2023, the *National Cybersecurity Strategy* outlines the U.S. government's approach to securing cyberspace, emphasizing collaboration between public and private sectors and reallocating responsibilities to entities best positioned to manage cyber risks. The Strategy recognizes that robust collaboration, particularly between the public and private sectors, is essential to securing cyberspace. It outlines two fundamental shifts in how the United States allocates roles, responsibilities, and resources in cyberspace.

Various industries are subject to sector-specific cybersecurity regulations. *The Health Insurance Portability and Accountability Act (HIPAA)* protects patient health information and mandates security measures for healthcare organizations. The *Gramm-Leach-Bliley Act (GLBA)* requires financial institutions to protect customer information. The *Securities and Exchange Commission (SEC) Cybersecurity Guidelines* require public companies to disclose significant cybersecurity incidents, including their nature, scope, timing, and impact. These laws and regulations are intended to work together to deter cybercriminal activities, safeguard sensitive information, and strengthen the resilience of critical infrastructure against cyber threats. The trouble with modernized laws is that when a law enforcement agent uploads a Trojan horse on a network, there could be any number of consequences: 1) The Trojan infects a particular individual or group of individuals or specific account names within a particular time frame for a particular reason; 2) The Trojan infects anyone connected to the LAN for a short time, or; The Trojan infects anyone by association, anywhere, anytime, for any reason.

COUNTER-CYBERTERRORISM IN EUROPE

News outlets don't typically cover training methods in counter-cyberterrorism, particularly lawful Trojan attacks. Instead, they focus on recent cyberterrorist incidents, threats, and laws and regulations related to internet privacy or identity theft. However, many countries are proactively addressing this issue to prevent the next major cyberattack by establishing guidelines for how member states should respond. Several news sources, for instance, reported that Germany's *Federal Criminal Police Office (BKA)* was using a Trojan Horse to access the smartphone data of suspected individuals before the information was encrypted (Burack, 2018). Although the desire to retaliate may be strong, hacking back can inadvertently empower the

Europeans are well aware of the necessity for up-to-date cyber-security training. Several countries in Europe have suggested that law enforcement agencies should learn to hack into computers or devices to access their data. But *what type of training is required—prevention or retaliation? Who requires this training?* For example, the Czech Republic provides a broad array of training, education, and awareness-raising initiatives for military personnel, judges and prosecutors, college students, K-12 students, as well as business and government officials. What specific *tasks* should be incorporated into the curriculum for cybersecurity training, education, or awareness-raising?

A WAY FORWARD

This chapter has demonstrated the need for cybersecurity prevention training. Veeam's *Cyber-Resilient Data Recovery Strategy Report* (2024) has recommended that "organizations invest in education and training programs to empower their workforce to become active participants in the cybersecurity risk management process. Clear communication and consistent reinforcement of cybersecurity policies and best practices are essential to create a shared sense of responsibility and vigilance" (Veeam Software, 2024, p.20).

The *CrowdStrike Global Threat Report* (Kurtz, 2025) also recommended educating users. "Provide regular security awareness training. Teach employees to recognize phishing attempts and social engineering tactics" (p.42). Also, "train Help Desk employees to exercise caution when taking password and reset request phone calls made outside of business hours, particularly if an unusually high number of requests is made in a short time frame or if the caller purports to be calling on behalf of a colleague" (p.19).

A study by illumio (2025) on the *Global Cost of Ransomware* recommended, "training programs should focus on how users can make better decisions about the content they receive through email, what they view or click in social media, how they access the web, and other common practices. As no cybersecurity control can prevent every attack, containment and response strategies were equally critical (Illumio, 2025). Some countries are utilizing their resources for training, while others are outsourcing to private firms. All seem eager to learn about the use of a Trojan Horse to collect data remotely from suspects.

What should cybersecurity prevention training look like? Who should provide the training – in-house or outsourced? Instructors who create their own digital materials want clearer directions on developing multimedia for learning, like a new model for making decisions about message design (Bishop, 2014). "Most instructors will use a fairly general and unstructured approach to preparation" (Roblyer 2015, p.5). However, "general principles of instruction, while more useful than general principles of learning, are not apt to be of much help to practitioners" (Gropper, 1983, p.111). Whatever it is, instructors want *something more*, without saying what "something more" entails or how it might be achieved. Assuming that most cybersecurity prevention training will be delivered online by a learning management system, instructors will need to follow a design guideline to get learners practicing skills and then provide error-contingent feedback on their practice. There is, however, more than one way to design instruction for learning. Table 1 summarizes eight design guidelines and corresponding definitions of learning from a multimedia environment.

Table 1. A summary of design guidelines and corresponding definitions of learning from a multimedia environment

Design Guideline	Supporting Definition of Learning
Favorite Feature	We design our programs based on the belief that the attributes in the latest technology are better than those in older technologies (Kurtz, 2025; Stansberry et al, 2019; Veeam, 2024).
Favorite Method	We design our programs based on the belief that one teaching method that is better than any other (e.g. Direct instruction is better than discovery method, Kirschner et al, 2006)
Design-By-Type	We choose to design our drill, tutorial, simulation, game, VR, or AR based on a well-known taxonomy of instructional software (Hannafin & Peck, 1988)
Maximum Impact	We design our programs based on a working memory model: a *visuo-spatial sketchpad* and a *phonological loop* an *episodic buffer* and a *central executive* (Baddeley, 1986)
Balance-the-Input	We design our programs based on a different working memory model: *imagens* for images, and *logogens* for printed or spoken language (Paivio, 1986)
Cognitive Load	We design our programs based on changing intrinsic and extrinsic cognitive loads into germane cognitive load (Chandler & Sweller, 1991; Sweller, 2005)

continued on following page

Table 1. Continued

Design Guideline	**Supporting Definition of Learning**
Structure a Sound Function	We design our programs based on using speech cues to focus attention on visuals on the user interface (Mann, 2009; 2025)
Whatever Works	We design our programs based on the belief that whatever worked for us last time will work this time. Methods over results. One size fits all, based on the intuition of the developers (Abrahamsson et al, 2002; Kupersmith, 2011).

(Mann, 2009)

Regardless of the chosen design guideline, the overall vision must prioritize *personalization* at the core of the learning environment (Redecker & Punie, 2025). "Personalized learning", according to World Schools (2025), means tailoring education to individual needs. So the starting point of cybersecurity prevention training should be to identify each student's unique learning needs with an in-depth assessment (Oxford Learning, 2025). The assessment will provide the details behind how a particular student learns, which will allow Educational Technology professionals to design a program to match those needs. "Personalized Learning Systems", according to the *Digital Learning Institute* (2025) and *Number Analytics* (2025), is one of the top 10 tech trends transforming modern education in 2025. "Personalized Learning Systems", also known as "Personalized Systems of Instruction," are not new. But that is a topic for another day.

REFERENCES

Abrahamsson, P., Salo, O., Ronkainen, J., & Warsta, J. (2002). Agile Software Development Methods: Review and Analysis, VTT Publications. 478.

Baddeley, A. D. (1986). *Working memory*. Clarendon.

Baker, K. (2023). The Zeus Trojan Malware: Definition and Prevention, CrowdStrike, https://www.crowdstrike.com/en-us/cybersecurity-101/malware/zeus-malware/

Beek, C. (2017). Emotet Downloader Trojan Returns in Force, McAfee, https://securingtomorrow.mcafee.com/other-blogs/mcafee-labs/emotet-downloader-trojan-returns-in-force/

Bishop, M. J. (2014). Reconceptualizing instructional message design: Toward the development of a new guiding framework. In Hokanson, B., & Gibbons, A. (Eds.), *Design in Educational Technology, Educational Communications and Technology: Issues and Innovations* (Vol. 1)., DOI: 10.1007/978-3-319-00927-8_9

Brown, R. (2019). Security Breach Update, https://tct.com.au/security-breach-update-15-march-2019/

Burack, C. (2018). German federal police use Trojan virus to evade phone encryption, *Deutsche Welle,* https://www.dw.com/en/german-federal-police-use-trojan-virus-to-evade-phone-encryption/a-42328466

Chandler, P., & Sweller, J. (1991). Cognitive load theory and the format of instruction. *Cognition and Instruction*, *8*(4), 293–332. DOI: 10.1207/s1532690xci0804_2

Constantin, L. (2012). Citadel banking malware is evolving and spreading rapidly, Researchers Warn, *PCWorld,* https://www.pcworld.com/article/474333/citadel_banking_malware_is_evolving_and_spreading_rapidly_researchers_warn.html

Eldridge, A. (2019). The ZeroAccess Rootkit Trojan, Nerds On Call, https://callnerds.com/the-zeroaccess-rootkit-trojan/

F-Secure. (2025). Trojan:W32/PFV-Exploit, https://www.f-secure.com/v-descs/pfv-exploit.shtml

Federal Bureau of Investigation. (2020). $3M Bounty for ZeuS Trojan Author, U.S. Department of Justice, https://www.fbi.gov/wanted/cyber/evgeniy-mikhailovich-bogachev

Federal Bureau of Investigation. (2025). Most Wanted, Evgeniy Mikhaylovich Bogachev, https://www.fbi.gov/wanted/cyber/evgeniy-mikhailovich-bogachev

Firewalls.com. (2025). https://www.firewalls.com/blog/security-terms/backdoor-trojan/?srsltid=AfmBOoqgA-oDEMZAjzTSdwTOf-wTGxleAyJ3tVmSEUcFlEbttGoQKoWj

Fortinet (2025). Trojan Horse Virus, *Fortinet, Inc.,* https://www.fortinet.com/resources/cyberglossary/trojan-horse-virus

Gropper, G. L. (1983). A behavioral approach to instructional prescription. In Reigeluth, C. M. (Ed.), *Instructional-design theories and models: An Overview of Their Current Status*. Lawrence Erlbaum Associates.

Hannafin, M. J., & Peck, K. L. (1988). *The Design, Development and Evaluation of Instructional Software*. MacMillan Publishing Co.

illumio (2025). The global cost of ransomware: Study, https://cdn.prod.website-files.com/63e25fb5e66132e6387676dc/679bc0561e9ed06d78d5d9c0_The-Global-Cost-of-Ransomware-Study.pdf

K12 Security Information eXchange (2023). *The K-12 Cyber Incident Map*, https://www.k12six.org/map

Kenton, W. (2018). Banker Trojan, Laws & Regulations Crime & Fraud, Investopedia, https://www.investopedia.com/terms/b/banker-trojan.asp

Kirschner, P. A., Sweller, J., & Clark, R. E. (2006). Why minimal guidance during instruction does not work: An analysis of the failure of constructivist, discovery, problem-based, experiential, and inquiry-based teaching. *Educational Psychologist, 41*(2), 75–86. DOI: 10.1207/s15326985ep4102_1

Krebs, B. (2014). Feds to Charge Alleged SpyEye Trojan Author, KrebsonSecurity, https://krebsonsecurity.com/2014/01/feds-to-charge-alleged-spyeye-trojan-author/

Krebs, B. (2014). 'Blackshades' Trojan Users Had It Coming, KrebsonSecurity, https://krebsonsecurity.com/2014/05/blackshades-trojan-users-had-it-coming/

Krebs, B. (2016). 'Blackhole' Exploit Kit Author Gets 7 Years, KrebsonSecurity, https://krebsonsecurity.com/2016/04/blackhole-exploit-kit-author-gets-8-years/

Krebs, B. (2020). DDoS Mitigation Firm Founder Admits to DDoS, KrebsonSecurity, https://krebsonsecurity.com/

Kupersmith, K. (2011). Agile is a Fad, The BA Times: Resources for Business Analysts, https://www.batimes.com/articles/agile-is-a-fad/

Kurtz, G. (2025). *CrowdStrike global threat report*. CrowdStrike, Inc.

Lau, H. (2019). Backdoor Trojan, Security Centre, *Symantec,* https://www.symantec.com/security-center/

MalwareBytes. (2025). Android banking trojans: How they steal passwords and drain bank accounts, *MalwareBytes,* https://www.malwarebytes.com/search/mobile%20banking%20trojan%20

Mann, B. L. (2009). Computer-aided instruction. In Wah, B. W. (Ed.), *Wiley Encyclopedia of Computer Science & Engineering* (Vol. 1, pp. 583–592). John Wiley & Sons, Inc. DOI: 10.1002/9780470050118.ecse935

Munson, L. (2019). The 6 Types of Trojans, Security-FAQs, https://www.security-faqs.com/admin-server-dos-log-steal-and-kill-the-6-types-of-trojans.html

National Cyber and Information Security Agency. (2015). Action Plan for the National Cybersecurity Strategy of the Czech Republic for the Period from 2015 to 2020, https://www.govcert.cz/download/gov-cert/container-nodeid-578/ap-cs-2015-2020-en.pdf

Nielson, T., & Staalesen, A. (2024). Norwegian police make an arrest in Russia-related espionage, *The Barents Observer,* https://www.thebarentsobserver.com/security/norwegian-police-makes-arrest-in-russiarelated-espionage/421016

Paivio, A. (1986). *Mental representations: A dual coding approach.* Oxford University Press.

ProRat Trojan. (2008), http://www.prorat.net/

36. Quraishi, A., Sen, A., Pham, S., Corral, A., & Johnston, T. (August 26, 2024). Ransomware attacks on schools threaten student data nationwide, *CBS News,* https://www.cbsnews.com/news/school-ransomware-attacks-threaten-student-data/

Roblyer, M. D. (2015). *Introduction to Systematic Instructional Design for Traditional, Online, and Blended Environments*. Pearson.

Sagduyu, Y. E., Erpek, T., Ulukus, S., & Yener, A. (2022). Vulnerabilities of deep learning-driven semantic communications to backdoor trojan attacks, arXiv:2212.11205v1 [cs.CR]

Solomon, A., & Evron, G. (September 2006). The world of botnets. *Virus Bulletin,* http://www.virusbtn.com

Stansberry, K., Anderson, J., & Rainie, L. (2019). The Internet will continue to make life better, *Pew Research Center,* https://www.pewresearch.org/internet/2019/10/28/4-the-internet-will-continue-to-make-life-better/

Sweller, J. (2005). Implications of cognitive load theory for multimedia learning. In Mayer, R. E. (Ed.), *Cambridge Handbook Of Multimedia Learning* (pp. 19–30). Cambridge University Press. DOI: 10.1017/CBO9780511816819.003

United States Secret Service. (2024). Network Intrusions and Ransomware, Investigations, https://www.secretservice.gov/investigations

U.S. Attorney's Office. (2017). Russian Citizen who Helped Develop the "Citadel" Malware Toolkit is Sentenced, U.S. Attorney's Office, Northern District of Georgia, *U.S. Department of Justice,* https://www.justice.gov/usao-ndga/pr/russian-citizen-who-helped-develop-citadel-malware-toolkit-sentenced-0

Veeam Software. (2024). Building a cyber-resilient data recovery strategy, https://webobjects2.cdw.com/is/content/CDW/cdw/on-domain-cdw/brands/veeam/veeam-nist-security-white-paper-cdw.pdf?ci=8722

Webroot (March 2019). Types of Trojan Horse software, https://www.webroot.com/us/en/resources/tips-articles/what-is-trojan-virus

Ying, T.-M. (2019). The evolution of mobile banking trojans, Symantec, https://medium.com/threat-intel/the-evolution-of-mobile-banking-trojans-608625c79143

Zorz, Z. (2012). Cross-platform Wirenet Trojan targets Mac and Linux users, HelpNetSecurity, https://www.helpnetsecurity.com/2012/08/30/cross-platform-wirenet-trojan-targets-mac-and-linux-users/

ADDITIONAL READING

Agence nationale de la sécurité des systèmes d'information (April 2019). Raising awareness on cybersecurity through cartoons, https://www.ssi.gouv.fr/en/actualite/raising-awareness-on-cybersecurity-through-cartoons/

Baddeley, A. D. (2002). Is working memory still working? *European Psychologist, 7*(2), 85–97. DOI: 10.1027//1016-9040.7.2.85

BBC News. 2019). U.S. and Taiwan hold first joint cyber-war exercise, https://www.bbc.com/news/technology-50289974

Carné de Carnavalet, X., & Mohammad Mannan, M. (2019). Privacy and Security Risks of "Not-a-Virus" Bundled Adware: The Wajam Case, arXiv:1905.05224v2

European Parliament. (2018). At A Glance. European Youth Event. Cyber-attacks: Not just a phantom menace, Prepared for the European Youth Event, taking place in Strasbourg, https://www.europarl.europa.eu/RegData/etudes/ATAG/2018/614759/EPRS_ATA(2018)614759_EN.pdf

European Telecommunications Standards Institute. (2015). Critical Security Controls for Effective Cyber Defence, Technical Report, https://www.etsi.org/deliver/etsi_tr/103300_103399/103305/01.01.01_60/tr_103305v010101p.pdf

Investigatory Powers Act. (2016). UK Legislation, Public General Acts, c. 25, https://www.legislation.gov.uk/ukpga/2016/25/contents/enacted

Krebs, V. (2008). Social Network Analysis, A Brief Introduction, OrgNet, http://www.orgnet.com/sna.html

Moore, M. (2018). Cisco and UK police team up for cybersecurity training, https://www.techradar.com/news/cisco-and-uk-police-team-up-for-cybersecurity-training

Pietrosanti, F., & Aterno, S. (2017). Italy unveils a legal proposal to regulate government hacking, *Boing Boing*, https://boingboing.net/2017/02/15/title-italy-unveils-a-law-pro.html

Sadoski, M., Paivio, A., & Goetz, E. T. (1991). A critique of schema theory in reading and a dual coding alternative. *Reading Research Quarterly*, *26*(4), 463–484. DOI: 10.2307/747898

Segura, J. (2012). Citadel: a cybercriminal's ultimate weapon? *Malwarebytes Lab,* https://securityintelligence.com/cybercriminals-use-citadel-compromise-password-management-authentication-solutions/

Shieh, C. (2007). OSI Model, DoD Model and the TCP/IP Protocol Suite, https://bit.kuas.edu.tw/~csshieh/teach/np/tcpip/index.html

Tamir, D. (2014). *Cybercriminals Use Citadel to Compromise Password Management and Authentication Solutions*. Security Intelligence.

UN General Assembly. (2016). The right to privacy in the digital age. A/C.3/71/L.39/Rev.1, pp. 2-3, https://www.un.org/Docs/journal/En/20161117e.pdf

VICE on HBO. (2017). How Israel rules the world of cybersecurity, *YouTube video,* https://www.youtube.com/watch?v=ca-C3voZwpM

Chapter 2
Hacking Then and Now

ABSTRACT

Hacking originally required exceptional computer skills and significant proficiency to access a computer system. Today, however, code libraries and automated tools enable anyone with the desire to learn to hack a computer network. Recently published reports recommend educating users to recognize phishing attempts while maintaining proactive monitoring to detect identity-based threats. Teach educators and lab managers to recognize phishing attempts and social engineering tactics, and provide them with regular security awareness training. Several universities offer short-term intensive training in cybersecurity, known as "boot camps," as well as Associate's, Bachelor's, Master's, and even Ph.D. programs in Cybersecurity. Counter-cyberterrorism has generated career opportunities for individuals skilled in scanning, hacking, and exploiting systems to evaluate vulnerabilities and reveal digital evidence that aids law enforcement in solving cases.

DEFINITIONS

Hacking

"Hacking" in a legal context is a term that describes an unconventional or illicit means of gaining unauthorized access to a digital device, computer system, or network. In the U.S., hacking is a federal crime under the *Computer Fraud and Abuse Act.* In the 1950s, the term "hacker" referred to students at the *Massachusetts Institute of Technology* who were exploring the limits of emerging computer technology. Early computer enthusiasts at the *Tech Model Railroad Club* used MIT's IBM 704 to control model-railroad signals, while curiosity-driven "phone phreaks" manipulated telephone tones in the early 1970s.

By the 1980s, the rapid spread of home computers and the rise of organized groups, such as the *Chaos Computer Club,* spurred legislators to act. Congress responded

DOI: 10.4018/979-8-3373-3126-3.ch002

by enacting the *Computer Fraud and Abuse Act (CFAA)* in 1986 to criminalize intentional, unauthorized access to protected computers. Amendments in 1994 and subsequent years expanded the CFAA's scope to include civil liability and extended jurisdiction to virtually any computer connected to interstate or foreign commerce.

Today, hacking has evolved into a complex ecosystem of state-sponsored espionage and organized crime. High-profile data breaches in 2025 exposed millions of records, from McDonald's job applicants to health-care patients, highlighting the persistent vulnerability of personal information.

Types of Hacks

Glastra (2020) outlined common types of hacks and the potential consequences. "Malware" is an umbrella term that encompasses various types of malicious software designed to impact the availability (ransomware), confidentiality (spyware), or integrity (viruses, worms, and other destructive types of malware) of data or networks.

A "man-in-the-middle" attack involves intercepting information sent or received over an unsecured network. Man-in-the-middle attacks can also access installed malware to process a victim's data. A "Distributed Denial-of-Service" attack makes a system or network unavailable by flooding it with traffic. DDoS attacks are often carried out through botnets. A "zero-day exploit" refers to vulnerabilities in hardware or software that have not yet been patched and can be exploited to install malware or gain access. A Structured Query Language ('SQL') Injection involves using malicious statements in data-driven applications to access a database and steal information.

Hacking Back

"Hacking back" is a practical term describing a specific type of action, not a legal concept; the legality of retaliating to a cyber-attack can be examined under different international law frameworks (Glastra, 2020). While the desire to retaliate against malicious actors is strong following global attacks like *Mirai, WannaCry, and NotPetya*, and hacking back can empower victims, most NATO countries agree that extensive counterattacks could be considered acts of war. Past efforts to hack back have often failed, partly due to fears of collateral damage. Additionally, hackers tend to hide their tracks by routing attacks through unsuspecting individuals' machines, sometimes involving thousands of devices (Drew, 2017; Giles, 2017). Cyber-attackers quickly adapt to situations where large organizations might start hacking back against each other, employing false-flag tactics to incite one company to target another.

The consensus has been that government action is preferable to private companies retaliating against attackers (Lemos, 2017). For instance, *BBC News* (2019) reported that the U.S. and Taiwan conducted their first joint cyber-war exercise. Taiwan's local government co-hosted the tests with the *American Institute in Taiwan*, which represents U.S. interests there. Taiwanese officials were targeted by phishing emails and texts as part of a week-long simulated cyber-war event advertised as the first of its kind. The exercises involved attempts to breach government websites by deceiving workers into accepting malicious communications.

Active Cyber Defence

Alternatively, "Active Cyber Defence" describes a range of offensive or destructive actions, including hacking back, that engage an adversary during or soon after an initial cyber attack. Active cyber defence does not include nonviolent actions such as diplomatic or economic sanctions (Iasiello, 2014).

Aggressive Cyber Defence

"Aggressive Cyber Defence" is a range of aggressive, passive and active defensive actions to be used in concert with one another that identify, deceive, and frustrate attackers into giving up and moving elsewhere. Examples include severing connections between targeted computers and the attacking command and control servers, as well as redirecting hostile traffic to a benign target or destination (Iasiello, 2014).

Passive Cyber Defence

There is always the option to employ "Passive Cyber Defence", which is a range of cyber defensive actions to protect the confidentiality, integrity, and availability of information systems and networks through the use of layered network security devices, processes, and countermeasures to protect the integrity of the information assets in an enterprise (Iasiello, 2014). Examples include firewalls, intrusion detection systems, and host-based intrusion detection systems.

Cyber Attack

A "Cyber Attack" is a set of actions ranging from network exploitation for information collection or data theft to denying, degrading, disrupting, or destroying an information system, an information network, or the content (Iasiello, 2014). Examples include distributed denial-of-service attacks and the insertion of malware designed to destroy information systems or the information resident on them, such as Stuxnet or Shamoon. In 2024, attacks related to initial access boomed, accounting for 52% of vulnerabilities (Kurtz, 2025).

In 2024, GenAI played a pivotal role in sophisticated cyberattack campaigns. It enabled *Famous Chollima* to create convincing fake IT job candidates that infiltrated victim organizations, and helped China, Russia, and Iran to conduct AI-driven disinformation and influence operations to disrupt elections (Kurtz, 2025).

Phishing

"Phishing" is the technique of using communication that falsely represents trusted contacts to get people to click a link or download a file. It can be used to gather information directly or as a means of installing malware. A 2024 study of phishing email click-through rates (Heiding, Lermen, Kao, Schneier & Vishwanath, 2024) indicated that AI-generated phishing messages had a significantly higher click-through rate (54%) than likely human-written phishing messages (12%). "Vishing" or voice phishing is very popular, especially callback and help desk vishing, to gain entry to organization networks. In 2024, voice phishing grew 442% (Kurtz 2025).

The OSI Model

The *Open Systems Interconnection Reference Model (OSI)* divides communication over a computer network into seven packet types or layers (Shieh, 2007). Examining each layer helps digital investigators construct a *modus operandi* about where digital evidence was left on a network (Casey, 2004). Digital investigators should have a solid understanding of OSI Network Layers to handle network evidence.

1. Physical layer
2. Data link layer
3. Network layer
4. Transport layer
5. Session layer
6. Presentation layer
7. Application layer

Layers 1 and 2: Physical and Data-Link

Layers 1 and 2 represent the elemental aspects of the OSI model. The Physical Layer describes the electrical signalling characteristics, modulation schemes, connector pin layouts, etc., which comprise the networking infrastructure. Note that traditional voice interception had operated at this layer through physical wiretaps.

The Data Link layer moves the IP packets or 'datagrams' between hosts. It is described by several protocols, including Ethernet, ATM, frame relay, Token Ring, etc. (Aqsacom, 2005). Lawful interception may include retrieving information from the Physical Layer of a computer network because all information sent and retrieved along a computer network passes through the physical layer. Relevant to this scenario is Casey's example wherein a suspect email was discovered to have been temporarily associated with the MAC address of another computer that belonged to an employee in the software development department of the company where he worked. The MAC address is part of the Data-Link layer and a source of identification of specific computers on an office-, home- or wide-area network (Casey, 2004).

Layers 3 and 4: Network and Transport

Whereas the Network Layer defines how data between hosts is routed to each other over one or more networks, the Transport Layer establishes the connection between two hosts, creating a virtual circuit (Casey, 2004). The most common protocol operating at the Network Layer is the Internet Protocol (IP) header, which contains critical information for lawful interception, such as the source and destination IP addresses. Network addresses are used to identify the hosts. Digital evidence also may be found at the network and transport layers.

The most common protocol supporting the Transport Layer is the Transport Control Protocol (TCP), which assures a solid connection between hosts through data flow control, error detection, and packet reception acknowledgment. Another popular Transport Layer protocol is the Universal Datagram Protocol (UDP). UDP is much lighter than TCP and does not have transport acknowledgment. Thus, it moves packets while "hoping for the best" in their delivery to the destination. Nevertheless, UDP is useful for supporting applications such as streamed voice and video, where point-to-point (or multipoint) data transfer in layers 3 and 4 must occur fast and with a minimum of latency (Aqsacom, 2005).

Layer 5: Session

The Session Layer controls the session (i.e., the connection) between computers on a network by establishing, managing and terminating the connections between a local and remote application. The OSI model made this layer responsible for the "graceful close" of sessions, which is a property of TCP, and also for session checkpointing and recovery (Wikipedia, 2019). "Commands can display information relating to specific sessions, provided they are still active" (Casey, 2004, p. 377). The Session Layer controls the setup and termination of communications sessions and the transfer mode of the data (simplex, half duplex, full duplex). When content is extracted from a communications link in layer 5, it is necessary to determine the transfer mode for lower-level interceptions (Aqsacom, 2005).

Layer 6: Presentation

The Presentation Layer is responsible for delivering and formatting information to the Application Layer for further processing or display. It relieves the Application layer of concern regarding syntactical differences in data representation within the end-user systems. Interception in the Presentation Layer is closely aligned with interception in the Application Layer; i.e., intercepted data formats from specific applications are defined through the Application Layer (Aqsacom, 2005).

Layer 7: Application

The Application Layer performs application services for computer application processes and provides services to user-defined application processes, but not to the end user. For example, the Application Layer defines a file transfer protocol, but the end user must go through an application process to invoke the TCP/IP file transfer (Wikipedia, 2019). This layer defines how applications communicate with each other over the network. Typical applications include email, file transfer, remote database queries, and remote terminal access. Some standard protocols operating at Layer 7 include FTP, Telnet, POP3, and HTTP. Lawful interception at the application level can reveal information exchanged by targets running such applications; however, the application data may not necessarily be readily available from network systems responsible for managing applications in layer 7, including web pages, Usenet posts, email messages, and IRC logs (Aqsacom, 2005). However, application data may not be readily available from the network system responsible for managing such applications (Casey, 2004).

Fast Flux Networks

After dismantling a network, investigators look for a Fast Flux network (Albors, 2017). "Fast Flux" is a network running several botnets that hide the domains that download malware or host phishing websites. Fast Flux can also refer to a type of P2P network used to host both the command and control centres or proxies used by these botnets, making them difficult to find and even more difficult to dismantle. A Fast Flux network has multiple IP addresses associated with a domain name, and they are constantly changing them quickly. In the case of Avalanche, more than 800,000 malicious domains have been used since 2009, with IP addresses being changed within periods as short as five minutes, which would initiate connections to different machines despite requesting to see the same website controlled by attackers. Two main types of Fast Flux networks exist: Single Flux and Double Flux.

Single Flux Network

The Single Flux network is characterized by multiple individual nodes registering and deregistering their IP addresses as part of a DNS (address) for a single domain name. These registrations have a very short lifespan (i.e., five minutes on average) and create a constantly changing flow of IP addresses when attempting to access a specific domain.

Double Flux Network

In a Double Flux network, zombie computers are used as proxies, which prevent the victim from interacting directly with the servers, hosting and serving the malware, making it challenging to locate. The Double Flux network uses components and methods that add layers, making locating the machine serving the malware difficult.

Phases of an Attack

Attackers have been known to attack a computer network in five phases (Chatterjee, 2019; Merisalo, 2020).

Phase 1. Reconnaissance

Reconnaissance is the initial phase of hacking, wherein the attacker gathers information about the target (Chatterjee, 2019). This process may include identifying the target and uncovering the target's IP address range, network, and DNS records. Attackers are usually motivated by financial gain, access to sensitive information, or brand damage; thus, the attacker's primary objective is to identify potential targets for their mission (Merisalo, 2020).

The attacker aims to obtain the names, positions, and email addresses of the targeted individuals or groups. They may collect information about the company from LinkedIn and the corporate website, map the supply chain, acquire building blueprints, and investigate security systems and available entry points. Furthermore, they might visit the company's premises, attend an event, or reach out to the secretary. The attacker may even create a fake company, register domains, and set up fraudulent profiles for social engineering purposes. Once the attacker assesses the defences in place, they choose their method. The selected approach is often challenging to prevent or detect, potentially involving a zero-day exploit, a spear-phishing campaign, or bribing an employee. Generally, the business impact is minimal. Ultimately, the attacker is ready to formulate a strategy for the attack.

Phase 2. Scanning

Scanning is the second phase of hacking (Chatterjee, 2019). In this phase, the attacker aims to breach the corporate perimeter and establish a persistent foothold within the environment (Merisalo, 2020). They might have spear-phished the company to acquire credentials, used valid credentials to access the corporate infrastructure, and downloaded additional tools like dialers, port scanners, network mappers, sweepers, and vulnerability scanners to scan the data.

This activity is almost untraceable. The attacker seeks details such as computer names, IP addresses, and user account numbers, which are used to facilitate the attack. The initial intrusion is escalated to long-term, remote access to the company's environment. They begin testing the network for other potential avenues of attack, employing various methods to map the network. The attacker then needs to reach out to determine which email server is currently in use. They are looking for an automated email, if possible, or, based on the information gathered thus far, to email HR with an inquiry about a job posting.

Phase 3. Gaining Access

Gaining access is the third phase of hacking (Chatterjee, 2019). During this phase, the attacker, having completed the enumeration and scanning of the network, now explores options for gaining access to it. Based on the data collected during Phases 1 and 2, the attacker develops a blueprint of the target network. Their objective is to fortify their foothold and identify the systems housing the target data (Merisalo, 2020). The attacker searches file servers for password files and other sensitive information while mapping the network to determine the target environment.

Using various media, such as a mobile app, email spoofing from websites, or other emails, the attacker dispatches a message to users, requesting them to log in to a new Google portal with their credentials. A *Social Engineering Toolkit (SET) is* also initiated for penetration testing, and an email is sent to users with the server address, masking it via *bitly* or TinyURL to shorten the URL and manage the links. A penetration test (pen test) is an authorized simulated attack performed on a computer system to evaluate its security (Black Duck, 2025).

Penetration testers use the same tools, techniques, and processes as attackers to find and demonstrate the business impacts of weaknesses in a system. Penetration tests usually simulate a variety of attacks that could threaten a business. They can examine whether a system is robust enough to withstand attacks from authenticated and unauthenticated positions, as well as a range of system roles. With the right scope, a pen test can dive into any aspect of a system (Black Duck, 2025). The attacker often impersonates an authorized user, making it challenging to identify them during this phase.

A pen test provides insight into eliminating dangerous security flaws. Pen testing can help an organization: Find weaknesses in the system, determine the robustness of controls, support compliance with data privacy and security regulations (e.g., PCI DSS, HIPAA, GDPR), and provide qualitative and quantitative examples of current security posture and budget priorities for management (Black Duck, 2025).

Phase 4. Maintaining Access

Maintaining access is the fourth phase of hacking (Chatterjee, 2019). With control over access channels and credentials acquired in the previous phases, the attacker now seeks to identify and gain the necessary level of privilege to achieve their objectives (Merisalo, 2020). The attacker has obtained multiple email accounts and begun testing these accounts on the domain. An administrator account is created based on the naming structure to blend in. As a precaution, the attacker identifies accounts that have not been used for a long time, assuming they are either forgotten or abandoned.

The attacker changes the password and elevates the privileges to administrator status to ensure permanent access to the network. No overt exploitation or attacks will occur at this time. If there is no evidence of detection, a waiting game is played, allowing the victim to believe that nothing has been disturbed. With access to an IT account, the hacker begins making copies of all emails, appointments, contacts, instant messages, and files to be sorted through and used later. Finally, the attacker gains access to the target data, compromising mail servers, document management systems, and customer data.

Phase 5. Covering Tracks

In phase 5, the attacker secretly removes customer data, corrupts critical systems, and disrupts business operations. They then eliminate any evidence using ransomware (Merisalo, 2020) and erase all sent emails, server logs, and temporary files (Chatterjee, 2019). Before the attack, the attacker alters their MAC address and routes their attacking machine through at least one VPN to hide their identity. Once access is acquired and privileges are escalated, the attacker will also look for signs of the email provider alerting the user or potential unauthorized logins on their account.

EUROPEAN STANDARDS AND THE OSI MODEL

The *European Telecommunications Standards Institute (ETSI)* sets the telecommunications standards for Europe. In 2015, ETSI advised that organizations create diagrams of their computer networks to pinpoint where potential failures in the system could occur.

Figure 1. Illustration of hardware devices on an organization's network. The system should be able to identify if new systems are introduced into the environment that have not been authorized by enterprise personnel

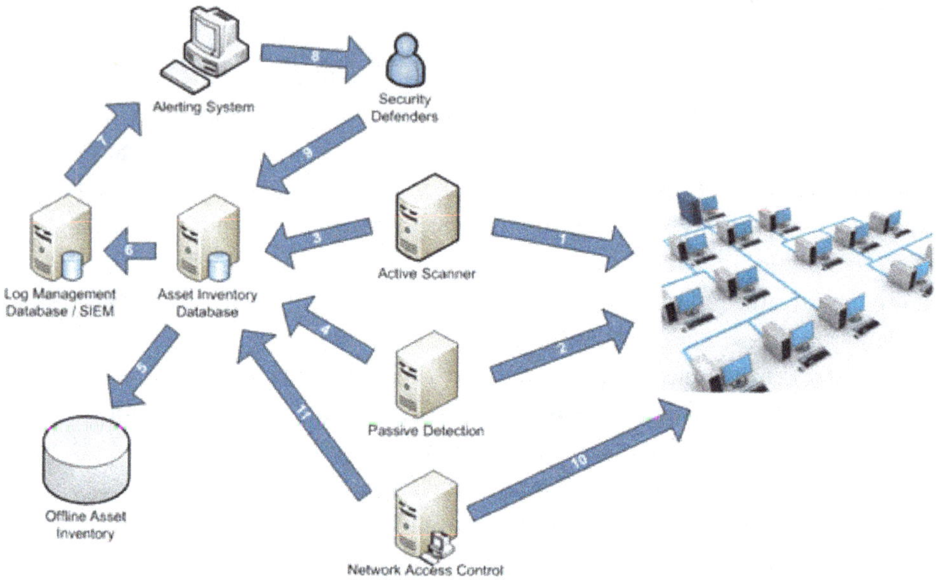

(ETSI, 2015)

The generalized architecture for lawful interception maps quite well onto the seven packet types or layers of the *Open Systems Interconnection (or OSI)* model, the concepts of which are highly relevant to lawful interception (Aqsacom, 2005). The OSI model is a conceptual framework that characterizes and standardizes the communication functions of a telecommunication system without regard to its underlying internal structure and technology (ETSI, 2015).

CYBERSECURITY TRAINING

Counter-cyberterrorism has generated career opportunities for individuals skilled in scanning, hacking, and exploiting systems to evaluate vulnerabilities and reveal digital evidence that aids law enforcement in solving cases.

Canada

In December 2023, the IT services at the *Marine Institute of Memorial University* were temporarily shut down (CBC, 2023). In the same month, the University of Sherbrooke was the victim of a cyberattack that was localized to two research laboratories (Radio-Canada, 2023). Some data from two research laboratories had been compromised. As a result, many colleges and universities in Canada offer cybersecurity programs or courses of study within existing programs, including the *University of Calgary, McGill University, Ontario Tech University, the University of Montreal, the University of Toronto, the University of Waterloo,* and the *University of British Columbia*, to name a few. For example, *Ontario Tech University* offers a one-year Master of Information Technology Security that prepares individuals to work in the high-demand IT security industry (Studyportals, 2025). The *University of Ottawa provide*s a two-year Master of Digital Transformation and Innovation. *Centennial College* and *Seneca College* in Toronto both offer a one-year Cybersecurity Postgraduate Certificate.

United States

In January 2025, the *University of Oklahoma* suffered a cyberattack that compromised employee data, financial information, and more, affecting 34,000 students (Greig, 2025). The following month, *St. Joseph's College of Maine* experienced a data breach that impacted 126,580 individuals in the state (Maine Attorney General, 2025). In March 2025, the website of *New York University* was hacked by @ bestn–gy, who replaced NYU's homepage with what appeared to be test scores and racial slurs (Schlott & Harris, 2025). "It's literally the raw data from NYU's own data warehouse," the hacker explained in a post. This was not the first time the hacker had targeted a university, boasting on X that they had previously taken over the *University of Minnesota's* website in a 2023 incident.

Several universities in the United States now offer short-term intensive training in Cybersecurity known as "boot camps," as well as Associate's, Bachelor's, Master's, and even Ph.D. programs in Cybersecurity, including *Arizona State University, Boston University, California State University at Sacramento, George Washington University, Georgia Institute of Technology, Johns Hopkins University, New York*

University, Northeastern University, Stanford University, and the University of Southern California, to name a few, (Cybersecurity Guide, 2024). These courses concentrate on specific issues about cybersecurity technology, cybersecurity law, digital forensics, policy, and related topics in either online or onsite formats, or both. Private companies offer training too. In August 2025, 4 days of on-site immersive DEF CON Training was held in Las Vegas with workforce tools to prepare registrants against attacks on IT infrastructure (DEF CON Training, 2025).

Want To Hack a U.S. Satellite? The U.S. Air Force allowed hackers to attempt to hijack an orbiting satellite at the Defcon Hacking Conference (Barrett, 2019). Before the start of the 2020 DefCon Hacking Conference selected researchers were invited to test their ideas during a 6-month trial run. The Air Force flew the winners to Defcon for a live hacking competition.

Figure 2. The US Air Force satellite

(Lockheed-Martin, 2019)

Black Hat U.S.A

In August 2025, the Mandalay Bay Convention Center in Las Vegas hosted Black Hat USA with a 6-day program. The event opened with four days of specialized cybersecurity Training, with courses for all skill levels. Also taking place during Black Hat USA was Summit Day on August 5, followed by a two-day conference featuring more than 100 selected briefings, dozens of open-source tool demos in Arsenal, a robust Business Hall, networking and social events.

Several European countries have proposed that law enforcement agencies learn to hack into computers or devices to access their data. Toward that end, the *European Parliament* published a collective case study of law enforcement hacking in six countries (Milt, Guteil, Liger, Heetman, Eager & Crawford, 2017). A collective case study aims to combine multiple cases into a single study (Mann, 2006, p.71). The study examined law enforcement's legal frameworks for hacking across six EU member states and three non-EU countries. The document reported policy proposals on law enforcement's use of hacking techniques (Milt *et al.*, 2017).

Europe's Certified Ethical Hacker

In Europe, the *EC-Council* offers a course called *Certified Ethical Hacker,* a qualification earned by demonstrating knowledge of assessing the security of computer systems by looking for vulnerabilities in a target system, using the same knowledge and tools as a malicious hacker, but lawfully and legitimately to assess the security posture of a target system (EC-Council, 2025). "Ethical Hacking" aka "penetration testing," or "pen testing," or even "White Hat Attacking."

The aim for the student Ethical Hacker is to learn the practice of testing a computer system, network, or web application to identify security vulnerabilities that an attacker could exploit.

Ethical hacking can be automated using software applications or performed manually. Either way, the process involves gathering information about the target before the test, identifying possible entry points, attempting to breach the system—whether through digital means or physical intrusion—and reporting the findings (EC-Council iClass, 2019). In any case, the Hacker Lab Modules encompass Footprinting and reconnaissance, scanning networks, system hacking, malware threats, social engineering, denial of service attacks, session hijacking, hacking web servers, web applications, wireless networks, mobile platforms, and evading firewalls.

In Europe, the pressure is on to maintain instrument-driven discourse across the member states to connect lawful hackers with the best instruction money can buy. While some European countries lack the technical ability to identify state-sponsored hacker groups (Lemos, 2017), others still lack the political will to call out their sponsors (Cerulus, 2019). A new EU protocol aims to better coordinate responses to large-scale disruptions such as *WannaCry* and *NotPetya* (Information Security Media Group, 2019). Numerous vendors, including Cloudflare, Google, Microsoft, and Symantec, have begun offering free services to help governments defend themselves more effectively against such attacks. This chapter outlines some of the main factors to consider in developing clarity of purpose for cybersecurity training, education, or awareness-raising.

PROTECTING THE GLOBAL FINANCIAL SYSTEM

The *Financial Action Task Force (FATF)* is the global money laundering and terrorist financing watchdog. Over 200 jurisdictions around the world have committed to the FATF. The FATF sets international standards that aim to prevent these illegal activities and the harm they cause to society. The *Financial Action Task Force* is an independent inter-governmental body that develops and promotes policies to protect the global financial system against money laundering, terrorist financing, and the financing of proliferation of weapons of mass destruction. The recommendations are recognized as the worldwide standard for anti-money laundering and counter-terrorist financing.

The mandate of the *Financial Action Task Force (FATF)* is to set standards and promote the effective implementation of legal, regulatory, and operational measures for combating money laundering, terrorist financing, the financing of proliferation, and other related threats to the integrity of the international financial system. Financial institutions that have set up programmes against money laundering and terrorist financing should include an ongoing employee training programme (FATF, p.77) and a financial intelligence unit conducting operational and strategic analysis (FATF, p.95).

Operational analysis identifies specific targets (e.g. people, assets, criminal networks and associations) to follow the trail of particular activities or transactions and to determine links between those targets and possible proceeds of crime, money laundering, predicate offences or terrorist financing. Strategic analysis identifies trends and patterns in money laundering and terrorist financing. This information then determines related threats and vulnerabilities from money laundering and terrorist financing. Strategic analysis may also help establish policies and goals for the financial intelligence unit.

Operation Avalanche

Operation Avalanche marked the largest-ever use of sinkholing to combat botnet infrastructures, with over 800,000 domains seized, sinkholed or blocked (Eurojust, 2017). “Sinkholing” is a research technique for redirecting the identification of the malicious command-and-control (C&C) server to law enforcement’s analysis server (Sancho & Rainer, 2019). This way, the malicious traffic from each client goes straight to the research box, ready to be analyzed.

Action Day for *Operation Avalanche* was postponed until late 2016 to allow for the identification of the perpetrators (Europol, 2016). Europol had set up a Command Post at its headquarters in The Hague. From there, representatives of the countries involved worked with Europol's *European Cybercrime Centre* (EC3) and Eurojust officials to ensure the success of the large-scale operation. The global effort to take down the perpetrator's network involved the support of prosecutors and investigators from 30 countries. The outcome was that five individuals were arrested, 37 premises were searched, 39 servers were seized, and 221 servers were put offline through abuse notifications sent to the hosting providers. The victims of malware infections were identified in 180 countries (Europol, 2016).

The story began, or at least was discovered, in 2012, when ransomware was detected, infecting several computer systems and blocking user access. A German investigation exposed a sophisticated technical infrastructure that infected millions of private and business computer systems with banking Trojans, enabling the operators to harvest bank and e-mail passwords (Eurojust, 2017). German prosecution and law enforcement authorities approached Eurojust and Europol for support. Several operational and coordination meetings were held at Europol and Eurojust, with both agencies cooperating closely. These brought together many Member States and third States, including the USA and Azerbaijan. Private sector partners included the German *Fraunhofer-Institut für Kommunikation, Informationsverarbeitung und Ergonomie,* the Shadowserver Foundation, Registrar of Last Resort and the *Internet Corporation for Assigned Names and Numbers (ICANN)* (National Telecommunications and Information Administration, 2008), INTERPOL, the *Ibero-American Network for International Legal Cooperation (IberRed),* which served as a liaison to Spanish-speaking countries.

DATA PROTECTION REGULATION IN EUROPE

The *General Data Protection Regulation (GDPR)* came into force in May 2018, designed to modernize older laws that protected the personal information of individuals, for example,

When it comes to trespassing in Europe, there shall be no interference by a public authority with the exercise of this right except such as is by the law and is necessary for a democratic society in the interests of international security, public safety or the economic well-being of the country, for the prevention of disorder or crime, for the protection of health or morals, or the protection of the rights and freedoms of others *(European Convention for the Protection of Human Rights and Fundamental Freedoms, 1950).*

Network and Information Security "Culture"

The *European Union Agency for Network and Information Security (ENISA)* is a centre of expertise for cybersecurity in Europe. The Agency is located in Athens, Greece, with a branch office in Heraklion, Crete. The ENISA contributes to a high level of Network and Information Security within the European Union by developing and promoting a culture of Network and Information Security in society to assist in the proper functioning of the European market.

Education, Awareness-Raising, Training

There are 44 countries in Europe, according to United Nations statistics (United Nations, 2024). Article 7 of Chapter II of the EU Directive concerning the security of network and information systems, mandates that each Member State adopt a national strategy for the security of network and information systems, defining the strategic objectives and appropriate policy and regulatory measures to achieve and maintain a high level of security of network and information systems (EU Directive, 2016). The national strategy is intended to indicate the training, education, and awareness-raising programmes on the security of networks and information systems (Chapter II, Article 7 sec 1d).

A Cooperation Group composed of representatives of the Member States, the Commission, and ENISA carry-out tasks based on biennial work programmes. The Cooperation Group exchanges information and best practices on training, education, and awareness-raising (Chapter III, Article 2, sec 1d) and discusses the work undertaken in exercises relating to the security of network and information systems and education programmes and training (Chapter III, Article 2, sec 3k).

THE EUROPEAN UNION COALITION

The European Union (EU) is a political and economic coalition of 28 member states. Together with the *Council of the European Union*, the European Parliament exercises the legislative function of the European Union. The European Parliament is the only parliamentary institution of the European Union that is directly elected by EU citizens. The European Union uses its leadership role to sort out disputes between member states and to resolve political crises and disagreements over controversial issues and policies. These days, the stakes are high (European Parliament, 2018).

United Kingdom

The United Kingdom joined the European Communities on 1 January 1973, and left the European Union officially on the last day in January 2020. It has always been a matter of concern whether the cybersecurity human resources were sufficient to meet the requirements of the time (EC-Council. 2019). In their latest cybersecurity strategy, the U.K. government promised to increase the investment in cybersecurity from GBP 869 million to GBP 1.9 billion. U.K. planners in the *National Police Chiefs' Council* have partnered with the network supplier Cisco to provide cybersecurity training to 120,000 police officers across England, Scotland, Wales, and Northern Ireland (Moore, 2018).

Equipment Interference

In 2016, the U.K. Parliament passed the *Investigatory Powers Act*. Provisions in the Act permitted police and intelligence agencies to carry out targeted equipment interference, that is, hacking into computers or devices to access their data and bulk equipment interference for national security matters related to foreign investigations. Material derived from equipment interference was then used in evidence (Fact Sheet, 2015). The next year, the *College of Policing* in Ryton advertised for a Technical Skills Trainer in Covert Surveillance. Later that same year, in November, at the *Police Conference on Creativity and Innovation in Policing,* Thomas Allmark of the Northumbria Police said,

The key takeaway of the conference was around digital training, some of the workshops around digital training, but also the conversations about online crime and the massive drive there needs to be within the force to adapt to that (College of Policing, 2017).

High Court Push-Back

In April 2018, the U.K. High Court ruled that the *Investigatory Powers Act* violated EU law. The government had until 1 November 2018 to amend the legislation. On 31 October 2018, the *Data Retention and Acquisition Regulations* came into force to address this ruling. These regulations increased the threshold for accessing communications data, that is, only for serious crimes. "Serious crimes" were offences capable of being sentenced to imprisonment for at least 12 months, and required that authorities consult an independent Investigatory Powers Commissioner before collecting the data. The regulations also included a loophole where rapid approval could be made internally without independent approval, a three-day expiry, and a subsequent review by the independent body. Since then, most debates about the regulations have been about the definition of the term "serious crime."

European Court Push-Back

Around the same time, the *European Court of Human Rights* issued a judgment in three consolidated cases challenging the U.K. government's mass interception program. The judgment found deficiencies in the legal framework governing mass interception, rendering the program unlawful under Articles 8 and 10 of the *European Convention on Human Rights (ECHR)*, which protects the rights to privacy and freedom of expression (ECHR, 2019).

In one case, a claimant, Mandy Richards, acting in person, brought wide-ranging proceedings against 22 defendants, including the Metropolitan Police, The Army, the Department of Health, and several Hospital Trusts (Richards v Investigatory Powers, 2017). The defendants subsequently applied for an extended civil restraint order against the Claimant.

I have, for over 18 months, asked the Police and others, where specifically appropriate to their agency, to look into reported incidents as they have occurred on malicious and unlawful interception, monitoring and manipulation of my communications and activities, unethical sharing of information, disruption to my personal and professional and political life, home intrusions, car tampering, electrical tampering, bike tampering and domestic disturbances resulting in a potentially lethal risk of harm to my person and my health (Richards v Investigatory Powers, 2017).

In another case, the *Investigatory Powers Tribunal* ruled against an application brought by Privacy International relating to the proper construction of section 5 of the *Intelligence Services Act 1994, (Intelligence Services Act 1994).* It held that the provision which empowered the Secretary of State to authorize "the taking … of such action as is specified in the warrant in respect of any property so specified" was wide enough to encompass computer and network exploitation or, in colloquial language, hacking of computers including mobile devices.

France

In March 2025, Université de Rennes, in Bretagne, France was cyberattacked by the ransomware group Funksec, according to ethical hacker SaxX. The cybercriminal group claims to have 50 GB of data, including sensitive documents of all kinds: PDFs, CSVs, databases, Gmail addresses, telephone numbers, invoices, passwords, SSH connection keys for different servers, student data, photos, etc". The cybercriminals threatened to publish the university's data in nine days. Six months earlier, France experienced a DDos attack at *Université de Reims Champagne–Ardenne in Reims,*

Grand Est (Gavois, 2024). One month before that, *Université Paris-Saclay at Gif-sur-Yvette* had a ransomware attack that exploited security flaws, then encrypted and locked its computer systems, demanding a ransom to unlock them (KD & AFP, 2024).

France has been a member of the EU since 1957. In 2015, France adopted a national cybersecurity strategy. This strategy aims to accompany French society's digital transition and address the new challenges of changing uses of digital technology and the associated threats (Ministry for Europe and Foreign Affairs, 2019). The main emphasis in the document "Paris Call for Trust and Security in Cyberspace" is on prevention: to prevent and recover from malicious cyber activities that threaten or cause significant, indiscriminate or systemic harm to individuals and critical infrastructure. A related overall concern is activity that damages the availability and integrity of the Internet, including interference in electoral processes through malicious cyber activity and the potential for theft of intellectual property, including trade secrets or other confidential business information, with the intent of providing competitive advantages to companies or commercial sector.

Legal provisions for the use of hacking tools by law enforcement in France have been governed solely by the *French Code of Criminal Procedure* and, more specifically, the amendments of LOI no 2016-731 of 3 June 2016, strengthening the fight against organized crime, terrorism and hacker financing. The French method of raising awareness about cyber-security has been to use humour and art (Agence nationale de la sécurité des systèmes d'information, April, 2019).

Figure 3. Illustration of the French method of raising awareness about cyber-security using humour and art. Translation: "I'm not falling for that. I am very cautious. I regularly change my smartphone password. One time it's 0000, another it's 1234"

(ANSSI, 2019)

In August 2019, BBC News reported that a team of French police called "Cybergendarmes" located and destroyed a virus that had infected 850,000 computers worldwide (BBC, 2019). The anti-virus company Avast first alerted France's *Digital Crime-Fighting Centre* to a private server that had sent a virus called *Retadup* to hundreds of thousands of Windows-operating computers in over 100 countries but mainly in Central and South America. The virus was sent via an email offering easy money or erotic pictures. Hackers were then able to use the virus to control the computers remotely without owners realizing it, to create the cryptocurrency *Monero,* extort money through "ransomware," and even steal data from hospitals in Israel as well as Israeli patients. The team first tracked down where the command server for the "botnet" network, then created a replica server and used it to render the virus inactive on some 850,000 computers. The botnet operators were believed to have made millions of Euros since they set up in 2016 and are still on the run. Whereas

France has developed a global approach to threats of cyberterrorism, other European countries have adopted a more conventional campaign of educational awareness.

The Czech Republic

The Czech Republic has been a member state of the *European Union* since 2004. The Czech Republic developed an *Action Plan for Security (2020)* that included education, awareness-raising, and training in information society development. Tasks defined by the Action Plan were fulfilled in cooperation and interoperability within the meaning of Czech law with other public institutions and were coordinated concerning the requirements and needs of the entities responsible for the task (European Union Agency for Cybersecurity, 2019).

The planners have established a laboratory for malware impacts on the information systems detection and testing (C.3.08) and implemented a honeypot system for cyber threat detection (C.3.05). Goal F in the Action Plan for the *National Cybersecurity Strategy of the Czech Republic* (2020) has been quite specific about training methods in counter-cyberterrorism.

Preparing Judges and Prosecutors

One of the most interesting initiatives in the Action Plan for the *National Cybersecurity of the Czech Republic, H.4.01* (2020) is to support cybersecurity-related education of the judiciary (i.e., Judges and Prosecutors) to provide imposition and enforcement of adequate sanctions in legal disputes related to cyber issues by education of the judges and prosecutors. Another is to train cybersecurity managers in the public administration in the detection and reporting of cybersecurity incidents, anomalies detection, and other possibilities of cooperation with the NCSC (F.3.02). A third means to raise the level of education in cybersecurity using modern teaching methods (F.3.04).

Preparing School-Age Students

School student "awareness" (goal F.1.01) purports to raise cybersecurity awareness and literacy among primary and secondary school students, as well as among the large public, i.e. end users, through the intermediary of supporting initiatives, awareness campaigns, and organizing public conferences.

Modernizing the school curriculum is another goal of the Action Plan (F.2.01), which is to modernize the existing primary and secondary school curricula and support new university study programs designed to produce cybersecurity experts. Preparing materials for school teachers is a third goal of the *National Cybersecurity*

Strategy of the Czech Republic, F.2.03 (2020), which means to prepare sufficient materials for school teachers, provide the teachers with education in the cybersecurity field, and prepare a sufficient amount of school materials for students.

Developing cyber-talent in students is a fourth goal of the Action Plan (F.2.06), to support, in coordination with universities, and develop student talent in the cybersecurity field. These goals in the Action Plan may be a cause for concern for some readers in that they may be construed by some as indoctrinating the youth in hacking, or at least, non-curricular content through the public education system.

Preparing University Students

Action Plan F.2.07 purports to offer cyber-internships to university students with the possibility of internships in the cybersecurity field in the Czech Republic and abroad. By F.2.08, plan administrators intend to cooperate with universities and colleges on the development of new curricula and implementation of these new programs, on the creation of new "study programs" in the cybersecurity and cyber-defence fields. In this way, the Czech Republic's Action Plan means to be consistent with ENISA's culture of *Network and Information Security in Society*, to assist in the proper functioning of the internal market. Meanwhile, some countries have taken the next step, namely, covert hackers.

Germany

Germany has been a member state of the European Union since 1958. In March 2008, *The Register* news service reported that the German government started hiring coders to develop "white hat" malware capable of covertly hacking into terrorists' PCs (SS8 Networks, 2007). Germany's *Federal Court of Justice* said the practice was not covered by existing surveillance legislation (Leyden, 2007).

Then, in 2015, upset by a cyber hack when intruders attacked the German parliament's network, Berlin prepared to "hack back," disrupting ongoing attacks by breaking back into the hacker's system to delete data and even destroy their system (Delcker, Honal & Ifenthaler, 2018). Berlin had revamped its tools for cyber counterstrikes, but the legislation lagged behind the changes.

Then again, in 2016, Germany's interior minister, Thomas de Maizière, detailed a wide range of measures that the German government was set to implement in response to a string of attacks.

We need a technology offensive. We must technically arm our security authorities much better than we have up to now in terms of personnel and equipment. We are planning the deployment of undercover cyber investigators on the dark net. These will be undercover investigators who will hone in on, for example, illegal weapons trading or communication between terrorists (Smale, 2016).

In Germany, law enforcement hacking tools are known as *StaatsTrojanern* or "State Trojans." This term essentially refers to malware that the police can use to infect targets' devices to give them the access they need to monitor communications and conduct searches. Germany's coalition government has extended police hacking powers by slipping a last-minute amendment into a law that's nominally dealt with driving bans. The *German Constitutional Court* has ruled on what the German press is calling "a new basic right," one that allows police to infiltrate a suspect's computer by using Trojan horses or rootkits. Whereas police had previously only been allowed to hack people's phones and computers in extreme cases such as terrorist threats, the change now allows them to use such techniques when investigating less serious offences (Meyer, 2017). Similarly, in the Netherlands, the lack of judicial oversight even extends after the fact.

The Netherlands

The Netherlands has been a member state of the EU since 1958. In December 2018, *Twickelerveld Intelligence and Investigations* completed the 8th Edition of its course in *Counterterrorism and Applied Intelligence* (UN General Assembly, 2016). Twickelerveld is located at Schiphol Airport in Northern Holland. Module 1 of the course focuses on "Cyber Awareness and Resilience," which concerns current cyber threats. Students learn how to protect themselves from threats through demonstrations of attack schemes and campaigns, including Trojan Horses.

There is no parliamentary oversight for lawful hacking by the police in the Netherlands, except by the Secret Service. Under Article 126nba of the *Code of Criminal Procedure* (*Kamer der Staten Generaal,* 2016), hacking can *only* be requested by the public prosecutor for investigations into crimes that are serious breaches of law or when the investigation requires it urgently. In practice, this law would allow law enforcement to access a computerized device used by a suspect, search the device to look at stored data and copy the data. This article permits the interception of private information (e.g., streamed data), including password capture and real-time monitoring of data traffic. Police Hackers can influence data by adjusting settings, turning on webcams or microphones, and sabotaging or turning devices off. Moreover, the law allows law enforcement to provide itself with access to the computerized device in different ways, including:

- Using a vulnerability in the system
- Intruding with a false identity or by brute force
- Using a Trojan to infect the device with malware

The national law does not require After-the-Hack supervision by judicial or other bodies, but assumes that After-the-Hack oversight will take place when the case goes to trial and the evidence resulting from the investigation measures is tested in court.

Italy

Italy has been a member of the EU since 1957. It is widely acknowledged that Italian law enforcement agencies use hacking tools in the process of criminal investigations. The technique of choice is the surreptitious installation of hidden Trojan horses (Vaciago & Ramalho, 2016). Rules governing the use of government Trojans concerning individual rights were drafted in 2016 by a multidisciplinary team of legal and technology experts, academia, law enforcement, and human rights groups. Whereas the use of Trojans is considered necessary to fight some forms of crime, often transnational, the use of cybersecurity tools should be consistent with constitutional guarantees. The law *should* establish criteria, conditions, and procedures for the use of Trojans by the judiciary. However, *Italian Criminal Procedure* does not contain such a regulation (Civici e Innovatori, 2017). There was a proposed requirement to notify individuals who have been the subject of invasion by such tools. Furthermore, evidence collected in a way that is outside the scope of the judge's authorization and the punishment will not be admissible.

Moreover, case-relevant and general provisions aiming to safeguard the use of the tools were included in the draft law (Pietrosanti & Aterno, 2017). Once an investigation has finished, the Trojan must be safely removed from the target device(s), either by law enforcement or through detailed instructions. Trojan production and use must be traceable. It was proposed that this is done through a *National Trojan Registry*, which would hold a 'fingerprint' of each version of the software. A Trojan's source code must be deposited in a specific authority and must be verifiable with a reproducible build process. Trojans must hold an annually reviewed certificate to ensure compliance with law and technical regulations.

Poland

Poland joined the European Union in 2004. Arguably, the most extreme policy to counteract cyberterrorism may be found in Poland. Poland's Counter-Terrorism Bill would give security service unchecked power (Council of Europe, 2016). The Bill consolidates sweeping powers, including enhanced surveillance capacity, in the hands of the *Internal Security Agency (ISA)*, with no independent oversight mechanism to prevent abuse and ensure proper accountability. The bill risks violating the rights to liberty, privacy, expression, association, peaceful assembly, and non-discrimination.

Amnesty International (2016) has also criticized the fast-track process for deliberating upon and passing the bill and the near absence of consultation and authentic debate with civil society in that process. Article 8. 1 of the Act states that to recognize, prevent and combat offences of a terrorist nature, the Head of the *Internal Security Agency* may order the following covert activities to be undertaken for a period no longer than three months concerning a person who is not a citizen of the Republic of Poland, and about whom there is a fear of possible involvement in terrorist activities:

- Obtaining and recording the content of conversations by technical means, including with the use of telecommunication networks
- Obtaining and recording the content of the image and sound of people from premises, means of public transportation and other venues other than public spaces
- Obtaining and recording the content of correspondence, including correspondence kept using electronic communication
- Obtaining and recording the data contained in data carriers, telecommunication end devices, as well as information and tele-information systems
- Obtaining access to and controlling the content of consignments

Article 41 introduced changes to the *Telecommunication Act of 2004*. By using the equipment or computer software, the *Internal Security Agency* may obtain access to information of which it is not an addressee by cracking or bypassing the electronic, magnetic, IT or any other safety measure or may obtain access to the IT and communications system. The information obtained by the *Internal Security Agency* as a result of the security assessment conducted remains a legally protected secret and cannot be used in the execution of the statutory tasks of the Internal Security Agency and is subject to immediate witnessed and recorded destruction.

Article 32b.1 refers to systems or data about the construction, functioning, and operational rules of the IT and communication systems in place, including computer passwords, access codes, and other data providing access to the system. Article 32b.1 is used to detect, prevent, or react to terrorist events in connection with systems or data and prosecute the perpetrators. *Amnesty International* has complained that the bill risks violating the rights to liberty, privacy, expression, association, peaceful assembly, and non-discrimination. *Amnesty International* has also criticized the fast-track process for deliberating upon and passing the bill and the near absence of consultation and authentic debate with civil society in that process (Amnesty International, 2016).

Spain

Spain has been a member of the EU since 1986. Spain relies on a mature legal framework for counterterrorism as a result of its long fight against the domestic terrorist group ETA. The *Spanish Criminal Code* specifically punishes any act of collaboration with the activities or purposes of a terrorist organization. Spain revised its penal code in 2015, empowering law enforcement agencies to prosecute individuals who glorify terrorism on social media, train remotely, operate without clear affiliation, or travel in support of non-state actors. Spain's counterterrorism capabilities, coordinated by the *National Intelligence Center for Counter-Terrorism and Organized Crime (CITCO),* have proven effective (U.S. Dept of State, 2016). *The National Police and Civil Guard* share responsibility for counterterrorism. Spain continued to implement its cybersecurity strategy to safeguard its critical information systems under the direction of the *Cyber Defense Committee*, charged with coordinating cybersecurity across government agencies.

Austria

Austria has been a member state of the European Union since 1995. Austria's government has announced a plan to spend nearly €290 million over four years to combat terror (Staff the Local, 2015). In the wake of the Charlie Hebdo attacks in Paris, the Austrian government announced the allocation of funds to combat terrorism, the funding to be used to hire new personnel trained in cybersecurity, crime-fighting, and forensics (Eerste Kamer der Staten Generaal, 2016). Some funding will help purchase IT upgrades and evidence-collection software. Notably, €126m will go into hiring new personnel with special skills, including specialists in cybersecurity, crime fighting and forensics. Technology investment is also planned, with €34m targeting special IT upgrades, such as the *Schengen Information System* database and evidence collection software.

Switzerland

Although Switzerland is one of only a handful of Western European countries that have not joined the European Union, the ties between Switzerland and the European Union are close. In October 2024, the *Vocational Training Center* or Berufsbildungszentrum (BBZ) in Switzerland was cyberattacked amid a wave of hacks targeting German-speaking institutions. The cybercriminals blocked access to several systems and demanded a ransom. The attack was carried out using encryption malware on the BBZ servers. The gateway was a security gap in the firewall. In collaboration with local police, the BBZ initiated the necessary technical measures to protect the IT infrastructure from further attacks and began restoring the systems. A report has been made to the police and the *Federal Office for Cybersecurity*. The BBZ has informed employees, parents, trainees and training companies about the cyberattack (Martin, 2024).

Before that, in 2023, the *University of Zurich*, Switzerland's largest university, announced it was the target of a "serious cyberattack". In the same year, the *Harz University of Applied Sciences* in *Saxony-Anhalt, Ruhr West University,* and the *EU/FH European University of Applied Sciences* all announced being impacted by cyberattacks. The *Vice Society Ransomware Group* claimed responsibility for a November attack against the *University of Duisburg-Essen* in Germany.

HS Swiss Training Security is located in Lugano, Switzerland. Security Agent Training at HS Swiss specializes in the latest equipment for completing tasks. Students learn all types of logistics preparation, either pre-intervention or during the intervention, providing both organizational assessments and on-site assistance. The investigative sector is equipped with a wide range of electronic and IT tools targeted and structured to ensure the highest level of professionalism at any level of service required (American Swiss Foundation, 2016).

The Swiss newspaper *SonntagsZeitung* reported that the *Swiss Department of the Environment, Transport, Energy and Communications* is examining the use of software to listen into VOIP conversations. The *Swiss Surveillance Act* does not allow for Trojan horse-type surveillance, said the SunntagsZeitung, but federal criminal regulations do allow software-based wiretaps as long as they are controlled in the same manner as other surveillance equipment, it said (American Swiss Foundation, 2016).

MOVING FORWARD

The historical progression of hacking has revealed a marked transformation in its scale and societal impact. Legal frameworks now confront a difficult balance between cybersecurity, public safety, and fundamental rights. Continuous innovations in attack methods, such as the exploitation of zero-day vulnerabilities and the abuse of cloud services, will require corresponding advancements in protective measures, legislative clarity, and frequent updates to the instructional design of cybersecurity training materials.

REFERENCES

Agence nationale de la sécurité des systèmes d'information (April 2019). Raising awareness on cyber-security through cartoons, https://www.ssi.gouv.fr/en/actualite/raising-awareness-on-cybersecurity-through-cartoons/

Albors, J. (January 2017). Fast Flux networks: What are they and how do they work? WeLiveSecurity, https://www.welivesecurity.com/2017/01/12/fast-flux-networks-work/

American Swiss Foundation. (2016). https://www.americanswiss.org/switzerland-and-the-european-union/

Amnesty International. (2016). Poland: Counter-terrorism bill would give security service unchecked power, https://www.amnesty.org/download/Documents/EUR3742632016ENGLISH.pdf

Aqsacom (2005). Lawful interception for IP networks. White Paper. Washington, DC, Layers 1 and 2, http://www.aqsacomna.com/us/articles/LIIPWhitePaperv21.pdf

Barrett, B. (2019). The US Air Force will let hackers try to hijack an orbiting satellite: At the Defcon Hacking Conference next year, the US Air Force will bring a satellite for fun and glory, *Wired, 09/17/2019,* https://www.wired.com/story/air-force-defcon-satellite-hacking/

BBC News. (2019). French 'cyber cops' dismantle pirate computer network, https://www.bbc.com/news/world-europe-49494927

Black Duck. (2025). Penetration testing, *Black Duck Software, Inc.,* https://www.blackduck.com/glossary/what-is-penetration-testing.html#:~:text=Definition,of%20weaknesses%20in%20a%20system

Casey, E. (2004). *Digital evidence and computer crime: Forensic science, computers and the Internet* (2nd ed.). Academic Press.

CBC. (2023). Cybersecurity issue affecting Grenfell Campus of Memorial University, CBC, https://www.cbc.ca/news/canada/newfoundland-labrador/grenfell-cybersecurity-issue-12-31-1.7071898

Cerulus, L. (February 2019). Europe hopes to fend off election hackers with 'cyber sanctions, POLITICO, https://www.politico.eu/article/europe-cyber-sanctions-hoped-to-fend-off-election-hackers/

Chatterjee, A. (2019). Five phases of hacking, *GeeksforGeeks, A Computer Science Portal for Geeks,* https://www.geeksforgeeks.org/5-phases-hacking/

Civici e Innovatori. (2017). Rules governing government Trojan use with respect to individual rights, https://issuu.com/civicieinnovatori/docs/sintesi_pdl_captatori_en

College of Policing. (November 2017). Coventry, UK, video, https://www.college.police.uk/About/Pages/Conference_-_Everyday-innovation.aspx

Council of Europe. (2016). Poland: On the Act of 15 January 2016 amending the Police Act and certain other Acts, Opinion No. 839/ 2016, Adopted by the Venice Commission at its 107th Plenary Session, Strasbourg, https://www.venice.coe.int/webforms/documents/default.aspx?pdffile=CDL-REF(2016)036-e

Cybersecurity Guide. (2024). Cybersecurity degree programs, https://cybersecurityguide.org/programs/

DEF CON Training. (2025). DEF CON Training Las Vegas, https://defcon.org/

Delcker, J., Honal, A., & Ifenthaler, D. (2018). Mobile device usage in higher education, *International Conference on Cognition and Exploratory Learning in the Digital Age,* https://files.eric.ed.gov/fulltext/ED571401.pdf

Directive (EU) 2016/680 of the European Parliament and of the Council of 27 April 2016, EUR-LEX, https://eur-lex.europa.eu/eli/dir/2016/680/oj/eng

Drew, D. (September 2017). The 'hack back' is not a defence strategy, IDG Contributor Network, https://www.csoonline.com/article/3228118/the-hack-back-is-not-a-defense-strategy.html

EC-Council. (2019). Certified Ethical Hacker, https://www.eccouncil.org/programs/certified-ethical-hacker-ceh/

EC-Council iClass (2019). EC-Council Academic Credits Program: Turn Certification into Education with Academic Credits, https://iclass.eccouncil.org/ec-council-academic-credits-program/

Eerste Kamer der Staten Generaal. (2016). Artikel 126nba, Gewijzigd Voorstel van Wet – *Computercriminaliteit III,* https://www.eerstekamer.nl/wetsvoorstel/34372_computercriminaliteit_iii

Eurojust (April 2017). Operation Avalanche: A closer look, The Hague, Netherlands, https://www.eurojust.europa.eu/doclibrary/Eurojust-framework/Casework/Operation%20Avalanche%20-%20A%20closer%20look%20(April%202017)/2017-04_Avalanche-Case_EN.pdf

European Convention for the Protection of Human Rights and Fundamental Freedoms, Article 8, https://www.echr.coe.int/documents/d/echr/convention_ENG

European Court of Human Rights. (1950). Convention for the Protection of Human Rights and Fundamental Freedoms, https://www.echr.coe.int/european-convention-on-human-rights

European Telecommunications Standards Institute. (2015). Critical Security Controls for Effective Cyber Defence, Technical Report, https://www.etsi.org/deliver/etsi_tr/103300_103399/103305/01.01.01_60/tr_103305v010101p.pdf

European Union Agency for Cybersecurity. (2019). National Cybersecurity Strategy 2015 – 2020, Czech Republic, https://www.enisa.europa.eu/about-enisa/structure-organization/national-liaison-office/news-from-the-member-states/czech-republic-national-cyber-security-strategy-2015-2020

Europol (December 2016). 'Avalanche' network dismantled in international cyber operation, https://www.europol.europa.eu/newsroom/news/%E2%80%98avalanche%E2%80%99-network-dismantled-in-international-cyber-operation

FATF. (2018). Recommendations, https://www.fatf-gafi.org/media/fatf/documents/recommendations/pdfs/FATF%20Recommendations%202012.pdf

Gavois, S. (20245). Cyberattack underway against the University of Reims Champagne-Ardenne, *Next Media*, https://next.ink/brief_article/cyberattaque-en-cours-contre-luniversite-de-reims-champagne-ardenne/

Giles, M. (2017). Hacking Back Makes a Comeback—But It is Still a Bad Idea, *MIT Technology Review*, https://www.technologyreview.com/s/609555/hacking-back-makes-a-comeback-but-its-still-a-really-bad-idea/

Glastra, J. L. (2020). The legality of hacking back under international law, Masters Thesis, *Faculty of Law, University of Oslo*, https://www.duo.uio.no/bitstream/handle/10852/79232/ICTL-Master-Thesis-candidate-9015.pdf?sequence=1&isAllowed=y

Greig, J. (2025). The University of Oklahoma isolates systems after 'unusual activity' on IT network, *The Record*, https://therecord.media/university-of-oklahoma-isolates-systems-unusual-activity

Heiding, F., Lermen, S., Kao, A., Schneier, B., & Vishwanath, A. (2024). Evaluating Large Language Models' capability to launch fully automated spear phishing campaigns: Validated on human subjects, https://arxiv.org/pdf/2412.00586

Information Security Media Group. (2025). https://ismg.io

Intelligence Services Act. (1994). UK Public General Acts 1994 c. 13, https://www.legislation.gov.uk/ukpga/1994/13/contents

Iasiello, E. (2014). Hacking back: Not the right solution," The U.S. Army War College Quarterly. *Parameters, 44*(3). Advance online publication. DOI: 10.55540/0031-1723.2732

Kamer der Staten Generaal. (2016) https://www.tweedekamer.nl/kamerstukken/kamervragen/detail?id=2018D34764&did=2018D34764

KD & AFP. (2024). Paris-Saclay University victim of a cyberattack, *BFM Tech & Co,* https://www.bfmtv.com/tech/cybersecurite/l-universite-paris-saclay-victime-d-une-cyberattaque_AD-202408130311.html

Kurtz, G. (2025). *CrowdStrike global threat report.* CrowdStrike, Inc.

Lemos, R. (2017). Why the hack-back is still the worst idea in cybersecurity, *TechBeacon,* https://techbeacon.com/security/why-hack-back-still-worst-idea-cybersecurity

Leyden, J. (2007). Germany seeks malware 'specialists' to bug terrorists, *The Register,* http://www.theregister.co.uk/2007/11/21/germany_vxer_hire_plan/

Mann, B. L. (2006). Conducting formative evaluations of online instructional material. In Mann, B. L. (Ed.), *Selected styles in web-based educational research* (pp. 232–242). Information Science Publishing. DOI: 10.4018/978-1-59140-732-4.ch016

Martin, A. (2024). Attack on IT infrastructure of the Vocational Training Center (BBZ) Schaffhausen, *The Record: Recorded Future News,* https://therecord.media/ransomware-attack-german-speaking-school-switzerland-bbz-schaffhausen

Merisalo, T. (2020). Five phases of a cyber attack: The attacker's view, F-Secure, blog, https://blog.f-secure.com/5-phases-of-a-cyber-attack-the-attackers-view/

Meyer, D. (June 23, 2017). Police get broad phone and computer hacking powers in Germany, ZDNet CBS Interactive, https://www.zdnet.com/article/police-get-broad-phone-and-computer-hacking-powers-in-germany/

Milt, K., Guteil, M., Liger, Q., Heetman, A., Eager, J., & Crawford, M. (2017). Legal Frameworks for Hacking by Law Enforcement: Identification, Evaluation and Comparison of Practices, The Policy Department for Citizens' Rights and Constitutional Affairs, *European Parliament Committee on Civil Liberties, Justice and Home (LIBE),* https://www.europarl.europa.eu/RegData/etudes/STUD/2017/583137/IPOL_STU(2017)583137_EN.pdf

Ministry for Europe and Foreign Affairs. (2019). France and Cybersecurity, *France Diplomatie,* https://www.diplomatie.gouv.fr/en/french-foreign-policy/defence-security/cyber-security/

National Telecommunications and Information Administration. (April 2008). ICANN. U.S. Department of Commerce. A statement on the Mid-Term Review of the Joint Project Agreement (JPA) Between NTIA and ICANN, Washington, DC, http://www.ntia.doc.gov/ntiahome/domainname/ICANN_JPA_080402.html

Pietrosanti, F., & Aterno, S. (2017). Italy unveils a legal proposal to regulate government hacking, Boing Boing, http://boingboing.net/2017/02/15/title-italy-unveils-a-law-pro.html

Radio-Canada. (2023). The University of Sherbrooke was the victim of a cyberattack, CBC, https://ici.radio-canada.ca/nouvelle/2033246/cyber-attaque-udes-universite-sherbrooke

SS8 Networks. (December 2007). The ready guide to intercept legislation: Germany, https://www.ss8.com/ready-guide.php

Sancho, D., & Rainer, R. (2019). Sinkholing botnets, A trend micro technical paper, https://www.trendmicro.com.tr/media/misc/sinkholing-botnets-technical-paper-en.pdf

Schlott, R., & Harris, C. (2025). Hacker claims responsibility for replacing NYU's website with apparent test scores, racial epithets, *AOL*, https://www.aol.com/nyu-website-seemingly-hacked-replaced-163744158.html

Shieh, C. (2007). OSI Model, DoD Model and the TCP/IP Protocol Suite, https://bit.kuas.edu.tw/~csshieh/teach/np/tcpip/index.html

Smale, A. (August 2016). Germany proposes tougher measures to combat terrorism, https://www.nytimes.com/2016/08/12/world/europe/germany-antiterrorism-measures.html

Staff Outlaw News. (November 2006). Swiss government may tap VoIP calls, OUT-LAW News, https://www.out-law.com/page-7379-theme=print

Staff The Local. (January 2015). Austria's €290m plan to fight terror, *The Local*, https://www.thelocal.at/20150121/austrias-290m-plan-to-fight-terror

Studyportals (2025). Master's degrees in Cyber Security in Canada, *Studyportals*, https://www.mastersportal.com/search/master/cyber-security/canada

United Nations. (2024). Department of Economic and Social Affairs Statistics, *United Nations Statistics Division*, https://unstats.un.org/UNSDWebsite/

U.S. Dept of State. (2016). Country reports on terrorism, https://www.state.gov/j/ct/rls/crt/2016/272231.htm

Vaciago, G., & Ramalho, D. (2016). The use of Trojans and other types of malware as means of obtaining evidence in criminal proceedings, *Digital Evidence and Electronic Signature Law Review, 13*, 88-96, https://journals.sas.ac.uk/deeslr/article/viewFile/2299/2252

Wikipedia. (2019). Internet protocol suite, TCP/IP, https://en.wikipedia.org/wiki/Internet_protocol_suite

ADDITIONAL READING

Digital Watch. (2020). National Cybersecurity Strategy of the Czech Republic: 2021-2025, https://dig.watch/resource/https-dig-watch-resource-national-cybersecurity-strategy-of-the-czech-republic

EC-Council United Kingdom. (2019). Training with EC-Council International Council of Electronic Commerce Consultants, https://www.eccouncil.org/get-certified-with-ec-council/

European Pariament. (2016). Article 7 of Chapter II of the EU Directive 1148, Security of network and information systems, https://www.europarl.europa.eu/RegData/etudes/BRIE/2020/654198/EPRS_BRI(2020)654198_EN.pdf

General Assembly of the United Nations. (2016). UN General Assembly, https://www.un.org/pga/71/2016/

Government of Canada. (2015). Fact Sheet, https://www.canada.ca/en/revenue-agency/news/newsroom/fact-sheets/fact-sheets-2015.html

Kondruss, B. (2025). Cyber attacks on universities: University ransomware attacks & data breaches worldwide, *KonBriefing Research,* https://konbriefing.com/en-topics/cyber-attacks-universities.html#Res340705

Office of Maine Attorney General. (2025). *Data Breach Notification,* https://www.maine.gov/agviewer/content/ag/985235c7-cb95-4be2-8792-a1252b4f8318/a5a9e39a-f847-4c4a-b745-a6e841c8f62f.html

Paistel, C. (2025). "We have taken measures": the University of Rennes is the victim of a cyberattack, *Ouest France*, https://www.ouest-france.fr/bretagne/rennes-35000/luniversite-de-rennes-victime-dune-cyberattaque-5559d17c-fd9b-11ef-96f1-e130525ba9af

Richards v Investigatory Powers Tribunal & Ors [2017] EWHC 560 (QB) (24 March 2017), http://www.bailii.org/ew/cases/EWHC/QB/2017/560.html

Veeam Software. (2024). Cyber-Resilient Data Recovery Strategy Report: Building a cyber-resilient data recovery strategy, https://webobjects2.cdw.com/is/content/CDW/cdw/on-domain-cdw/brands/veeam/veeam-nist-security-white-paper-cdw.pdf?ci=8722

Chapter 3
Surveillance and Moral Panic

ABSTRACT

The current climate of shootings in schools has generated moral panic among school administrators and campus police. "Moral panic" is a form of irrational social action that amplifies a genuine threat posed by a social group. In this climate, some administrators have opted for sophisticated surveillance systems that exceed standard security networks, employing automated license plate readers, ostensibly to enforce parking regulations. Campus police have even utilized drones to scrutinize activism on campus. Others have installed gunshot detection sensors that use artificial intelligence and devices capable of picking up other loud noises on campus, resulting in excessive policing where they are deployed. Additionally, some school administrators are implementing advanced biometric software to determine whether students can dine in the cafeteria. There currently exists little or no justification why a school would require such technology, other than to propagate moral panic among lawmakers, parents, and students.

SURVEILLANCE TECHNOLOGY

The title refers to monitoring tools and practices used to oversee student behaviour, activities, and communications in both physical spaces and digital environments. The implementation of these tools and practices has fostered a culture of surveillance in schools. This culture is driven by concerns about safety, discipline, and academic integrity; however, it raises critical questions regarding privacy, control, and the

DOI: 10.4018/979-8-3373-3126-3.ch003

effects on students' mental health and development (Marlow, Greytak, Duarte & Sun, 2023).

Proponents argue that surveillance tools protect students from harm by identifying instances of bullying, violence, or even mental health issues such as depression and suicidal thoughts. For example:

- Most university police departments in the U.S. have instituted body-worn cameras since 2017.
- The *University of Maryland Police Department* implemented ShotSpotter gunshot detection technology in 2015.
- The *University of California, San Diego Police Department*, and the *Hampton University Police Department* both began using ShotSpotter gunshot detection technology in 2018.
- The *University of Connecticut Police Department* began using ShotSpotter in 2016.
- Police Departments at *East Carolina University, Michigan State University,* and *MIT* have been using Social Sentinel social media monitoring since 2015.
- The *University of Oregon Police Department* and the *University of West Georgia Police Department* began using Social Sentinel social media monitoring in 2018.
- The *University of Kansas* and *Elon University Campus Police Department* have both been using automated license plate readers since 2015.
- The *Binghamton University Police Department* and the *Ohio University Transportation and Parking Services* began using them in 2018.
- The *New Mexico State University Police Department* even operates a surveillance drone, as of 2018.

Whereas this culture of surveillance in schools has been driven by concerns about safety, discipline, and academic integrity, it also raises critical questions about privacy, control, and the impact on students' mental health and development.

SCHOOL SHOOTINGS

Despite assurances from technology companies, surveillance in American schools has not improved student safety. Instead, constant monitoring has only damaged the school environment, with K-12 students becoming less likely to report dangerous behaviour (Marlow et al., 2023). Some students have said they felt like their every move was being watched. Critics argue that, over time, persistent surveillance erodes student trust and teaches them to accept intrusion as normal.

An ACLU study examined a sample of school shootings between 1999 and 2023 (Marlow et al., 2023). 1,602 schools reported having surveillance technology installed during the incidents. Some schools, especially in urban or high-risk areas, use metal detectors or conduct random searches to prevent weapons or drugs from entering the premises.

SURVEILLANCE PRODUCTS AND PRACTICES

The second aspect of the study was a thorough review of the products and practices within the Surveillance Technology industry. Specifically, the authors examined materials from credible journalistic sources, surveillance technology websites, promotional materials, opinion pieces, advocacy organizations' websites, resources, and legal and scholarly research (Marlow et al., 2023). Technologies such as RFID and digital monitoring claim to enhance administrative tasks, making attendance tracking or campus security more effective. In 2021, K-12 schools and colleges across Canada spent an estimated $3.1 billion on security products and services (Singer, 2022). The ACLU identified ten major surveillance technologies being marketed to and utilized by school districts (Marlow et al., 2023).

Surveillance Cameras

Many schools have installed surveillance cameras in hallways, classrooms, and common areas to prevent misbehaviour, violence, and vandalism. These cameras allow schools to monitor students through live video feeds and record footage, sometimes with sound. Recent providers include *Aegis Protective Solutions, Avigilon (Motorola), Axis, Fusus, NetTalon, and Verkada.* Some cameras give law enforcement real-time access to their footage, including controlling their operation and viewing the feeds anytime. However, the ACLU's review of mass shootings in K-12 schools revealed that surveillance cameras were present in 8 of the 10 schools that experienced these shootings, suggesting their deterrent effect on student safety was limited (Marlow et al., 2023).

Furthermore, the rationale for acquiring surveillance cameras did not align with their usage; "rather than being used to prevent school shootings, surveillance cameras are used to identify students who commit minor infractions of school rules" (Morrison, 2021). While cameras integrated with police technology granted officers real-time access to school cameras, which may be useful during an extremely rare active shooter situation, allowing police to monitor schools continuously in the absence of an emergency does not benefit students, and risks alienating at-risk students, students with disabilities, or low-income students.

Surveillance cameras undermine school environments, implicitly branding students as untrustworthy and potential criminals just as they are forming their identities. Students who know or feel they are constantly being watched may feel compelled to avoid behaviours or associations that could be deemed unpopular, embarrassing, subject to misinterpretation, or that they do not wish to be recorded.

Facial Recognition Technology

In some schools, facial recognition technology has been deployed to identify students and staff as they enter the campus or navigate the premises, generating a comprehensive log of movements. This technology is often utilized alongside surveillance footage. Some recent providers include *Aegis, FaceFirst, Oosto (formerly AnyVision), SAFR (RealNetworks), SN Technologies, TriCorps/FacePRO (Panasonic), Visitor Aware, and Verkada.*

Figure 1. Facial recognition in a school

(Lacey, n.d)

Images are captured by still and video cameras and compared with database images to identify individuals deemed as "suspects." Captured images can be analyzed either in real-time or retrospectively by applying the technology to photographs and video recordings. This technology can track and analyze the movements and interactions of every student, teacher, staff member, and school visitor. However, facial recognition technology is not infallible and demonstrates higher error rates in identifying people of colour, women, and young people, which increases the likelihood of false identifications and discriminatory applications within a youthful K-12 school population compared to the general public (Grother, Ngan & Hanaoka, 2019).

When the faceprints of students, teachers, or staff are stored without proper data protection, that personal information can end up in the hands of malicious hackers. Furthermore, when students know or believe that technology is in use to identify and track them wherever they go within the school and to determine and create a record of all the people they associate with, they may hesitate to engage in positive behaviour (Marlow et al., 2023).

For instance, the implementation of face surveillance in schools could discourage students from vulnerable populations (e.g., LGBTQ+ or politically active students) from participating in relevant clubs and affinity groups. In some communities, the presence of this surveillance technology might even dissuade certain students from associating with peers from vulnerable groups, as doing so could be perceived as too risky.

Access Control

Access control often combines the use of still or video cameras with facial recognition technology to screen visitors at schools. Recent providers include *Dormakaba* and *Visitor Aware*. Due to the limitations of facial recognition technology, this system may inadvertently exclude legitimate visitors (e.g., a parent attending a teacher conference), a mistake that is more likely to occur when the visitor is a person of colour (Marlow et al., 2023). Additionally, standards for exclusion, such as a database hit indicating that a parent was previously incarcerated or is undocumented, may expose private, irrelevant information and be used to discriminate or take other actions against a visitor, potentially embarrassing, isolating, or otherwise harming a student.

Behaviour Detection

Behaviour detection involves the use of "behavioural recognition," commonly referred to as "video analytics." Video analytics is a type of artificial intelligence that aims to automatically extract meaning from a video feed. This artificial intelligence software is employed to identify anomalies in student behaviour (e.g., AI-driven tools assessing student interactions to detect bullying or stress). Behaviour detection technology can misinterpret or misunderstand certain student activities due to cultural, community, ability, or age differences. This misinterpretation could lead to various interventions, ranging from being removed from class for questioning to suspensions for behaviour that is neither dangerous nor unlawful (Marlow et al., 2023). This risk is particularly heightened for students of colour and students with disabilities.

For instance, a student might lightly punch a friend in the arm as a greeting in the hallway, only to have AI interpret and flag that action as the start of an assault. The consequences of such false notifications can be particularly problematic for overpoliced and overdisciplined student populations, including students of colour and those with disabilities (Maas, 2021). Moreover, certain student populations who may demonstrate different traits and behaviours than a nondisabled student, such as autistic students who already face challenges in school, may have their disability-related behaviours flagged as threatening, even when they are not.

Video Analytics

The goal of video analytics is "scene understanding", which differs from "motion detection". Recent providers include *Avigilon, Axis, BriefCam (Cannon), and Verkada.* In addition to detecting motion, video analytics qualifies a motion as "an object", "understands" the context around the object, and "tracks" the object throughout the scene (Gagvani, 2008). Suspicious activities, such as loitering or entering an unauthorized area, are automatically flagged and reported to security personnel. Examples include tracking individuals across an area, zone or perimeter protection, identifying and detecting deviations from "normal" movement patterns in an area, and detecting abandoned objects (Stanley, 2012).

Social Media Monitoring Software

Schools have been utilizing software to monitor students' online activities, including their browsing history, emails, and social media, especially on devices or networks owned by the school. Tools like *GoGuardian* or *Bark* can identify inappropriate content or potential security threats. Social media monitoring software examines students' public social media accounts for terms and phrases identified by the school and/or the product provider as concerning, even when they are off campus (Mahanoy Area School District v. B.L., 2021).

When the technology detects a concerning post, it notifies the provider and the school authorities. Some recent providers include *DigitalStakeout* and *Social Sentinel.* By monitoring students, schools aim to enforce rules, maintain order, and uphold academic honesty, thereby reducing incidents of cheating, cyberbullying, and harmful behaviour.

Students who are aware or suspect that their school is monitoring their social media posts may cease using these platforms to communicate with their peers. This encompasses online support and affinity groups for LGBTQ+ students or those facing mental health challenges. Students might even lose trust in "private" groups and chats for discussing sensitive topics, such as accessing reproductive health resources.

Social media companies employ proprietary algorithms to save and filter content, which can be biased (Blodgett, Green & O'Connor, 2016). AI systems will sometimes disproportionately focus on marginalized students, particularly those in underfunded or high-risk schools, and have faced criticism for racial or gender biases, such as facial recognition systems being less accurate for people of colour. Specific words used to trigger alerts while monitoring student communications can reflect a discriminatory bias of the technology provider or school, such as "gay," "lesbian," or "queer," which may result in a student being outed or targeted by individuals who may be hostile toward LGBTQ2SIA+ individuals

Some schools have infringed upon students' First Amendment rights by scrutinizing those who share harmless opinions about their community during their own time outside of the school setting, as highlighted by the 2021 *United States Supreme Court* ruling in *Tinker v. Des Moines Independent Community School District* (Cole, 2021). Social media monitoring can prompt schools to regulate and penalize students for speech unrelated to school safety yet closely tied to free expression (Madfisa, Hirschfield & Addington, 2021).

Such monitoring could also worsen a student's mental health struggles if they discover that their private communication has been intercepted and shared with an unintended audience. Being under surveillance can lead to increased stress and anxiety, especially in teenagers who are already navigating complex emotional and social dynamics. Students may alter their natural behaviours, fearing they are constantly being watched. This can suppress creativity, critical thinking, and social interaction as students become more guarded.

Student Communications Monitoring

Scans of private student electronic communications, including emails and documents created on school accounts and software applications, for words and phrases considered problematic by the technology provider and/or school, are shared concerning communications with the provider and/or school. Recent providers include *Bark, Gaggle, Securly, and Social Sentinel.* These technologies can scan private student communications, such as emails and documents created on school accounts and software applications, for words and phrases regarded as problematic by the technology provider and/or school and shared concerning communications with the provider and/or school.

Cell-Site Simulators

Cell-site simulators, also known as Stingrays or IMSI catchers, are eavesdropping devices designed to intercept cell phone traffic and track the source of cell phone data. A cell phone connects to the site with the strongest signal, which is typically the nearest site. Law enforcement officers use cell-site simulators to pinpoint the mobile devices of targeted suspects.

Figure 2. A cell-site simulator can determine a cell phone's location and intercept its calls and text messages

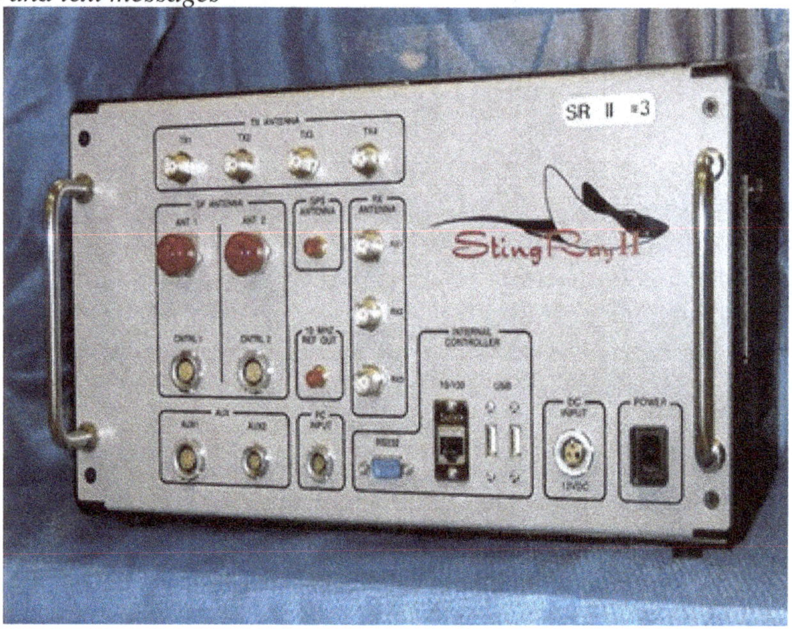

(U.S. Patent and Trademark Office)

These devices can be handheld by an officer or mounted in vehicles, airplanes, helicopters, or drones equipped with global positioning systems. They are used either to locate a specific cell phone, or to identify someone who is not already known. In both instances, they capture location information not only about a target but also about anyone who happens to be nearby. By gathering information in real-time, cell-site simulators eliminate the need for police to rely on service providers for data collection.

R. v. Bedi, 2016. Maple Batalia already had a successful career underway as a model and actress and was studying to become a medical doctor at Simon Fraser University in Canada. Maple and her boyfriend, Gurjinder Dhaliwal, who was not a student, had been in a relationship for four years, which Maple had recently ended. Gurjinder attempted to reconcile with her, his phone showing he had made numerous calls and texts, which only led to two angry face-to-face confrontations.

Figure 3. Maple Batalia was murdered by her ex-boyfriend, Gurjinder "Gary" Dhaliwal (middle). Gary was sentenced to 21 years in prison. His friend, Gursimar Bedi (right), was found guilty of being accessory to the murder

(Diakiw, 2011)

One night, as she was leaving the library, Gurjinder (Gary) shot Maple three times and stabbed her eleven times, to which he later pleaded guilty to second-degree murder. The case turned on the role that a cell-site simulator played in apprehending Gursimar Bedi for assisting Gurjinder (Gary) Dhaliwal after Gary murdered Maple Batalia on the university campus.

There is also evidence in the form of records of calls to and from cell phones alleged to have been in Mr. Bedi and Mr. Dhaliwal's possession that night, as well as records of the sites in relevant locations that were contacted by those phones... Accordingly, I find Mr. Bedi guilty of the count of accessory after the fact to murder with respect to the incidents that I have described. (Justice T.A. Schultes, R. v. Bedi, 2016, at 194).

Prince Jones v. United States. In 2014, Prince Jones was convicted of rape and robbery. Police used a cell-site simulator to apprehend Mr. Jones. The police did not have a search warrant authorizing them to use the cell-site simulator for this purpose, but Mr. Jones's motion to suppress the evidence obtained by the cell-site simulator was denied. Prince Jones appealed in February 2016, with an amicus brief filed in the D.C. Court of Appeals by the ACLU. In September 2017, the court reversed Mr. Jones's conviction, stating that the police needed a search warrant to use a cell-site simulator.

The *U.S. Department of Homeland Security Office of the Inspector General* has looked at deployments of cell-site simulators by the Secret Service and *U.S. Immigration and Customs Enforcement (ICE)* and found that neither department has adhered to Federal statute when using cell-site simulators during their investigations (Claburn, 2023). The Inspector General subsequently issued a memorandum stating that the department must use cell-site simulators consistent with the protections of the U.S. Constitution, including the Fourth Amendment and the Pen Register Statute.

The *fourth amendment* of the *United States Constitution* is the right of the people to be secure in their persons, houses, papers, and effects, against unreasonable searches and seizures, shall not be violated, and no Warrants shall be issued, but upon probable cause, supported by Oath or affirmation, and particularly describing the place to be searched, and the persons or things to be seized *(U.S. Const. amend. IV).*

The *Fourth Amendment* prohibits unreasonable search and seizure and sets requirements for issuing search warrants. Warrants must be issued by a judge or magistrate, justified by probable cause, supported by oath or affirmation, and must describe the places to be searched and the persons or things to be seized (Claburn, 2023). *Fourth Amendment* case law deals with three main issues:

1) What government activities constitute "a search" and "seizure"
2) What constitutes "probable cause" to conduct a search and seizure
3) How violations of *Fourth Amendment* rights should be addressed

United States v. Ellis. In 2009, a federal judge in Oakland, California, reached the same conclusion as the DC court. However, in that case, *United States v. Ellis*, US District Judge Phyllis Hamilton found that there was exigency, which is the notion in American criminal procedure that law enforcement can search or seize persons or things if there are imminent circumstances where bodily harm or injury is in process, evidence is being destroyed, or a suspect is in flight. In such situations, warrants aren't required.

United States v. Lambis. In July 2016, a federal judge in New York ruled in a case known as *United States v. Lambis*, following the DC Court of Appeals precedent. US District Judge William Pauley wrote that without a search warrant; the Government may not turn a citizen's cell phone into a tracking device.

In 2017, the *District of Columbia Court of Appeals* ruled that the warrantless use of a cell-site simulator violated the Constitution when a man suspected of sexual assault and robbery was located by local police. In a 2-1 opinion, the DC Court of Appeals, effectively the equivalent of a state supreme court, agreed with the lower court's ruling that using the device, also known as a stingray, was unconstitutional.

In addition, the judges went further: they found the violation so egregious that any evidence derived from the stingray should be excluded from the case, overturning the conviction.

Cell-site simulators can determine a cell phone's location by spoofing a cell tower. In some cases, cell-site simulators can also intercept calls and text messages. Once deployed, the devices intercept data from a target phone and information from other nearby phones. At times, police have falsely claimed the use of a confidential informant when they have deployed these particularly sweeping and intrusive surveillance tools.

While intercepting private communications is usually unconstitutional, it can change when students use school-provided equipment to communicate. Nevertheless, monitoring students' communications, including emails and what they write in private documents using school-provided resources, may chill the contemplation and discussion of unpopular or private subjects.

Pen Registers

Pen registers are surveillance devices that capture the phone numbers dialled on outgoing calls and the numbers identifying incoming calls. They are not meant to reveal the content of communications, nor do they identify the parties involved in a communication or indicate whether a call was connected; they merely show that one phone dialled another. However, in an increasingly connected world, a record of every telephone number dialled, and the source of every call received can create a comprehensive picture or profile of a person's associations, habits, contacts, interests, and activities. For this reason, pen registers and trap-and-trace devices are very useful to law enforcement, though they raise significant privacy concerns.

Figure 4. A pen register records all numbers called from a particular telephone line

(U.S. Patent and Trademark Office)

Government investigators are required to get a court order to use a pen register unless there are exigent circumstances. However, as the report by the *Office of Inspector General* at the *U.S. Department of Health and Human Services* notes, government investigators often fail to do that. A 1986 federal law requires a court order to use such devices, but the standard for approval was so low as to be nearly worthless. Consequently, a prosecutor does not have to justify their request, and a judge is required to approve every request.

That said, recent judgments have held that cell-site simulators require a "search" under the *Fourth Amendment*, barring exigent circumstances or other known exceptions. This opinion joins the growing chorus of courts holding that the Fourth Amendment protects against the warrantless use of invasive, covert technology to track people's phones. The court's recognition that constitutional protections must keep pace with advancing technology is an important reminder of what is at stake as the Supreme Court takes up the issue of police requests for historical cell phone location data (ACLU attorney Nate Wessler)

A person's awareness that the government can locate and track him or her using their cell phone should not be sufficient to negate that person's otherwise legitimate expectation of privacy (Prince Jones v. United States, 2017).

ONLINE MONITORING AND WEB FILTERING

"Online monitoring" or "Web filtering" can track a student's online behaviour, including what websites they visit, and flag particular kinds of behaviour deemed suspect by the technology provider or school. Some recent providers include *Gaggle, GoGuardian, and Bark.* Website content considered to be inappropriate by the school can then be blocked. In this way, children over 13 years of age can become targets for data collection from data brokers who collect their information from social media apps, shopping history, location tracking services, and more. Data brokers then process and sell the data. This collection of massive amounts of personal data raises concerns about who has access to it, how it is stored, and whether it could be misused or fall into the wrong hands, mainly as private companies run many systems.

Deleting the advertising IDs from a teen's devices can increase their privacy and stop advertisers from collecting their data. However, there is an age restriction on tracking teenagers in a U.S. jurisdiction. When they turn 13, children age out of the data protection provided by the *Children's Online Privacy Protection Act (COPPA).* Teenagers between the ages of 13 and 17 can be tracked online using identifiers known as "Advertising IDs" (McClellan & Portnoy, 2024).

RAND research reported a consensus among school staff, technology company representatives, healthcare professionals, and advocacy group members that AI-based suicide risk monitoring tools could identify students in the K–12 sector who were at risk for suicide and thereby provide reassurance for school staff and parents (Ayer, Boudreaux, Paige, Holmes, Blagg & Mendon-Plasek, 2023). Their report went on to say, however, that prior research showed that AI-based suicide risk prediction algorithms, and, by extension, student activity monitoring in schools, can compromise student privacy and, in so doing, perpetuate existing inequalities. Key community members, including pediatric providers, mental health counsellors, and caregiver, play important roles in the implementation of these tools, but they might be unaware of how K–12 schools use them to detect student suicide risk.

Harms

(1) Monitoring students' online activities may chill the use of the internet and internet-based tools for the research and contemplation of potentially unpopular or private subjects (e.g., sexual orientation, gender identity, locally unpopular political candidates and viewpoints, reproductive care resources, and mental health resources), even when such research and writing is part of an academic project.

(2) Some schools have unlawfully weaponized web filtering tools to engage in viewpoint discrimination, including a Missouri school that used the technology to block LGBTQ+ content.
(3) When students use school-mandated education apps on their home computers, even in some cases after they are logged off the app, the monitoring continues and can scan and report the online activities of nonstudents in the same household.

WEAPON DETECTION

Some companies have responded to school shootings by touting surveillance technology that can detect and warn schools about the presence of a weapon. Recent providers include *Actuate, AnyVision, Evolv, Xtract One, SN Technologies, SoundThinking (formerly ShotSpotter), Virtual eForce, and ZeroEyes.* There have been several instances of false notifications; however, such as mistaking a broomstick, a three-ring binder, or a Google Chromebook laptop for a weapon, which has resulted in an armed police response to the notification. Sending police into a school with weapons drawn, thinking they are facing an armed student or potential active shooter, could have life-threatening impacts on innocent students and school staff.

Murder on School Property

On April 20th, 1999, grade 12 students Eric Harris and Dylan Klebold killed 12 students and a teacher and wounded 24 others at *Columbine High School* before taking their own lives. The shooting was among the first national tragedies in the era of cell phones. Science Teacher Theresa Miller and several students in the room maintained contact by phone with police outside the school (Associated Press, 2002; Cullen, 2009). Some students could not get through on their phones due to overloaded emergency services, so they called news stations.

Figure 5. A security video capture showing Eric Harris and Dylan Klebold in the cafeteria during the Columbine High School shooting where on April 20, 1999, they murdered 12 students and a teacher

Since Columbine, over 74 copycat cases have been reported in the United States, 21 of which resulted in attacks, while the rest were thwarted by law enforcement (Jones, 2015). In many of them, the perpetrators cited Harris and Klebold as heroes or martyrs. Debates surfaced in social media about American gun culture and gun control laws, high school cliques, subcultures (e.g. goths), outcasts, and school bullying, as well as teenage use of pharmaceutical antidepressants, the Internet, and violence in video games and movies.

The *Sandy Hook Elementary School* shooting occurred on December 14, 2012, in Newtown, Connecticut. The shooter, Adam Lanza, killed 26 people, including 20 children and six adults, at the school before taking his own life. Before the school shooting, Lanza also killed his mother at their home. Laura Feinstein, a reading specialist at the school, gathered two students from outside her classroom and hid with them under desks after they heard gunshots (Lenoir, 2012). Feinstein called the school office and tried to call 911 but could not connect due to a lack of reception on her cell phone. She hid with the children for approximately 40 minutes, at which point law enforcement came to lead them out of the room (WTOP News, 2012). This tragic event was one of the deadliest school shootings in U.S. history and sparked a significant national debate on gun control and mental health issues.

On February 14, 2018, 19-year-old Nikolas Cruz opened fire on students and staff at *Parkland High School*, killing 17 people and injuring 17 others. Police say Cruz was armed with multiple magazines and at least one AR-15-style rifle. The suspected shooter bought the firearm in the past year and had passed the background check to make the purchase, according to a U.S. official briefed on the investigation.

Figure 6. A security video capture from February 14, 2018, showing Nikolas Cruz on the second floor during the Parkland High School shooting where he killed 14 students and three staff members

Social media platforms like *YouTube* (Chen, Hurley & Karim, 2005), *Instagram* (Systrom & Krieger, 2010), and *Facebook* (Zuckerberg, Saverin, McCollum, Moskovitz & Hughes, 2004) have played major roles in providing a platform for planning and advertising an active shooter's scenario. On social media, Nikolas Cruz made quite clear his desire to perpetrate the exact type of violence of which he later stood accused. His digital profile contained troubling content about guns and violence-related posts on social media, his posts rife with racial slurs against Blacks and Muslims (McLaughlin & Park, 2018). On his Instagram page, Cruz posted a photo of a shotgun, a BB gun, and several long knives. His disturbing behaviour had several threatening comments on a vlogger's YouTube page, including: "I wanna shoot people with my AR-15", "I wanna die fighting, killing a s**t ton of people", "I am going to kill law enforcement one day they go after the good people", "I am going to be a professional school shooter."

On May 24, 2022, 18-year-old Salvador Ramo killed 19 students and 2 teachers and injured 17 others at *Robb Elementary School* in Uvalde, Texas. In 2023, Uvalde County District Attorney Christina Mitchell convened a grand jury to evaluate whether law enforcement could be held criminally responsible for their response on the day of the shooting. District Police Chief Pedro Arredondo was charged with ten counts of child endangerment, a state felony. Another officer, Adrian Gonzales, was charged with 29 counts.

Figure 7. A security video capture shows 18-year-old Salvador Ramos at Robb Elementary School in Uvalde, Texas where on May 24, 2022, he killed 19 students and 2 teachers and injured 17 others

School shootings have become a significant concern in the United States, where they have increased in frequency and severity. In May 2024, families of the victims of the Uvalde school shooting filed a lawsuit against Meta, the parent company of

Instagram, as well as Daniel Defense, the maker of the AR-15 rifle, and Activision, the publisher of the "Call of Duty" video game series (Kessler & Martinez, 2022). The lawsuit alleges that these companies played a role in promoting the gun used in the shooting to young people. The families argue that Meta, through Instagram, contributed to the shooter's exposure to weapons and violent content, which they claim influenced his actions.

GUNSHOT DETECTION AND ANALYTICS

Gunshot detection and analytics is an audio-based system that, in some cases, will also record video used to detect and report gunshots. The primary identifying characteristic of gunfire is its impulsivity, a sharp and loud onset of sound followed by a quick dissipation (Maher & Routh, 2016). Some recent providers include *CLS Technology, Databuoy, and SoundThinking,* formerly *ShotSpotter.*

SoundThinking promotes *ShotSpotter* as a high-tech improvement on traditional 911 calls, marketing its *ShotSpotter* forensic gunshot detection method to police departments and prosecutors as a reliable method for detecting and locating gunfire incidents in urban environments and generating admissible evidence for use in criminal prosecutions (Max, 2023). The *ShotSpotter* method involves networks of microphones deployed in urban settings, which are tasked with detecting the impulsive sounds of gunfire and transmitting the sound recordings to *SoundThinking's* black-box algorithm and human examiners for forensic analysis. If the impulsive noises are suspected to have originated from gunfire, *SoundThinking* alerts local police departments so that officers can quickly respond and investigate (Max, 2023).

Complicating this classification task is the common occurrence of similar impulsive noises that can be mistaken for gunfire. So potential harm includes the false detection of a gunshot, which could be triggered by something as innocuous as the sound of firecrackers or a car backfire (Rodriguez, 2011), a loud muffler (People v. Reed, 2017), a jackhammer, nail gun or manual hammer strike (Grant, 2020), a loud truck or helicopter (People v. Reed, 2017), and college campus noises (Crowe, 2023) such as a dropped textbook or slammed door. This plethora of impulsive noises poses a significant scientific challenge for ShotSpotter's algorithm during the classification process (Max, 2023).

Police officers in Greenwood, Arkansas, responded to *Greenwood High School* after devices in the school bathrooms detected gunshots, a noise that later was determined to be a slammed door, officials said (KFSM-TV, 2023). Sending police into a school, thinking there is an active shooter, could have life-threatening impacts. There is also a risk that the microphones may be repurposed into general listening and audio recording surveillance devices.

REMOTE VIDEO MONITORING /PROCTORING

"Remote video monitoring" or "proctoring" means using the integrated video camera on a student's computer to monitor that student's attendance, focus, and compliance with anti-cheating rules on assignments or tests. Some recent providers include *ExamSoft, Gauge, GoGuardian, and Nestor Analytics.* During exams, tools like *ProctorU* or *ExamSoft* monitor students' screens and webcams to prevent cheating by analyzing gaze, facial expressions, and surroundings.

Related harms can include attendance-taking, which can produce false results if facial recognition fails—breaches of personal privacy, watching students at home through their computer system. The lawsuit *Robbins v. Lower Merion School District* was filed after 15-year-old high school sophomore (second-year student) Blake Robbins was disciplined at school for his behaviour in his bedroom (Doctorow, 2010; Nasaw, 2010). The school based its decision to discipline Robbins on a photograph that had been secretly taken of him in his bedroom via the webcam in his school-issued laptop.

Without telling its students, the school remotely accessed their school-issued laptops to secretly take pictures of students in their homes, chat logs, and records of the websites they visited. The school then transmitted the images to servers, where school authorities reviewed them and shared the snapshots with others (Martin, 2015). In one widely published photo, the school had photographed Robbins in his bed (U.S. Dept of Education, 2022).

Finally, neurodivergent students, such as those with attention-deficit/hyperactivity disorder (ADHD), may appear not to be focusing on their screen during class or repeatedly looking off camera during a test when such behaviour is reflective of a disability or behaviour that has nothing to do with academic integrity. Students with certain physical disabilities, such as those who require more time for bathroom breaks, might also be flagged for suspicious conduct.

A federal court in Ohio recently found that such monitoring violates the *Fourth Amendment's* prohibitions against unreasonable searches (*Ogletree v. Cleveland State University,* 2022). However, due to its limited geographic applicability, very few students were directly impacted by that ruling. In what is undoubtedly a worst-case scenario, a teacher in a Philadelphia suburb used this remote access technology to secretly activate a student's webcam and watch him while he was sleeping and partially undressed (*Robbins v. Lower Merion School District, 2016*).

This list was not intended to be an exhaustive list of all types of student surveillance technologies in 2023, and it most certainly does not include all the companies currently providing or marketing these technologies.

NATIONAL SURVEY & FOCUS GROUPS

A third component in the ACLU national study was a national survey for the online survey with a sample size of 502 youths 14-18 years old (Marlow *et al.*, 2023). Approximately one third of 14-18-year-old students surveyed (32%) reported that surveillance made them "always feel like I am being watched." Nearly a quarter of the students surveyed (24%) were concerned about how school surveillance limited their online resources. Approximately 1 in 5 students (21%) surveyed were concerned that surveillance technology was used to identify students seeking reproductive health care, including abortion. Approximately a quarter of students surveyed (27%) were concerned about how surveillance could be used to discipline them, and how surveillance could be shared with law enforcement (22%).

A fourth stage of the study was 11 one-hour virtual focus groups with a total of 47 students in grades 9-12 (Marlow *et al.*, 2023). The ACLU conducted four focus groups with a total of 15 "aware" students and seven focus groups with 32 "general" students, resulting in 11 focus groups and 47 student participants.

MORAL PANIC

Recent shootings at schools and universities have sparked moral panic. "Moral panic" is typically understood as a unique form of irrational social action that amplifies the actual threat posed by a social group (Heir, 2016). Goode and Ben-Yehuda (2013) identified five characteristics of moral panic.

- *Concern,* a heightened anxiety level over a perceived social threat
- *Hostility,* a consequence of an "us-versus-them" point of view
- *Consensus,* agreement about the threat and its potential to cause harm
- *Panic,* disproportional to its actual occurrence,
- *Volatility,* when the panic disappears as abruptly as it started.

Numerous high-profile school rampage attacks have instilled such widespread fear and anxiety across Canada and the U.S. that even schools with minimal crime have turned into sites of heightened surveillance and security (Madfisa et al, 2021). However, mental health advocates contend that most security measures, such as metal detectors, armed staff, and surveillance cameras, do not effectively prevent extreme incidents like school shootings. The surveillance culture in schools reflects broader societal trends toward data collection and monitoring, but it also highlights the delicate balance between safety and privacy. While the intentions behind surveillance often stem from concerns about student welfare, the long-term consequences on trust, autonomy, and freedom are important to consider. Schools must navigate these issues carefully to protect both students' well-being and their rights.

REFERENCES

Associated Press. (December 5, 2002). Teacher Praised for Heroism at Columbine, *L.A. Times Archives,* https://www.latimes.com/archives/la-xpm-2002-dec-05-me-miller5-story.html

Ayer, L., Boudreaux, B., Paige, J., Holmes, P., Blagg, T., & Mendon-Plasek, C. (December 5, 2023). Artificial intelligence–based student activity monitoring for suicide risk considerations for K–12 schools, caregivers, government, and technology developers, *RAND Research Report,* https://www.rand.org/pubs/research_reports/RRA2910-1.html

Bedi, R. v. (2016) BCSC 1930, https://www.canlii.org/en/bc/bcsc/doc/2016/2016bcsc1930/2016bcsc1930.html?resultId=0c46ec9329ed414c86a04f4f3ba3b0a1&searchId=2025-07-24T01:30:37:999/10cdd435aa6d41bdbe7277d9b6a17b15

Blodgett, S. L., Green, L., & O'Connor, B. (2016). Demographic dialectal variation in social media: A case study of African-American English, *Proceedings of the 2016 Conference on Empirical Methods in Natural Language Processing,* pgs. 1119–1130, Austin, Texas, November 1-5. DOI: 10.18653/v1/D16-1120

CBS News Staff. (November 27, 2001). Most Columbine Lawsuits Dismissed, *CBSNews.com,* https://www.cbsnews.com/news/most-columbine-lawsuits-dismissed/

Chen, S., Hurley, C., & Karim, J. (2005). YouTube, https://www.youtube.com/

Claburn, T. (2023). *Secret Service, ICE break the law over and over with fake cell tower spying*. Security.

Cole, D. (June 23, 2021). The Supreme Court teaches students an important lesson on free speech, *Washington Post,* https://www.washingtonpost.com/opinions/2021/06/23/cheer-case-supreme-court-speech/

Crowe, K. C. (2012). Troy will turn off Shotspotter, *Times Union,* https://perma.cc/Y4MSSNSP

Cullen, D. (2009). Columbine. Hachette Book Group, https://en.wikipedia.org/wiki/

Dhaliwal, R. v. 2019 ONCA 398 (CanLII), https://www.canlii.org/en/on/onca/doc/2019/2019onca398/2019onca398.html?resultId=15530ec8d6d0428a98184741dde73502&searchId=2025-07-24T01:32:49:499/e990f65ad42849be8e553e09fa1863aa

Doctorow, C. (February 17, 2010). "School used student laptop webcams to spy on them at school and home." *Boing Boing,* https://boingboing.net/2010/02/17/school-used-student.html

Gagvani, N. (2008). Introduction to video analytics, *EE Times,* https://www.eetimes.com/Introduction-to-video-analytics/?pageNumber=1/

Goode, E., & Ben-Yehuda, N. (2013). *Moral panics: The social construction of deviance* (2nd ed.). Wiley-Blackwell.

Grant, K. (2020). ShotSpotter sensors send SDPD Officers to false alarms more often than advertised, *Voice of San Diego*, https://perma.cc/NRY8-JU3G

Grother, P., Ngan, M., & Hanaoka, K. (December 2019). Face RecognitionVendor Test (FRVT) Part 3: Demographic Effects, *U.S. Department of Commerce, National Institute of Standards and Technology,* https://nvlpubs.nist.gov/nistpubs/ir/2019/NIST.IR.8280.pdf

Heir, S. (2016). Moral panic, moral regulation, and the civilizing process. *The British Journal of Sociology*, *67*(3), 414–434. DOI: 10.1111/1468-4446.12201 PMID: 27444132

Jones, M. (October 5, 2015). "How Columbine Spawned Dozens of Copycats".

Kessler, B., & Martinez, M. (July 12, 2022). Disturbing new footage shows Salvador Ramos roaming Uvalde school halls, cops running away from gunshots, *U.S. News,* https://nypost.com/2022/07/12/cops-ran-away-from-gunshots-during-uvalde-school-shooting-video/

KFSM-TV. (February 23, 2023). Greenwood Police assure high school is safe after false alarm leads to lockdown, https://www.5newsonline.com/article/news/local/false-alarm-greenwood-high-school-gunshot-detector/527-be4f0e9b-b096-4aee-bdea-25339135f998

Lenoir, A. (2024). The Columbine High School shooting: The massacre that shook America, *Mahanoy Area School Dist. v. B.L., 141 S. Ct. 2038, 2021*, https://www.supremecourt.gov/opinions/20pdf/20-255_g3bi.pdf

Maas, D. (March 9, 2021). Scholars Under Surveillance: How Campus Police Use High Tech to Spy on Students, *Electronic Frontier Foundation*, https://www.eff.org/deeplinks/2021/03/scholars-under-surveillance-how-campus-police-use-high-tech-spy-students

Madfisa, E., Hirschfield, P., & Addington, L. A. (2021). School securitization and its alternatives: The social, political, and contextual drivers of school safety policy and practice. *School Psychology Review, 50*(2-3), 191–205. DOI: 10.1080/2372966X.2020.1855063

Mahanoy Area School District v. B.L., (2021). https://www.oyez.org/cases/2020/20-255

Maher, R. C., & Routh, T. K. (September 2016). Wideband audio recordings of gunshots: Waveforms and repeatability, 141ST *Audio Eng'g Soc'y Convention*, at 3, https://perma.cc/TRZ3-SJ3K

Marlow, C., Greytak, E., Duarte, K., & Sun, S. (October 2, 2023). Digital dystopia: The danger in buying what the edtech surveillance industry is selling, report, *American Civil Liberties Union,* https://www.aclu.org/publications/digital-dystopia-the-danger-in-buying-what-the-edtech-surveillance-industry-is-selling

Martin, J. P. (April 16, 2015). "Lower Merion schools". *The Philadelphia Inquirer.*

Max, B. (2023). SoundThinking's black-box gunshot detection method: Untested and unvetted tech flourishes in the criminal justice system. *Stanford Technology Law Review: STLR: An Online High-Technology Law Journal from Stanford Law School, 26*, 193.

McLaughlin, E. C., & Park, M. (2018). Social media paints picture of racist professional school shooter, CNN, https://web.archive.org/web/20180216085130/https://edition.cnn.com/2018/02/14/us/nikolas-cruz-florida-shooting-suspect/index.html

McClellan, M., & Portnoy, E. (October 1, 2024). How to stop advertisers from tracking your teen across the Internet, *Electronic Frontier Foundation,* https://www.eff.org/deeplinks/2024/09/how-stop-advertisers-tracking-your-teen-across-internet

Morrison, J. (2021). Cameras are being used to punish students, not stop school shooters, *Forbes,* https://www.forbes.com/sites/nickmorrison/2021/04/11/cameras-are-being-used-to-punish-students-not-stop-school-shooters/?sh=6d9842f83669

Nasaw, D. (2010). U.S. school district spied on students through webcams, court told. *The Guardian,* https://en.wikipedia.org/wiki/Robbins_v._Lower_Merion_School_District#cite_note-guardian1-6

Ogletree v. Cleveland State University, 1:21-cv-00500 (Dec. 20, 2022), https://www.govinfo.gov/content/pkg/USCOURTS-ohnd-1_21-cv-00500/pdf/USCOURTS-ohnd-1_21-cv-00500-0.pdf

Okla. Admin. Code tit. 210, ch. 20, subch. 29 - *Standards of Performance and Conduct for Teachers,* https://www.law.cornell.edu/regulations/oklahoma/title-210/chapter-20/subchapter-29

People v. Reed, No. 16015117 (July 6, 2017) (Cal. Super. Ct. S.F. County)

Robbins v. Lower Merion School District 2016, Pennsylvania Eastern District Court.

Rodriguez, I. (November 22, 2011). Broward Sheriff Dropping Gunshot Detection System, S. FLA. *Sun-Sentinel*, midnight), https://perma.cc/Z473-ZQ3M

Singer, N. (June 26, 2022). Schools are spending billions on high-tech defence for mass shootings," *New York Times,* https://www.nytimes.com/2022/06/26/business/school-safety-technology.html

Stanley, J. (2012). Video analytics: A brain behind the eye? *ACLU,* https://www.aclu.org/news/national-security/video-analytics-brain-behind-eye

Systrom, K., & Krieger, M. (2010). Instagram, https://www.instagram.com/

Tinker v. Des Moines Independent Community School District (1969). https://www.oyez.org/cases/1968/21

United States v. Ellis, 206 U.S. 246 (1907), https://supreme.justia.com/cases/federal/us/206/246/

United States v. Lambis, 197 F. Supp. 3d 606, 609 (S.D.N.Y. 2016), https://case-law.vlex.com/vid/united-states-v-lambis-893647076

U.S. Dept of Education. (April 2022), Institute of Education, National Center for Education Statistics (NCES), https://nces.ed.gov/programs/digest/d21/tables/dt21_214.30.asp?current=yes

Zuckerberg, M., Saverin, E., McCollum, A., Moskovitz, D. & Hughes, C. (2004). The Facebook, computer program.

Chapter 4
Delete, Delete, Hang Up on Social Media

ABSTRACT

Five years ago, social media were described as handlers of user-generated content that was harming the users (Mann, 2020). Five years later, not much has changed. The connection between social media use and suicide is significant. Meanwhile, "doxing" is carried out to intimidate targeted individuals and publicly reveal their private information without their consent. "Shadowbanning" is a practice employed by social media wherein a user's posts are obscured from other users without their knowledge. "Swatting" in schools is also a disturbing trend. False 911 calls or online tips are made claiming there's a shooter or bomb on campus. Social media companies acknowledge it but call it "de-amplification". The "Chromebook Challenge" is also a problem, wherein social media encourages students to stick paperclips into the USB port of their Chromebook to start it smoking or catch fire. Many are calling for social media companies to take stronger action to protect individuals from having their information leaked and from these various forms of cyberbullying.

A COALITION OF THE WILLING

Social networks aim to help people connect within their communities, similar to a *town square* (Zuckerberg, 2021) or a *global village*—"a place where you don't necessarily have harmony; instead, you have an extreme concern for everyone else's business and much involvement in everybody else's life" (McLuhan & Lapham, 1994). The global village is where both the young and the not-so-young eagerly share their opinions and personal data, forming a coalition of the willing.

While most social media users eagerly exercise their legal right to express themselves freely, some seem unwilling or unable to recognize the significant risks of sharing information about their most private thoughts, interests, opinions, work,

DOI: 10.4018/979-8-3373-3126-3.ch004

and health status, particularly during times of psychological distress or personal tragedy. This silent agreement to disclose personal data and preferences to third parties effectively releases those parties and the Internet Service Provider from any liability outlined in the license.

SO, WHAT'S THE PROBLEM?

The problem arises when these global villagers overlook or neglect to read crucial instructions and feedback presented in text and other visual formats, leading to a clickwrap license that grants permission to disclose their data to third parties (Mann, 2009). The clickwrap license is a contract that releases those parties and the ISP from liability should they become aware of the content (Mann, 2015). This is a result of an omission on the villagers' part, reflecting a state of *non compos mentis*. This raises a question: Why do they act this way? There appear to be several possible answers (Boyd, 2006):

- To be nice to people that I hardly know, like other students
- To keep face with people I know but don't like
- To look cool, to have status
- To keep up with everyone's posts
- To circumvent the privacy constraints
- It's easier to say "yes" than "no" when I'm not sure
- As a way of acknowledging someone I think is interesting

Five years ago, social media was described as user-generated content that was harming its users (Mann, 2020). Five years later, not much has changed. Chamath Palihapitiya, a former Vice President of Facebook, expressed immense guilt about Facebook and forbade his children from using it. "I think that we have created tools that are tearing apart the social fabric of how society functions," he stated in an interview at *Stanford's Graduate School of Business*. "I feel tremendous guilt… We all knew in the back of our minds, even though we pretended there were no bad unintended consequences... It's the short-term, dopamine-driven feedback loops we've created. "Likes" are ruining how society operates (Sulleyman, 2017).

SOCIAL MEDIA SUICIDE

The connection between social media use and suicide is particularly significant among youth, a demographic characterized by both a high suicide rate and a considerable presence on platforms like Facebook, Twitter, and Instagram (Coyle, 2014). This underscores the tragic suicides of young individuals who have been bullied by their peers on social media.

"I Hope I Am Dead When U Get Home"

So said Courtney Brown, 17, in a text to her mother moments before her parents found her hanging in the basement (Scott, 2015). Courtney was a victim of bullying, both at school and online, according to her parents. She was afraid to go outside and wouldn't even take the family dogs for walks.

Jenna Bowers-Bryanton, 15, also died by suicide after being bullied and cyber-bullied by her peers at school and on social media (CBC News, 2011). The parents of Courtney Brown and Jenna Bowers-Bryanton revealed that the RCMP questioned a 19-year-old Truro man who admitted to posting on Facebook, boasting about counselling 15 of his friends to bully the girls, naming them specifically.

Figure 1. A small sample of suicide victims from cyberbullying on social media platforms.

Top row: American teenager Carson Bride (left), British teen Molly Russell (middle), and Canadian teenager Courtney Brown (right). Bottom row: Emily McNamara (left), Jamie Hubley (middle), Rehtaeh Parsons (right)

"Depression Pins You May Like"

Two weeks before her death, British teenager Molly Russell, 14, received an email from *Pinterest* titled "Depression Pins You May Like," which featured an image of a bloody razor. *Instagram* was facilitating Molly's discovery of new depression content. In the six months leading up to her death, she shared, liked, or saved over 2,000 posts related to suicide, self-harm, and depression on the platform (Meaker, 2022). The Senior Coroner for North London concluded that it was more accurate to state that Molly "died from an act of self-harm while suffering from depression and the negative effects of online content" (Beever, 2022).

Similarly, Emily McNamara, 14, of Sackville, Nova Scotia, who hanged herself in the garage of their family home in 2011, had saved messages that suggested that her continued use of social media had contributed to her distress (Boesveld, 2012).

Jamie Hubley, 15, committed suicide after battling depression from being bullied over the fact that he was the only openly gay teenager at his high school. He left a suicide note on his blog site, "It's so hard, I'm sorry, I can't take it anymore" (Edwards, 2011).

Rehtaeh Parsons, 15, attempted suicide by hanging herself in 2011, which put her in a coma and eventually led to the decision to switch off her life support. Rehtaeh had gone with a friend to a home in which she was allegedly raped by four teenage boys. Her death was attributed to online distribution of photos of the gang rapists that occurred 17 months before her suicide (Segal, 2015).

Todd Loik, 15, loved shop class and dreamed of becoming a welder. He was looking forward to taking his driver's licence test on his 16th birthday, but he was tormented by being bullied at school and online over his sexuality, with hate-filled comments on social media. On September 9, 2013, Todd took his own life after years of being tormented by bullies.

Amanda Todd, in Her Own Words

Amanda Todd hanged herself at her home in Port Coquitlam, British Columbia. Amanda was a 15-year-old Canadian student cyberbullied by Aydin Coban, a Dutch Turkish man already imprisoned in the Netherlands for sexual blackmail. A month before her death, Amanda posted a video on YouTube that described how she had been tormented by persistent bullying online (Leung & Bascaramurty, 2012).

Figure 2. Amanda Todd posted a video on YouTube in which she used a series of flashcards to tell her experience of being blackmailed into exposing her breasts via webcam on Blogger and being bullied and physically assaulted

(Amanda Todd Legacy Society, 2024)

The cyberbully, Aydin Coban, was found guilty on all charges against Amanda Todd. He was sentenced to 13 years in prison by the BC Supreme Court. On November 24, 2022, Aydin Coban was extradited to the Netherlands, where he will continue serving his sentence from 2017. Coban was released on December 21, 2023. The Dutch courts ruled that Coban's sentence would be reduced to 6 years, which he would need to serve after completing his current sentence in the summer of 2024.

SOCIAL MEDIA ADDICTION

Despite the absence of "social media addiction" in the *Diagnostic and Statistical Manual of Mental Disorders* (DSM-5, 2013), the *American Psychiatric Association* (AMA, 2025) and several law firms (e.g., Lanier Law, 2025) have nevertheless acknowledged "social media" has become a form of technology addiction. Accordingly, a group of 33 states, including California and New York, are suing Meta Platforms Inc. for harming young people's mental health and contributing to the youth mental health crisis by knowingly designing features on *Instagram* and *Facebook* that addict children to its platforms.

New York Addictions

In January 2024, New York City filed a lawsuit against major social media companies, including Meta (Facebook, Instagram), Snap (Snapchat), and TikTok. The lawsuit alleges that these companies have intentionally designed their platforms to be addictive to children and young adults, worsening a mental health crisis among youth. It highlights how features like notifications and content algorithms encourage prolonged and compulsive usage, which has been linked to higher rates of depression, anxiety, and suicidal thoughts among teenagers (NYC Press Office, 2024).

In February 2024, a lawsuit was filed in California Superior Court by the City of New York, the DOE (the largest school district in the nation), and NYC H+H (the most extensive public hospital system in the country). This lawsuit seeks to hold the companies operating *TikTok, Instagram, Facebook, Snapchat,* and *YouTube* accountable for their role in creating the youth mental health crisis in New York City.

The lawsuit alleges that these companies intentionally designed their platforms to manipulate and tempt children and teens to continue to use social media. The complaint specifically asserts that the companies' negligence has significantly contributed to fueling a youth mental health crisis, which constitutes a public nuisance, affecting schools, hospitals, and communities. In New York City, over 38 percent of high school students reported feeling so sad or hopeless during the past year that they stopped participating in their usual activities. As a result, the city has had to spend significant resources to address the issue.

Nevada Addictions

The *Nevada Attorney General* has filed lawsuits against social media companies such as *Meta, Snapchat,* and *TikTok*, alleging that their platforms are designed to be addictive and detrimental to young users. These lawsuits draw parallels between social media addiction and substance abuse, highlighting the platforms' role in cyberbullying and the promotion of harmful content related to self-harm and eating disorders (Miller, 2024; Ritter, 2024).

Indigenous Addictions

The *Menominee* and *Spirit Lake* tribes of the Menominee Indian Reservation in Wisconsin, along with the *Spirit Lake Tribe* located in east-central North Dakota on the southern shores of Devils Lake, are the first among 575 federally recognized tribes to challenge companies such as *Meta, SNAP, Alphabet,* and *ByteDance*. They claim that these platforms exploit vulnerable populations through manipulative design features that foster addiction and mental health issues (Kaeding, 2024). The *Menominee Indian Tribe of Wisconsin*, along with the *Spirit Lake Tribe* in North Dakota, filed a lawsuit in a Los Angeles County court against companies that own social media platforms such as *Facebook, Instagram, TikTok, YouTube,* and *Google*.

We are demanding that these social media corporations take responsibility for intentionally creating dangerous features that ramp up the compulsive use of social media by the youth on our Reservation (Menominee Tribal Chair Gena Kakkak, April 2024).

Seattle Addictions

The *Social Media Victims Law Centre* in Seattle, Washington, filed three lawsuits, one against *Meta Platforms, Inc.*, and two against *Meta, Snap Inc.*, and *ByteDance*, for the wrongful deaths of three children in Louisiana. The Law Centre alleges that dangerous and defective applications of these social media platforms have led to addiction, anxiety, depression, and ultimately, the deaths of the three youths. The addictive design and distribution of harmful content were made available to minors without their parents' consent or knowledge, which directly contributed to several teen suicides (Lofton, 2022).

Colorado Addictions

The *Coalition of State Attorneys I*n a significant federal case, over 33 states have sued Meta for deceptive practices that harm youth mental health. The lawsuit alleges that Meta prioritizes profit over the well-being of young users by designing features that promote addictive behaviour and failing to disclose the known risks of their platforms (NAAG, October 2024).

Collectively, these lawsuits aim to hold social media companies accountable for the mental health crisis affecting youth, advocating for both financial compensation and reforms in how these platforms function to safeguard young users better.

THE CHROMEBOOK CHALLENGE

A recent trend on the TikTok social media platform encourages students to stick paperclips or pencils inside of their school-assigned Google Chromebooks' USB ports to start a cloud of smoke or even a fire (Cross, 2025). In the United States, the "Chromebook Challenge" has become a problem in several school districts.

What most people don't know is that the lithium batteries inside the Chromebooks can reignite. So, they'll bring it back into the house or we'll put it away, thinking it's OK, and then hours later we'll have a problem (ABC Eyewitness News, 2025).

Figure 3. A smoking school computer, a consequence of "the chromebook challenge" appearing on social media

(Wilburn, 2025)

Belleville, New Jersey

The Chromebook Challenge gained international attention after a 15-year-old high school student in Belleville, New Jersey, was arrested and charged with third-degree arson and criminal mischief for intentionally manipulating his Chromebook (Wilburn, 2025). The laptop, which was left outside the classroom while students and staff evacuated the school, emitted smoke and was charred when police and firefighters arrived.

Southington, Connecticut

In the same month, two students at Southington High School in Connecticut were arrested after they set a laptop on fire in class as part of the so-called TikTok Chromebook challenge (Dempsey, 2025). The juveniles were each charged with reckless burning, reckless endangerment, criminal mischief and second-degree breach of peace. They are scheduled to appear in juvenile court.

Long Beach, California

Around the same time, a 13-year-old girl from Lindsay Academy in Long Beach was arrested after she took the Chromebook Challenge (Gile, 2025). She is accused of arson after she short-circuited her Chromebook by shoving a foreign object into the USB port.

Toronto, Canada

In recent years, students have been injured and suspended for participating in these activities on school property, and fire departments have already responded to "several" incidents, according to a post on X from Ontario's fire marshal (Shea, 2025). The Toronto Catholic District School Board sent an email warning parents about a slew of social media trends, including the Chromebook Challenge.

Calgary, Alberta

The Public-School Board in Calgary, Alberta, confirmed one incident. In Edmonton, four cases have been confirmed, with several others under investigation (Culture Magazine, 2025). Schools across Alberta are now actively reminding students of the serious dangers of misusing school-issued technology.

London, Ontario

Meanwhile, Ben Sontag is a Grade 7 student at Northridge Public School in London, Ontario, has said he has seen classmates attempt the "Chromebook Challenge" at his school, which has resulted in student suspensions (Seguin, 2025). Grade 7 Northridge student Ben Sontag said, "I feel like you'll get in trouble and you're going to have to pay a lot of money to fix it. I don't think it's worth it." TikTok has taken action and has blocked the search option for Chromebook fires and other similar searches.

SCREEN TIME

New York City

In 2021, 77 percent of high school students in New York City reported spending an average of three or more hours per school day in front of screens, excluding time spent on schoolwork. At the time of writing, the U.S. Congress has expressed concern about national security regarding TikTok's data collection practices. However, the fate of *TikTok* for U.S. citizens will rest with President Donald Trump, who stated, "There is a warm place in my heart."

France

Politico Europe reported that French President Emmanuel Macron stated he would give his government a month to review the proposals from an expert group regarding screen time, aiming to translate them into action (Herrero, 2025). The report indicates age restrictions intended to prevent access to the most popular social networks until individuals turn 18 years of age. The French government has strengthened its stance on fundamental issues, particularly the proposal to establish a digital minimum age of 15, as previously suggested in a bill by lawmaker Laurent Marcangeli. In a speech last month, Macron urged its implementation at the European level. However, the *Alliance française des industries du numérique (Afnum)* criticizes a report that portrays the industry negatively: "There are several unsubstantiated allegations," including regarding the age limits, stated a representative of the lobby.

China

The *Cyberspace Administration of China* (CAC) has proposed regulations aimed at limiting smartphone screen time for individuals under the age of 18 to a maximum of two hours per day, to curb and prevent addiction to apps and smartphones among this age group (Kharpal, 2023). While children under three should primarily be shown songs and audio-focused content, those between the ages of 12 and 16 may be exposed to educational and news content. Moreover, children under eight should be restricted to a maximum of 40 minutes a day on their smartphones, while kids aged eight to 16 can use their phones for no more than one hour per day. Individuals aged 16 to 17 can use a handset for a maximum of two hours. If these rules are enacted, they could impact companies such as Tencent and ByteDance, which operate some of China's largest mobile apps. The regulations have not yet been finalized and remain open for public consultation.

Canada

Four major school boards in Canada, represented by a new coalition called *Schools for Social Media Change*, claim that students are facing an "attention, learning, and mental health crisis" due to the "prolific and compulsive use of social media products," according to a news release (Alphonso, 2024). The federal government has prohibited TikTok's business operations in Canada over national security concerns, but Canadian citizens can still access the app.

TIKTOK TIPS

Assuming TikTok stays put, Arzt and Abulhosn (2023) recommend eight tips to help reduce or eliminate your time on TikTok:

1. Set a timer: Set timers for how long you want to use TikTok at a time.
2. Create 'TikTok Free' places and times: Have locations/times where you don't engage with TikTok at all. This sets clear boundaries for your use.
3. Focus on alternative hobbies: Spend more time engaging in hobbies that feel meaningful to you.
4. Put your phone in the other room: Try to get in the habit of putting your phone in another location if you find yourself scrolling mindlessly.
5. Have an accountability partner: Find a friend or family member who understands your goals and will support you in spending less time on TikTok.
6. Practice more mindfulness: Acknowledge that you will feel some anxiety when you reduce using TikTok and practice letting the discomfort pass.
7. Know your triggers: Think about when you're most likely to waste time on TikTok and consider what you can do during that time instead.
8. Take a full detox/reset: Commit to spending at least a week off TikTok. You may feel uncomfortable, but you will also cultivate more insight into how you want to move forward with your TikTok habits.

DOXING

"Doxing" is a cyber-attack that publicly reveals someone's private or personally identifiable information online without their consent. This information can include names, addresses, phone numbers, workplace details, or other sensitive data. Doxing is typically carried out to harass, intimidate, or harm the targeted individual. Doxing is illegal in many jurisdictions when it involves harassment, stalking, or the unauthorized use of private information. If you are a victim of doxing, consider reaching out to law enforcement and taking steps to secure your personal information. Doxing has increasingly impacted Canadian educators and students, leading to significant personal and professional repercussions (Gilmour, 2025). Many are calling for social media companies to take stronger action to protect individuals from having their information leaked and from various forms of cyberbullying.

The U.K.'s Crown Prosecution Service

The *U.K.'s Crown Prosecution Service* published social media guidelines to help prosecutors determine which online actions are illegal. The guidelines cover doxing, inciting virtual mobbing (i.e., encouraging others to engage in online harassment), and fake social media profiles used for online abuse, among others, four categories of offences related to communications sent via social media (Crown Prosecution Service, 2024). There are four types of offences specific to prosecuting cases involving communications sent through social media.

Category 1. Threats of violence to a person or damage to property.
Category 2. Stalking, harassment, and the non-consensual disclosure of private sexual images are included in this section. It also encompasses individuals in intimate or family relationships attempting to control each other's behaviour. This category does not solely refer to an ex-partner engaging in revenge porn; rather, the revenge porn offence will encompass anyone who retweets or forwards such material without consent. However, anyone who sends the message simply because they found it humorous would not be committing the offence.
Category 3 involves communication that amounts to a breach of a court order.
Category 4 offences include grossly offensive communications that don't fit the other categories. These communications would likely be prosecuted under the *Malicious Communications Act* or section 127 of the *Communications Act.*
Standard methods of doxing include:

- *Social Media Scraping*. Collecting publicly available information from social media profiles.
- *Hacking*. Gaining unauthorized access to accounts or systems to retrieve personal data.
- *Reverse Lookup*: Using tools like reverse phone lookups or IP tracing to gather details.
- *Data Breaches*. Exploiting leaked information from security breaches.
- *Search Engines*. Digging through search engine results for obscure or forgotten information.
- *Phishing*. Trickery to obtain sensitive data through fake communications.

Consequences of Doxing

- Harassment and threats.
- Identity theft.
- Damage to reputation and personal relationships.
- Financial harm or job loss.
- Emotional distress.

University of Glasgow

In 2019, Shelby Judge, a female tutor of English Literature at the University of Glasgow, became a victim of doxing after her tweet critiquing a new children's book in the "Mr. Men" series titled "Mr. Clever," suggested that the book promoted regressive gender roles (McKay, 2023). Following an interview in *The Telegraph*, Dr. Judge's personal information was shared online, leading to thousands of rape and death threats. The harassment escalated to the point where individuals sent her photos taken outside the university's English department, causing her significant distress and impacting both her personal and professional life.

Yale University

Doxing is not limited to social media (McKay, 2023). In November 2023, a doxing truck drove around New Haven, Connecticut, as part of the conservative advocacy group *Accuracy in Media's* "Campus Accountability Campaign" (Hernandez & Okutan, 2023). The truck appeared on Yale's campus, displaying the names and photos of students labelled as "leading antisemites." This led to significant distress among the targeted students. In response, over 100 Yale faculty and staff members signed an open letter defending the students' rights to free expression and condemning the harassment.

Figure 4. Conservative advocacy group accuracy in media displayed the personal information of Yale and Harvard students on its doxing truck in New Haven, Connecticut

(Hernandez & Okutan, 2023)

The faculty members who signed the letter included 19 from the American Studies Department, 17 from the History Department, 15 from the Women's, Gender, and Sexuality Studies Department, 14 from the English Department, 13 from the Ethnicity, Race, and Migration Department, 10 from the African American Studies Department, and 11 from the School of the Environment (Raab, 2023).

Marquette University

The *Wisconsin Supreme Court* heard arguments in a case involving John McAdams, a Marquette University Professor who doxed Cheryl Abbate, a graduate student and Philosophy instructor, for telling an undergraduate student that everybody agrees with gay rights and there was no reason to discuss it (McCoy, 2018). McAdams felt that Abbate mishandled the conversation with the student. But instead of expressing his concerns directly to Abbate in a face-to-face discussion, McAdams published her name and contact information on his blog. He also promoted the blog post to local media, increasing the reach and exposure of the woman's contact information. As a result, Abbate received hateful, threatening messages; more than 100 direct communications, including comments that she should be raped or killed. She feared for her safety, and the situation escalated until she no longer felt safe on campus (Johnson, 2018). The constant psychological stress and fear eventually led her to withdraw from Marquette University and transfer to a different graduate program. Marquette's attorney noted that Professor McAdams was suspended by a unanimous vote of seven of his peers on the Marquette faculty.

Preventing Doxing

These cases highlight the severe impacts of doxing on educators and students, stressing the need for robust policies and support systems to protect individuals from this form of online harassment.

- ***Limit Public Information***. Minimize the personal details you share online.
- ***Use Strong Passwords***. Secure your accounts to prevent unauthorized access.
- ***Enable Two-Factor Authentication***. Add an extra layer of security to your accounts.
- ***Be Careful with Links***. Avoid clicking on unknown or suspicious links that might be phishing attempts.
- ***Use Privacy Tools***. Employ VPNs, private browsing, and anonymization tools.
- ***Monitor Your Online Presence***. Regularly search for yourself online to understand what's publicly available.

SWATTING

Swatting in U.S. schools is a disturbing and growing trend. False 911 calls or online tips are made claiming there's a shooter or bomb on campus. These reports often mimic real threats, including fake gunfire sounds or videos. Law enforcement responds as if the threat is real: armed officers, building sweeps, evacuations, and sometimes even helicopters. Many of these incidents are coordinated across multiple schools or states in a single day, often resulting in lockdowns, SWAT team deployments, and widespread panic among students, staff, and parents. Swatting incidents typically occur when an attacker has gained access to their victim's personal information, such as their home or work address (Fortinet, 2025).

During the school year, 446 false reports of active shooters were recorded in American schools, marking a 546% increase from the previous school year. These incidents accounted for 63.8% of all violent threats in schools during this timeframe (Klinger & Klinger, 2024). The *Educator's School Safety Network* reported there were 158 swatting incidents in 2023-2024, down 64% from the 446 swatting incidents recorded in the previous school year (Klinger & Klinger, 2024). Although swatting and false reports have decreased, the trend over time indicates that violent incidents in schools continue to increase year over year. In the 2023-2024 school year, the four most common incidents of violence were (1) a false report of an active shooter, (2) a gun found on campus, (3) outside violence spilling into the school, and (4) a shooting in the school or on school grounds.

Figure 5. Threats and violent incidents in schools 2016-2024. Not included were those not reported in the media

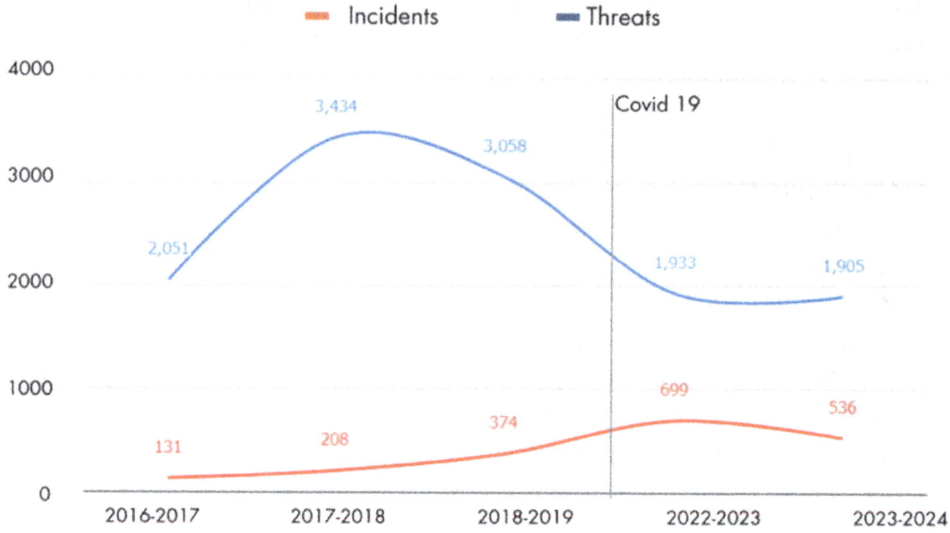

(Klinger & Klinger, 2024)

One of the most high-profile swatting cases involved Los Angeles resident Tyler Barriss making a false claim against Andrew Finch in Kansas in 2017. Andrew Finch, a 28-year-old father of two young children, was shot to death with a sniper rifle by Wichita Police Officer Justin Rapp less than 10 seconds after Andrew stepped out on his front porch. Andrew had committed no crime. He was not armed. He had not threatened the officers or anyone else. The police had been called to his home because of a swatting prank that they failed to investigate before surrounding Andrew's home.

Tyler Barriss had made a hoax call to emergency services, reporting Finch for killing a member of his family and holding two others hostage. Police arrived at Finch's house and shot and killed him. Barriss was arrested and given 20 years in prison. Andrew's killing was one of 23 police shootings in the city of Wichita over the preceding five years, none of which were meaningfully investigated and none of which resulted in meaningful discipline for the officers involved (Van Brunt & Anand, 2025). Officer Rapp went on to be promoted to detective by the Wichita Police Department.

Reposting Liability

Copying someone else's post without explicit permission constitutes a clear violation of copyright law (Miller, 2024). Whether it's a text post, photo, or video, every piece of content on social media is protected by copyright as soon as it is created. Reposting without permission exposes you to potential lawsuits, and claiming ignorance will not protect you from legal action. Attribution alone is inadequate.

Giving credit to the original creator does not eliminate the need for permission. While acknowledging the creator can help foster goodwill, it does not legally relieve you of responsibility. Attribution is important, but it cannot replace obtaining proper consent. Just because you tag someone does not mean you have the right to use their work. Social media platforms facilitate sharing legally. The safest way to share content is by using the platform's built-in sharing features. These tools automatically credit the original creator and ensure that your repost aligns with both the platform's policies and copyright law. Ignoring these tools and choosing to repost directly may result in legal consequences.

SHADOWBANNING

Shadowbanning is a contentious practice employed by social media platforms in which a user's posts or activities are partially or completely obscured from other users without their awareness (Gilbert, 2024). Consequently, while the user can still create posts and engage as usual, their content remains considerably less visible or entirely unseen by others, thus diminishing their reach and interaction.

How It Works

Shadow banning limits the broader visibility of a user's content without their knowledge. A Facebook or Instagram post that's been subjected to shadow banning remains on the original poster's profile page, but it might appear less often, or not at all, in the timelines of other users (Gilbert, 2024). Posts from a shadowbanned user may not show up in search results, hashtags, or the feeds of other users. Interactions from other users are limited, resulting in fewer likes, comments, and shares. The affected user is generally unaware of their shadowbanned status, as they view their posts and activities as normal. Part of this method's power of shadow banning is that it's nearly impossible to uncover, even by policymakers or software engineering experts.

Social media companies acknowledge it, though they prefer to use terms such as "deamplification" and "reducing reach" (Fowler, 2022). Reduction started as an effort to tamp down spam, but its use has expanded to content that doesn't violate the rules but gets close to it, from miracle cures and clickbait to false claims about Sept. 11 and dangerous stunts. Whistleblower Frances Haugen revealed a complex system for ranking content in Facebook, with algorithms scoring posts based on factors such as their predicted risk to societal health or their potential to be misinformation and then demoting them in the Facebook feed (Fowler, 2022).

Reasons for Shadowbanning

Users may be shadowbanned for violating platform policies, such as posting inappropriate content or engaging in spammy behaviour.

Automation and Bots. Excessive use of automation tools, bots, or repetitive actions can trigger shadowbanning to curb artificial engagement.

Algorithmic Triggers. Platforms may use algorithms to detect and limit the visibility of content deemed undesirable or harmful.

Platforms Known for Shadowbanning

Instagram users have reported sudden drops in engagement and visibility, often attributed to shadowbanning linked to hashtag misuse or policy violations. Users have claimed that shadowbanning occurs due to political content or breaches of Twitter's terms of service. Similar concerns arise when TikTok users discover their videos are not reaching the anticipated audience.

Controversy and Criticism

Lack of Transparency. Users often criticize the lack of clear communication from platforms about why shadowbanning occurs and how to resolve it.

Impact on Free Speech. Some view shadowbanning as a suppression of free speech, especially when it targets specific viewpoints or content.

Effectiveness and Fairness. Questions arise about the effectiveness and fairness of shadowbanning as a moderation tool, particularly regarding false positives and inconsistent enforcement.

How to Address Shadowbanning

Review and Adjust Content: Ensure that posts comply with the platform's community guidelines and avoid spammy behaviour.

Engage Authentically: Avoid using bots or automated tools excessively and focus on genuine interactions.

Appeal Process. Some platforms offer an appeal process where users can request a review of their account status.

By understanding shadowbanning, users can better navigate social media platforms and maintain compliance with their policies to avoid reduced visibility and engagement.

NUDIFICATION

Nudification applications enable users without technical or even Photoshop skills to artificially generate intimate imagery of someone without their consent. The resulting image is a *Synthetic, Non-Consensual, Explicit AI-Created Imagery*, or SNEACI (Gibson, Olszewski, Brigham, Crowder, Butler, Traynor, Redmiles & Kohno, 2024).

In October 2023, 14-year-old Francesca Mani heard that some boys had naked photos of female classmates. She soon learned her picture was among them. Still, the images were doctored - created with artificial intelligence using what's known as a "nudify" website or app, which turns real photos of someone fully clothed into real-looking nudes. Francesca Mani knew nothing about nudify websites when she discovered she and several other girls at Westfield High School in New Jersey had been targeted. According to a lawsuit later filed by one of the other girls through her parents, a boy at the school uploaded photos from Instagram to a site called "Clothoff."

Despite the increasing awareness of such applications and their potential to infringe on the rights of image subjects and cause downstream harm, no systematic study of the nudification application ecosystem across multiple platforms has been conducted to date. As of this writing, there have been 30 similar incidents in schools across Canada and the U.S. over the last 20 months, with many more reported globally (Cooper, 2024).

SELFIES

Selfies are not new. In 1839, the first selfie was taken on a Daguerreotype by American photographer Robert Cornelius. As for the selfie stick, Indonesia was one of the first countries to use it. Some locals referred to it as the narcissist stick, which quickly spread to Malaysia and the Philippines. The rest of the world was still stretching their arms to get a selfie (Wendling, 2014).

Figure 6. (a). In 1839, American photographer Robert Cornelius took the first selfie (U.S. Library of Congress) (b) In 1925, Arnold and Helen Hogg in the UK demonstrate their makeshift selfie stick

In November 2000, the first camera phone went on the market, with a resolution of 110,000 pixels, which was an impressive innovation at the time. when Japan-based SoftBank Corporation launched the world's first mobile phone with a fully integrated camera. The built-in, back-facing camera

KILLFIES

In 2011, Tom Ryaboi dangled his feet over the edge of a tall building in Toronto and took a picture straight down, Figure 7. He posted it on Flickr and Reddit. The picture became a viral hit.

Figure 7. Tom Ryaboi's selfie of his feet dangling over the edge of a tall building in Toronto

(Ryaboi, 2011)

After that event, a new generation of Instagrammers, YouTubers, and members of other social networks began to cultivate the craft of risking life and limb to post heart-pounding pictures and videos of dangerous stunts. Risk-taking social media photography deaths and injuries roughly tripled in number from the beginning of 2014 to the end of 2015, according to a media analysis conducted by medical researchers in Turkey (Dokur, Petekkaya & Karadağ, 2018).

A subculture has emerged in the past eight years of people who seek out death-defying situations for the likes, followers, and adulation of fans on social media. More than 250 people across the world have died in the pursuit of the perfect selfie (Scherzer, 2019). The majority of these "killfies" were caused either by drowning, being hit by a car or train, or falling from a great height. All around the world, selfie and photo deaths have increased (Baker, 2017).

Figure 8 shows an Instagram post of Meenakshi sitting on the edge of a rock over the Grand Canyon, taken by her husband, Vishnu. The caption read, "A lot of us, including yours truly, are fans of daredevilry attempts to stand at the edge of cliffs and skyscrapers. Are our lives just worth one photo?" Months later, they would both be dead. They were killed in an 800-foot fall at Yosemite National Park, an accident that occurred while they were on the edge of a cliff and taking pictures for their Instagram account (Elgan, 2019).

Figure 8. A posting to an Instagram account showing a photo of Meenakshi Moorthy taken by her husband Vishnu. Months later, they would both be dead from a fall

(Elgan, 2019)

Researchers at *Carnegie Mellon University* and the *Indraprastha Institute of Information* reported that India recorded the highest number of 'killfies' globally, caused by drowning, being hit by trains or cars, or falling from great heights, all in pursuit of the perfect photo (Lamba, Bharadhwaj, Vachher, Agarwal, Arora & Kumaraguru, 2017).

In response to the surge in fatalities, the Mumbai Police and the state tourism ministry announced 16 'no-selfie zones,' planning to station volunteers and police in these perilous locations, such as beaches, dams, and forts, fortifying them by using public address systems and social media to spread the word. The Indian state of Goa identified 24 "no-selfie zones" along its coastline following a rise in deaths and injuries. Eight years later, selfie-seekers are still risking their lives for the perfect photo, and the much-hyped 'no-selfie zones' are conspicuously absent (Das, 2024).

WHERE IT ALL STARTED

In March 2003, the *U.S. Patent and Trademark Office* received a technology patent application from Jonathan Abrams for "Friendster," defined as a system, method, and apparatus for connecting users in an online computer system based on their relationships within social networks. His patent was approved two years later. Soon after, social media platforms with catchy names began to populate the Internet.

Since then, social media has been criticized for negatively influencing children and young adults, contributing to issues such as violence and suicide. Lawsuits have been brought against some social media companies alleging that their platforms negatively influence young people. Social media operators need to be held more accountable for the harms their products cause, not just encouraged to innovate. Social media entices young and not-so-young participants to put themselves in harm's way for admiration and respect from their peers. These companies must be subjected to liability frameworks that expose them to meaningful financial losses should they be found responsible for harm.

The changing social interactions that this technology has brought about have outpaced our values and attitudes, an anthropological condition known as "cultural lag" (Mann, 1993). The recommendation taken in this chapter is ultimately that the solution is in the hands of its victims, who need to put down the mouse and step away from the computer, and no one else will get hurt (Aftab, 2016).

REFERENCES

ABC7 Eyewitness News. (2025). Teen charged after laptop fire at New Jersey high school believed to be part of TikTok challenge, https://abc7chicago.com/post/chromebook-challenge-teen-charged-laptop-fire-new-jersey-high-school-believed-part-tiktok-trend/16417860/

Acton, B. & Koum, J. (2009). WhatsApp. Computer program.

Aftab, P. (2016). Put down the mouse and step away from the computer…and no one will get hurt! Stop Cyberbullying, *WiredSafety.org*, http://www.stopcyberbullying.org/teens/index.html

Alphonso, C. (2024). Five more Canadian school boards sue social media giants, alleging harm to students' mental health, *The Globe and Mail Inc.,* https://www.theglobeandmail.com/canada/article-school-boards-sue-byte-dance-meta-snap/

AMA. (2025). American Psychiatric Association, https://rarediseases.org/organizations/american-psychiatric-association/

APA. (2025). Technology Addictions: Social Media, Online Gaming, and More, *American Psychiatric Association,* https://www.psychiatry.org/Patients-Families/Technology-Addictions-Social-Media-and-more/Expert-Q-A-Technology-Addiction

Arzt, N., & Abulhosn, R. (7 July 2023). TikTok addiction: Causes, signs, & how to stop, choosing therapy, https://www.choosingtherapy.com/tiktok-addiction/

Baker, E.-R. (July 19, 2017). People are dying and injuring themselves for the perfect Insta snap, *Vice Magazine,* https://www.vice.com/en/article/people-are-literally-dying-and-injuring-themselves-for-the-perfect-insta-snap/

Beever, S. (September 30, 2022). Social media content contributed to the tragic teenager Molly Russell, HullLive, https://www.hulldailymail.co.uk/news/uk-world-news/social-media-content-contributed-tragic-7648709

Bergstrom, I. (2008). Facebook can ruin your life. And so can MySpace, Bebo… *The Independent,* https://www.independent.co.uk/life-style/gadgets-and-tech/news/facebook-can-ruin-your-life-and-socan-myspace-bebo-780521.html

Boesveld, S. (2012). RCMP launch probe into Facebook post after man brags of tormenting teens who committed suicide, *National Post,* https://nationalpost.com/news/canada/n-s-rcmp-launch-probe-into-facebook-post-after-man-brags-of-tormenting-teens-who-committed-suicide

Boyd, D. (September 2006). Facebook's privacy trainwreck: Exposure, invasion, and drama, *Apophenia Blog,* https://www.danah.org/papers/FacebookAndPrivacy.html

CBC News. (28 March 2011), Bullied teen's death sparks campaign, https://www.cbc.ca/news/canada/nova-scotia/bullied-teen-s-death-sparks-campaign-1.996424

Chen, S., Hurley, C. & Karim, J. (2005). YouTube, a computer program.

Constitution of the United States. (1789). https://guides.loc.gov/constitution

Cooper, A. (December 15, 2024). Schools face a new threat: "nudify" sites that use AI to create realistic, revealing images of classmates, 60 Minutes, *CBS News,* https://www.cbsnews.com/news/schools-face-new-threat-nudify-sites-use-ai-create-realistic-revealing-images-60-minutes-transcript/

Coyle, S. (2014). Social media and suicide prevention, *Social Work Today, 14,* 1, https://www.socialworktoday.com/archive/012014p8.shtml

Cross, G. (2025). What is the Chromebook Challenge? The trend that has students destroying school laptops, *USA Today,* https://www.usatoday.com/story/tech/2025/05/20/chromebook-challenge-tiktok-trend/83730941007/

Crown Prosecution Service. (2024). Cybercrime definitions: Doxing, https://www.cps.gov.uk/legal-guidance/cybercrime-prosecution-guidance

Culture Magazine. (2025). Students Intentionally Setting Laptops on Fire for TikTok Sparks Safety Concerns in Canadian Classrooms, *Asian-English Culture Magazine,* https://culturemagazin.com/students-intentionally-setting-laptops-on-fire-for-tiktok-sparks-safety-concerns-in-canadian-classrooms/

Das, M. (July 28, 2024). As 'killfie' threat mounts, no-selfie zones planned in 2016 a non-starter, *The Times of India,* https://timesofindia.indiatimes.com/city/mumbai/as-killfie-threat-mounts-no-selfie-zones-planned-in-2016-a-non-starter/articleshow/112074139.cms

Dempsey, C. (2025). Connecticut students arrested for TikTok 'Chromebook Challenge' fire, *Journal Inquirer,* https://www.firerescue1.com/arson-investigation/conn-students-arrested-for-tiktok-chromebook-challenge-fire

Dokur, M., Petekkaya, E., & Karadağ, M. (2018). Media-based clinical research on selfie-related injuries and deaths. *Ulusal Travma ve Acil Cerrahi Dergisi = Turkish Journal of Trauma & Emergency Surgery : TJTES, 24*(2), 129–135. DOI: 10.5505/tjtes.2017.83103 PMID: 29569684

DSM-5 (2013). Diagnostic and Statistical Manual of Mental Disorders, https://psychiatryonline.org/doi/book/10.1176/appi.books.9780890425787

Éducaloi. (2019). Cyberbullying, https://www.educaloi.qc.ca/en/youth/capsules/cyberbullying

Edwards, B. (2011). 'I wish I could be happy,' *Ottawa East News,* https://www.insideottawavalley.com/news-story/3800605--i-wish-i-could-be-happy-/

Elgan, M. (2019). People are falling off buildings in search of the perfect Instagram shot, *Fast Company,* https://www.fastcompany.com/90287323/people-are-falling-off-buildings-in-search-of-the-perfect-instagram-shot

Fortinet (2025). Swatting: The danger of false emergency calls, https://www.fortinet.com/resources/cyberglossary/swatting

Fowler, G. A. (2022). Shadowbanning is real: Here's how you end up muted by social media, *The Washington Post,* https://www.washingtonpost.com/technology/2022/12/27/shadowban/

Gibson, C., Olszewski, D., Brigham, N.G., Crowder, A., Butler, K.R.B., Traynor, P., Redmiles, E.M., & Kohno, T. (November 14, 2024). Analyzing the AI nudification application ecosystem, arXiv.org; Ithaca, NY.

Gilbert, K. (2024). How shadow banning can silently shift opinion online, *Yale Insights,* https://insights.som.yale.edu/insights/how-shadow-banning-can-silently-shift-opinion-online

Gile, N. (2025). Long Beach teenager arrested for arson after viral "Chromebook Challenge" prank sparks fire, *KCAL News,* https://www.cbsnews.com/losangeles/news/long-beach-teenager-arrested-for-arson-after-viral-chromebook-challenge-prank-sparks-fire/

Gilmour, M. (2025). Dawson College teachers say government probe into tensions on campus creating climate of fear, *CTV News,* https://www.ctvnews.ca/montreal/article/dawson-college-teachers-say-government-probe-into-tensions-on-campus-creating-climate-of-fear/

Hernandez, T., & Okutan, E. (2023). 'Doxxing truck' appears on Yale's campus, displays student names and photos, *Yale News,* https://yaledailynews.com/blog/2023/11/17/doxxing-truck-appears-on-yales-campus-displays-student-names-and-photos/

Herrero, O. (2025). Why Macron is obsessed with banning social media for kids, *POLITICO,* https://www.politico.eu/article/emmanuel-macron-france-social-media-ban-minors-big-tech/

Intimate Images and Cyber-protection Act. SNS 2017, c 7, https://nslegislature.ca/legc/bills/63rd_1st/1st_read/b027.htm

Johnson, S. (April 19, 2018). State Supreme Court hears arguments over suspension of Marquette Professor, *Wisconsin Public Radio,* https://www.wpr.org/justice/state-supreme-court-hears-arguments-over-suspension-marquette-professor

Kaeding, D. (April 12, 2024). Wisconsin tribe sues social media companies over suicide rates among Native youth, *Wisconsin Public Radio,* https://www.wpr.org/news/menominee-indian-spirit-lake-tribe-sues-social-media-suicide-rates-native-youth

Kharpal, A. (August 2, 2023). China floats two-hour daily limit of smartphone screen time for kids, *CNBC,* https://www.cnbc.com/2023/08/02/china-floats-two-hour-daily-limit-of-smartphone-screen-time-for-kids.html#:~:text=Time%20restrictions&text=Children%20under%20the%20age%20of%20eight%20should%20be%20restricted%20to,a%20maximum%20of%20two%20hours

Klinger, A., & Klinger, H. (2024). Violent Threats and Incidents in Schools: An Analysis of the 2023-2024 School Year, *The Educator's School Safety Network,* www.eSchoolSafety.org

Lamba, H., Bharadhwaj, V., Vachher, M., Agarwal, D., Arora, M., Sachdeva, N., & Kumaraguru, P. (2017). From camera to deathbed: Understanding dangerous selfies on social media, *Proceedings of the Eleventh International AAAI Conference on Web and Social Media, 11,* 1, https://ojs.aaai.org/index.php/ICWSM/article/view/14956

Lanier Law Firm. (2025). Social Media Addiction Statistics, Redefining Legal Care, https://www.lanierlawfirm.com/social-media-addiction/statistics/

LeLievre v. Gould, [1893] 1 Q.B. 491 at 497.

Leung, W., & Bascaramurty, D. (12 October 2012). Amanda Todd tragedy highlights how social media makes bullying inescapable, The Globe and Mail Inc, https://www.theglobeandmail.com/news/national/amanda-todd-tragedy-highlights-how-social-media-makes-bullying-inescapable/article4611068/

Lofton, C. (July 21, 2022). Suicide deaths of 2 area teens subject of lawsuit against social media companies, *Fox 22,* https://abc17news.com/cnn-regional/2022/07/21/suicide-deaths-of-2-area-teens-subject-of-lawsuit-against-social-media-companies/

Mann, B. L. (1993). Technology orientation for educators: Learning from the industrial subculture. *New Morning Watch: Educational & Social Analysis, 20*(3), 18–25.

Mann, B. L. (2009). Social networking websites: A concatenation of impersonation, denigration, sexual and aggressive solicitation, cyber-bullying and happy slapping videos. *International Journal of Law and Information Technology, 17*(3), 252–267. DOI: 10.1093/ijlit/ean008

Mann, B. L. (2015). Social networking websites: A concatenation of impersonation, denigration, sexual and aggressive solicitation, cyber-bullying and happy slapping videos, in Philip Leith (Ed.). *Privacy in the Information Society* (pp. 493–503), Part VI. Social Networks, Volume II of a 3-volume series. The Library of Essays on Law and Privacy. London, U.K.: Ashgate Publishing. January.

Mann, B. L. (2020). *Applying Internet Laws and Regulations to Educational Technology, Public Policy and Administration Book Series*. IGI Global.

McCoy, D. (May 1, 2018). When studying, doxing gets you doxed, *Huff Post,* https://www.huffpost.com/entry/opinion-mccoy-doxing-study_n_5ae75ec7e4b02baed1bd06cc?utm_source=chatgpt.com

McKay, K. (February 22, 2023). Doxxing – A 21st Century Crime, *Glasgow Guardian*, https://glasgowguardian.co.uk/2023/02/22/doxxing-a-21st-century-crime/?utm_source=chatgpt.com

McLuhan, M., & Lapham, L. H. (1994). *Understanding Media: The Extensions of Man*. McGraw-Hill.

Meaker, M. (2022). How a British teen's death changed social media, *Wired,* https://www.wired.com/story/how-a-british-teens-death-changed-social-media/

Miller, S. (February 15, 2024). Nevada attorney general's lawsuits against social media companies underscore impact on youth, Las Vegas Weekly, https://lasvegasweekly.com/news/2024/feb/15/nevada-attorney-generals-lawsuits-social-media/

NAAG. (February 21, 2024). A Bipartisan Coalition of 39 State Attorneys General Urge Congressional Action on Pharmacy Benefit Manager Reform, *National Association of Attorneys General,* https://www.naag.org/press-releases/a-bipartisan-coalition-of-39-state-attorneys-general-urge-congressional-action-on-pharmacy-benefit-manager-reform/

NYC Press Office. (February 14, 2024). Mayor Adams announces lawsuit against social media companies fueling nationwide youth mental health crisis, *City of New York,* https://www.nyc.gov/office-of-the-mayor/news/125-24/mayor-adams-lawsuit-against-social-media-companies-fueling-nationwide-youth-mental-health?ref=upstract.com#/0

OUT-LAW News. (July 2006). Friendster patents social networking, http://www.outlaw.com/default.aspx?page=7092

Raab, R. (November 27, 2023). Faculty pen letter pledging to defend doxxed students, including 'nonviolent direct action, up to and including arrest,' *Yale Daily News,* https://yaledailynews.com/blog/2023/11/27/faculty-pen-letter-pledging-to-defend-doxxed-students-including-nonviolent-direct-action-up-to-and-including-arrest/?utm_source=chatgpt.com

Ritter, K. (January 31, 2024). Nevada AG launches lawsuits against social media firms in state court, Associated Press, Las Vegas Sun, https://lasvegassun.com/news/2024/jan/31/nevada-ag-launches-go-it-alone-lawsuits-against-so/

Ruskin, B. (2015). Court strikes down anti-cyberbullying law created after Rehtaeh Parsons's death, CBC News, https://www.cbc.ca/news/canada/nova-scotia/cyberbullying-law-struck-down-1.3360612

Scherzer, A. (2019). Why is India the world capital for selfie deaths, and what's being done to stop it? ABC News, https://www.abc.net.au/news/2019-03-08/selfie-deaths-india-world-capital-killfies/10874536

Scott, J. P. (2015). Courtney Brown's suicide and the tragic effects of bullying, Canadian Living, Transcontinental Media, http://www.canadianliving.com/life/community/courtney_browns_suicide_and_the_tragic_effects_of_bullying.php#.UQ12Imtij9g.twitter

Segal, M. (2015). Independent review of the police and prosecution response to the Rehtaeh Parsons case, https://novascotia.ca/segalreport/Parsons-Independent-Review.pdf

Seguin, K. (2025). Students describe a dangerous social media 'challenge' that's made its way to London, Ontario, https://www.cbc.ca/lite/story/1.7555022?feature=random

Shea, C. (2025). The Toronto Catholic District School Board is begging students to stop blowing up their laptops, *Toronto Life,* https://torontolife.com/city/toronto-catholic-district-school-board-students-blowing-up-laptops-chromebook-challenge/

Sulleyman, A. (2017). Facebook is 'destroying' society and making users feel 'vacant and empty,' former exec says, *The Independent*, https://www.independent.co.uk/life-style/gadgets-and-tech/news/facebook-society-destroy-social-media-network-users-damage-communicate-connect-chamath-palihapitiya-a8105131.html

The eGirls Project (3 June 2015). https://egirlsproject.ca/the-project/what-we-are/

Van Brunt, A.V. & Anand, E. (2025). Police abuse: Finch v. Rapp, *Roderick & Solange MacArthur Justice Center,* media@macarthurjustice.org

Wendling, M. (December 10, 2014). #BBCtrending: Twitter declares 2014 the year of the 'selfie', BBC News.

Wilburn, C. (2025). Houston-area schools warn parents about Chromebook Challenge damaging school property, *Houston Chronicle,* https://www.houstonchronicle.com/news/houston-texas/trending/article/tiktok-chromebook-challenge-houston-schools-20321671.php

Zuckerberg, M. (6 March 2021). A privacy-focused vision for social networking, Facebook, https://www.facebook.com/notes/mark-zuckerberg/a-privacy-focused-vision-for-social-networking/10156700570096634/

Zuckerberg, M., Saverin, E., McCollum, A., Moskovitz, D. & Hughes, C. (2004). Facebook, computer platform.

Chapter 5
Legal Initiatives:
The U.K., the U.S., and Europe

ABSTRACT

There have been recent attempts in the U.K., the U.S. and Europe to prevent harm to young and not-so-young members on social media through legislation and educational initiatives, highlighting several existing programs as standards of care. In the UK, the Online Safety Act came into force in 2025, which requires social media companies to enforce their age limits consistently and protect their child users. In the U.S., a school's "duty of care" arises from negligence law, which mandates that school administrators take reasonable steps to protect students from foreseeable harm despite potential breaches of privacy and freedom of speech, hence the controversy over the Kids Online Safety Act. According to critics, KOSA is essentially a censorship regime disguised as a "duty of care" that would suppress lawful, important speech online, especially for young people.

THE PAISLEY SNAIL

In August 1928, May Donoghue drank a bottle of Stevenson's ginger beer at the Wellmeadow Café in Paisley, Scotland. After drinking the ginger beer, she discovered a decomposed snail in the bottle. Consequently, Mrs. Donoghue suffered severe gastroenteritis and shock. She later sued the ginger beer manufacturer, David Stevenson.

DOI: 10.4018/979-8-3373-3126-3.ch005

Figure 1. Left: Mrs. May Donoghue of the "Paisley snail" case with her grandchildren. Right: A bottle of Stevenson's ginger beer similar to the one she was served

(Olijnyk, 2022)

At trial, the House of Lords ruled that Mr. Stevenson, the manufacturer of Stevenson's ginger beer, owed a duty of care to Mrs. Donoghue, which was breached because it was reasonably foreseeable that failing to ensure the product's safety could harm consumers. *Donoghue v Stevenson (1932)* became a landmark case in English tort law that established the modern concept of negligence and laid the foundation of the modern law of negligence in common law jurisdictions worldwide, establishing general principles of the duty of care.

Before the Paisley Snail

Before the Paisley Snail, the law of negligence was only invoked if there was a contractual relationship in place. Before the Paisley Snail and the associated court case *Donoghue v Stevenson (1932)*, the manufacturer would have owed no duty of care to the consumer if they had no contract, unless the manufacturer was aware at the time that the product was defective, and that that information was concealed from the consumer (*Levy v Langridge 150 E.R., 1838; Longmeid and Wife v Holliday 155 E.R. 752, 1851*), or if the product was dangerous and the manufacturer failed to warn the consumer *(Heaven v Pender, West India Graving Dock Co., 1883)*. Before Mrs. Donoghue's decomposing snail, Mr. Stevenson would not have been liable for negligence to Mrs. Donoghue.

DUTY OF CARE IN BRITAIN

"Duty of care" is the foundation for all negligence claims. Lord Atkin articulated "the neighbour principle," which established the modern law of negligence by outlining general principles of the duty of care.

You must take reasonable care to avoid acts or omissions that you can reasonably foresee would likely injure your neighbour. Who, then, in law, is my neighbour? The answer appears to be individuals who are so closely and directly affected by my actions that I ought reasonably to have them in contemplation as being thus affected when I focus on the acts or omissions in question *(Donoghue v Stevenson, 1932, 580).*

The "neighbour principle" is a legal doctrine that requires a person to take reasonable care to avoid actions or omissions that could reasonably foreseeably harm their neighbour. In this context, a "neighbour" refers to anyone directly affected by the action or omission in question. This principle was expanded by the House of Lords in a series of cases culminating in *Anns v. Merton London Borough Council (1977).* In that case, Lord Wilberforce established a two-stage test for determining the duty of care:

First, one must ask whether a sufficient relationship of *proximity exists* such that carelessness on the part of the former may likely cause damage to the latter, thereby giving rise to a *prima facie* duty of care.

Secondly, if the first question is answered affirmatively, it is essential to consider whether any factors might negate, reduce, or limit the scope of the duty, the *class of person* to whom it is owed, or the *damages* that may arise from a breach of it.

Since *Donoghue,* the whole world has become a neighbour online. Since *Donoghue,* the "neighbour principle" has been extended to *anywhere*, at *any time*. Today, everyone takes *anywhere, anytime* for granted; the law has yet to catch up (Currie, 2004). Before this case, the manufacturer could not be held liable for negligence to the consumer without a prior contractual relationship.

Once a duty of care is established, the standard of care can be determined by either law or policy. The "standard of care" is evaluated by examining what actions a reasonable person would take in similar circumstances. A breach of duty of care is assessed based on factual considerations.

A School's Duty of Care

Schools have a duty of care to all students to prevent and address bullying among children and adolescents (Foody & Samara, 2018). A person suing a school, for example, must prove that the school or school board owed them a duty of care, that it breached that duty by failing to meet the required standard of care, and that the student suffered injury or harm as a result.

British Initiatives

In September 2024, the Department for Education in England published an updated version of the *Statutory Safeguarding and Child Protection Guidance for Schools in England*, entitled "Keeping Children Safe in Education." The guidance sets out what schools and colleges in England must do to safeguard and promote the welfare of children and young people under the age of 18.

The UK's *Online Safety Act* came into force in 2025 (GovUK, 2025). The Act requires social media companies to enforce their age limits consistently and protect their child users. Ofcom is the independent regulator of Online Safety in the U.K. It devises the steps that providers can take to fulfil their safety duties in codes of practice.

Ofcom has a broad range of powers to assess and enforce providers' compliance with the framework. Services must assess any risks to children from using their platforms and set appropriate age restrictions, ensuring that child users have age-appropriate experiences and are shielded from harmful content. Ofcom is supposed to focus on the rules that social media platforms set and monitor whether they are adhering to their stated commitments (Hern, 2024). Ostensibly, this means that a platform that wants to provide minimal censorship can, provided it doesn't give users a false sense of security by claiming otherwise. Service providers who use measures to prevent access to their service for children under a certain age must specify in their terms of service what measures are being used to enforce this age limit and enforce this consistently.

A Negative Right

Since 1998, British citizens have had a negative right to freedom of expression, according to Article 10 of the *European Convention on Human Rights,* as applied in British law through the *Human Rights Act.* A "negative right" is an obligation not to be subjected to an action of another person or group, such as a government, usually occurring in the form of abuse or coercion. This freedom includes expressing one's views on social media. Article 10 of the *United Kingdom's Human Rights Act* (1998) states that,

> *Everyone has the right to freedom of expression, which includes the freedom to hold opinions and to receive and impart information and ideas without interference by public authority and regardless of frontiers (UK's Human Rights Act, 1998).*

That said, the United Kingdom has ramped up its censorship efforts, now taking the extraordinary step of jailing its citizens for making "hateful" social media posts and threatening to extradite the citizens of other countries, including the U.S., for "hate speech" and other speech violations (Standing Staff, 2024). Two men have been sent to prison for stirring up hatred and violence online in the first cases of their kind linked to the recent riots seen across England (Murray & Syal, 2024). Jordan Parlour, 28, was jailed for 20 months after pleading guilty to inciting racial hatred with Facebook posts in which he advocated an attack on a hotel in Leeds as part of the violent public disorder that swept England. In Northampton, Tyler Kay, 26, was given three years and two months in prison for posts on X that called for mass deportation and for people to set fire to hotels housing asylum seekers.

Director of Public Prosecutions Stephen Parkinson stated that there are dedicated police officers who scour social media looking for this material and then follow up with identification and arrests. London Metropolitan Police Commissioner Sir Mark Rowley stated that the arrests won't be confined to British citizens, warning that the government would extradite citizens of other countries.

DUTY OF CARE IN EUROPE

In Europe, the duty of care for students, particularly in higher education, is a complex and evolving area of legal and ethical debate. While not universally defined, it generally encompasses a school or university's obligation to take reasonable measures to protect students from foreseeable harm and to provide appropriate support services. This duty is often viewed as a responsibility to exercise reasonable care and skill when teaching and providing support services. Whereas the specific legal frameworks vary across European countries, the principle of the duty of care to students is widely recognized.

Table 1. The principle of duty of care to students has been applied across European countries

Country	Key Principle	Legal Source
France	Schools have a strict liability for students during school hours and activities.	Code de l'éducation; based on administrative liability (i.e., responsabilité de l'État)
Germany	Supervisory duties are regulated by state law (Länder), not federal. Teachers must prevent foreseeable harm.	Landesrecht (state laws); Civil Code (BGB) for liability
Netherlands	Duty of care is part of general tort law. Schools must act as a "reasonably acting institution" would.	Civil Code (Burgerlijk Wetboek)
Sweden	Schools must protect students from physical and psychological harm.	Education Act; Work Environment Act
Italy	Schools and teachers are liable for student safety unless they prove absence of fault.	Article 2048 Civil Code; Ministry of Education guidelines

continued on following page

Table 1. Continued

Country	Key Principle	Legal Source
Spain	Teachers and schools have a duty to supervise and protect students at all times.	Ley Orgánica de Educación; Civil liability law
Finland	Teachers have a general legal obligation to ensure student safety and intervene in risk situations.	Basic Education Act; Government Decree on Pupil Welfare

European Legal Initiatives

Children are big users of social media. Article 24 of the *EU Charter* states that (2) a child's best interests must be a primary consideration, and that (1) children shall have the right to such protection and may express their views freely (EU Charter, Article 24). Article 8 of the *Charter of Fundamental Rights of the European Union* (2000) states that everyone has the right to the protection of personal data, and that everyone has the right to access the data that has been collected about him or her, and the right to have it rectified.

In Europe, the duty of care for students using social media is multifaceted, encompassing parental consent, age restrictions, and school policies. Many countries, like Germany and Belgium, have established a minimum age for social media access, often with parental consent required for younger users. Germany requires parental consent for children between 13 and 16. There are currently no plans to go further. However, child protection advocates say controls are insufficient and call for existing rules to be better implemented. There are currently no plans to go further (Reuters, 2024). However, child protection advocates say controls are insufficient and call for existing rules to be better implemented. Belgium mandates a minimum age of 13 for creating accounts without parental permission. While the Netherlands doesn't have any laws regarding a minimum age for social media use, the government did ban mobile devices in classrooms from January 2024 to reduce distractions (Reuters, 2024). Exceptions apply for digital lessons, medical needs or disabilities. In Italy, children under the age of 14 need parental consent to sign up for social media accounts, while no consent is required from that age upwards.

Whereas Norway is not a member state of the European Union, it is closely associated with the EU through its participation in the *European Economic Area (EEA),* an agreement that brings together all the EU member states and three EFTA countries (Iceland, Norway, and Liechtenstein) to create a single market. In October 2024, the Norwegian government proposed raising the age at which children can consent to the terms required to use social media to 15 years from 13 years currently, although parents would still be permitted to sign off on their behalf if they are under the age limit. The centre-left government also said it had begun work on legislation to set an absolute legal minimum age limit for social media use.

Schools in Europe also play a crucial role in educating students about responsible social media use and online safety. This includes addressing potential risks like cyberbullying, privacy concerns, and the impact of online content on mental health. Schools educate students about online risks and promote responsible social media use, while also considering data privacy and consent, particularly for younger students.

DUTY OF CARE IN THE UNITED STATES

In the United States, there is no single federal policy explicitly defining "duty of care". Legislation is established through case law. So, a teacher's duty of care in the U.S. arises from the principles of negligence law. Schools have a legal obligation to take reasonable measures to protect students from foreseeable harm, ensuring their safety and well-being while on school premises or participating in school activities, which includes providing adequate supervision, maintaining safe facilities, and responding appropriately to potential risks. Key aspects of a teacher's duty of care include:

- Actively monitoring students to prevent accidents or injuries
- Maintaining a safe learning environment by addressing any hazards, reporting unsafe conditions, and following safety protocols
- Intervening in situations that could lead to harm, such as bullying, violence, or unsafe activities
- Providing adequate instruction to ensure students understand how to perform tasks safely
- Preparing to respond appropriately in emergencies, such as medical crises or natural disasters

In the U.S., duty of care is used in tort law to determine when an individual is liable for an injury to another person. The legal standards governing the duty of care differ by state, as each state has its own tort laws. If a person's actions fall below the standard, they may be deemed negligent and held liable for any resulting damages. For instance, in *Oklahoma Admin. Code § 210:20-29-5 (Principle III),* a career teacher may face dismissal or non-reemployment for:

- Willful neglect of duty
- Repeated negligence in the performance of duty
- Mental or physical abuse of a child

- Incompetency
- Instructional ineffectiveness
- Unsatisfactory teaching performance
- Any reason involving moral turpitude
- Abandonment of contract

AMERICAN INITIATIVES

In the United States, lawsuits by school districts against social media companies are multiplying. Over 200 school districts have now taken legal action against major social media companies concerning the youth mental health crisis. What began as a single lawsuit filed by Seattle public schools has evolved into a widespread offensive against the social media platforms that adolescents use habitually. Although this legal battle is still in its early stages, experts indicate it could have significant implications for K-12 education—whether there is a win, loss, or settlement. The First Amendment of the *United States Constitution,* adopted in 1791, safeguards the civil rights and liberties associated with life in the U.S. The First Amendment states that,

> *Congress shall make no law respecting an establishment of religion or prohibiting the free exercise thereof, or abridging the freedom of speech, or of the press; or the right of the people peaceably to assemble, and to petition the Government for a redress of grievances" (U.S. Constitution, 1789).*

The principle applies whether the "speech" is shared in a classroom or on the Internet. That said, social media platforms are private companies and, as such, are not bound by the First Amendment, which means they can moderate the content that people post on their websites without violating those users' First Amendment rights. It also means the government cannot tell social media sites how to moderate content. Many state laws that have tried to regulate how social media companies can moderate their content have failed on First Amendment grounds.

Government Overreach

Americans know all too well what can happen when government officials assert broad discretionary power over telecommunications networks. For over 20 years, the U.S. government has deputized internet service providers and systems to surveil Americans and their correspondents without meaningful judicial oversight (McSherry, Guariglia, Gilligan & Crocker, 2024). The U.S. government continues to collect digital communications data as long as the surveillance is directed at foreigners located outside the United States and does not intentionally target Americans. Once collected, the FBI can query the communications of specific individuals. In

2021, the FBI conducted up to 3.4 million warrantless searches to find Americans' communications.

KIDS ONLINE SAFETY ACT (KOSA)

The recent adoption of the *Kids Online Safety Act (KOSA) by the U.S. Senate* responds to the prevailing moral panic among certain American school administrators and campus police, a form of irrational social action that amplifies a genuine threat posed by shootings in some American schools (Heir, 2016). If signed into law, KOSA would mandate Internet service providers to adhere to a "duty of care" provision aimed at diminishing and preventing harmful practices toward minors, such as bullying and violence (Blumenthal, 2024). KOSA's goal was to establish guidelines to protect minors from harmful material on social media platforms through a "duty of care" system and require covered platforms to disable "addicting" design features for minors (Felner, 2024). The Act mandated that:

- Online platforms take reasonable measures to prevent and mitigate harm to minors, including cyberbullying, sexual exploitation, and exposure to harmful content.
- Platforms provide parents and guardians with tools to supervise and manage their children's online activities, such as controlling privacy settings and monitoring usage.
- Platforms disclose information about their algorithms and data collection practices and report on potential risks to minors.

In September 2024, U.S. Senators Richard Blumenthal and Marsha Blackburn reported on the results of a new poll of 1,200 online interviews (Felner, 2024). The report stated that 86 percent of respondents supported the *Kids Online Safety Act.* Support for the bill crossed partisan lines, with 87 percent of Republicans, 88 percent of Democrats, and 82 percent of independents favouring it. Seventy-six percent of Republican voters were also more likely to vote for a candidate for Congress who supports the *Kids Online Safety Act.* Advocacy groups, parents, and some tech companies endorse KOSA as a necessary step to protect children from online dangers. Proponents of this view are legal positivists who argue that laws must conform to a system of rules that dictate our actions.

KOSA Criticism

The *Electronic Frontier Foundation* and its supporters have been critical of KOSA since it was introduced in 2022 and have even labelled the *Kids Online Safety Act* "dangerous" because it threatens protected speech and will initiate privacy-invasive age verification requirements and content restrictions for many users wishing to access social media (Kelley, 2025). KOSA opponents have expressed concerns that the Bill could lead to over-censorship and restrict access to important information for marginalized groups, including LGBTQ+ youth (Bonesteel & Greer, 2024). Proponents of this view argue that laws must be justified by their moral content (Dyzenhaus, Moreau & Ripstein, 2007; Fuller, 1969). Students seeking access to social media should not have to limit their freedom of speech or their access to online content for the sake of personal privacy (Kelley, 2025).

The bill passed in the Senate by a 91–3 vote in 2024, after which it stalled in the House of Representatives due to concerns over free speech and content moderation. KOSA reflects a genuine bipartisan desire to address the harms children and teens face on social media, but it also encapsulates a larger cultural and political clash over free speech, privacy, and the role of the state in regulating digital life (Kimery, 2025). In May 2025, The Kids Online Safety Act (KOSA) was back in the Senate, its supporters claiming again that the latest version won't censor online content (Mullin, 2025

CHILDREN AND TEENS' ONLINE PRIVACY PROTECTION ACT

The *Children and Teens' Online Privacy Protection Act (CTOPPA)* is a proposed U.S. federal law that aims to expand and modernize the protections offered under the existing *Children's Online Privacy Protection Act (COPPA),* which currently safeguards the online privacy of children under 13. CTOPPA is designed to extend those protections to teenagers up to age 16 and to strengthen enforcement mechanisms, considering evolving digital threats. Although this Act does not directly protect students in schools, colleges, or universities, many social media platforms accessed by young students would be required to comply. Schools, colleges, and universities may need to revise their digital policies and vendor contracts with their ISPs. The core provisions are that:

- Data privacy protection would be extended to users aged 13–16, preventing websites from collecting or using personal information without the teen's consent. Platforms must explain how and why data will be collected and used.

- Data deletion rights would be strengthened, permitting children and youth to request deletion of their personal data.
- Targeted advertising would be banned to minors without their parents' consent, which is particularly relevant on platforms like TikTok, Instagram, and Snapchat

Meta's Fact-Checking Replaced by User Moderation

In January 2025, Meta Platforms, the parent company of Facebook, Instagram, and WhatsApp eliminated independent fact-checking to "restore free expression" and moved to a "Community Notes" model on Facebook, Instagram, and Threads, like Elon Musk's X platform (Capoot & Vanian, 2025). In a video posted alongside a blog post by the company, Meta's CEO Mark Zuckerberg said third-party moderators were "too politically biased", and that it was "time to get back to our roots around free expression" (McMahon, Kleinman & Subramanian, 2025).

Meta's fact-checking program, launched in 2016, referred posts that appeared false or misleading to an independent organization to assess their credibility. Posts tagged as inaccurate had labels added to provide viewers with more information and were moved lower in users' feeds. This has been replaced by community notes. Dr. Kate Klonick, Associate Professor of Law at St John's University Law School, said that "The private governance of speech on these platforms has increasingly become a point of politics," and that the change reflects a radical swing in the opposite direction from building trust and safety mechanisms that address issues like harassment, hate speech, and disinformation (McMahon et al, 2025).

State-Level Legislation

Several states enacted laws addressing social media harms in educational environments. Florida, Texas, and Louisiana were advancing bills to limit social media use in schools and impose penalties on platforms for harm to minors. The *Social Media Regulation Act (2023)* in Utah required age verification and parental consent for students under 18 years old. The Act permitted parents to access their children's accounts. Social media platforms were required to block access during overnight hours. Arkansas passed the *Social Media Safety Act (2023),* which targeted social media platform liability for harm to minors, and similar parental verification and age-gating requirements for children's accounts.

THE TAKE IT DOWN ACT

Take It Down is a federal law enacted in the United States that was introduced by Senator Ted Cruz in June 2024, passed by both houses in April 2025, and was signed into law by President Trump on May 19, 2025. *Take It Down*, or "The Tools to Address Known Exploitation by Immobilizing Technological Deepfakes on Websites and Networks" Act is aimed at non-consensual intimate imagery ("revenge porn") or deepfakes posted to online sites and social media applications, typically made with assistance through artificial intelligence.

Electronic Frontier Foundation (EFF), a digital rights advocacy group have said that Take It Down is the wrong approach to helping people whose intimate images are shared without their consent. Lawmakers should be strengthening and enforcing existing legal protections for victims, rather than inventing new takedown regimes that are ripe for abuse. The bill mandates online platforms must remove flagged content within 48 hours, with no safeguards to prevent abuse. According to their website, "the 48-hour takedown deadline means that online service providers, particularly smaller ones, will have to comply quickly to avoid legal risks. That time crunch will make it impossible for services to verify the content meets the NCII definitions found in the bill.

LAST WORD

Before the Paisley Snail, the law of negligence was narrow and could only be invoked if there was a previous contractual relationship. A social media company could not have been held liable for negligence without a prior agreement with a school. After the Paisley Snail, a contract was no longer required to establish negligence. *Donoghue v Stevenson (1932)* set the precedent for "duty of care". Since liability would, by default, attach to the platform, not the user, the worry is that social media platforms would silence even remotely controversial speech to keep their business safe. Or, more likely, services will rely on automated filters, infamously blunt tools that frequently flag legal content, from fair-use commentary to news reporting" (EFF, 2025).

REFERENCES

Anns v Merton London Borough Council [1977] UKHL 4, [1978] AC 728, https://www.bailii.org/uk/cases/UKHL/1977/4.html

Arkansas State Legislature. (2023). Social Media Safety Act 689, https://arkleg.state.ar.us/Bills/Detail?id=sb396&ddBienniumSession=2023%2F2023R

Blumenthal, R. (September 13, 2024). New Polling Shows Massive Public Support for the Kids Online Safety Act, *U.S. Senator,* https://www.blumenthal.senate.gov/newsroom/press/release/icymi_new-polling-shows-massive-public-support-for-the-kids-online-safety-act Richard Blumenthal

Bonesteel, A., & Greer, E. (2024). This Bill purports to protect kids from big tech. For LGBTQ+ Youth, It's a Grave Danger, *Them,* https://www.them.us/story/kids-online-safety-act-kosa-youth-lgbtq-content?utm_source=chatgpt.com

Capoot, A., & Vanian, J. (2025). Meta scraps fact-checking, brings back political content in latest Trump-friendly move, *CNBC,* https://www.cnbc.com/2025/01/07/meta-eliminates-third-party-fact-checking-moves-to-community-notes.html

Charter of Fundamental Rights of the European Union. (2016), https://www.refworld.org/legal/agreements/eu/2007/en/13901

Charter of Fundamental Rights of the European Union (2000). Official Journal of the European Communities, C 364/01, Article 8, https://www.europarl.europa.eu/charter/pdf/text_en.pdf

Congress.gov. (2000). Children's Online Privacy Protection Act (COPPA), https://www.govinfo.gov/content/pkg/PLAW-105publ277/pdf/PLAW-105publ277.pdf

Congress.gov. (2023). Children and Teens' Online Privacy Protection Act (CTOPPA), https://www.congress.gov/bill/118th-congress/senate-bill/1418/text

Council of Europe (1950). *Convention for the Protection of Human Rights and Fundamental Freedoms,* Council of Europe Treaty Series 005,

Currie, R. J. (2004). Of neighbours and netizens, or, duty of care in the tech age: A comment on Cooper v. Hobart. *Canadian Journal of Learning and Technology, 3*(2). https://digitalcommons.schulichlaw.dal.ca/cjlt/vol3/iss2/2/

Department for Education. (2024) Keeping children safe in education 2024: statutory guidance for schools and colleges, London, U.K: Department for Education, https://assets.publishing.service.gov.uk/media/66d7301b9084b18b95709f75/Keeping_children_safe_in_education_2024.pdf

Dyzenhaus, D., Moreau, S. R., & Ripstein, A. (2007). *Law and Morality: Readings in Legal Philosophy* (3rd ed.). University of Toronto Press.

EFF. (2025). Tools to Address Known Exploitation by Immobilizing Technological Deepfakes on Websites and Networks, *Electronic Frontier Foundation,* https://www.eff.org/document/take-it-down-act-one-pager

Felner, L. (July 30, 2024). Senate passes the Kids Online Safety Act, *The Verge,* https://www.theverge.com/2024/7/30/24205718/senate-passes-kids-online-safety-act-kosa-content-moderation

Foody, M., & Samara, M. (2018). Considering mindfulness techniques in school-based anti-bullying programmes. *Journal of New Approaches in Educational Research,* 7(1), 3–9. DOI: 10.7821/naer.2018.1.253

Gov, U. K. (2025). What does the Online Safety Act do? Department for Science, Innovation & Technology, https://www.gov.uk/government/publications/online-safety-act-explainer/online-safety-act-explainer#:~:text=The%20Act%20requires%20social%20media,are%20shielded%20from%20harmful%20content

Heaven v Pender (t/a West India Graving Dock Co) (1883) L.R. 11 Q.B.D. 503, CA.

Heir, S. (2016). Moral panic, moral regulation, and the civilizing process. *The British Journal of Sociology, 67*(3), 414–434. DOI: 10.1111/1468-4446.12201 PMID: 27444132

Hern, A. (2024). What is the UK's Online Safety Act and what powers will it provide? *The Guardian News & Media Ltd.,* https://www.theguardian.com/law/article/2024/aug/08/what-is-uk-online-safety-act-new-legislation-laws

Kelley, J. (January 1, 2025). Kids Online Safety Act continues to threaten our rights online: 2024 in Review, *Electronic Frontier Foundation,* https://www.eff.org/deeplinks/2024/12/kids-online-safety-act-continues-threaten-our-rights-online-year-review-2024

Kids Online Safety Act (KOSA), H.R. 7891 (2023). https://www.congress.gov/bill/118th-congress/senate-bill/1409/text

Kimery, A. (2025). Congress renews fight over kids online safety with revived KOSA bill, *Biometrics Research Group,* https://www.biometricupdate.com/202505/congress-renews-fight-over-kids-online-safety-with-revived-kosa-bill

Levy v Langridge 150 E.R. 1458, (1838) 4 M. & W. 337Longmeid and Wife v Holliday 155 E.R. 752, 1851)

Mann, B. L. (2009). Social networking websites: A concatenation of impersonation, denigration, sexual and aggressive solicitation, cyber-bullying and happy slapping videos. *International Journal of Law and Information Technology*, *17*(3), 252–267. DOI: 10.1093/ijlit/ean008

Mann, B. L. (2015). Social networking websites, in Philip Leith (Ed.). *Privacy in the Information Society* (pp. 493–503), Part VI Social Networks, Volume II of 3-volume series The Library of Essays on Law and Privacy, London, U.K: Ashgate Publishing. January.

McMahon, L., Kleinman, Z., & Subramanian, C. (January 7, 2025). Facebook and Instagram get rid of fact-checkers, *BBC News,* https://www.bbc.com/news/articles/cly74mpy8klo

McSherry, C., Guariglia, M., Gilligan, B., & Crocker, A. (June 6, 2024). Security, surveillance, and government overreach – the United States set the path, but Canada shouldn't follow it, *Electronic Frontier Foundation,* https://www.eff.org/deeplinks/2024/06/security-surveillance-and-government-overreach-united-states-set-path-canada

Mullin, J. (2025). The Kids Online Safety Act Will Make the Internet Worse for Everyone, *Electronic Frontier Foundation, https*://www.eff.org/deeplinks/2025/05/kids-online-safety-act-will-make-internet-worse-everyone

Murray, J., & Syal, R. (August 2024). Two men jailed for social media posts that stirred up far-right violence, *Guardian News & Media,* https://www.theguardian.com/politics/article/2024/aug/09/two-men-jailed-for-social-media-posts-that-stirred-up-far-right-violence

Oklahoma Admin. Code § 210:20-29-5 (Principle III)

Olijnyk, Z. (2022). The 'Paisley snail' again emerges as legal community celebrates Donoghue case of spoiled ginger beer, *Canadian Lawyer,* https://www.canadianlawyermag.com/practice-areas/litigation/the-paisley-snail-again-emerges-as-legal-community-celebrates-donoghue-case-of-spoiled-ginger-beer/366977

Ortutay, B. (2025). President Trump signs Take It Down Act, addressing nonconsensual deepfakes. What is it? *Associated Press,* https://apnews.com/article/take-it-down-deepfake-trump-melania-first-amendment-741a6e525e81e5e3d8843aac20de8615

Reuters (2024). What countries do to regulate children's social media access, https://www.reuters.com/technology/what-countries-do-regulate-childrens-social-media-access-2024-11-28/

United Kingdom's Human Rights Act (1998). https://www.legislation.gov.uk/ukpga/1998/42/contents

United States Constitution, (1789). https://guides.loc.gov/constitution

Utah State Legislature. (2023). Utah Social Media Regulation Act, https://le.utah.gov/~2023/bills/static/SB0152.html

v Stevenson, D. [1932] A.C. 562. Legal Case Summary, *LawTeacher,* https://www.lawteacher.net/cases/donoghue-v-stevenson.php

Chapter 6
Legal Initiatives:
Canada

ABSTRACT

Until recently, hands-off legislation, toothless policy statements, unknowing parents, uncaring participants, and unwilling social network intermediaries unintentionally conspired to invite impersonation, denigration, sexual and aggressive solicitation, and cyberbullying to the young members of many social media platforms. The situation was serious because the user-generated content displayed on-screen was having a devastating impact on their lives. Then, in 2024, there was some movement. A coalition of four major school boards filed lawsuits against some of the world's largest social media companies, alleging that the platforms disrupted student learning and were highly addictive for children. Also, in 2024, the CEOs of Meta, TikTok, X and other social media companies were questioned on the effects of social media on young people's lives. Meanwhile, the Department of Justice has compiled a list of twelve Criminal Code offences that they say apply to cyberbullying.

DUTY OF CARE

In Canadian law, the duty of care refers to a legal obligation that requires individuals and organizations to exercise reasonable care when performing any act that could foreseeably harm others. It is a foundational concept in negligence law, a branch of tort law. A duty of care arises when: 1) It is reasonably foreseeable that a person's actions (or inaction) could cause harm to another person; 2) There is a sufficiently close relationship between the parties; and 3) imposing the duty is fair, just, and reasonable in light of broader societal concerns. This test was formalized in the landmark *Supreme Court of Canada* case *Cooper v. Hobart (2001),* refining the earlier *Anns test* from English law. Some examples:

DOI: 10.4018/979-8-3373-3126-3.ch006

- Teachers and schools owe a duty of care to students.
- Doctors owe a duty of care to patients.
- Drivers owe a duty of care to other road users.
- Occupiers (e.g., store owners) owe a duty of care to people on their premises.

If a duty of care is established and breached, and harm results, the person or institution may be found negligent and liable for damages. To prove negligence in Canada, a plaintiff must show: 1) a duty of care was owed; 2) that the duty was breached; 3) that the breach caused damage, and 3) the damage was not too remote.

A LEGAL FRAMEWORK FOR SAFE SCHOOLS

In Canada, courts have long recognized that schools owe a duty of care to students, with the standard being that of a reasonably prudent parent. The legal framework for ensuring safe schools includes the *Criminal Code of Canada (1985), the Young Offenders Act (1985), the Canadian Charter of Rights and Freedoms (1982),* provincial school acts, and the common law. For example, the standard of care owed to students by administrators under common law is consistent with that of a reasonably prudent parent in similar circumstances. The options available for exercising such prudence and care are intricate, covering both civil and criminal law, as well as federal and provincial legislation, thereby defining a school administrator's moral and legal responsibilities to maintain violence-free environments in schools.

Schools for Social Media Change (2024)

Section 2 of *the Canadian Charter of Rights and Freedoms* (1982) states that everyone in Canada has the freedom of thought, belief, opinion and expression, including freedom of the press and other media of communication (Charter, 1982, at s.2). However, in March 2024 a coalition of four major school boards called *Schools for Social Media Change* filed lawsuits against some of the world's largest social media companies, alleging that the platforms had disrupted student learning and were highly addictive for children. The district school boards of Toronto, Peel and Ottawa-Carleton, along with Toronto's Catholic school board, sued for $4.5 billion in total damages from Meta Platforms Inc., Snap Inc. and ByteDance Ltd., which operate the platforms Facebook and Instagram, Snapchat and TikTok, respectively, alleging students were experiencing "attention, learning, and mental health crises" as a consequence of using social media.

CANADIAN CENTRE FOR CHILD PROTECTION

The *Canadian Centre for Child Protection* delivers programs across Canada to increase the personal safety of children and to reduce their risk of sexual exploitation.

Kids in the Know (2025)

Kids in the Know (2025) is one of their educational programs that increases the personal safety of children and reduces their risk of online victimization. The program engages students with interactive activities to help build skills that increase their safety and reduce their risk of victimization online. Designed for children from kindergarten to high school, it focuses on building self-esteem through teaching critical problem-solving skills. The core foundation of the program is based on seven Root Safety Strategies and 4 Root Safety Environments (Kids in the Know, 2025).

Cybertip.ca (2025)

Cybertip.ca (2025) is another of their programs' tip lines to report the online sexual exploitation of children to the police. The Government of Canada also has a site called *Get CyberSafe* that was set up to increase awareness of common online threats and to make cyber safety a part of daily life (Cybertip.ca, 2025).

MediaSmarts (2025)

Another federal initiative is *MediaSmarts* (2025), a Canadian not-for-profit charitable organization for digital and media literacy. The vision is that children and youth have the critical thinking skills to engage with media as active and informed digital citizens (MediaSmarts, 2025).

PREVNET (2025)

Most Federal and Provincial governments offering support for cyberbulied victims refer to the *Promoting Relationships and Eliminating Violence Network* (PREV-Net, 2025). PREVNet created a website for parents that is specifically designed to meet their needs and answer their questions about cyberbullying and keeping children and youth safe online. It features articles, blog posts and interactive content based on the latest research and information.

PREVNet (2025) is an umbrella network of 130 leading Canadian research scientists and 62 national youth-serving organizations. Launched in 2006 with the

Networks of Centres of Excellence, PREVNet's mission is to stop bullying in Canada and to promote safe and healthy relationships for all Canadian children and youth. Co-founded by Dr. Debra Pepler of York University and Dr. Wendy Craig of Queen's University, this national network was the first of its kind in Canada to change the way we understand and deal with bullying problems in Canada.

Alberta's StopCyberbullying (2025)

Perhaps the best Alberta resource on cyberbullying is the StopCyberbullying (2025) interactive website with the motto "Don't Stand By, Stand Up". It claims to be the first cyberbullying prevention program in North America, with specially trained young volunteers who design and deliver community programs to help their peers address cyberbullying. Teens and tweens staff their text messaging support line for other young people, build apps to promote kindness, and provide student peer support in their schools.

British Columbia's AWARE Campaign (2021)

Is the teacher also a victim? Instead of student resources, the *BC Teachers' Federation (2023)* offers its teachers a cyberbullying web page to help *them* cope with cyberbullying in their classrooms and their personal lives. Similarly, the BC AWARE campaign (2021) wants to assemble like-minded IT security, privacy, governance, risk, and assurance organizations in BC to hold their own security, privacy or information risk awareness events.

Manitoba's Cyberbullying Prevention Act

Manitoba Bill 214 Cyberbullying Prevention Act, was created as a new tort for cyberbullying. The victim may sue the person engaging in cyberbullying. A person who subjects another person to cyberbullying commits a tort against that person (s 19). In awarding damages in an action for cyberbullying, the court must have regard to all of the circumstances of the case, including (20.2a):

(a) Any vulnerabilities of the plaintiff
(b) All aspects of the conduct of the defendant
(c) The nature of any existing relationship between the plaintiff and the defendant

Manitoba was also the first province to test and convict someone on the revenge porn offence (section 162.1 of the Criminal Code). A Winnipeg man was sentenced to 90 days in jail after admitting to posting three explicit photos of his ex-girlfriend on Facebook for allegedly cheating on him (Southall & Foderaro, 2016). Manitoba provides access to a PREV-Net website about the rights and responsibilities concerning cyberbullying.

New Brunswick's PREV-Net (2025)

New Brunswick's Education Act 1997 was amended in 2012 to include a description of a "positive learning and working environment" as "a safe, productive, orderly and respectable learning and working environment free from bullying, cyberbullying, harassment and other forms of disruptive or non-tolerated behaviour or misconduct, including behaviour or misconduct that occurs outside school hours and off the school grounds to the extent the behaviour or misconduct affects the school environment. "Serious misconduct" means any behaviour exhibited by a person that is viewed by the school or school district officials as extreme and unacceptable in the New Brunswick public education system, including (a) bullying, (b) cyberbullying…" (*An Act to Amend the Education Act, SNB 2012).*

New Brunswick provides access to a PREV-Net website about the rights and responsibilities concerning cyberbullying. PREV-Net stands for *Promoting Relationships and Eliminating Violence Network* (PREV-Net, 2025). PREVNet has four strategies: education, assessment, intervention and policy to stop bullying and victimization and create environments where children feel safe.

Newfoundland & Labrador's Bullying Awareness & Prevention (2025)

The Government of Newfoundland and Labrador has initiated a *Bullying: Awareness and Prevention* program (Government NL, 2025). The *Education and Early Childhood Development* webpage has several links to educational resources (Education & Early Childhood Development, 2019).

Nova Scotia's Intimate Images & Cyber-Protection Act (2018)

In July 2018, Nova Scotia proclaimed the *Intimate Images and Cyber-Protection Act* (IICP) to protect victims of cyberbullying and non-consensual sharing of intimate images (Intimate Images and Cyber-Protection Act, 2017). Victims and parents of victims could now participate in restorative approaches to resolve disputes, get protection orders for alleged offenders to stop the activity, request removal of online content, prohibit further contact, and even seek compensation. The IICP Act was developed through consultation with targeted stakeholders – including lawyers, academics, police, *CyberScan, Victims' Services, and Status of Women, Families and*

Victims. Under this law, Nova Scotians can access support and pursue alternatives to criminal prosecution. The IICP Act of 2018 replaced the *Cyber-Safety Act of 2013,* which the Supreme Court of Nova Scotia struck down.

Anything that hurts anybody's feelings, if it is done online, is called "cyberbullying." It's Draconian (Ruskin, 2015).

Of the 820 investigations under the Cyber-safety Act, 378 involved cyberbullying between adults. It was an adult case of cyberbullying, *Crouch v. Snell,* in 2015, in which the Cyber Safety Act was struck down in its entirety. The court held that the Cyber-Safety Act violated sections 2(b) and 7 of the Canadian Charter of Rights and Freedoms. As a result, the Protection Order granted against the Respondent was void and of no effect.

Ontario's Safe & Accepting Schools (2025)

The *Ontario Ministry of Education* has created a *Safe and Accepting Schools* website (2025). Each school in Ontario has a safe school team working to promote a safer and more welcoming learning environment. Teams include the school principal, a teacher, a student (where appropriate), a parent and a member of the broader community. In *R. v. Pengelley, 2009,* Nicholas Pengelley, the Chief Law Librarian at York University, was charged with attempting to lure a young girl over the Internet. Pengelley was alleged to have had sexually explicit conversations in an online chat room with an undercover police officer posing as a 12-year-old girl.

PEI's Taking Stock of Cyberbullying (2025)

The Prince Edward Island (PEI) *Department of Environment, Labour and Justice* have partnered with the *PEI Department of Education* and *Women's Network PEI* on a project called *Taking Stock of Cyberbullying: A Scan of the PEI Context (2025).* In 2014, the objective was to complete a community needs assessment, an environmental scan, and to produce a discussion paper (MacCallum, 2014). Notably, this report is cited in the *Annual Report of the Justice* and *Public Safety Victims of Crime Act 2015-2016* (MacLauchlan, 2016). This report aimed to address cyberbullying in PEI using the results of a broad-based community consultation and environmental scan. This aim was to explore ways that cyberbullying could be prevented and addressed in PEI. The project's discussion paper was primarily intended for use in creating a better understanding of the issue of cyberbullying and youth on PEI and may be used to inform future actions.

The conclusion of the report stated that, whereas there were serious cases where victims were profoundly affected by harassment, threats and other toxic behaviours, the majority of youth identified cyberbullying as a nuisance and something that happened to everyone. Areas in which the community would like to see work done include the use of evidence-based, effective "healthy relationship" programming in schools and extra-curricular activities, creating protocols that are consistent and effective to address cyberbullying as it arises, and programs for parents to understand more about the issues associated with cyberbullying.

It's no good telling parents, "You should monitor your kid's Twitter."
You can't monitor your kid's Twitter (Kutcher, 2016).

Quebec's Éducaloi (2025)

Quebec's approach to cyberbullying is éducaloi (2025) la loi expliquée en un seul endroit, or "the law all in one place". In 1996, the Quebec Bar set up a committee on legal information and education and began looking for funding. Claude Masse, president of the Quebec Bar, obtained funding from the Department of Justice Canada. Since then, Éducaloi has had a website dedicated to legal education with free resources for teachers. A team of 29 specialists in law, communications, and education carry out the organization's mission, which is to help citizens understand their legal rights and responsibilities. Students in law and communications contribute throughout the year. The team also works with many outside collaborators and volunteers.

In November 2018, police investigated an anonymous Instagram account shaming students at Riverdale High School with disparaging comments and rumours (Gilmour, 2018). When the *Lester B. Pearson School Board* learned about the account, it sent an email home to parents asking them to speak with their kids. Instagram was also contacted by the school and by parents to shut down the account, but Instagram refused, reiterating its code of conduct. Health counsellors were made available to students at Riverdale. The school principal said that the staff is using this as a teaching opportunity, trying to change kids' understanding of social media and this moving experience.

Saskatchewan's Be Kind Online (2025)

The Ministry of Education has partnered with SaskTel *Be Kind Online* to provide grants of up to $1,000 for youth-led initiatives to address cyberbullying in Saskatchewan (Gilmour, 2018). The goal is to empower youth to take action in their communities to spread kindness, positivity, and connectedness. The grant provides youth the opportunity to collaborate with others to find solutions to stop bullying and inspire others to do the same. The *Be Kind Online* program includes a *Student Reporting Tool* embedded in the webpage. According to police, *the City of Regina* enacted an anti-bullying bylaw in 2006 that resulted in just one conviction in 2015. Bylaw infractions are charged the same way as traffic tickets, marked by a fine instead of a criminal record; the maximum fine for cyberbullying is $2,000.

Northwest Territories Safe Schools Plan (2025)

The *Government of the Northwest Territories (GNWT)* has a bullying prevention website that links to federal and provincial government websites on bullying and cyberbullying (GNWT, 2019). The *Safe Schools Plan* includes guidelines, templates and tools to assist boards and schools in creating, implementing and evaluating their policies and procedures for the safety of their school communities.

Moreover, this Government is committed to eliminating bullying behaviour. On November 1, 2013, the Legislative Assembly passed *Bill 12: An Act to Amend the Education Act,* which defines bullying, including cyber-bullying, and requires the Government to create regulations that establish the *Territorial School Code of Conduct* and prescribe the matters to be addressed in Safe Schools plans by *District Education Authorities and Divisional Education Councils.* The GNWT has a territory-wide campaign to denounce bullying, including cyber-bullying, and is gathering information and developing resources for schools, teachers, parents, victims and bystanders.

Nunavut's Connecting Nunavummiut (2025)

The Government of Nunavut (2025) has a website called "Connecting Nunavummiut: How to Protect Children Online." Nunavut is Canada's newest, largest, and northernmost territory. It also has a Facebook page called *stopbullyingnunavut.* On April 1, 1999, the *Nunavut Act* and the *Nunavut Land Claims Agreement Act* officially separated Nunavut from the Northwest Territories.

Yukon 's PREV-Net (2025)

The Yukon Territory provides access to a PREV-Net website about the rights and responsibilities concerning cyberbullying. PREV-Net stands for *Promoting Relationships and Eliminating Violence Network* (PREV-Net, 2025). PREVNet has four strategies: education, assessment, intervention and policy to stop bullying and victimization and create environments where children feel safe.

High-profile Canadian cases have demonstrated that lawmakers have largely failed to respond adequately to online victims. Critics, however, have argued against a punitive emphasis on criminalizing cyberbullying, suggesting that a focus on punishment promotes an after-the-fact approach, which does little to address the cultural changes necessary in schools (Short, 2013). Instead, they advocate for solutions to cyberbullying that conceptualize it as an educational issue (Bailey, 2014). Responses from the criminal justice system should be seen as a last resort due to their reactive and severe nature. Educational responses and multi-faceted support for youth should take precedence (Dodge & Spencer, 2018). Effective responses to sexualized cyberbullying, including the non-consensual distribution of intimate images, require multi-pronged strategies that involve proactive educational initiatives (Shariff & DeMartini, 2015, p. 282). Consider employing different coping strategies at various times.

CYBERBULLYING LEGISLATION IN CANADA

Although contemptible, there is still no consensus on a clear and working definition of "cyberbullying" in either the scholarly or the criminal context (Arntfield, 2015). By all accounts, "cyberbullying" is an omnibus term comprising several possible criminal offences, not all relevant in every case. The conceptual elasticity of cyberbullying has been used to push for a tougher crime agenda while obscuring the tragedy of the suicides in Canadian federal parliamentary debates (Bailey, 2014).

Bill C-13 Protecting Canadians from Online Crime Act

Bill C-13 came into force in Canada on March 10, 2015, impacting domestic and international criminal search powers. *Bill C-13, the Protecting Canadians from Online Crime Act*, ostensibly aimed at prosecuting cyberbullying, more accurately increased new police powers – especially warrantless search of members' files held by the Internet Service Provider. Most of Bill C-13 was about lawful access, not defeating cyberbullying. However, increasing police powers was not necessary since Canada already had rules to deal with cyberbullying. Bill 13 and Bill S-4 were *ex post facto* laws and, as such, would do nothing for the many thousands of teenagers and their parents who were experiencing cruelty from their peers. One possible solution would have been to repeal Bill 13 or at least modify it. Another solution would have been to recommend educational initiatives for coping with social media.

Privacy Commissioner Daniel Therrien characterized Bill C-13 as going well beyond cyber-intimidation (OpenMedia, 2015). It grants immunity to telecom providers who disclose private information about their customers to law enforcement without a warrant. The Bill also makes it far easier for the government to obtain deeply revealing metadata on targets based merely on suspicion. Despite being promoted as an anti-cyberbullying bill, C-13 could make things worse for teens online by undermining their right to privacy.

Under Bill C-13, a wide range of government officials and public officers could access Canadians' personal information without their knowledge or consent. The officers obtaining that information without a warrant could be anyone from a local Police Officer, a Tax Agent, a Justice of the Peace, a CSIS Agent, or even the Mayor (Ling, 2014). Whereas Bill C-13 provided these officials with substantial power over your information, it left the targets of such surveillance with little by way of legal recourse, not least because they were not even informed that their privacy had been breached.

This kind of overreach by the government isn't unique. The UK's *Investigatory Powers Act 2016* (aka Snoopers' Charter), which gives vast spying powers to virtually all public bodies, has caused numerous controversies over the last decade — including a 2008 incident where it came to light that Dorset City Council was using state surveillance powers to snoop on the families of children that they suspected were attending the wrong schools (Investigatory Powers Act 2016). Provisions in the Act permit police and intelligence agencies to carry out targeted equipment interference, that is, hacking into computers or devices to access their data and bulk equipment interference for national security matters related to foreign investigations. Material derived from equipment interference can then be used in evidence. Catching online bullying, in all its forms, shouldn't require government overreach.

CYBERBULLYING AND THE CRIMINAL CODE OF CANADA

On their website entitled *Cyberbullying and the Non-Consensual Distribution of Intimate Images,* the Department of Justice (DOJ) compiled a list of twelve Criminal Code offences that the DOJ says "may apply to instances of cyberbullying" (Department of Justice Canada, 2017):

S 163.1 Child pornography
S 319 Inciting Hatred
S 264 Criminal Harassment
S 261.1 Uttering Threats
S 423(1) Intimidation
S 403 Identity Fraud
S 346 (S)extortion
S 372 False Messages, Indecent or Harassing Telephone Calls
S 241. Counselling Suicide
S 298-301. Defamatory Libel
S 430(1.1) Mischief About Data
S 342.1 Unauthorized Use of a Computer

S 163.1 Child Pornography

According to the Department of Justice Canada, child pornography is a criminal offence that appears to fit cyberbullying behaviours. Child pornography, as defined by s. 163.1(1) of the Criminal Code, is inherently harmful to children and society. The harm exists independently of dissemination or any risk of dissemination and flows from the existence of the pornographic representations, which on their own violate the dignity and equality rights of children *(R. v. Sharpe, 2001).* Section 163.1 (1) defines *child pornography* as: A photographic, film, video or other visual representation, whether or not it was made by electronic or mechanical means, that shows a person who is or is depicted as being under the age of eighteen years and is engaged in or is depicted as engaged in explicit sexual activity, or the dominant characteristic of which is the depiction, for a sexual purpose, of a sexual organ or the anal region of a person under the age of eighteen years. It is any written material, visual representation or audio recording that advocates or counsels sexual activity with a person under the age of eighteen years that would be an offence under this act. It is any written material whose dominant characteristic is the description, for a sexual purpose, of sexual activity with a person under the age of eighteen years that would be an offence under this act or any audio recording that has as its dominant characteristic the description, presentation or representation, for a sexual purpose, of sexual activity with a person under the age of eighteen years that would be an offence under this act.

R. v. Sharpe (2001) was a constitutional rights case pitting the societal interest to regulate child pornography against the right to freedom of expression. John Sharpe was charged with two counts of possession of child pornography under s. 163.1(4) of the Criminal Code and two counts of possession of child pornography for distribution or sale under section 163.1(3). First, the court considered the Charter under freedom of expression and whether possession of expressive material (child pornography) was protected by the right to freedom of expression under the *Canadian Charter of Rights and Freedoms,* section 2(b). The crown conceded that the Criminal Code prohibition of possession of child pornography had infringed on freedom of expression.

Second, the court considered the Charter under the right to liberty and whether the Criminal Code's prohibition of possession of child pornography infringed his right to liberty. Third, the court considered the scope of the definition of "child pornography" under section 163.1 of the *Criminal Code of Canada,* where "child pornography" includes visual representations that show a person who is depicted as under the age of 18 years and is engaged in explicit sexual activity, and visual representations. The dominant characteristic is the depiction of a sexual organ for a sexual purpose or the anal region of a person under the age of 18 years.

Counselling Underage Sex

Child pornography, which includes written material or visual representations that advocate or counsel sexual activity with a person under the age of 18, is an offence under the *Criminal Code of Canada.* Before his trial, the accused brought a preliminary motion challenging the constitutionality of s. 163.1(4) of the Code, alleging a violation of his constitutional guarantee of freedom of expression. The Crown conceded that section 163.1(4) had infringed section 2(b) of the *Canadian Charter of Rights and Freedoms* but argued that the infringement was justifiable under s. 1 of the Charter.

Both the trial judge and the majority of the *British Columbia Court of Appeal* ruled that the prohibition of the simple possession of child pornography as defined under s. 163.1 of the Code was not justifiable in a free and democratic society. John Robin Sharpe was given a four-month conditional sentence for his conviction of possessing child pornography. After sentencing, Lorna Dueck, with the *National Coalition of Concerned Mothers,* said that this was a "hugely symbolic case" that was a missed opportunity to protect children. A child advocacy group says the sentence made Sharpe the champion for people who want to engage in sex with children (CBC News, 2002).

S 172.1 Internet Luring

Section 172.1 Internet luring is not on the DOJ's list but should be added. In *R. v. S.H., 2018,* Jonathan Regan was acquitted of the offence of Internet luring. The Crown appealed the acquittal on the basis that the Trial Judge erred in his interpretation of the elements of the offence by requiring the Crown to prove that the Respondent had the intention to commit the underlying offence of which the alleged luring was intended to facilitate. The acquittal was set aside, and the matter was remitted to the Provincial Court for a new trial. Three elements of the offence under Section 172.1(1)(c) had been established from the previous case *R. v. Legare (2009)*:

> *An intentional communication by computer with a person whom the accused knows or believes to be under 14 years of age, and for the specific purpose of facilitating the commission of a specified offence as mentioned in Section 172.1(1)(c)*

In *R. v. Dragos (2012),* Bogdan Dragos was convicted of Internet luring, sexual interference, indecent exposure, sexual assault, invitation to sexual touching and possession of child pornography. The accused met the 13-year-old complainant on an Internet chat room site and asked her how old she was. She told him that she was 14. He never again inquired about her age, notwithstanding many comments she made which should have caused him to make additional inquiries about her age, including a statement that she was in grade 9.

When the complainant's mother discovered the accused's telephone number on her telephone bill and learned that the complainant had met the accused in a chat room, the mother called the accused, told him that the complainant was "way underage," and warned him that she would call the police if the contact persisted. The accused and the complainant continued to communicate over the Internet, and the accused arranged a clandestine meeting with the complainant at a hotel, where they engaged in various sexual acts short of sexual intercourse. The accused was 24 years old at the time of the offences and had no criminal record. He was sentenced to a total of 23 months incarceration (18 months for Internet luring, four months consecutive for sexual interference, one month consecutive for possession of child pornography and one month concurrent for indecent exposure), followed by three years of probation.

S 319. Inciting Hatred

Incitement of hatred would seem to be an obvious characteristic of the cyberbully's method of engagement, communicating statements in any public place and inciting hatred against any identifiable group, which is likely to lead to a breach of the peace.

One example is the case *R. v. Topham,* in which Mr. Topham was charged under section 319(2) with promoting hatred to the students in his high school class through his website by re-publishing materials from the Internet. Topham's lawyer noted that the circumstances of this case were different from those in *R. v. Keegstra,* who similarly had been charged under section 319(2) of the Criminal Code with promoting hatred through communications to the students in his high school class.

In the Keestra case, the accused, an Alberta high school teacher, was charged under section 319(2) of the Criminal Code with willfully promoting hatred against an identifiable group by communicating antisemitic statements to his students. That court dismissed the application on the ground that section 319(2) of the Code did not violate freedom of expression as guaranteed by section 2(b) of the Canadian Charter of Rights and Freedoms. Here, too, although Mr. Topham alleged to have promoted hatred through his website by re-publishing materials which were widely available on the Internet, the defence application was dismissed. "Incitement of hatred" seems to be part of a perpetrator's method of engagement for cyberbullying.

S 264 Criminal Harassment

Section 264 of the *Criminal Code of Canada* describes "criminal harassment" as a person causing another person to fear for their safety or the safety of someone known to them. The conduct comprises repeatedly following the person from place to place; repeatedly communicating with, either directly or indirectly; besetting or watching where the other person resides, works, carries on business; or engages in threatening conduct directed at them or any member of their family.

In *R. v Gardner (2018),* for example, Shane Gardner pleaded guilty to one count of criminal harassment for sending a series of violent and chilling threats to Terry Murphy via Facebook. The threats caused Terry Murphy to fear for his safety. The Court held that general deterrence and denunciation are paramount considerations when social media is used to criminally harass another person.

S 261.1 Uttering Threats

Uttering a threat is a statement of intent to cause bodily harm or death to a person - to burn, destroy or damage real or personal property; or to kill, poison or injure an animal or bird that is the property of the person. In December 2018, for example, the entire Lord Selkirk School Division north of Winnipeg closed all 15 of its schools due to threats on social media (CBC News, 2018). The RCMP released the name of one of the young perpetrators charged in connection with the threats to Selkirk-area schools. The School Division put the schools into a "hold-and-secure" status and sent emails to families to alert them of their new security measures.

In January 2019, two boys, aged 12 and 13, were arrested for allegedly threatening three Winnipeg schools on social media. The boys had no access to weapons and likely didn't think they'd get caught (CBC News, 2019). Police urged parents to use the arrests as a learning opportunity to talk to their children about the effects of social media after the anonymous online threats resulted in a $45,000 police investigation and heightened security at the schools.

S 423(1) Intimidation

Intimidation describes a preliminary form of cyberbullying behaviour. Intimidation is characterized in the Criminal Code as stopping another person from doing something that he or she has a lawful right to do or using violence or threats of violence to them or their spouse or children or injuring his or her property. Intimidation further describes persistently following that person and hiding or depriving him or her of their property. For example, a worker alleged that she had been bullied by her co-workers both in the workplace and through social media. The worker further alleged that her employer's failure to respond to her complaints of bullying and harassment contributed to her mental disorder. The worker filed a claim with the *British Columbia Workers' Compensation Board* for compensation for a mental disorder under that Act (1996). In her application for compensation, the worker said that she had been bullied by three co-workers. The worker described silent bullying, being ridiculed in front of her co-workers, and being threatened on a social media platform. The worker wrote that she felt humiliated, intimidated, offended, and psychologically unsafe.

The worker reported that she had informed her manager of the co-workers' behaviours around the time that they occurred but did not file a formal written complaint with her employer until October 2016. The worker believed that the social media posts were about her as they were posted on the same day of interactions at work. The worker felt threatened by a "punch in the throat" comment. She was humiliated, intimidated and offended. The worker felt psychologically unsafe. The Chair denied the worker's appeal, finding that the worker was not entitled to compensation for a mental disorder and that the significant stressors of online bullying and harassment did not arise out of and during the worker's employment. Perhaps, in this case, section 423 was too narrowly defined.

S 403 Identity Fraud

Not everyone thinks identity fraud, scamming, and cyberbullying fit the same category because cases of cyber-blackmail are less prominent than cyberbullying but can have the same devastating impact on victims (Kiss, 2013). The position taken here is that cyberbullying becomes the new *modus operandi* once the victims become aware of the scam. They may harass you, intimidate you, threaten you, blackmail you, or extort you.

Romance scammers fraudulently impersonate another person with the intent to gain advantage for themselves, consistent with section 403 of the Criminal Code. Romance scammers take advantage of people looking for romantic partners, often through dating websites, mobile apps, or social media, by pretending to be prospective companions with the intent to cause disadvantage to the person being impersonated or person being victimized. They play on emotional triggers to get them to send money, gifts or personal details (Scamwatch, 2019). Conversations between scammers and victims often go on for months. The con artists will find different ways to ask for money. In some cases, they pretend they are flying to see the woman but get stuck in an airport with no passport and need to ask for some quick money. In one instance, a woman in Brazil took out a $500 loan to help the man she thought she was dating (Cassidy, 2014).

Figure 1. Romance scam showing false identity of Dr. Alec Couros, a Canadian Professor at the University of Regina

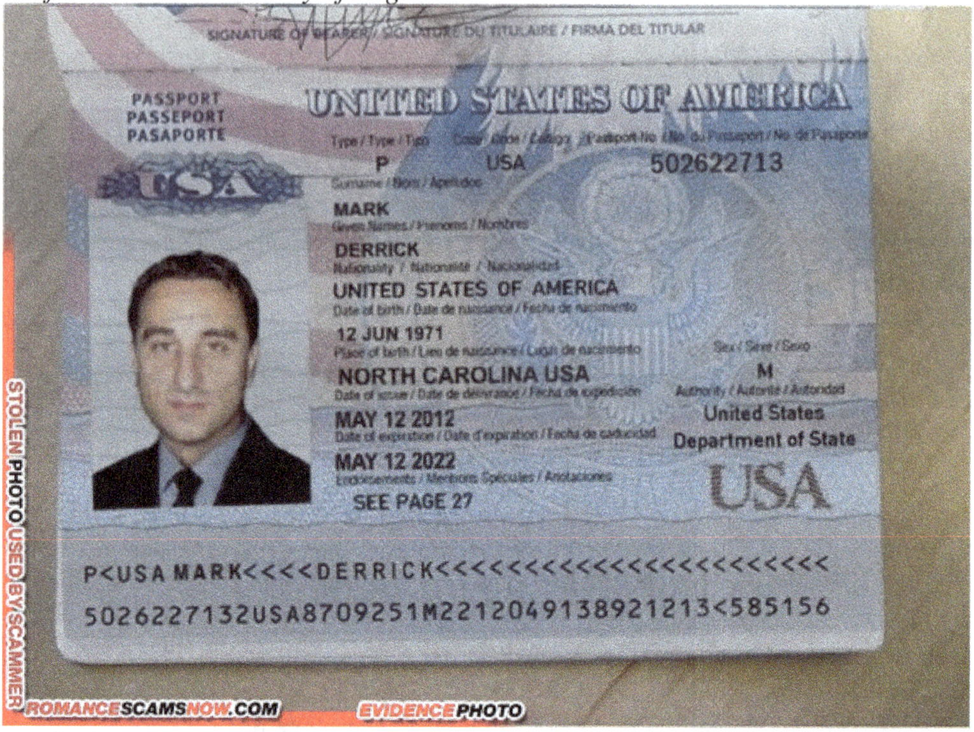

(Used by permission of Dr. Couros)

For many years, scammers have been using the photos of Dr. Alec Couros and his family to commit identity fraud, Figure 1. Dr. Couros is a Professor of Educational Technology and Media at the University of Regina (Couros, 2015). Couros hears from new scam victims daily as they frequently find the "real" him through his writings on the topic. Unfortunately, many victims find out too late, often after they have already sent significant amounts of money to these scammers and have developed a significant emotional attachment. A complex crime that relies on a victim's capacity for love, trust, and goodwill for the execution of fraud (Scamwatch, 2019).

S 346. (S)extortion

Extorting sexually explicit material online, or "sextortion," is a form of cyberbullying that uses threats, accusations, menaces or violence. *R v MacFarlane* describes a case of sextortion heard in a Manitoba court *(R v MacFarlane, 2018).* The complainant was a friend of the sister of the accused, Blair MacFarlane.

In 2010, MacFarlane (then age 19) surreptitiously video-recorded the complainant (then age 17) undressing and showering when she was in the bathroom of his family home in Winnipeg. In a different relationship five years later, MacFarlane decided to attempt to extort sexually explicit material from the complainant by threatening to disseminate intimate images of her. To carry out his sextortion plan, MacFarlane created multiple email accounts under pseudonyms. He extracted several nude or semi-nude still images from the recording and manipulated the images using software to hide their source. He sent emails with intimate images to the complainant and her sister. The emails were menacing. The emails said that cooperating with his demands was the only way to avoid Internet publication. The complainant's sister replied to an email asking what he wanted. MacFarlane said, to start, he wanted a picture of the complainant in a bra. The complainant did not acquiesce to the demand.

The gravity of the extortion offence was serious. The judge called the crimes "cold and calculating" and imposed 18 months' imprisonment, allocated as 12 months on the extortion offence, six months concurrent on the distribution-of-an-intimate-image-without-consent offence, and six months consecutive on the voyeurism offence.

S 372. False Messages, Indecent or Harassing Telephone Calls

Cyberbullying can also include false messages, with the intent to injure or alarm someone by conveying information that they know is false. In *R. v. J.M.D* (2018). The complainant was a highly accomplished nurse who worked in a palliative care facility and taught nursing on a part-time basis. Mr. J.M.D. was a single father of two teenage children. Mr. J.M.D. was charged with harassing the complainant by repeatedly text messaging her and engaging in conduct that reasonably caused the complainant to fear for her safety. Despite clear instructions not to contact the complainant, Mr. J.M.D. texted or e-mailed the complainant ten or more times over a few days. He chided the complainant, telling her that the school authorities considered her treatment of his children to be abuse. This statement was completely fabricated as, on inquiries being made with the school authorities, it was apparent that Mr. J.M.D. had not even spoken to the school authorities about the breakup.

As expected, however, it did cause the complainant anxiety. Judge McKimm surmised that Mr. J.M.D's complaint had threatened the livelihood of a professional woman pregnant with her first child. Even without the earlier references to threatening her reputation or taking her child, Judge McKimm found Mr. J.M.D. guilty on both counts.

S 241. Counselling Suicide

Counselling, encouraging or assisting a person to die by suicide may be considered an extreme form of cyberbullying. Counselling suicide is an indictable offence and is liable to imprisonment for a term of up to 14 years.

The Momo Challenge

Police in the U.K. have issued a warning about the "Momo Challenge" that is urging kids to commit self-harm (Police Service of Northern Ireland in Craigavon, 2018). Figure 2 shows the bug-eyed girl with women's breasts and chicken legs known as "Momo," which has been popping up on social media since 2018, urging kids to kill themselves or else, "Momo's going to kill you."

Figure 2. Screenshot of Momo

(Facebook, 2018)

The suicide 'challenge' called “Momo” has raised concern in multiple countries and is serving as a warning to parents about the dangers of their child's media consumption (Flanagan, 2019). There are numerous variations. For example, while watching the British preschool animated television series *Peppa Pig* or playing the popular video game *Fortnite,* children encounter the Momo image with an ominous voice telling the child to take a knife to their own throat. Another version threatens their family if the challenge is not completed.

R. c. Morin, 2014

In this case, the Crown accused Jonathan Morin of counselling X to commit suicide and thereby committing an indictable offence (R. c. Morin, 2014). On September 27, 2012, the victim and Y were chatting on Facebook and trading insults. Y sent some excerpts from their conversation to her boyfriend, Jonathan Morin. Angry about the comments the victim had made to his girlfriend, the accused sent her several insults and told her that she should kill herself. Y, too, suggested that the victim should hang herself. Sadly, after this interchange, the victim attempted suicide. Before this conversation on September 27, she had felt fine and had not been thinking about suicide. The dialogue she had on Facebook with Y and Jonathan Morin is what triggered her suicide attempt.

S **298-301. Defamatory Libel**

Defamatory libel, under certain conditions (i.e., published online, using one or more communication technologies,) can be considered cyberbullying. A defamatory libel is a text or other media that is published to a chat room or social media site that is likely to injure the reputation of any person by exposing him to hatred, contempt or ridicule or that is designed to insult the person of or concerning whom it is published. Concerning the mode of expression, a defamatory libel may be expressed directly or by insinuation or irony, either in words legibly marked on any substance or by any object signifying a defamatory libel other than by words.

For example, the appellant in *R. v. Simoes, 2014,* heard at the Ontario Court of Appeal, was a restaurant owner. The complainant repeatedly called the appellant's restaurants to complain and posted negative reviews on an online restaurant review site. This triggered a flurry of online postings, e-mails and letters from the appellant, the complainant and her lawyer. E-mails inviting sexual activity were sent to the complainant's employer from fake e-mail accounts set up in the complainant's name. The same sexually explicit message was posted on an adult cyber-dating website. That posting also included the complainant's photo. At trial, counsel conceded that the e-mails to the complainant's employer and the posting on the cyber-dating website amounted to defamatory libel as defined in s. 298 of the Criminal Code.

CRIMINAL ACTS, BUT NOT CYBERBULLYING

Cyberbullying requires a computer or cell phone as an instrument of a crime. Two other categories of computer-related offences have been defined by the U.S. Department of Justice (1989) however, that do not seem to constitute cyberbullying behaviour or intent: the computer is the "object" of the crime (e.g., the theft of computer hardware or software); and the computer as the "subject" of the crime (viruses, worms, etc.), that incapacitate normal computer functioning)

S 430(1.1) Mischief About Data

Section 430 covers offences in which a computer was the "subject" of the crime, where computer data was destroyed or altered, or where the transmission was obstructed, interrupted or interfered with the lawful use of computer data, or denies access to computer data to a person who is entitled to access to it. Typically, the offender will advance an attack in five phases: reconnaissance, scanning, gaining access, maintaining access, and covering tracks (Chatterjee, 2019). A Trojan Horse, for example, is a malicious computer program that pretends to be a benign application. A Trojan Horse will purposefully do something to the user's computer that the user does not expect, from a variety of temporary harmful effects to permanent damage, such as logging keystrokes to steal information, passwords or credit card numbers (Wikipedia, 2008). They are distinct from viruses.

With a Trojan horse on a compromised computer, you could do whatever you wanted. That computer would be as good as your own. You would own it. Now imagine that you owned 100,000 such computers scattered worldwide, each running and being looked after in someone's home, office, or school. Imagine that with just one command, you could tell all of these computers to do whatever you wanted (Solomon & Evron, 2006).

The case of the *United States v. Baratov 2017* in the Court of Appeal for Ontario sought to prosecute Mr. Karim Baratov for conduct that corresponded to the Canadian offence of unauthorized use of a computer, contrary to s. 342.1 of the Criminal Code, R.S.C. 1985, c. C-46. He allegedly worked as a hacker-for-hire to gain unauthorized access to email accounts *(United States v. Baratov, 2017)*. The offender, in this case, may have been more interested in the behaviours of the machine rather than the reactions of the machine owner. It should not be considered a case of intentional cyberbullying.

S 342.1 Unauthorized Use of a Computer

Unauthorized use of a computer is a criminal offence where the computer itself is *the subject,* not the instrument of a crime. Four separate offences can be identified under Section 342.1 as follows: (1) the obtaining offence, (2) the interception offence, (3) the user offence, and (4) the enabling offence. To trigger the application of this section, the unauthorized acts must have been committed fraudulently. It is important to note that these two elements are cumulative and, therefore, must both be present for a court to find the accused guilty of any of the four offences mentioned above.

In *R. c. Paré,* the Court of Quebec, a police officer was charged with having acted fraudulently in obtaining computer services *(R. c. Paré, 1987).* The accused admitted to his absence from the right to obtain the services. However, he denied acting fraudulently. The Court had to establish that the act was not qualified as fraudulent simply because it was not authorized. The Defendant's conduct must also have been dishonest and morally wrong. The Defendant tried to minimize the gravity of his actions by conceding that his superiors knew and had tolerated the situation. However, the Court found his conduct equivalent to willful blindness and disregard and that his attempt to justify his use did not remove his fraudulent intentions.

SOME COPING STRATEGIES

The time has come for the partial liability to rest with the user and the intervening SNI. The position taken here is that any person intending to join a social media platform should be obliged to take reasonable steps to protect their data from being viewed, re-used, or sold. What follows are some coping strategies from various sources:

> ***The Super-Logoff.*** Delete the account that prevents others from searching for information, writing on a user's wall, or tagging photos when they are not online (Tucke, 2014).
> ***The Whitewash.*** Deactivate the account to prevent others from posting messages to the wall, to send messages privately, or to surreptitiously browsing the content.
> ***Delete*** every wall message, status update, and "like" shortly after it's posted (Boyd, 2010). This one is consistent with Zuckerberg's vision to reduce the permanency of messages.
> ***Cloak*** messages in code are intended only for certain friends who can decipher the code (Madden et al., 2013).

> ***Use multiple platforms.*** There are many hundreds to choose from, wherein a particular platform is used for certain kinds of audiences. Facebook, for example, may be used for family-oriented communications, while Instagram may be the place for close friends (Madden et al., 2013). Zuckerberg has a privacy-focused vision for social networking, enabling interoperability between Messenger, Instagram and WhatsApp (Zuckerberg, 2019).

In 2024, the CEOs of Meta, TikTok, X and other social media companies went before the *U.S. Senate Judiciary Committee* to testify on the effects of social media on young people's lives (Associated Press, 2024). These bosses were told that sexual predators, addictive features, suicide and eating disorders, unrealistic beauty standards, and bullying were some of the issues young people are still dealing with on their social media platforms, and these companies were not doing enough to protect them. The Senators pointed to internal company documents that showed that Meta declined to strengthen the teams devoted to tracking online dangers to teens (Le Monde, 2025). Throughout the hours-long event, parents who lost children to suicide silently held up pictures of their dead loved ones. Zuckerberg addressed them directly,

I'm sorry for everything you have all been through. No one should go through the things that your families have suffered... Meta continues to invest and work on industry-wide efforts to protect children.

REFERENCES

Arntfield, M. (2015). Toward a Cybervictimology: Cyberbullying, routine activities theory, and the anti-sociality of social media, Canadian Journal of Communication 40(3)

Associated Press. (2024). Zuckerberg apologizes to families at heated U.S. Senate hearing on social media child safety, CBC News, https://www.cbc.ca/news/world/social-media-senate-hearing-child-safety-exploitation-1.7100952

Bailey, , J. (2014). Time to unpack the juggernaut? Reflections on the Canadian federal parliamentary debates on cyberbullying. *SSRN*, *37*(2), 662–707. doi:10.2139/ssrn.2448480DOI: 10.2139/ssrn.2448480

BC Aware Campaign. (2021). Reboot Communications, https://www.rebootcommunications.com/bcaware/

BC Teachers' Federation. (2023). Kids matter, Teachers care, https://www.bctf.ca/

Boyd, D. (2010). Risk Reduction Strategies on Facebook Apophenia: making connections where none previously existed, online, https://www.zephoria.org/thoughts/archives/2010/11/08/risk-reduction-strategies-on-facebook.html

British Columbia Workers Compensation Act, RSBC (1996) c 492, https://www.canlii.org/en/bc/laws/stat/rsbc-1996-c-492/latest/rsbc-1996-c-492.html

Canadian Charter of Rights and Freedoms. (1982). Part I of the Constitution Act, c 11, Justice Laws Website, https://laws-lois.justice.gc.ca/eng/const/page-15.html

Cassidy, T. (October 2014), "Regina man's identity used in online romance scamming," *CBC News,* [Podcast], https://www.cbc.ca/news/canada/saskatchewan/regina-man-s-identity-used-in-online-romance-scamming-1.2800046

CBC News. (28 March 2011), Bullied teen's death sparks campaign, https://www.cbc.ca/news/canada/nova-scotia/bullied-teen-s-death-sparks-campaign-1.996424

CBC News. (Dec 04, 2018) RCMP release name of youth charged in connection with threats to Selkirk-area schools, https://www.cbc.ca/news/canada/manitoba/selkirk-school-threats-students-return-1.4931490

CBC News. (Jan 23, 2019). Children, ages 12 and 13, charged for allegedly threatening Winnipeg schools: Incredibly complex investigation had police working with overseas social media company to identify anonymous users, https://www.cbc.ca/news/canada/manitoba/winnipeg-school-threats-arrests-1.4989564

CBC News. (May 03, 2002) Sharpe sentenced in B.C. child pornography case, https://www.cbc.ca/news/canada/sharpe-sentenced-in-b-c-child-pornography-case-1.315991

Chatterjee, A. (2019). The 5 Phases of Hacking, *Geeks for Geeks*, https://www.geeksforgeeks.org/5-phases-hacking/

Constitution of the United States. (March 4, 1789). First Amendment, https://constitution.congress.gov/constitution/amendment-1/

Couros, A. (October 2015). Romance Scams Continue, and I Need Your Help, [Blog], https://educationaltechnology.ca/couros/2627

Criminal Code *(R.S.C., 1985, c. C-46),* https://laws-lois.justice.gc.ca/PDF/C-46.pdf

Currie, , R. J. (2004). Of neighbours and netizens, or, duty of care in the tech age: A comment on Cooper v. Hobart. *Canadian Journal of Learning and Technology, 3*(2). https://digitalcommons.schulichlaw.dal.ca/cjlt/vol3/iss2/2/

Cybertip.ca. (2025). Canadian Centre for Child Protection Inc., https://cybertip.ca/en/

Department of Justice Canada (2017). Cyberbullying and the non-consensual distribution of intimate images, https://www.justice.gc.ca/eng/rp-pr/other-autre/cndii-cdncii/p4.html

Department of Environment, Labour and Justice (2025). Taking Stock of Cyberbullying: A Scan of the PEI Context, https://www.princeedwardisland.ca/sites/default/files/publications/taking_stock_of_cyberbullying.pdf

Dodge, , ASpencer, , D. C. (2018). Online sexual violence, child pornography or something else entirely? Police responses to non-consensual intimate image sharing among youth. *Social & Legal Studies, 27*(5), 636–657. doi:10.1177/0964663917724866DOI: 10.1177/0964663917724866

Donoghue v Stevenson. (1932) A.C. 562. Legal Case Summary, *LawTeacher,* https://www.lawteacher.net/cases/donoghue-v-stevenson.php

Dyzenhaus, D., Moreau, S. R., & Ripstein, A. (2007). *Law and Morality: Readings in Legal Philosophy* (3rd ed.). University of Toronto Press.

éducaloi (2025). la loi expliquée en un seul endroit, https://educaloi.qc.ca/

Felner, L. (July 30, 2024). Senate passes the Kids Online Safety Act, *The Verge,* https://www.theverge.com/2024/7/30/24205718/senate-passes-kids-online-safety-act-kosa-content-moderation

Flanagan, R. (2019). Police in U.K. issue warning about 'Momo Challenge' urging kids to self-harm, *CTV News,* https://www.ctvnews.ca/sci-tech/police-in-u-k-issue-warning-about-momo-challenge-urging-kids-to-self-harm-1.4313148

Foody, , MSamara, , M. (2018). Considering mindfulness techniques in school-based anti-bullying programmes. *Journal of New Approaches in Educational Research, 7*(1), 3–9. doi:10.7821/naer.2018.1.253DOI: 10.7821/naer.2018.1.253

Fuller, L. (1969). *The Morality of Law.* Yale University Press.

Gilmour, M. (2018). West Island high school targeted by Instagram cyberbully, https://www.cjad800.com/news/west-island-high-school-targeted-by-instagram-cyber-bully-1.8575283.html

Government of Newfoundland and Labrador. (2025). Bullying: Awareness and Prevention, https://www.gov.nl.ca/education/k12/bullying/

Government of Nunavut. (2025). Connecting Nunavummiut: How to Protect Children Online, https://www.gov.nu.ca/en/connecting-nunavummiut/how-protect-children-online

Government of the Northwest Territories. (2025). Education, Culture and Employment, Digital Literacy - Teacher Resource, https://www.ece.gov.nt.ca/en/services/resources-current-education-staff/digital-literacy-teacher-resource

Heaven v Pender. (1883). *(t/a West India Graving Dock Co)* L.R. 11 Q.B.D. 503, CA.

Heir, , S. (2016). Moral panic, moral regulation, and the civilizing process. *The British Journal of Sociology, 67*(3), 414–434. doi:10.1111/1468-4446.12201 PubMedDOI: 10.1111/1468-4446.12201 PMID: 27444132

Investigatory Powers Act (2016). U.K. Legislation, https://www.legislation.gov.uk/ukpga/2016/25/contents

Kelley, J. (January 1, 2025). Kids Online Safety Act continues to threaten our rights online: 2024 in Review, *Electronic Frontier Foundation,* https://www.eff.org/deeplinks/2024/12/kids-online-safety-act-continues-threaten-our-rights-online-year-review-2024

Kids in the Know. (2025). Canadian Centre for Child Protection, https://www.kidsintheknow.ca/app/en/

Kiss, J. (2013). Cyber scams take advantage of hope and trust, The Guardian, https://www.theguardian.com/society/2013/aug/16/cyber-scams-take-advantage-hope-trust

Le Monde. (2024). Zuckerberg apologizes in US Congress after tech grilling, https://www.lemonde.fr/en/pixels/article/2024/02/01/zuckerberg-apologizes-in-us-congress-after-tech-grilling_6483502_13.html

Levy v Langridge (1838) *150 E.R. 1458,* 4 M. & W. 337

Longmeid and Wife v Holliday (1851) *155 E.R. 752,* 6 Ex. 761.

MacLauchlan, W. (2016). Report of the Justice and Public Safety Victims of Crime Act 2015-2016, Minister of Justice and Public Safety and Attorney General, https://www.princeedwardisland.ca/sites/default/files/publications/april_1_2015-march_31_2016_victims_of_crime_annual_report_1.pdf

Manitoba (2013). Bill 214. Cyberbullying Prevention Act, https://web2.gov.mb.ca/bills/40-2/b214e.php

Mann, , B. L. (2009). Social networking websites: A concatenation of impersonation, denigration, sexual and aggressive solicitation, cyber-bullying and happy slapping videos. *International Journal of Law and Information Technology, 17*(3), 252–267. doi:10.1093/ijlit/ean008DOI: 10.1093/ijlit/ean008

Mann, B. L. (2015). Social networking websites, in Philip Leith (Ed.). *Privacy in the Information Society* (pp. 493–503), Part VI Social Networks, Volume II of 3-volume series, The Library of Essays on Law and Privacy, London, U.K: Ashgate Publishing. January.

MediaSmarts. (2025). Centre of Digital Media Literacy, https://mediasmarts.ca/

Ontario Ministry of Education. (2025). Creating safe and accepting schools, https://www.ontario.ca/page/creating-safe-and-accepting-schools

OpenMedia. (2015). Communication Security Establishment is monitoring our private online activities on a massive scale and sharing sensitive data with other governments, https://openmedia.org/press/item/breaking-spy-agency-cse-monitoring-our-private-online-activities-massive-scale-and-sharing

Police Service of Northern Ireland in Craigavon. (2018). Momo Image: *Facebook,* https://www.facebook.com/PSNI.Craigavon/photos/a.390441237658321/2097736956928732/?type=3

PREVNet Inc. (2025). Promoting Relationships & Eliminating Violence Network, https://www.prevnet.ca/

R. c. Morin. (2014) QCCQ 1609, https://www.canlii.org/en/qc/qccq/doc/2014/2014qccq1609/2014qccq1609.html?resultIndex=1

R. v Dragos. (2012) ONCA 538, http://canlii.ca/t/fs9ps

R v Gardner. (2018) ONCA 584, https://www.ontariocourts.ca/decisions/2018/2018ONCA0584.pdf

R. v J.M.D. (2018) BCPC 211, http://canlii.ca/t/htm3x

R. v Legare. (2009) 3 SCR 551, 2009 SCC 56, https://www.canlii.org/en/ca/scc/doc/2009/2009scc56/2009scc56.html?resultIndex=1

R. v MacFarlane. (2018) MBCA, https://bcsth.ca/what-to-do-if-someone-has-shared-or-threatened-to-share-your-intimate-image/

R. v Paré. (1987) 2 SCR 618, 1987, https://www.canlii.org/en/ca/scc/doc/1987/1987canlii1/1987canlii1.html?resultIndex=1

R. v Pengelley. (2009) 19936 (ON SC), http://canlii.ca/t/239jh

R. v S. H. (2018) NLSC 218, https://www.canlii.org/en/nl/nlsc/doc/2018/2018nlsc218/2018nlsc218.html?searchUrlHash=AAAAAQAZUi4gdi4gUy5ILiwgMjAxOCBOTFNDIDIxOAAAAAAB&resultIndex=1

R. v Sharpe. (2001) 1 SCR 45, 2001 SCC 2, https://scc-csc.lexum.com/scc-csc/scc-csc/en/item/1837/index.do

R. v Simoes. (2014) ONCA 144, https://www.canlii.org/en/on/onca/doc/2014/2014onca144/2014onca144.html

R. v Spencer. (2014) 2 SCR 212, 2014 SCC 43, https://www.canlii.org/en/ca/scc/doc/2014/2014scc43/2014scc43.html?resultIndex=1

R. v Topham. (2017) BCSC 551 (CanLII), <https://canlii.ca/t/h3cv5>

Ruskin, B. (2015). Court strikes down anti-cyberbullying law created after Rehtaeh Parsons's death, CBC News, https://www.cbc.ca/news/canada/nova-scotia/cyberbullying-law-struck-down-1.3360612

SaskTel. (2025). Be Kind Online, https://bekindonline.com/

Scamwatch (2019). Australian Competition and Consumer Commission, https://www.scamwatch.gov.au/types-of-scams/dating-romance

Shariff, S. & DeMartini, A. (2015). Defining the legal lines: eGirls and intimate images, https://muse.jhu.edu/pub/192/edited_volume/chapter/1579702

Short, D. (2013). AV v Bragg Communications Law's next steps: Should bullying be a tort... or even a crime? Manitaoba Law Journal, 37(1), 341-352.

Solomon, A. & Evron, G. (September 2006). The world of botnets.

Southall, C., & Foderaro, A. R. (2016). Social media in the educational workplace, *Manitoba Association of School Superintendents*. Fillmore Riley LLP.

StopCyberbullying. (2025). Don't Stand By, Stand Up, http://www.stopcyberbullying.org/index2.html

United States v Baratov. (2017) ONCA 481, http://canlii.ca/t/h46t7

Young Offenders Act, R.S.C. (1985), *c. Y-1,* https://laws.justice.gc.ca/PDF/Y-1.pdf

Chapter 7
Adverse Effects Discrimination

ABSTRACT

Legal writers refer to this situation in Canada as "adverse effects discrimination" (Yorke, 2016), in the U.K. as "indirect" discrimination (Priest v. Canada, 2022), and in the U.S. as "adverse impact discrimination" (R. v. Sharma, 2022) or "adverse discrimination effect" (Regehr, Kanani, McFadden & Saini, 2016, p. 36). These terms describe a policy intended to treat everyone equally, but that ends up harming a protected group. One of the most notable cases in legal history was Gosselin v. Quebec (Attorney General), which challenged parts of Quebec's social welfare scheme that provided lower social assistance rates to individuals under 30 who did not participate in retraining programs. This court decision largely hinged on "The Law's Test". This chapter offers an overview of various opinions published about this case. Gosselin is part of a needs assessment for judicial guidance in deciding equity cases. Other examples of age-based discrimination are also discussed.

YOU'RE STILL YOUNG – JUST RETRAIN YOURSELF

The government's short-term plan in the 1980's was to get recipients under 30 years old into work and training programs that would supplement their base income while they developed valuable skills to secure permanent jobs. Most of these individuals lacked the necessary technological skills required for permanent employment. Meanwhile, schools, colleges, and libraries were actively experimenting with personal computers at that time (Mann, 1994).

DOI: 10.4018/979-8-3373-3126-3.ch007

Figure 1. A typical classroom of the 1980's showing adults upgrading their skills for permanent work placement

(Glendale Community College)

At the very least, approximately 55,000 people in this same age group would have been forced to subsist on less than $200 per month at some point during this period. Given the average monthly living costs at the time, less than $200 per month was inadequate to meet their basic needs (Hodes, 2008). Inadequate educational attainment is a central contributor to poverty and is a prominent concern in *Gosselin.* The issues raised concerning education, poverty, and the right to economic security at a level that at least ensures bare subsistence were of particular importance to all marginalized groups (Grover, 2005).

BACKGROUND

Under this program, individuals under 30 who were not enrolled in government-approved education, training, or workfare initiatives received only $170 per month. In contrast, those aged 30 and older were entitled to $466 per month. The rationale for this policy was to encourage young people to enter the workforce and acquire skills, thereby decreasing long-term dependence on welfare. However, Louise Gosselin was ineligible to receive training under Quebec welfare regulations for several reasons.

1. Gosselin was *under* 30 years of age. Whereas single recipients aged 30 and older were entitled to receive $466 a month, recipients under 30 who were capable of work, would receive no more than $170 a month, under government regulation. Louise Gosselin was under 30 years old. Individuals under 30 could increase

their benefits by participating in one of three "employability programs": the *Education Program,* the *Community Work Program,* or the *Remedial On-the-Job Training Program.* Participation could raise one's welfare rate for the duration of involvement.

2. The training programs had a limited number of spots, which meant that not all eligible young welfare recipients could enroll. Quebec's *Social Assistance Program* only allowed 30,000 training placements for the 85,000 welfare recipients under age 30. Even if someone wanted to participate, they might not have been able to due to a lack of available space.
3. Third, some programs imposed strict entry requirements that excluded certain individuals based on their skills, work history, or personal circumstances. Gosselin, like many others, may not have satisfied these criteria.
4. Fourth, Louise Gosselin experienced significant hardship, including periods of homelessness, mental health struggles, and precarious living conditions. Ms. Gosselin had to depend on social assistance throughout much of her adult life. At times, she attempted to work, taking on roles such as cook, waitress, salesperson, and nurse's assistant, among others. However, work either drained her energy or induced stress, causing her to quit.
5. Many training programs at the time had rigid schedules and attendance requirements, which could be difficult for individuals facing unstable housing, health issues, or other personal challenges. Related to scheduling, even if she had wished to participate in a training program, Gosselin would have found that there were intervals between the completion of one program and the starting of another, during which the amount of her social assistance benefit would have plunged (Sampson, 2006).

Under these living conditions, Louise Gosselin was unable to access the very programs that would have allowed her to receive higher welfare benefits. As a result, she was forced to live on a significantly lower welfare amount of $170 per month, which was insufficient for her basic needs. This situation formed the basis of a legal argument that the regulation was discriminatory and violated her Charter rights.

ANALYSIS

Ms. Gosselin's court case failed because, when confronted with a complex claim rooted in deep systemic inequalities, it was easier under the current section 15 of the Charter to highlight the government's good intentions and assert that they should refrain from intervening in resource allocation within complex benefit schemes. Ms. Gosselin encountered numerous disadvantages: poverty, physical and psychological health issues, a lack of employability, substance abuse, and harassment, which the majority merely referred to as "personal difficulties" without examining the broader context or the systemic inequalities that may underpin these disadvantages.

Gosselin's lawyer argued that, at the time (the mid-1980s), section 29(a) of the *Regulation Respecting Social Aid, RRQ (1981)* violated the security of the person's interest under section 7 of the *Charter* and discriminated based on age under section 15. She also argued that the regulation breached section 45 of the *Quebec Charter. However,* the Court determined that section 29(a) of the regulation did not infringe section 15 of the *Charter,* nor did it violate the security of the person's interest under section 7. The Court also ruled that section 29(a) of the regulation did not breach section 45 of the *Quebec Charter.* The appeal was dismissed, and the regulation was upheld under the Constitution.

Despite pressing contextual concerns, poverty contributed to, and even caused, the under-30 group to refrain from employability programs. McLaughlin J. did not conclude that this reflected discrimination against one group over another, noting the relatively weak rationale that individuals over 30 have more difficulty finding employment than those under 30. Justice L'Heureux-Dube did not seem to dispute her colleague's viewpoint regarding employability challenges for those over 30 but rather emphasized that under-30s would be disadvantaged if they could not enter the job market, leading to personal hardship.

The Law's Test

This decision of the court turned, or at least partly turned, on what is called "The Law's Test ", which originated in *Law v. Canada (Minister of Employment and Immigration) [1999].* In that case, Nancy Law was a thirty-year-old woman in the 1980s with no dependent children or disability who was denied survivor's benefits under the Canada Pension Plan (*Canada Pension Plan, R.S.C. 1985).* The threshold age to receive benefits under the Plan was thirty-five. The Court held that the age distinction was justified because Nancy Law did not demonstrate that the purpose or effect of the impugned legislative provisions violated her human dignity. The test comprised the following three pillars or broad inquiries:

First pillar: Does the impugned law:

(1) Create a *formal distinction* between the claimant and others based on one or more personal characteristics, or

(2) Neglect to consider the claimant's already disadvantaged position within Canadian society, resulting in substantively *differing treatment* between the claimant and others based on one or more personal characteristics?

Second pillar: Is the claimant subject to *differential treatment* based on one or more enumerated or analogous grounds?
Third pillar: Does the *differential treatment* discriminate by imposing a burden on the claimant or withholding a benefit in a way that reflects the stereotypical application of the presumed group? Or are there personal characteristics that otherwise suggest the individual is less capable or worthy of recognition and value as a human being or member of Canadian society, equally deserving of concern, respect, and consideration?

NEGATIVE LAW

The *Supreme Court of Canada ruled* that the government had no positive obligation under section 7 of the *Canadian Charter* to protect the liberty or security of the person. This reflects the traditional interpretation of *Section 7 of the Canadian Charter*. Rather, the government was not required to infringe upon an individual's *Section 7* rights in a way that does not align with the principles of fundamental justice.

Everyone has the right to life, liberty, and security, and not to be deprived of them, except by the principles of fundamental justice (Charter, 1982, S7).

By "not infringing", the government was saying that they were not required to act to protect the person's liberty or security. In this way, the rules in *Section 7* made it possible for grossly inadequate benefits under a welfare scheme to be viewed as an incentive for young people to seek employment and earn their dignity. More to the point, the "security of the person" did not apply to the benefit of social assistance because such a right would require the state to take positive actions.

As a consequence of the *Gosselin* decision, a negative stereotype of "poor young adults" was perpetuated in the media. The majority of Justices in the case determined that Louise Gosselin and others like her (i.e., young, poor, unemployed, or underemployed women), who were resilient individuals, were merely lazy, possessing enormous but untapped human potential, and just needed "tough love." This stereotype underpins the evidentiary findings of the trial judge and forms the basis of the majority opinion of the *Supreme Court of Canada.*

Arbour's "Two Rights"

In *Gosselin*, Arbour J. proposed that *Section 7* protects two rights, not just one. First, it safeguards an individual's right to life, liberty, and security. Second, it defends the right not to be deprived of one's life, liberty, or security except in accordance with principles of fundamental justice. Traditionally, *Section 7* has been interpreted as protecting only the second right. Arbour J. rejected this conventional interpretation through textual, purposive, and contextual analysis. The purposive analysis is particularly intriguing. Arbour J. noted that conventional reading ultimately diminishes the meaningful content of the right to life under *Section 7*.

I do not believe that *Section 7* of the *Charter* can be read merely as a negative right. In Gosselin, it can be argued that the government's silence on the right to subsistence-level welfare for all recipients combined with the so-called 'incentive program' reinforced negative stereotypes of the welfare recipient as undeserving and malingering (Grover, 2005).

In her dissent, however, Justice Arbour highlighted what MacDonnell viewed as a critical weakness in her approach (MacDonnell, 2012). The existence of a "free-standing" right to life, liberty, and security of the person would eliminate the necessity for a separate right to be free from deprivations of those rights, save for the principles of fundamental justice, since the latter could quickly fall under the former. For this reason, constructing a theory of the protective function on the "two rights" interpretation of s. seven proposed by Justice Arbour proved unwise.

An extreme interpretation of the events in *Gosselin* is what the feminist writer Judith Butler referred to as "the deployment of sovereignty as a tactic," which renders its effectiveness aligned with its aim (Butler, 2004). Sovereignty thus becomes the very instrument of power through which law is either tactically employed or suspended; populations are monitored, detained, regulated, inspected, interrogated, made uniform in their actions, fully ritualized, and subjected to control and regulation in their daily lives.

Some members of the Court's apparent indifference to the unnecessary suffering of young women and men living in poverty seems to conflict with fundamental Canadian and Quebec values. McLachlin J., for instance, asserted that any adverse effects are "unwitting, accidental." McLachlin wrote for the majority and found no violation of *Section 15*, arguing that the regulations enhanced the claimant's dignity by considering her more employable and, therefore, more deserving of training and education than older adults.

Under *Section 15* of *the Charter,* every individual is equal before and under the law and has the right to equal protection and equal benefit of the law without discrimination, particularly without discrimination based on race, national or ethnic origin, colour, religion, sex, age, or mental or physical disability. Subsection 1 does not preclude any law, program, or activity aimed at improving the conditions of disadvantaged individuals or groups, including those disadvantaged due to race, national or ethnic origin, colour, religion, sex, age, or mental or physical disability *(Canadian Charter of Rights and Freedoms, 1982).*

L'Heureux-Dube J. proposed that a neutral distinction, or one that "unwittingly" leads to a negative effect, is not based on a negative stereotype. Such distinctions produce, without justification, disproportionately negative impacts on groups recognized as being within the scope of an equality provision's protection.

SOVEREIGN POWER

Unlike in the U.S., where supreme power resides within the court system, supremacy over constitutional issues in Canada firmly rests within the legislature (Walchow, 2014). Plaxton (2008) argues that in Gosselin, Arbour J.'s dissent reveals an inherent flaw in the concept of "rights"; namely, that they presuppose the authority of the sovereign to exclude entire populations from the protection of the law. Through various and subtle suspensions of the rule of law, an unaccountable version of sovereign power has emerged that focuses on managing security with or without the law (Pavlich, 2011). One hallmark of systemic discrimination is its ability to cloak itself in "common sense" and erase the realities faced by those suffering from discrimination (Kim & Piper, 2003). According to feminist writer Judith Butler (2004), the future becomes lawless when it surrenders to the discretionary decisions of designated sovereigns who are beholden to nothing and no one except the performative power of their choices.

Past federal budgets have neglected many vital social programs and contributed to the ongoing gender imbalance in the allocation of Canada's resources (Sampson, 2006). While it may seem overly simplistic, adverse effect discrimination is rarely intentional and often emerges from a policymaker's effort to treat all parties relatively and equally. Consequently, policymakers find it challenging to anticipate which policies might lead to discrimination complaints, due to the unique characteristics of individuals or groups (e.g., varying age groups) and penalties or restrictions not imposed on others (Regehr et al., 2016, p. 36). Additionally, the Supreme Court of Canada's analytical approach to section 15(1) of the *Canadian Charter of Rights and Freedoms* has made it difficult for equality claimants to successfully present their claims of this nature (Hamilton & Koshan, 2015).

NEGATIVE DISCRIMINATION

Plenty of other examples support the principles of gender inequality, ageism, and, in this case, differential provisions for workforce training. Justice McIntyre remarked,

> *Discrimination can be defined as a distinction, whether intentional or not, based on the personal characteristics of an individual or group. This can result in imposing burdens, obligations, and disadvantages on such individuals or groups that are not placed on others, or it may withhold or limit access to*

opportunities, benefits, and advantages available to other members of society. Distinctions made solely based on an individual's association with a group are unlikely to avoid the label of discrimination, while those based on an individual's merits and abilities are usually not classified as such (Andrews v. Law Society of British Columbia, 1989).

The Motherhood Penalty

Mothers in the workforce experience additional disadvantages compared to women who are not mothers (Correll, Benard & Paik, 2007). The "motherhood penalty" may account for a significant proportion of the gender gap in pay, as the pay gap between mothers and non-mothers could, in fact, be larger than the pay gap between men and women. Mothers also face additional disadvantages compared to childless women and men. Some studies show that visibly pregnant women are judged as being less committed to their jobs, less dependable, less authoritative, more emotional, and more irrational than otherwise equal, non-pregnant female managers (Correll et al., 2007). Previous studies have found it difficult to distinguish between whether actual differences in productivity between mothers and non-mothers are behind the motherhood penalty, or whether it is rooted in discrimination.

Consider the discriminatory impact of having young children on a woman's employment during the COVID-19 pandemic, often referred to as "the motherhood penalty," which was particularly evident among less-educated and single mothers. Those who became pregnant or had young children were the most affected; in this case, they lost their jobs more frequently, worked fewer hours per week, and required support for a longer duration than men. In *R.L. v Canada Employment Insurance Commission (2023),* R.L. argued that the Act had a discriminatory impact on her during the COVID-19 pandemic, especially as she had claimed both regular and special benefits.

In *Gosselin,* the disadvantage was economic. Some new mothers couldn't benefit from the credit of hours needed to qualify for a second claim for EI benefits, specifically maternity and parental benefits. As a result, they were unable to receive all or part of those benefits. These mothers could not take advantage of the credit of hours because it had already been applied to their previous claim for regular benefits, even if those hours were not necessary for qualification at that time.

"It's Only Political, Not Legal"

In a hearing of *Card v. Ontario Ministry of Training, Colleges & Universities* in 2024 by the *Human Rights Tribunal of Ontario*, Adjudicator Mark Hart stated that the applicant, Daryl Card, failed to establish a violation of his rights under the

Code by the respondent. This decision does not imply that the applicant's desire for programming suitable to his abilities and for such programming to be funded by the provincial government is not a worthy goal. Rather, the solution may reside more in the political arena than the legal one. Following the decision of the Supreme Court of Canada in *Gosselin.*

Crafting a social assistance plan to meet the needs of young adults is a complex issue for which there is no ideal solution. Regardless of the government's measures, there will always be some individuals for whom a different set of measures might have been more suitable. The fact that some people may slip through the cracks of a program does not indicate that the law fails to consider the overall needs of the group affected, nor does it imply that distinctions in the law amount to discrimination in the substantive sense intended by *Section 15(1)* of the Charter (Adjudicator Hart, 2024).

While the *Gosselin* decision was made in the context of *Section 15(1)* Adjudicator Hart stated that its reasoning equally applied to the proper interpretation of what constituted "discrimination" under the Code, especially when evaluating a program funded by the provincial government. The Adjudicator believed that the applicant's assertion that the *Ministry of Training, Colleges & Universities* should provide funding for a literacy program like the Hoff program is essentially a demand for the respondent's funding of such programs to align perfectly with the needs of every individual who may gain some benefit from these offerings. In his view, such a conclusion could not be justified as a basis for claiming discrimination against the applicant due to disability in violation of the Code.

AGE-BASED DISCRIMINATION, YET AGAIN

The opposite view was expressed in *Okanagan College v Okanagan College Faculty Association, 2024*. In *Gosselin,* where welfare recipients under the age of 30 received lower benefits as an incentive to participate in employment training programs, the court referenced the stereotyping of older individuals (paras. 32-33). This does not imply that age is a "lesser" ground for s. 15 purposes. However, existing disadvantages and historical patterns of discrimination against a particular group are part of the contextual evaluation to determine whether a distinction is discriminatory, as outlined in *Law v. Canada (Minister of Employment and Immigration), 1999.*

Concerns about age-based discrimination typically involve discrimination against older individuals who are assumed to lack abilities they may actually possess. Young people do not share a similar history of being undervalued. While this does not resolve the discrimination issue, it may be relevant, as it was in Law. Generally, and based on the evidence and our understanding of society, young adults as a group do not appear particularly vulnerable or undervalued.

Discrimination Affecting Older Adults

In 2011, the *Law Commission of Ontario* published a report (Bates, 2011) regarding regulations under the *Employment Standards Act* that allow employers to provide employees aged 65 or older with fewer or no benefits compared to younger employees, based on the assumption that these older employees no longer have the same need for benefits as younger ones. Additionally, the Ontario Works social assistance program requires those receiving benefits to seek employment, volunteer, or pursue retraining opportunities. However, the *Ontario Works Act* specifically exempts recipients aged 65 or older from these participation requirements. In other words, the Ontario Works program assumes that individuals aged 65 and older, unlike their younger counterparts, will not return to the workforce and does not require them to make efforts toward doing so.

An Unfavourable Law

An unfavourable law rendered Louise Gosselin ineligible to obtain the education necessary for securing employment to support herself. Her case serves as a poignant illustration of the dire consequences individuals face when they cannot afford life's essentials due to being denied social assistance (Brodsky, Cox, Day & Stephenson, 2006). While some legal writers may dismiss the artificiality of a separate inequality category, there is a consensus on the importance of retaining the adverse effects of discrimination as a valuable tool for analyzing section 15(1) claims. Furthermore, recognizing and addressing the adverse effects of discrimination is considered essential for achieving substantive equality. Nevertheless, the Supreme Court of Canada's analytical approach to section 15(1) of the *Canadian Charter of Rights and Freedoms* has posed challenges for equality claimants trying to mount successful claims of this nature (Hamilton & Koshan, 2015).

PRIEST V. CANADA (ATTORNEY GENERAL)

Mr. Priest, the Applicant in this matter, is an employee of the *Canada Revenue Agency (CRA)*. He works in the unit that administers the *Scientific Research and Experimental Development (SRED)* program. Like other employees, when the CRA instituted new minimum educational requirements for his job Mr. Priest was granted acquired rights based on his previous education and experience.

Mr. Priest was hired by the CRA in 2009 as a Research Technology Advisor in the SRED program area, a position classified at the CO-02 level. At the time of his hiring, he held a Bachelor of Science degree (magna cum laude) from McMaster

University, which he obtained in 1975, as well as various additional training courses in computer science. In addition, Mr. Priest had teaching and job experience in that field.

When the CRA posted a job opportunity that would have been a promotion for Mr. Priest, he applied together with an accommodation request. He claimed that the minimum job requirements for the position discriminated against him based on age, because when he obtained his degree, programs in computer science were not available at the university level. He asked for an exemption from the educational requirements. This was refused, and Mr. Priest was screened out of the competition. A brief summary of these decisions will be helpful to understand the nature of Mr. Priest's claim on this issue.

HOMER V CHIEF CONSTABLE OF WEST YORKSHIRE POLICE

In *Homer v Chief Constable of West Yorkshire Police, [2012] UKSC 15,* the case concerned a claim of adverse effect discrimination (referred to in the United Kingdom as "indirect" discrimination) based on age, arising from the imposition of education requirements. Mr. Homer had retired from the police force at the age of 51 and then began working with a specialized unit that provided legal advice and support to police forces in the United Kingdom. He was not a lawyer but was hired based on his lengthy experience with the criminal justice system. Over time, the education requirements for this unit were increased, and towards the end of his career, Mr. Homer was denied a promotion because he did not have a law degree. His claim of indirect discrimination was upheld because it was not realistic to expect him to obtain a law degree at the age of 62, given that he would be forced to retire at 65. The U.K. Supreme Court found "(a) requirement which works to the comparative disadvantage of a person approaching compulsory retirement age is indirectly discriminatory on grounds of age".

LUCAS V DEPARTMENT OF FINANCE

In the case of *Lucas v Department of Finance*, heard by the Industrial Tribunal of Northern Ireland, Lorraine Lucas claimed that online testing favoured younger candidates. It was therefore part of the claimant's case that use of online tests was a provision, criterion or practice by which she and others in her age group were identifiable as being at a disadvantage, compared to those in a younger age grouping. It was also the claimant's case that advertising the post externally, as opposed to internal promotion, operated against her and others in her age group, thereby placing the claimant at a substantial disadvantage in comparison to younger candidates.

The claimant's stance regarding the perceived discrimination arising from online testing was based upon the interpretation of evidence from statistics showing the relative success rates of applicants across five bands of age groups. Those were divided into: 16-24; 25-34; 35-40; 41-49; and 50+ (the last being the claimant's age group). However, the Tribunal unanimously ruled that the respondent did not treat the claimant less favourably on the grounds of age. Her complaint is therefore dismissed in its entirety.

THE RISE IN AGE DISCRIMINATION LAWSUITS IN AMERICA

Recently, there has been an increase in age discrimination lawsuits in the U.S. One reason for the increase is that the average age of retirement has increased. Another reason is that employers tend to associate age with digital skills and therefore focus on recruiting younger employees to keep up with the changes in technology. However, disqualifying otherwise eligible employees solely for their age is unlawful (Faruqi & Faruqi, 2022).

In the United States, the Age Discrimination in Employment Act (ADEA) prohibits employment discrimination against individuals 40 years or older. To prove age discrimination, an employee must establish that (1) he or she is in the protected age class; (2) he or she was subjected to an adverse employment action; (3) he or she was qualified for the job; and (4) a younger person filled the position. Under the ADEA the employer's adverse action must be made solely based on the employee's age (also known as "but-for" causation).

A NEEDS ASSESSMENT FOR JUDICIAL INSTRUCTION

The opinions expressed in this paper regarding Adverse Effects Discrimination and Indirect Discrimination may serve as part of a needs assessment for judicial instruction on adjudicating cases related to equity. Candidates aspiring to the bench should embrace the virtue-centred theory of judging, which entails a unique approach to cases involving equity considerations (Solum, 2003). In this context, "Equity" can rectify generalities in the law by allowing exceptions in instances where the rule results in unforeseen and unjust outcomes, as seen in the *Gosselin* and *Law* cases.

According to Solum, "Equity, the practice, should only be executed by judges who embody equity, the virtue" (Solum, 2003, p.27).

Perhaps moral education could be a way to prevent unequal treatment—or, more accurately, inequitable treatment—by revising legal curricula in law schools to place greater emphasis on the distinctions between legal positivist and natural law theories (Pavlich, 2011). The curriculum might incorporate decisions that compare act- and rule-utilitarian logic with deontological logic, including Kant's categorical imperatives (Kant, 1785) and Rawls' principles of justice (Rawls, 1999). I hope that graduates will deliver better legal decisions, more compassionate than the one issued by the majority of the Supreme Court of Canada in *Gosselin v. Quebec*.

REFERENCES

Andrews v. Law Society of British Columbia, 1989 CanLII 2 (SCC), [1989] 1 S.C.R. 143, at para. 19.

Bates, L. (June 2011). The law as it affects older adults, The Law Commission of Ontario, www.lco-cdo.org

Brodsky, G., Cox, R., Day, S., & Stephenson, K. (2006). Gosselin v. Quebec (Attorney General). *Canadian Journal of Women and the Law, 18*, 189. http://www.thecourt.ca/the-womens-court-of-canada-gosselin-v-quebec-attorney-general-2006-1-w-c-r-193/

Butler, J. (2004). *Precarious life: The power of mourning and violence*. Verso.

Canada Pension Plan, R.S.C. 1985, c. C-8, https://laws-lois.justice.gc.ca/eng/acts/c-8/index.html

Canadian Charter of Rights and Freedoms, https://laws-lois.justice.gc.ca/eng/const/page-15.html

Card v. Ontario (Ministry of Training, Colleges and Universities), 2017 HRTO 35 (CanLII), https://canlii.ca/t/gwwtb

Correll, S., Benard, S., & Paik, I. (2007). Getting a job: Is there a motherhood penalty? *American Journal of Sociology, 112*(5), 1297–1339. DOI: 10.1086/511799

Faruqi & Faruqi, LLP (2022). Faruqi & Faruqi, LLP, New York office.

Gosselin v. Quebec (Attorney General), [2002] 4 S.C.R. 429, 2002 SCC 84, https://scc-csc.lexum.com/scc-csc/scc-csc/en/item/2027/index.do

Grover, S. (2005). The Equality and Liberty Rights of the Destitute: A Canadian Charter Case Example. *International Journal on Minority and Group Rights, 12*(1), 43–61. DOI: 10.1163/1571811053890416

Hamilton, J. W., & Koshan, J. (2015). Adverse Impact: The Supreme Court's Approach to Adverse Effects Discrimination in Section 15 of the Charter, 19:2. *Review of Constitutional Studies*, 191–235. https://ssrn.com/abstract=2528157

Hodes, C. (2008). Dignity and the conditions of truth: What equality needs from the law. *Canadian Journal of Women and the Law, 19*(2). https://www.researchgate.net/publication/254942986_Dignity_and_the_Conditions_of_Truth_What_Equality_Needs_from_Law

Homer v Chief Constable of West Yorkshire Police, [2012] UKSC 15

Kant, I. (1993). *[1785]. Groundwork of the Metaphysics of Morals* (3rd ed.). (Ellington, J. W., Trans.). Hackett.

Kim, N., & Piper, T. (2003). Gosselin v. Quebec: Back to the Poorhouse. *McGill Law Journal. Revue de Droit de McGill, 48*, 749.

Law v. Canada (Minister of Employment and Immigration), [1999] I S.C.R. 497, https://scc-csc.lexum.com/scc-csc/scc-csc/en/item/1691/index.do

Lucas v Department of Finance (Discrimination - Age) [2022] NIit 17429_19it, https://www.bailii.org/nie/cases/NIIT/2022/17429_19it.html

MacDonnell, V. A. (2012). Protective function and section 7 of the Canadian Charter of Rights and Freedoms. *Review of Constitutional Studies, 17*(1).

Mann, B.L. (1994). Computing then and now. *New Morning Watch: Educational & Social Analysis, 22* (1-2).

Okanagan College v Okanagan College Faculty Assoc., 2024 CanLII 88299 (BC LA), https://canlii.ca/t/k6w2z

Pavlich, G. (2011). *Law & Society Redefined.* Oxford University Press.

Plaxton, M. (2008). Foucault, Agamben, and Arbour J.'s dissent in Gosselin. *Canadian Journal of Law and Jurisprudence, 21*(2), 2. DOI: 10.1017/S0841820900004471

Priest v. Canada (Attorney General), 2022 FC 1598, https://canlii.ca/t/jt41v

Rawls, J. (1999). *A Theory of Justice.* Cambridge University Press. DOI: 10.4159/9780674042582

Regehr, C., Kanani, K., McFadden, J., & Saini, M. (2016). *Essential Law for Social Work Practice in Canada* (3rd ed.). Oxford University Press.

Regulation Respecting Social Aid, RRQ (1981) c A-16, r 1

R.L. v Canada Employment Insurance Commission, 2023 SST 2056 (CanLII), https://canlii.ca/t/k5vh6

Sharma, R. v. 2022 SCC 39, https://canlii.ca/t/jssdp

Sampson, F. (2006). Gosselin Impact Study, Women's Legal Education and Action Fund, Toronto.

Solum, L. B. (2003). Virtue jurisprudence: A virtue-centred theory of judging. *Metaphilosophy, 34*(1-2), 2. DOI: 10.1111/1467-9973.00268

Waluchow, W. (2014). "Constitutionalism", *The Stanford Encyclopedia of Philosophy (Spring),* Edward N. Zalta (ed.), https://plato.stanford.edu/archives/spr2014/entries/constitutionalism/

Yorke, C. (March 7, 2016). Understanding adverse effect discrimination, MacDonald & Associates, https://macdonaldassociates.ca/2016/03/07/understanding-adverse-effect-discrimination/

Chapter 8
Online Dispute Resolution:
Structured Argument and Technology

ABSTRACT

Most people in a dispute would likely be attracted to online dispute resolution (ODR) rather than formal litigation because it is less costly, more convenient, operates outside the formal court structure, and does not require legal representation. However, these reasons that attract most people to online dispute resolution also attract more affluent, more powerful clientele with the money to hire lawyers with more significant resources than their less fortunate counterparts. Whereas formal definitions of 'online dispute resolution' have remained similar over the years, there isn't a single classification system for online dispute resolution. The technological emphasis in an online dispute aims to support the delivery of communication messages. The structured argument emphasis in an online dispute aims to support language-based communication between the disputing parties.

TECHNOLOGY EMPHASIS

In 1996, the first articles about online dispute resolution (ODR) appeared in a law review. Meanwhile, there was a growing number of disputes stemming from online activities. Online disputes at the time mostly involved university students. Face-to-face conferences about ODR were held through the late 1990s. Many of the same issues that contributed to disputes could also be employed to resolve disputes (Katsh, 2011). It wasn't long before ODR was brought in to resolve traditional kinds of disputes occurring offline. Originally focused on disputes exclusively related to

DOI: 10.4018/979-8-3373-3126-3.ch008

online activities, ODR is now used in online and offline disputes. Moreover, instead of finding disputes that can use ODR, the new challenge is finding tools that can provide trust, convenience, and expertise for many different kinds of conflicts (Katsh, 2011).

The technological focus of online dispute resolution aims to facilitate the delivery of communication messages. These include text via e-mail, asynchronous postings to e-mail, email attachments, social media, private breakout meeting rooms, virtual courtrooms, synchronous text messaging, audio and video podcasting, website streaming, video conferencing, real-time voice-over protocols like *Zoom*, and, more recently, ChatGPT. Figure 4 presents an evaluation of virtual communication design in a courthouse.

Figure 1. Evaluating virtual design communication for a courthouse

(Nichols, 2018)

Westermann, Savelka, and Benyekhlef (2023) introduced *LLMediator*, an experimental platform designed to enhance online dispute resolution by leveraging the capabilities of state-of-the-art large language models like GPT-4. In the context of high-volume, low-intensity legal disputes, alternative dispute resolution methods such as negotiation and mediation provide an accessible and cooperative approach for laypeople. LLMediator aims to improve the efficacy of these processes by using GPT-4 to reformulate messages, making them less inflammatory, and to suggest or directly send interventions to negotiating parties (Westermann, Savelka, & Benyekhlef, 2023).

Katsh, Osterweil, Sondheimer, and Rainey (2006) argued that a technology-intensive approach should be considered to be "the fourth party in dispute resolution" that can play different roles in consensus building, decision-making, and the interaction between the disputing parties and a third-party neutral. One feature of an ODR system is its influence on communication and negotiation, which adds value to the third party by providing an ally or assistant (Katsh, 2002). Cortés (2008) determined that Internet technology has not only changed the status of ODR from an alternative method to the primary method of dispute resolution, but has also changed the way disputes are resolved.

Similarly, Out-Law.com has reported that 'the Internet may become a popular medium for dispute resolution. In the U.S., virtual *courtroom* initiatives have already been launched. The European Union and organizations such as *the International Chamber of Commerce* are also exploring the potential of online services aimed at more efficient dispute resolution (Out-Law.com, 2008).' Dieguez (2008) goes further, stating that technology can even *replace* human expertise in dispute resolution: 'It [the software] has proven to be very effective, achieving 85 percent of cases settled through online-assisted negotiation.' His favourite feature is 'the electronic form,' where 'ICT must implement the use of ADR to effectively address disputes arising from e-commerce.'

A SHORT HISTORY OF ODR PLATFORMS

The first platforms for Online Dispute Resolution (ODR) emerged in the mid-1990s as a response to the growth in e-commerce. Some of the earliest and most notable ODR platforms included:

- *Virtual Magistrate (1996).* One of the first experimental ODR platforms, designed to resolve disputes involving internet service providers and users.
- *Online Ombuds Office (1996-1999).* Developed at the University of Massachusetts Amherst, this was one of the earliest attempts to provide online mediation services.
- *SquareTrade (1999).* Originally partnered with eBay, SquareTrade was one of the first large-scale ODR platforms used for resolving disputes between buyers and sellers.
- *CyberSettle (1998).* An automated blind bidding system is designed for insurance and legal disputes.
- *ECODIR (2001).* A European ODR project initiated by the University of Namur, Belgium, focusing on consumer disputes.

2000s Through the 2010s

From the 2000s through the 2010s, Online Dispute Resolution gained legal recognition and was integrated into formal dispute resolution processes.

- *UNCITRAL's Work on ODR (2010s).* The United Nations Commission on International Trade Law (UNCITRAL) began developing frameworks for ODR in cross-border e-commerce.
- *Court-Integrated ODR.* Courts in Canada, the U.S., and the UK started implementing ODR systems for small claims and family disputes (e.g., British Columbia's Civil Resolution Tribunal in 2016).
- *European Union ODR Platform (2016).* The EU launched an ODR platform to help resolve consumer disputes across member states.

At this writing, ODR has expanded beyond e-commerce into family law, employment disputes, and government services, using technologies like artificial intelligence, chatbots, and blockchain.

AI and Machine Learning. Platforms like Modria (acquired by Tyler Technologies) use AI to assist in dispute resolution.

Blockchain-based ODR. Emerging in smart contracts and decentralized finance (DeFi), ensuring automated enforcement of dispute resolutions

Global Court Adoption. More jurisdictions are implementing ODR in courts, especially post-COVID-19, as remote resolution gains traction.

Online Dispute Resolution has evolved from an experimental concept to a widely adopted system in e-commerce, courts, and international dispute resolution. The future of ODR will likely involve greater AI automation, smart contracts, and global legal frameworks to handle digital disputes more efficiently.

CLASSIFICATION SYSTEMS

There isn't a single classification system for online dispute resolution. A review of the literature for this chapter found no evidence that any one classification system was superior to others. Therefore, the following list and description of existing classification systems for online dispute resolution are intended to be illustrative, not exhaustive.

Rosener-McAveney's Spectrum

Rosener-McAveney's Spectrum refines Schiavetta's concept of 'varying degrees of Internet use.' Although originally intended as a classification system for mediation only, the Rosener-McAveney spectrum (Rosener & McAveney, 2006) may apply to various *forms* of online dispute resolution (Schafer, 2008).

The Technology-Support Role

At the far end of the Rosener-McAveney spectrum, in a technology-support role, traditional mediation is employed alongside Internet technology. A case commences when parties agree to use the free service, register with the service, and start negotiating directly via email, chat rooms, listservs, and videoconference software. 'SquareTrade' is one example of traditional mediation utilizing online technologies.

Software and a Neutral Third-Party

Positioned toward the middle of the spectrum is the combination of software and a neutral third-party facilitator. The software generates suggestions based on the preferences and concessions of the parties involved. Neutral third-party facilitators using this software collaborate with the parties to develop a mutually agreeable settlement. If they accept the same package, the dispute is resolved. 'Smartsettle' serves as an example of such a service.

Fully Automated Computer System

At the other end of the Rosener-McAveney spectrum is the fully automated computer system capable of generating high-speed settlements by matching offers and demands through an online, double-blind bidding system. 'Cybersettle' serves as a prime example of such a system. Another is 'Second Life'. Law students in a dispute resolution class at the University of Dayton Law School are refining their mediation skills in Second Life, where each participant's avatar communicates via their presenter's voice or through text messages (Wagner, 2007). Besides the general communication within the group, separate private instant messages can occur simultaneously. The presenter's personality, as noted by DeBrosse (2008), is reflected in how the avatars are dressed and how they move; biases based on appearance or voice are eliminated, although gestures and facial expressions, which are vital to communication, are also absent (DeBrosse, 2008).

Hart's Categories

Another popular classification system is Hart's (1999) categories. Hammond (2001) suggests that Hart's ODR classification is preferred among dispute resolution professionals because it describes the process of dispute resolution as a function of third-party intervention in the dispute: starting from no intervention in an *unassisted negotiation* between two or more parties to the facilitation of communication between parties who wish to resolve *conciliation and mediation*; progressing to advisory decision-making in a *neutral third-party evaluation*; and, ultimately, reaching full decision-making in arbitration.

WIPO's Categories

The *World Intellectual Property Organizati*on (WIPO) identified four categories of dispute resolution: mediation, arbitration, expedited mediation, and expert determination (WIPO, 2008). WIPO's "Expedited Arbitration" is a time-sensitive form of arbitration that may, based on the parties' choice, be preceded by mediation or expert determination (Motion, 2003). WIPO's "Expert Determination" is a process wherein a dispute or difference between the parties is submitted to one or more experts who assess the matter referred to by the parties. The determination is binding unless the parties have agreed otherwise. Depending on the parties' choice, expert determination may be preceded by mediation or followed by (expedited) arbitration (Wissler & Rak, 2004).

Hörnle's Categories

Julia Hörnle (2002) classified six categories of online dispute resolution (ODR) that are still in use today: documents-only arbitration, online evaluation, mock trial, online mediation, automated settlement systems, and complaints assistance. Hörnle's "Evaluation" involves a neutral third party making decisions based on the disputants' written submissions and documentary evidence. However, unlike arbitration, the decision serves as a non-binding recommendation. The non-binding nature of online evaluation encourages greater participation. In Hörnle's Mock Trial (also known as a summary jury trial), the neutral third party is replaced by several volunteers (Internet users) who act as an online jury in a civil trial. This jury of peers arrives at a non-binding determination of the issues through a web-based platform. The website i-courthouse exemplifies a mock trial. Complaints Assistance includes a self-help system and a job aid that functions as an online law centre to enhance ODR performance.

Motion's Categories

Paul Motion (2005) identified five general categories of ODR: Mediation, arbitration, automated negotiation, assisted negotiation, and the UDRP (Uniform Dispute Resolution Procedure). Notably, only Motion included domain name disputes, referred to as "The UDRP," in his listing of ODR providers. The UDRP aims to resolve disputes between trademark holders and domain name owners, as companies and organizations often use domain names as their trademarks. A domain name holds significant value as both a trademark and an intellectual property asset (Roos, 2003).

However, even the UDRP exhibits inequities—specifically, an uneven impact that often predictably favours complainants while disadvantaging respondents due to its procedures (Komaitis, 2005). Another inequity is known as domain kiting. 'Domain kiting removes millions of valuable names from the system, rendering them unavailable for the purposes for which they were originally intended. It places an unnecessary burden on every registry (Parsons, 2006).'

A FORMAL DEFINITION

Formal definitions of 'online dispute resolution' have consistently remained similar over the years. In 2003, for example, ODR was defined as *an omnibus term* that described various classifications of dispute resolution systems or procedures (Goodman, 2003). Four years later, it was characterized as *a broad category* encompassing any mediation, arbitration, or dispute resolution that occurs outside of court and at least partially online. Farah (2005) conservatively defined "online dispute resolution" as the use of information technology, particularly the Internet, in alternative dispute resolution processes. Zondag and Lodder (2007) described the process of 'online dispute resolution' as an effort to utilize the Internet to mainstream alternative dispute resolution (Zondag & Lodder, 2007). Schiavetta (2004) included dispute resolution conducted exclusively online, as well as those supported to varying degrees by the Internet.

OVERLAPPING TERMINOLOGY

Sometimes, various terms refer to the same or comparable concepts in different classification systems. Below are a few examples of overlapping meanings.

Arbitration

According to Motion's (2003) classification, arbitration, also known as documents-only arbitration (Hart 1999; Hörnle 2002), is a neutral process in which one or more arbitrators review the dispute and issue a binding decision. Documents-only arbitration has been employed for a significant duration to resolve consumer disputes. Depending on the preferences of the parties involved, arbitration may be preceded by mediation or expert determination. Expedited arbitration is a process conducted within a short timeframe and at a lower cost.

Automated Negotiation

Paul Motion's (2005) term "Automated Negotiation," which Hörnle (2002) describes as "an Automated Settlement System", is well-suited for monetary claims and can serve as a negotiation tool in another dispute resolution process. The procedure involves the parties submitting successive blind bids, meaning the bids remain undisclosed to each other. Disputants enter their bids using the web form until the bids are within 30% of one another (and sometimes even less). A "Settlement" is achieved based on the average of the bids.

Mediation

"Mediation" for Motion is a non-binding process in which a neutral intermediary, known as the mediator, assists the parties in resolving their dispute. Online mediation is particularly well-suited for small consumer disputes. Depending on the parties' preferences, mediation may be followed, if no settlement is reached, by arbitration, expedited arbitration, or expert determination. In both conciliation and mediation, the third party promotes communication between the parties seeking a resolution (Hart, 1999). The three main categories in the Rosener-McAveney (2006) spectrum discussed earlier are designed to illustrate online mediation along a technology-intensive continuum, ranging from technology-supported to fully automated. The presence of a neutral intermediary does not eliminate the necessity for a good job aid or tutorial for ODR novices.

Synchronous or Asynchronous?

Finally, there is a tendency to discuss technology-intensive approaches that compare synchronous and asynchronous technologies to determine which is best suited for a particular purpose. However, synchronous communication and asynchronous communication, for example, differ from one another. For that reason, they cannot be fairly compared. Unsurprisingly, a recent comparison of synchronous versus asynchronous communication in dispute resolution produced conflicting results (Poblet & Casanovas, 2007). This finding is consistent with previous technology comparisons (Mann, 2006). The same can be said for synchronous and face-to-face communication, as well as asynchronous and face-to-face communication. The interactions are simply not comparable and, therefore, should not be compared. Nonetheless, this outcome has not deterred individuals from seeking large grants and publishing chapters to do just that.

A more accurate comparison of a technology-intensive approach would be email versus fax machines, as both are synchronous and text-based, offering no possibility for nonverbal communication. Another valid comparison would be an audio conference and voice-over IP. This tendency to compare technologies has fueled critics' rebuttals of the technology-intensive approach to ODR as 'technocentric.' This term, derived from Piaget's concept of 'egocentric' (Papert, 1988), instead argues that "electronic forms," by themselves, cannot resolve a dispute. Rather, it may be more precise to say that for some, ODR is preferable to ADR (e.g., for cross-border disputes) and court litigation (i.e., lower costs), but not as effective in other cases (e.g., those concerning the equality of bargaining power between consumers and sellers of products or services).

DISCUSSION

The relatively recent history listed other factors affecting disputants' abilities to function effectively online, including the context in which the discussions occur, the type of conflict and its intensity, the prior relationship between the dispute and the physical conditions such as time and level of comfort with technology (Hammond, 2001). Rabinovich-Einy (2003) suggested that differences between parties may be more extreme in writing capabilities than with oral speech due to unequal literacy levels (p.45). Additional factors bearing on the effectiveness of online mediation, in particular, might pertain to the disputant's belief in the process, trust in the mediator, quality of mediator interventions, and ability of the online environment to accommodate the parties' need to engage interactively. However, these hypotheses are as yet untested in ODR conditions. In the wider social context, it is also hoped that this chapter may improve ODR literacy and be a practical resource for the ODR Developer seeking new ways to assist inarticulate, novice and lesser dispute-wise claimants in designing their presentations more effectively. Notably, some problems are solely administrative, others political. An important last point is that judging presentations and presenters should always be a private matter, not a committee decision. The agreed solution to resolving a dispute should be recorded and made available to the parties by the body responsible for the procedure to avoid later uncertainty or misunderstanding.

THE STRUCTURED ARGUMENT EMPHASIS

The structured argument emphasis in an online dispute aims to support language-based communication between the disputing parties. Winograd and Flores (1986) characterized the Platonic approach to structuring an argument as follows:

- Has identifiable objects and well-known properties
- Finds general rules that apply to situations associated with those objects and properties
- Applies rules logically in the situation of concern, concluding what should be done (Winograd & Flores, 1986, pp. 14-15, 30-31).

Plato predominantly wrote about resolving disputes through his character Socrates.
Socrates: You, Gorgias, like myself, have had great experience of disputations, and you must have observed, I think, that they do not permanently terminate in mutual edification or in the definition by either party of the subjects which they are discussing, but disagreements are apt to arise-somebody says that another has not spoken indeed or clearly; and then they get into a passion and begin to quarrel, both parties conceiving that their opponents are arguing from personal feeling only and jealousy of themselves, not from any interest in the question at issue (Plato, 380 B.C., Gorgias).

Winograd and Flores (1986) chose to reject the objective stance introduced in Plato's rationalistic orientation (i.e., that the physical world is the primary reality) as well as his subjective stance (i.e., that my feelings and thoughts are the primary reality), arguing instead, alongside Heidegger, that one cannot exist without the other. Aakhus accurately noted that Winograd and Flores' pragmatic approach to communication aligned with those of Simon, Searle, and Habermas. Therefore, the ideal outcome of communication for Winograd and Flores was "intersubjectivity" and "consensus." For them, the design of technology involves integrating into the flow of human interaction in a way that assists people in collaboratively managing breakdowns through a network of commitments (Winograd & Flores, 1986, p.176). Just as Winograd and Flores acknowledged Plato for his influence on dispute resolution, Fodor (1980) recognized Aristotle for his impact on Artificial Intelligence (AI) decision support systems.

Placating the Listener

Aristotle developed modes of persuasion as the essence of rhetoric and the counterpart to dialectic. His syllogistic logic comprises a minor premise, a major premise, and a conclusion. Similar to Plato, Aristotle noted that modes of persuasion could appeal to human emotions and, at times, distort our judgment.

In a *political debate,* the man forming a judgment decides his vital interests. There is no need, therefore, to prove anything except that the facts are what the supporter of a measure maintains they are.

In *forensic oratory,* however, this is not enough; to placate the discontent in the listener is what pays here. Other people's affairs are to be decided so that the judges, intent on their satisfaction and listening with partiality, surrender themselves to the disputants instead of judging between them (Aristotle, 350 B.C., Rhetoric, 1355a).

Aristotle introduced a *Belief-Desire-Intention Model of Reasoning* and presented implicit premises of practical reasoning within deliberation *endoxa*, or reputable opinions, because these are either accepted by all, endorsed by the majority, or acknowledged by the wise (Aristotle, 350 B.C., Topics, 100b22-24). When making and defending a proposal, the argumentation often hinges on generally accepted opinions of the audience that are not explicitly stated as premises.

Aristotle's Syllogism

Aristotle's theory of syllogism has exerted an unparalleled influence on the history of Western thought. "Syllogisms" are assertions that can be either true or false. Each sentence must maintain the same structure: a subject and a predicate, which must either affirm or deny the predicate concerning the subject. Therefore, every assertion represents either the affirmation or denial of a single predicate of a single subject. However, Walton and Godden (2005) suggested that inferences based on *endoxa* in public deliberations tend to be fallible and are inherently subject to critical questioning.

Assertoric propositions, in Aristotelian logic, indicate whether something *is* true *or false*. A statement is considered assertoric when it claims that something exists without determining the truth of its existence. Such a statement must be verified empirically, meaning it must refer to something outside itself. For example, "Pine trees grow in Siberia" and "Chicago is larger than Omaha" are assertoric propositions.

Problematic propositions, however, assert the possibility of something being true. The statement is considered a problematic proposition when it indicates that something *could* be true even though nothing in the statement itself prevents it from being true. For example, "Rottweilers run faster than leopards" or "A corporation could be wealthier than a country" is problematic.

Apodeictic propositions assert things which are self-evidently or necessarily either true or false. A statement is apodictic if it must be true (or false). For example, "A triangle has three sides" or "Two plus two equals four" are apodeictic propositions. Immanuel Kant incorporated these categories directly from Aristotle. In his book Critique of Pure Reason, Kant contrasted "apodictic," "problematic," and "assertoric," which he called the modality of a judgment. "The modality of judgments is a quite special function of judgments, which is distinctive in that modality contributes nothing to the content of the judgment but rather concerns only the value of the copula about thinking in general" (Kant, 1781, p.A70/B95).

ARGUMENT STRUCTURES: ARISTOTLE VS. TOULMIN

Muecke and Stranieri (2007) proposed an alternative to Aristotle's syllogistic logic and *endoxa* to capture expert reasoning for online disputes (Walton & Godden, 2005) based on Toulmin's (1958) argument structure. Toulmin argued that although Aristotelian logic was well-suited to analytical argument, it was inadequate for other arguments (Toulmin, 1958). The argument structure proposed by Muecke and Stranieri (2007) and illustrated in Table 1 may well be compatible with the three innovations proposed in this document, though they are as yet untested in a dispute resolution context.

Table 1. Two arguments are shown in the same format.

Argument A: Typical Aristotlean Syllogism[1]	
Premise 1: Socrates is a man in town.	A particular, affirmative proposition, is True.
Premise 2: All men in town are stonecutters.	A universal, affirmative proposition, is True.
Conclusion: Socrates is a stonecutter in town.	A valid syllogistic argument.
Argument B: Toulmin's Qualifiers & Exceptions[2]	
Premise 1: Mustafa is an Arab in town.	A particular, affirmative proposition, is True.

continued on following page

Table 1. Continued

Argument A: Typical Aristotlean Syllogism[1]	
Premise 2: Most (Aristotle would say 'Some') Arabs in town are Muslims.	A conditional, affirmative proposition, is True. (Thus far, still consistent with Aristotlean logic).
Conclusion: Mustafa is most likely a Muslim in town.	An inconclusive argument, invalid. (As Aristotlean syllogism, this argument would require at least one and likely two more premises, to sort 'Some Arabs are Muslim' from 'Some Arabs are Not Muslim'). In Toulmin's logic, these premises and conclusion could constitute the *thesis* in the claim.
Data on Mustafa's beliefs in town, the Muslims and non-Muslims in town, Arabs and non-Arabs in town, etc. Warrant on the connection between Mustafa, the Muslims and Arabs in town, etc. Backing. Maybe this is all hearsay. Nobody has seen Mustafa in months. Maybe he got married and left town. Where's the evidence? Qualifiers. Is there more than one "Mustafa" in town, especially if the town is located in an area where there is likely to be more than one. Counter-arguments. Religious conviction is a private matter, and nobody else's business. Limitations. Mustafa was seen with a Sikh girl (it is customary for Muslims and Sikhs to keep their distance).	Toulmin's argument would then provide *data* to support the claim, followed by a *warrant* to show why the data supports the claim, some *backing* of facts or reasoning to legitimize the warrant, a *qualifier* to narrow the focus of the claim, a *rebuttal* or counter argument, and a *reservation* or any limitation of the argument that might invalidate the warrant. In sum, an argument supported by true premises and conclusion is not always justified, due to counter-argument, as noted in Lodder and Verheij (1999).

Argument A shows a typical Aristotlean syllogism with two True propositions yielding a Valid conclusion. Argument B shows how Muecke and Stranieri's adaptation of Toulmin's argument structure can be imposed-over and extends a syllogism
(Mann, 2009, p.88)

In sum, the emphasis on the structured arguments approach for online dispute resolution requires information technology and a legal knowledge system to manage extant knowledge and develop a model of legal argumentation and legal ontology, as in Table 1. The field is interdisciplinary (Lodder & Bol, 2003).

A primary concern with the structured argument approach is the tendency to interrupt during synchronous communications exchanges (e.g., during text messaging in a Chat, wall-writing on a social networking website, or voice-over IP, which gives the faster typist an unfair advantage (Rule, 2002). Walton and Godden (2005) believe that interrupting the other party in this way violates Grice's principles of cooperation.

Figure 2. Online dispute resolution explained

(ADR Times (2021)

Text-Based ODR

From 2020 to 2022, the *Resolution Systems Institute* and the *University of California, Davis* conducted a series of six focus groups to explore why court text-based online dispute resolution was underused (Feinstein & Shack, 2024). The groups were held at locations that were geographically and demographically diverse across the United States, with participants resembling self-represented litigants. These focus groups included whites in rural New Hampshire (n=6), Latinos in Houston, Texas (n=14), and African Americans in Baltimore, Maryland (n=15).

The study aimed to determine why court text-based online dispute resolution was underutilized (Feinstein & Shack, 2024). Results showed that most participants were interested in using ODR and appreciated the option of settling a case from the comfort of their homes without the inconvenience of going to a courthouse. However, the focus group discussions also indicated negative responses (Feinstein & Shack, 2024, p.6):

Unsure How to Respond Correctly

Participants said they would feel intimidated at the prospect of being sued, at having to understand the amount of information provided to them, and at the formatting of the court documents. They also said they would feel a lack of self-confidence in navigating the ODR system without the help of court staff (Feinstein & Shack, 2024).

Text-Based Communication

Participants expressed significant reservations about text-based ODR. They were concerned about potential misunderstandings or the other party's lack of civility during negotiations. Many preferred having someone moderate or facilitate their communications with the other party to ensure accountability. While most leaned towards mediating via video rather than text, many still favoured text-based communication (Feinstein & Shack, 2024).

Skepticism & Lack of Trust

Many participants were concerned about being scammed and wanted reassurance that the mailed court documents, such as the Notice and the ODR platforms, were legitimate. They noted that the court seal and contact information added to the sense of legitimacy (Feinstein & Shack, 2024).

Lack of Clarity

Word choice appeared to affect whether the information was understood. Participants responded best to plain language and wanted legal terms to be defined early in a document. They also noted a preference for step-by-step instructions, which they found easy to follow (Feinstein & Shack, 2024).

COMMON MISTAKES WITH CONFLICT RESOLUTION

Part of successful conflict resolution involves being aware of the common mistakes people make when resolving conflicts. Having this knowledge can help you avoid these mistakes and correct them in your conflict resolution process. As you begin to implement conflict resolution in your school or organization, keep the following mistakes in mind (Jacobson, 2025):

- Avoiding conflict
- Being defensive
- Over-generalizing
- Being right
- Psychoanalyzing
- Forgetting to listen
- Playing the blame game
- Trying to "win" the argument
- Making character attacks
- Stonewalling

REFERENCES

Aakhus, M. (August 2001). Constituting deliberation as "buy-in" through GDSS design and implementation. *SIGGROUP 22,* (2).

Aristotle. (350 B.C.) Rhetoric. Translated by W. Rhys Roberts. In Lee Honeycutt (ed.). Aristotle's Rhetoric: A hyper-textual resource, http://classics.mit.edu/Aristotle/rhetoric.html

Cortés, P. (2008, February). Effective disputes. *The New Law Journal, 158*, 7306.

Cybersettle (2025). https://www.cybersettle.com/

DeBrosse, J. (March 2008). UD Law Prof using the innovative website to teach mediation skills. Cox Ohio Publishing, Dayton, Ohio, USA.

Dieguez, J. (2008). Does the proposed European procedure enhance the resolution of small claims? *Civil Justice Quarterly*, *27*(1), 83–97.

ECODIR. (2001). Electronic Consumer Dispute Resolution (ECODIR), https://www.arbitration-adr.org/resources/?p=serviceproviders&a=show&id=40

EvalCommunity. (2024ab). Understanding Effectiveness Evaluation: Definition, Benefits, and Best Practices, https://www.evalcommunity.com/career-center/effectiveness-evaluation/

Farah, C. (2005). Critical analysis of online dispute resolution: The optimist, the realist and the bewildered. *Computer and Telecommunications Law Review*, *11*(4), 123–128.

Feinstein, R., & Shack, J. (2024). Making ODR more accessible to self-represented parties: Focus group perspectives, Resolution Systems Institute, https://s3.amazonaws.com/aboutrsi/591e30fc6e181e166ffd2eb0/Final-Report-OPEN-16April2024-R.pdf

Fodor, J. (1980). Methodological Solipsism Considered as a Research Strategy in Cognitive Science. *Behavioral and Brain Sciences*, *3*(1), 63–73. DOI: 10.1017/S0140525X00001771

Goodman, J. (2003). The pros and cons of online dispute resolution: An assessment of cyber-mediation websites. *Duke L. & Tech. Rev. 0004.*

Hammond, A.-M. (2001). The effectiveness of online dispute resolution. Department of Conflict and Management. Masters thesis. Royal Roads University.

Hart, C. (1999). Online dispute resolution and avoidance in electronic commerce. The chapter was presented at the *Uniform Law Conference of Canada.* August.

Hörnle, J. (2002) Online Dispute Resolution in Business-to-Consumer E-commerce Transactions. *Journal of Information, Law and Technology, (2).*

Jacobson, S. (2025). Common mistakes with conflict resolution, *The Conover Company,* https://www.conovercompany.com/common-mistakes-with-conflict-resolution/

Kant, I. (1781). Transcendental Analytic: First Book, The Analytic of Concepts, Section II. On the logical function in Judgments 4, 100, Critique of Pure Reason. Translated and edited by Paul Guyer and Allen W. Wood.

Katsh, E. (2002). Online dispute resolution: The next phase. *Lex Electronica, 7*,(2),

Katsh, E. (2011). ODR: A Look at History – A Few Thoughts About the Present and Some Speculation About the Future. In Abdel Wahab, M. S., Katsh, E., & Rainey, D. (Eds.), *Online Dispute Resolution: Theory and Practice: A Treatise on Technology and Dispute Resolution*. Eleven International Publishing., https://www.ombuds.org/odrbook/Table_of_Contents.htm

Katsh, E., Osterweil, L., Sondheimer, N., & Rainey, D. (2006). Experimental application of process technology to the creation and adoption of online dispute resolution. Project highlights proceedings. *The National Center for Technology and Dispute Resolution.* http://www.odr.info/nmb/DGo2006%20Project%20Highlights%20proceedings%200303061.pdf

Komaitis, K. (2003). *ICANN: Guilty as charged?* Journal of Information, Law, &. *Technology (Elmsford, N.Y.)*, 1.

21. Komaitis, K. (2005). Pandora's box is finally opened: The Uniform Domain Name Dispute Resolution Process and Arbitration. *International Review of Law Computers & Technology*, *19*(1), 99–116. DOI: 10.1080/13600860500051697

23. Lodder, A., & Bol, S. (2003). Towards an online negotiation environment: legal principles, technical requirements and the need for close cooperation. In A. Lodder, E. Clark, T. Gordon, E. Katsh, C. Rule, E. Thiessen, B. Verheij, D. Walton and J. Zeleznikow (Eds.). *Essays on legal and technical aspects of Online Dispute Resolution,* Chapters from the ICAIL 2003 ODR Workshop, Edinburgh, Scotland, UK, http://odrworkshop.info/odrworkshopproceedings2003.pdf

Lodder, A. & Verheij, B. (1999). Computer-mediated legal argument: Towards new opportunities in education. *Journal of Information, Law and Technology, 2.*

Lodder, A., & Zeleznikow, J. (2005). Developing an online dispute resolution environment: Dialogue tools and negotiation support systems in a three-step model. *Harvard Negotiation Law Review*, *10*(287), 302.

Mann, B. L. (2006). Making your own educational materials, part II: Multimedia design for learning. *International Journal of Instructional Technology & Distance Learning, 3*(10).

Mann, B. L. (2009). Smoothing some wrinkles in online dispute resolution. *International Journal of Law and Information Technology, 17*(1), 83–112. DOI: 10.1093/ijlit/ean017

Motion, P. (2005). Article 17: Encouragement of alternative dispute resolution – Online dispute resolution: A view from Scotland. In Edwards, L. (Ed.), *The new legal framework for e-commerce in Europe* (pp. 137–169). Hart Publishing.

Muecke, N., & Stranieri, A. (2007). An argument structure abstraction for Bayesian belief networks: Just outcomes in online dispute resolution. *Proceedings of the APCCM,* 35-40.

Online Ombuds Office. https://ombuds.org/

Out-Law.com. (2008). *Dispute resolution*. Pinsent Masons LLP.

Papert, S. (1988). *A critique of technocentrism in thinking about the school of the future. Children in the Information Age*. Elsevier.

Parsons, B. (May 2006). Domain Kiting: A serious problem gets worse, *Go Daddy,* http://www.bobparsons.com/DomainKiting.html?serendipity[searchTerm]=404+pages#c16179

Plato. (380 B.C.). Gorgias. Translated by Benjamin Jowett. In D.C. Stevenson (ed.). *The Internet Classics Archive,* http://classics.mit.edu/Plato/gorgias.html

Poblet, M., & Casanovas, P. (2007). Emotions in ODR. *International Review of Law Computers & Technology, 21*(2), 145–155. DOI: 10.1080/13600860701492146

Rabinovich-Einy, O. (2003). The Ford-Firestones of the future: Resolving offline disputes in an online society. In A. Lodder et al, (Eds.). *Essays on legal and technical aspects of Online Dispute Resolution,* June 28, Edinburgh, UK, http://odrworkshop.info/odrworkshopproceedings2003.pdf

Roos, F. (2003). First Come, Not Served': Domain Name Regulation in Sweden. *International Review of Law Computers & Technology, 17*(1), 63–72. DOI: 10.1080/1360086032000063129

Rosener, J., & McAveney, S. (2006). Controlling chaos - frameworks for governing virtual relationships: Part II Substantive law issues. *Intellectual Property & Technology Law Journal, 18*(7), 11–20.

Rule, C. (2002). *Online dispute resolution for business: For e-commerce, B2B, consumer employment, insurance and other commercial conflicts*. Jossey-Bass.

Schafer, B. (2008). Personal communication. School of Law. UK: University of Edinburgh.

Schiavetta, S. (2004). Relationship Between e-ADR and Article 6 of the European Convention of Human Rights under the Case Law of the European Court of Human Rights. *Journal of Information, Law and Technology*, (1).

Staff (August 2006). Colin Rule. Workout Business Processes, http://www.ework-out.co.uk/

Staff (March 2006). Canada backs Sikh dagger rights. BBC News, http://news.bbc.co.uk/2/hi/americas/4770744.stm

Toulmin, S. (1958). *The uses of argument*. Cambridge University Press.

UNCITRAL. (2025). United Nations Commission on International Trade Law, https://uncitral.un.org/

Wagner, J. (July 2007). Second Life Avatar sued for copyright infringement. Giga Omni Media, Inc., http://gigaom.com/2007/07/04/second-life-avatar-sued-for-copyright-infringement/

Walton, D., & Godden, D. (2005). Persuasion dialogue in online dispute resolution. *Artificial Intelligence and Law*, *13*(2), 273–295. DOI: 10.1007/s10506-006-9014-0

Westermann, H., Savelka, J., & Benyekhlef, K. (2023). LLMediator: GPT-4 Assisted Online Dispute Resolution, *Workshop on Artificial Intelligence for Access to Justice,* Braga, Portugal. June 19.

Winograd, T., & Flores, F. (1986). *Understanding computers and cognition: A new foundation for design*. Addison-Wesley.

WIPO. (June 2008). ADR Procedures, https://www.wipo.int/amc/en/center/wipo-adr.html

Wissler, R., & Rak, R. (2004). Assessing mediator performance: The usefulness of participant questionnaires. *Journal of Dispute Resolution*, 229.

Zondag, B., & Lodder, A. (2007). Constructing computer-assisted dispute resolution systems by developing a generic language to analyze information exchange in conflict discourse. *International Review of Law Computers & Technology*, *21*(2), 191–205. DOI: 10.1080/13600860701492203

ENDNOTES

1 Based on Aristotle's examples, in Categories, The Rhetoric, and Metaphysics.

2 Muecke and Stranieri's example.

Chapter 9
Online Dispute Resolution:
The Presentation Design and Evaluation

ABSTRACT

The design of a persuasive presentation for an online dispute can be critical to the satisfactory resolution of a dispute. Some disputants, however, may not be able to afford the cost of a professional multimedia company to develop their online dispute presentation and may need direction on how to design a persuasive presentation for an online dispute. The desired effect is that the opposing party will focus their attention on a preferred point of view, legal reminders, a character's background or a personality trait, which can make the presentation persuasive in an online dispute. Maintaining attention during an online dispute is just as important as the choice of technology platform and the tone and use of voice in the language. This chapter describes a three-step procedure for designing and evaluating a presentation for an online dispute.

INTRODUCTION

Dispute resolution platforms can combine multimedia capability with functionality in a user-friendly interface (Rabinovich-Einy & Katsh, 2014). Communication can include text presentation via email, asynchronous text postings in email, instant messaging, bulletin boards, or social networking websites, synchronous text messaging, audio and video podcasting, website streaming, video conferencing

DOI: 10.4018/979-8-3373-3126-3.ch009

and real-time voice-over protocols. Multi-channel capability enables the display of multiple screens, as well as voice and video.

Visuals can be displayed on computer screens of any size. The visual can be a character in a video or graphic, such as a computerized tutor, coach or mentor (human likeness or cartoon), appearing as an avatar or agent (static or moving). The visual event can be a sketch, diagram, photo, static or moving image, animated GIF or cartoon, or linked reference. A visual can include formatted text, unformatted text or hypertext, scanned handwriting, a static or animated photograph, a pictograph, film or video.

During online disputes, sound cues can be used to: maintain vigilance (alerting attention network), provide context (orienting attention network) or resolve a conflict (executive attention network) to balance uneven conditions that favour reputable or wealthy disputants and leave inarticulate and lesser dispute-wise participants (Mann, 2025). Either party can attach a digital exhibit, such as a digital photograph or scanned image of medical records. A dispute over a property or an undelivered purchased item is are example where not all the information would be available electronically. That said, electronic evidence, such as a doorbell video or digital photo of the damaged product, might still be of help (Lodder & Zeleznikow, 2005).

MAINTAINING ATTENTION

The problem of unequal bargaining conditions between novices and more experienced respondents can be exacerbated by instructions that are not explicit enough for some disputants, intimidating written instructions, FAQs that are too long or too short, or few or no pictorial renditions of the meeting space. Other times, disputes may arise through, and sometimes because of, online communication methods that can not maintain attention (Mann, 2020).

Attention is invaluable to human life (Eysenck & Kean, 2020). Today, brain-scanning technologies offer a new perspective on "attention"; that attention is not one thing as previously thought, but three things, three interdependent networks comprising an attention system: an *alerting attention network,* an *orienting attention network,* and an *executive attention network* (Hopkins, 2021; Posner & Barbey, 2020). Figure 1 illustrates the approximate locations of the three attentional networks comprising the human attention system.

Figure 1. Anatomy of the three attentional networks comprising the human attention system in the brain: an alerting network, an orienting network and an executive attention network

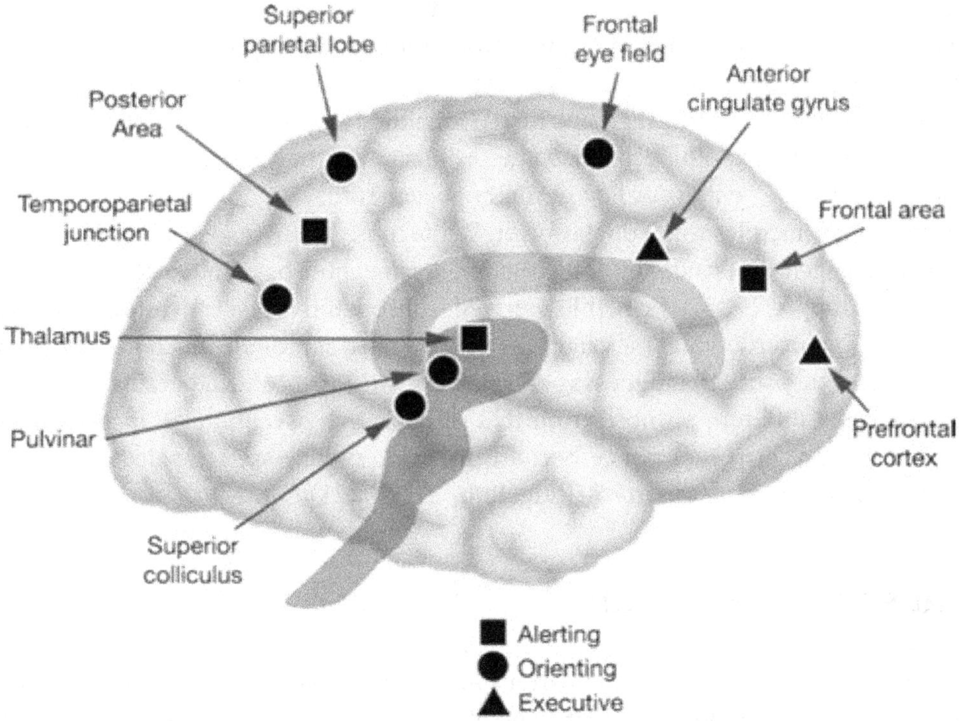

(Posner & Rothbart, 2007)

Cueing the Executive Attention Network

This chapter is only concerned with the *executive attention network,* which functions to resolve conflicts among our thoughts, feelings, and responses. Resolving a conflict during an online dispute, therefore, can be accomplished by design - first by leaving the details in the visuals (i.e., in on-screen text, detailed illustrations, or animations), and then by separating-out the gist from the details, and presenting it as sound cues to focus attention on critical information in the visual events. Using this approach, users better comprehend a presentation when the visuals and sound do not require them to divide their attention between multiple sources of mutually referring information (Mann, 2025).

Most designers wishing to create their digital materials look to guidance for help in developing their presentations. Some have expressed a desire for advice on whether the sound should replace or replicate onscreen explanations (Barron &

Kysilka, 1993; Koroghlanian & Klein, 2004). Others seek purposeful advice that is grounded in strong cognitive principles (Mayer, 2021). Still, some want more than simply narrated screen text (Bishop, Amankwatia & Cates, 2008) or mere word lists (Gyselinck, Jamet & Dubois, 2008). Will audio convey hints or warnings that may only be overlooked if presented only through text and images? (Jaén, Bohigas & Novell, 2009)? Some desire a designer sound for computer systems (Buxton, 1987, p.1). Others prefer a more pragmatic focus (Smaldino & Lowther, 2007). Regardless, developers seek something beyond the ordinary, yet they *do* not articulate what "something more" entails or how it might be achieved.

General principles won't do, however. While more useful than general principles of learning, general principles of instruction are not apt to be of much help to practitioners (Gropper, 1983). "Principles derived from cognitive research remind us how *not* to design instructional messages, as they do not yet provide much guidance on how to design instructional messages" (Bishop, 2013, p.146). Rather, instructional design has a different purpose from that of cognitive psychology. "Instructional design is a prescriptive science because its primary purpose is to determine *the optimal methods of instruction*" (Reigeluth, 1999, p.21).

PRESENTATION DESIGN

Sound cueing in online presentations has demonstrated good long-term results across various ages and different content (Mann, 2025). Sound stimulation can evoke responses in visual areas of the brain, even in very young children (Goswami, 2004). Also, memory for material presented in sound is durable and resistant to interference from other modalities (Baddeley, 1986). Yet sound alone is insufficient to learn from multimedia, hence the need for purposeful advice on how to enhance learning from technology with sound.

During online disputes, sound cues can be used to resolve a conflict and balance uneven conditions that favour reputable or wealthy disputants and leave inarticulate and lesser dispute-wise participants (Mann, 2009). Either party can attach a digital exhibit, such as a digital photograph or a scanned image of a medical record. A dispute regarding a purchased item that is not delivered or was damaged on arrival is an example where not all information is available electronically. That said, electronic evidence, such as a digital picture of the damaged product, might be of help (Lodder & Zeleznikow, 2005, p.302).

Essentially, the ODR Developer has two concerns. The first is the 'dispute-wisdom of the ODR process', and *not only* the features on the ODR site. Four traits identified in "most dispute-wise" negotiators are particularly relevant in an online dispute (Hammond, 2001, p.21). Under the right conditions, these traits could be acquired by a "lesser dispute-wise" negotiator:

1) Have a primary focus on reviewing contracts and agreements
2) Spend a lot of time on highly complex and technical issues
3) Acquire a good understanding of the broader issues involved
4) Take an assertive approach.

The second concern of the ODR Developer is to determine which function of sound works well with the visual events in the presentation. Sound is critical in contemporary presentation software because of its durability in human memory and resistance to interference and forgetting (Mann, 2008).

Given a purpose or *function*, a sound prompt will alert, caution, warn, remind or direct the presenter to visual events displayed by a computer program or Internet site. The desired effect is that the opposing party will focus their attention on the desired point of view, character's background, etc, which makes the presentation useful in preparing for an online dispute. Table 1 shows five different functions for sound for cueing a visual event.

Table 1. The sound cues to resolve a conflict, identify a problem, make a decision, reduce ambivalence, or remove a doubt

Temporal Sound Cue >	• A negotiated solution • A reminder, hint, partial feed-back • *estoppel*[1]
Point of View Sound Cue >	• A conflict of opinions • A dilemna • Opposing political opinions[2]
Locale Sound Cues >	• The *windows in your house* illustration[3]
Atmosphere Sound Cues >	• A map and directional voice-over[4] • *quid pro quo*[5]
Character Sound Cues >	• A personal conflict, *mea culpa*[6] • NPC *Windrunner* in WoW reads for *Horde* characters [7] • Attacked *ad hominem*[8]

(Mann 2009)

Temporal Sound

During a conflict, temporal sound cues can serve as an effect or spoken cue (either human or computerized) that alerts, warns, or guides the viewer regarding a future event or reminds them of a past event. It may originate from a tape or digital file, a virtual coach or agent within a computer application or website, a voice-over IP, or a podcast.

Blackboard, Inc. v. Desire2Learn Inc.

Blackboard did not contact Desire2Learn before filing its patent infringement suit, yet Blackboard asked the court to award treble damages for "willful" infringement, according to Desire2Learn CEO John Baker (Jones, 2006). Blackboard and Desire2Learn are both learning management systems (LMSs), ranking among the top ten concerns for technology leaders in higher education (Camp & DeBloois, 2007). LMSs offer developers and content providers presentation, instruction, teaching, and assessment tools, all typically enclosed behind a password-protected shell. In doing so, LMSs have redefined the stakeholders in online distance education and expanded the scope of intellectual property protection (Mann, 2008). Initiating an online dispute early on might have helped prevent the intense reactions in higher education (Hawkins, 2007), legal magazines (Carnevale, 2007), and peer-reviewed journals (Nicholas, 2007) over the threat of a patent infringement lawsuit. Clear temporal sound cues could have saved significant costs and anxiety by guiding the viewer's attention to *prior art,* which is considered when examining an invention's novelty and non-obviousness, and would not include everything made public before the filing date.

Locale Sound

During a dispute, locale sound cues can fill an informational role when it is associated with a visual event presented in a video clip, graphic, or a paragraph of formatted text. Most often, familiar sounds are used to establish a place, real or imaginary, as in a virtual world dispute, or in a reconstruction of events to present evidence or clarify a situation to the arbitration panel.

Eros LLC v. Leatherwood

In a typical example from the virtual world, Second Life player Kevin Alderman (also known as Stroker Serpentine) filed a lawsuit in a U.S. court against fellow Second Lifer Volkov Catteneo for selling copies of Alderman's Eros SexGen bed, seeking damages equal to three times the amount Eros suffered or three times the defendant's profits. A more cost-effective out-of-court settlement might have been possible by comparing the beds and voice-overs to demonstrate *where* there were allegedly *significant* similarities. The use of location or locale sounds could also have been provided to clarify the coding.

POV Sound

When a point of view (POV) sound cue is presented during a dispute, it can provide more information about a person's perspective than what is stated in the visual event. A point of view (POV) sound cue can reflect the *emphasis* in the differing opinions between differing political opinions, or a deeply felt moral, cultural or religious belief, all potentially critical to a morally- or culturally-sensitive issue.

Multani v. Commission Scolaire Marguerite-Bourgeoys

The Supreme Court case of Canadian Sikhs not being allowed to wear a ceremonial dagger to school could have been settled more quickly and cost-effectively out of court. An online dispute resolution version of the kirpan dispute could have had an online presentation prepared by Balvir Singh Multani using point-of-view sound to explain that Orthodox Sikhs had been required to carry a kirpan since the 17th century, and then insisting it is not a weapon. Spoken language would inform the viewer about *how* the object in the graphic or picture (i.e. the kirpan) should be interpreted, explaining the religious and spiritual significance of the kirpan and its various kinds displayed in a document-sharing area. Similarly, a presentation by the other party would have shown a different POV.

A POV sound prompt in the presentation by Claude Bouchard, *Quebec Federation of Parents' Committees*, for example, would emphasize personal safety in the school, perhaps quoting statistics of increasing violence in some school districts. "As a parent, is the life and safety of a child more important than religious freedom? I think so," and perhaps yet another POV by a representative from *la Commission Scolaire de Marguerite-Bourgeoys.*

MacLeod v. Newsquest

In a case before Lord Macphail, Angus Macleod, Scottish Political Editor of *The Times* and contributor to BBC radio and television, sued the publishers *ofThe Sunday Herald* for alleged defamation in an item in "Alan Taylor's Diary". The court action for defamation was dismissed 'as it was manifest from the language used that the article concerned was in no way an attack upon Mr Macleod; the ordinary reader would have understood that the article had been written for his or her entertainment in a cheerful, irreverent and playful spirit, and had contained elements of fantasy'. The outcome may have been different if arbitrators, peers and disputants in an online dispute were asked to "listen to the words being read" from a podcast with all its intended emphasis, rather than "read the words" silently from a page or screen.

Atmosphere Sound

During a conflict, atmospheric sound cues can provide a context for events not shown or partially shown visually. Atmosphere sound might help to determine culpability in happy slapping cases. 'Happy slapping' is a form of cyberbullying recorded on video and uploaded as a video clip to social media to impersonate, denigrate or aggressively solicit a victim (Mann, 2009, 2015). Happy slapping videos depict small groups of aggressive, poorly educated youths known in England as 'chavs' (in Scotland, 'neds') hitting a random person in a school, on a bus, or at a street corner, while the event is recorded on a cell phone camera. The victims can be the same age as the attackers, but not always, as in the following example.

Anderson, R. v EWCA

In a video clip, a 27-year-old man can be seen shouting into the camera of his cell phone, "This is YouTube material," as he urinates on a disabled 50-year-old woman who lay in the street. The woman later died in the hospital. Aside from visual evidence of the recorded assault, the atmospheric sound may have further helped investigators to establish whether there was the intent of the attackers or whether the 'victim' had taunted the attackers, and whether the video would later be used to denigrate the victim on social media.

Character Sound

A character sound cue refers to a character or personality trait of a person played during a visual event. Consider two examples where character or personality sound could have filled in information lacking in the visuals.

Koon, S. v United States

Sound could have helped to define a person's character in this case. Consider the example of the videotaped incident of black motorist Rodney King as he was being clubbed and kicked by four white Los Angeles police officers in 1991. The officers claimed that King had resisted arrest. Videotaped footage of the event was the central piece of evidence for both sides in this case. However, the poor quality of the video made it difficult to determine who started the fight and who was hitting whom. In a frame-by-frame analysis of the videotape, the expert police witness supported the prosecutor's contention that only reasonable force was used against King.

No one questioned the act of freeze-framing the events in the video clip. In the detailed account, which recounted the event of the beating, the defence presented the photographs in sequence.

The chilling effects of warping the video into freeze-frame photography cannot be underestimated. The temporization that reading video [and listening to the audio] entails is halted by spatial determinations that can reconfigure the violence to which Mr. Rodney King was subjected (Ronell, 2005, p.211).

This shifted the experience from watching a film to viewing pictures. By arguing that every individual 'mini-action' was legal and in compliance with regulations, they implied that the overall action was also legal, thereby undermining the impression conveyed by the film as it is perceived as a whole.

After the trial, a television station analyzed the sound on the videotape with the assistance of sound evidence expert George Papcun. Notably and relevant to this essay was Dr Papcun's analysis of the words shouted by men on that videotape that added context to the visual event and the *character* of the arresting officers, taken here from Dr. Papcun's transcript:

> 12:53:04 Voice 1: "Hands behind your back!"
> 12:53:09 Voice 2: "Hands behind your back!"
> 12:53:13 Voice 2: "Behind your back, n*gger!"

Again, character sound could have helped to define the intent and character of the police officers in this case.

Necessary Force With a Taser

The second example of sound defining a person's character is clear from the recording of Robert Dziekanski dying after being Tasered by federal police at Vancouver Airport (Pritchard, 2007). Robert Dziekański was a 40-year-old Polish immigrant who had taken his first airplane ride to visit his mother in Canada. In the video, he can be seen taking office chairs and putting them in front of the security doors (CBC News, 2007).

> Officer: 'Hit him again. Hit him again.'
> Several loud cracking sounds
> Second Officer: Code red!

An ambulance team arrived a few minutes later, and he was declared dead (Haines, 2007). Did the use of a Taser by police officers in this case constitute 'necessary force'? Will the visual events in the Dziekanski video be depicted without the audio, as in the Rodney King trial? Perhaps the outcome will be the same. In previous cases, where the subjects refused to comply with directions or commands by police officers, the decisions had been mixed (R v. Walcott, 2008).

EVALUATING THE PRESENTATION

Most evaluations of online disputes focus on their *effectiveness*. An "effectiveness evaluation" involves measuring the outcomes and impacts of a program to determine whether it is achieving the desired results and addressing the needs of the target population (EvalCommunity, 2024b). An "effectiveness evaluation" poses the question, "To what extent is the program *effective* in attaining its goals?" (Patton, 1982). Effectiveness evaluation explores the degree to which a program, policy, or intervention meets its intended objectives or goals.

Outcome evaluations, which are the focus of this chapter, are objective and systematic. They require the collection and analysis of data to determine whether the outcomes are significant and beneficial to the target population (EvalCommunity, 2024b). This includes considering human variables such as empathy, compassion, competing values, and the availability of mercy that cannot be replicated by machines (Costabel, 2023, p.84). Outcomes evaluation poses the questions, "To what extent are desired client outcomes being attained? And what are the effects of the program on clients?" (Patton, 1982).

Expert-Peer Online Assessment

The Expert-Peer method of ODR online assessment exemplifies outcomes evaluation (Mann, 2005, 2006, 2009). This method originates from common statistical techniques aimed at improving accuracy rates from multiple assessors (Tweedie & Mengersen, 1999). The online version of this approach and formula was initially applied to evaluate the unique learning style of Australian Aboriginal students, which could not be adequately assessed through conventional means (Mann, 1998). The validity of the method and formula was tested (Mann, 2005) and further developed in 2006, introducing anonymity and accountability measures to prevent ceiling effects and peer bias. A comprehensive discussion of the method's development is accessible elsewhere (Wadhwa, Schulz & Mann, 2006).

The current iteration of this method and formula has been modified from its predecessor to better accommodate the limitations and requirements of presentations for online dispute resolution. Figure 2 illustrates the four steps in expert-peer online assessment of an online dispute presentation.

Figure 2. The expert-peer online assessment process

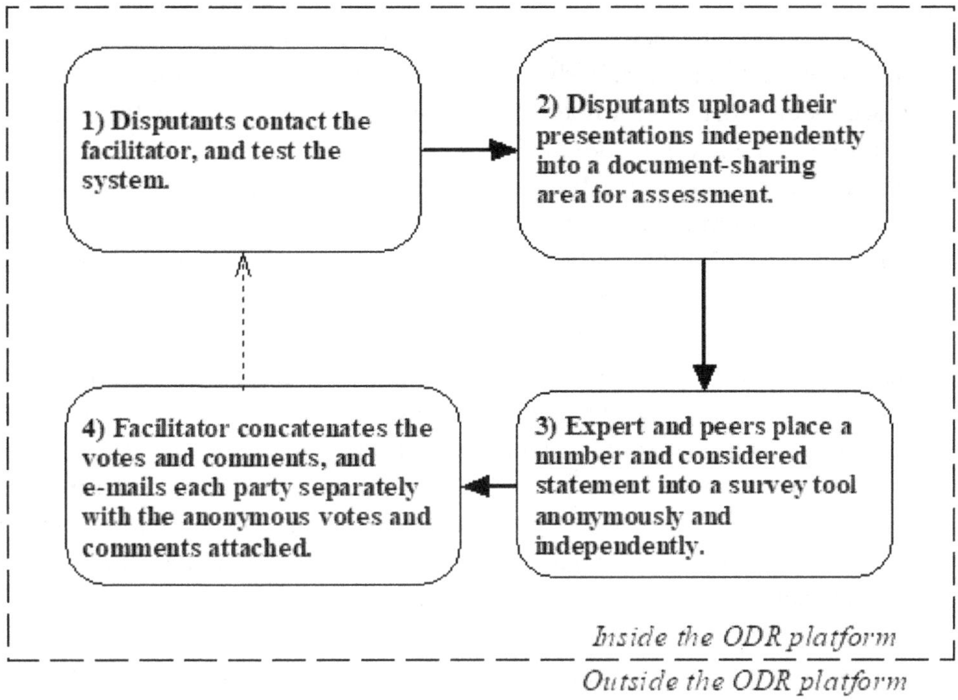

(Mann 2009)

The Expert-Peer online assessment of an online dispute presentation requires claimants and respondents to post their cases independently in a secure area. Subsequently, two or more peers review the cases, assign a numerical mark, and provide comments on each presentation without knowledge of the expert's assessment. A designated expert independently assigns a numerical mark and writes comments, separate from the peers. The scores are tallied and compared with the comments (Mann, 2005).

An ODR version of the kirpan dispute, for instance, could have featured an online presentation prepared by Balvir Singh Multani, utilizing point-of-view sound on a Zoom platform to clarify that Orthodox Sikhs have been required to carry a kirpan since the 17th century and maintain that it is not a weapon. VoIP recordings like Zoom facilitate two-way, real-time audio discussions and ongoing instant messaging during interactive slide presentations. Colin Rule, ODR Director for eBay and PayPal, has stated that VoIP is becoming mainstream and that for ODR services, this advancement is a significant turning point, as disputants can now communicate synchronously over their computers at low or no cost.

The process is somewhat more intricate than just annotating and saving screen recordings because much occurs in real time.

1. Disputants should generate ideas for the presentation, create a chapter mock-up, and prepare the slides. Early on, it is advisable to email the ODR facilitator to access the VoIP platform and discuss some preliminary ideas for potential inclusion in the real-time presentation.
2. Disputants enter the VoIP software in real time, where one party receives "moderator" status from the facilitator. The facilitator then uploads PowerPoint slides to the whiteboard, a document presentation area, and begins to speak to them, introducing each slide and responding to their spoken and instant text messages. Upon conclusion, the entire real-time session is saved as a playable file.
3. Assessors review the recording, then log into the ODR platform and enter a numerical score and comments into a survey tool on the secure ODR platform. In the case before the Supreme Court, the interveners included representatives from the World Sikh Organization of Canada, the Canadian Civil Liberties Association, the Canadian Human Rights Commission, and the Ontario Human Rights Commission. These may also serve the purpose of online out-of-court dispute resolution.

Expert-peer online assessment may also be suitable for evaluating annotated screen recordings. Annotated screen recordings are playable computer files that can be independently reviewed and assessed. Screen recording software allows the developer or user to capture onscreen actions. The process includes recording what occurs on the screen as a compressed video file, narrating the screen recording with a microphone based on the script, and previewing the recorded clip. Assessors would review the recorded clip sent to them as frequently as necessary, then log in to the ODR platform to input a numerical score and comments into a survey tool on the secure ODR platform. This format could have served as a suitable platform in the patent dispute between LMS competitors Blackboard, Inc. and Desire2Learn.

Finally, crimes recorded by video camera also record sound, as in the Rodney King beating, the Dziekanski Tasering death, and the happy slapping video, which can encourage discussion and debate of audio-visual evidence in a criminal investigation.

Expert-Peer Formula

- What if there existed a standard method of counting the votes and comments of an arbitrator or expert that included anonymity for the assessors?

- And what if inter-rater and intra-rater consistency data were used to weigh the assessments (votes) of each peer, arbitrator or expert?

The expert-peer assessment formula shown in Figure 2 is recommended as a response to the third research question, "How should the assessments of experts and peers be used to judge online dispute presentations?" The expert-peer formula was modified for online dispute presentation from its predecessor used for online peer assessment in post-secondary education. The original version has high statistical validity and the side effect of democratizing the online assessment process (Mann, 2005). The new version uses the same mathematics as the original, except the update proposes qualitative changes to its use for evaluating online dispute presentations that include an appointed arbitrator or expert and volunteers or "peers."

In its present form, the evaluation formula for online dispute presentations could accommodate such a scenario. Figure 3 shows the expert-peer assessment formula for evaluating online dispute presentations.

Figure 3. Expert-peer assessment formula

$$\text{Judgment of the group} = \frac{\text{Appointed Expert} + \dfrac{\text{Peer 1} + \text{Peer 2} + \text{Peer 3} + \text{Peer 4}}{4}}{2}$$

(Mann 2009)

The formula in Figure 3 can accommodate online disputes in which the neutral third party is replaced by several interested volunteers (peers) acting as if they were an online jury in a civil trial, as in Hörnle's Mock Trial (e.g. a summary jury trial) (Hörnle, 2002), and the neutral third party could also be retained, all as bona fide voting members. The "Arbitration" process described in Motion's (2005) Hart's (1999), and Hörnle's (2002) classification systems, for example, is similar to the neutral procedure of WIPO's "Expert Determination" (2008) wherein the dispute is submitted to one or more arbitrators/experts who make a decision on the matter presented before them by the parties.

Assessing the Kirpan in Schools Dispute

The procedural alternative to deciding the kirpan in schools dispute could have been to:

1) Choose a voting arbitrator or legal expert, plus four peers – i.e., a member of the Sikh community, a representative from the Parents' Committee at the School, a School Board official, an Orthodox Sikh elder, or a representative from any of the organizations associated with the case that were mentioned earlier.
2) Everyone remains anonymous.
3) Experts and peers review the online presentations anonymously and independently from one another, assigning each presentation a mark and justifying their mark in writing.
4) Intra-rater consistency (written/numerical). The next step in the process is to total the scores according to the formula and determine intra-rater consistency between the scores and the written justification, as determined by a facilitator. If there is a discrepancy, expert and peer reviewers could be asked to remove the discrepancy between their written and numerical assessments. Figure 4 shows some hypothetical concatenated scores of online presentations in the Kirpan dispute.

Figure 4. Hypothetical concatenated scores of online presentations in the kirpan dispute

Complainant's Dispute Presentation: Commission Scolaire de Marguerite-Bourgeoys	***Respondent's Dispute Presentation***: Balvir Singh Multani
6.9125 = 6.5+6+5+7/4= 6.125 + 7.7/2	7.20 = 7+6+6+7/4=6.5+7.9/2

One further step can be taken. Intra-rater consistency (by occasion), where the scores assigned by each rater for evaluating dispute presentations, can also be used to rate the raters to ensure high-quality raters in online dispute resolution. Experts and peer reviewers could be rated by other reviewers (peer assessment), by program administrators, and even by themselves (self-assessment). The results could be used for job placement and promotion, or self-improvement. The procedure in the evaluation formula for online dispute presentations could easily accommodate the opinions of the disputants, self-assessments, and those of a program administrator.

Wissler and Rak's (2004) study on attorneys' assessments of particular mediators, for example, revealed information that could be helpful to both prospective employers and novice mediators. However, there were issues with the research design. The first issue was that the reported percentiles could not reflect the variation within the group scores for any specific mediator.

A better approach, given that all attorney assessments were given equal weighting, would have been to obtain a single number - the average (the mean or median) of all attorney assessments, and associated standard deviations and effect sizes. A second problem with the method of analysis was that all the raters had equal impact. A better method would have been to use a weighting formula like the evaluation formula for online dispute presentations (Mann, 2005) to include the "rater's experience" or "rater's skill level" in the analysis of a particular mediator. A third problem is that percentiles should not have been compared against one another, as rater assignment across mediators was not random. Care should be taken to compare scores across mediators.

CONCLUSION

The busy field of online dispute resolution is an excellent place to start a discussion about the executive attention network because the business of executive attention is to manage conflict. After all, conflict is the raison d'être of online disputes. Online dispute resolution usually works smoothly when there are only two parties and when the substance of the dispute is only monetary. However, when the dispute is difficult, emotional, or there's a large amount of money in dispute, there are many parties, or when there is a perception of judicial bias or prejudice (Katsh & Rule, 2016), substandard presentations made by inarticulate and lesser dispute-wise disputants can make the bargaining conditions uneven (American Arbitration Association, 2006) compared to professionally-presented cases of more dispute-wise respondents (Hörnle, 2002). In any case, those of us who must consider attention in the design of audio-visual communications should know the new perspective on gaining and maintaining attention in an online dispute.

REFERENCES

American Arbitration Association. (2006). Arbitration & ADR Services, https://www.adr.org/

Baddeley, A. (1986). *Working memory. Clarendon Press*. University Press.

Baddeley, A. (2013). On applying cognitive psychology. *British Journal of Psychology, 104*(4), 443–456. DOI: 10.1111/bjop.12049 PMID: 24094277

Barron, A., & Kysilka, M. (1993). The effectiveness of digital audio in computer-based training. *Journal of Research on Computing in Education, 25*(3), 277–289. DOI: 10.1080/08886504.1993.10782051

Bishop, M. J. (2013). Reconceptualizing instructional message design: Toward the development of a new guiding framework. In Hokanson, B., & Gibbons, A. (Eds.), *Design In Educational Technology: Design Thinking, Design Process, and the Design Studio*. Springer.

Bishop, M. J., Amankwatia, T. B., & Cates, W. M. (2008). Sound's use in instructional software to enhance learning: A theory-to-practice content analysis. *Educational Technology Research and Development, 56*(4), 467–486. DOI: 10.1007/s11423-006-9032-3

Buxton, W. (1987). The audio channel. In Baecker, R. M., & Buxton, W. A. S. (Eds.), *Readings in Human-Computer Interaction: A Multidisciplinary Approach* (pp. 393–399). Morgan Kaufman Associates.

Camp, J. S., & DeBloois, P. B. (2007). [IT issues *Educause Review,* May/June.]. *Top (Madrid)*, 10.

Carnevale, D. (2007). Supreme Court's patent ruling could spell trouble for Blackboard and others [May.]. *The Chronicle of Higher Education, 53*, 37.

CBC News. (2007). https://www.cbc.ca/news

Eros LLC v. Leatherwood, https://virtuallyblind.com/files/eros_default.pdf

EvalCommunity. (2024a). Understanding Effectiveness Evaluation: Definition, Benefits, and Best Practices, https://www.evalcommunity.com/career-center/effectiveness-evaluation/

Eysenck, M. W., & Keane, M. T. (2020). *Cognitive Psychology: A Student's Handbook* (8th ed.). Psychology Press. DOI: 10.4324/9781351058513

Goswami, U. (2004). Neuroscience, education and special education. *British Journal of Special Education, 31*(4), 175–183. DOI: 10.1111/j.0952-3383.2004.00352.x

Gropper, G. L. (1983). A behavioural approach to instructional prescription. In Reigeluth, C. M. (Ed.), *Instructional-design theories and models: An Overview of Their Current Status*. Lawrence Erlbaum Associates.

Gyselinck, V., Jamet, E., & Dubois, V. (2008). The role of working memory components in multimedia comprehension. *Applied Cognitive Psychology, 22*(3), 353–374. DOI: 10.1002/acp.1411

Haines, L. (2007). Canadian taser death caught on camera: Vancouver Airport amateur footage shocker, *The Register,* https://www.theregister.com/2007/11/15/taser_death_video/#:~:text=Vancouver%20Airport%20amateur%20footage%20shocker,more%20Taser%20shot%20into%20Dziekanski

Hammond, A.-M. (2001). The effectiveness of online dispute resolution. Department of Conflict and Management. Masters thesis. Royal Roads University.

Hannafin, M. J., & Peck, K. L. (1988). *The Design, Development and Evaluation of Instructional Software*. Macmillan. Publishing Company.

Hart, C. (1999). Online dispute resolution and avoidance in electronic commerce. The chapter was presented at *the Uniform Law Conference of Canada.* August.

Hawkins, B. (2007). Letter from Brian Hawkins, President of EDUCAUSE, to Blackboard CEO Michael Chasen, https://www.educause.edu/ir/library/pdf/EPO0711.pdf

Hopkins, K. (2021). Neuroscience as a contemporary science domain to contextualize the nature of science instruction. *Science & Education, 30*(3), 463–500. DOI: 10.1007/s11191-020-00187-7

Hörnle, J. (2002). Online Dispute Resolution in Business-to-Consumer E-commerce Transactions. *Journal of Information, Law and Technology. (2).*

Jaén, X., Bohigas, X., & Novell, M. (2009). Semi-virtual classroom for physics contents, *EAEEIE Annual Conference.*

Jones, P. (2006). The Blackboard patent: Where's Waldo? Eklektix. Inc. https://lwn.net/Articles/197535/

Katsh, E., & Rule, C. (2016). What we know and need to know about online dispute resolution, South Carolina Law Review, 67(2), 329-344, https://scholarcommons.sc.edu/sclr/vol67/iss2/10 67(2)

Koon v. United States | 518 U.S. 81 (1996), https://supreme.justia.com/cases/federal/us/518/81/

Koroghlanian, C., & Klein, J. (2004). The effect of audio and animation in multimedia instruction. *Journal of Educational Multimedia and Hypermedia, 13*(1), 23–46.

Lodder, A., & Zeleznikow, J. (2005). Developing an online dispute resolution environment: Dialogue tools and negotiation support systems in a three-step model. *Harvard Negotiation Law Review, 10*(287), 302.

MacLeod v. Newsquest (Sunday Herald) Ltd | [2007], https://www.casemine.com/judgement/uk/5a8ff84a60d03e7f57ebdf28

Mann, B. L. (2005). Testing the validity of Post and Vote Web-based peer assessment, in David Williams. Scott Howell and Mary Hricko (Eds.). *Online Assessment, Measurement and Evaluation: Emerging Practices* (pp. 132-153) Hershey, PA: Information Science Publishing, http://www.stemnet.nf.ca/~bmann/HigherEd99.htm

Mann, B. L. (2008). Copyright protection and the new stakeholders in online distance education. *First Monday, 13*(7). http://www.uic.edu/htbin/cgiwrap/bin/ojs/index.php/fm/article/viewArticle/2095/1997. DOI: 10.5210/fm.v13i7.2095

Mann, B. L. (2008). Computer-aided presentations. In Wah, B. W. (Ed.), *Encyclopedia of Computer Science and Engineering*. John Wiley & Sons Inc., https://www.cdli.ca/~bmann/0_ARTICLES/Mann_CAI_Wiley.pdf

Mann, B. L. (2008). The evolution of multimedia sound, *Computers and Education: An International Journal 50(*4), 1157-1173, https://www.cdli.ca/~bmann/0_ARTICLES/Mann_ComputersEd_08.pdf

Mann, B. L. (2009). Smoothing some wrinkles in online dispute resolution. *International Journal of Law and Information Technology*, *17*(1), 83–112. DOI: 10.1093/ijlit/ean017

Mann, B. L. (2009). Social networking websites: A concatenation of impersonation, denigration, sexual and aggressive solicitation, cyber-bullying and happy slapping videos. *International Journal of Law and Information Technology, 17*(3), 252–267. DOI: 10.1093/ijlit/ean008

Mann, B. L. (2015). Social networking websites: A concatenation of impersonation, denigration, sexual and aggressive solicitation, cyber-bullying and happy slapping videos. In Philip Leith (Ed.). *Privacy in the Information Society* (pp. 493–503), Part VI. Social Networks, Volume II of a 3-volume series. The Library of Essays on Law and Privacy. London, U.K.: Ashgate Publishing. January

Mann, B. L. (2025). Speech cueing curricular multimedia: Instructional design that activates the orienting attention network. *Journal of Interactive Learning Research, 36*(2), 191–214. DOI: 10.70725/115195dejbne

Mayer, R. E. (2021). *Multimedia learning* (3rd ed.). Cambridge University Press.

Mayer, R. E., & Moreno, R. (1998). A split attention effect in multimedia learning: Evidence for dual processing systems in working memory. *Journal of Educational Psychology, 90*(2), 312–320. DOI: 10.1037/0022-0663.90.2.312

Motion, P. (2003). Internet arbitration clauses: Shock and awe? *The Journal: Magazine of the Law Society of Scotland*, p. 42.

Motion, P. (2005). Article 17: Encouragement of alternative dispute resolution – Online dispute resolution: A view from Scotland. In Edwards, L. (Ed.), *The new legal framework for e-commerce in Europe* (pp. 137–169). Hart Publishing.

Multani v. Commission scolaire Marguerite-Bourgeoys, [2006] 1 S.C.R. 256, 2006 SCC 6, https://decisions.scc-csc.ca/scc-csc/scc-csc/en/item/15/index.do

Nicholas, R. (2007). Trouble in the classroom. *Patent World., 190*, 12–13.

Patton, M. Q. (1982). Qualitative methods and approaches: What are they? *New Directions for Institutional Research, 1982*(34), 3–15. DOI: 10.1002/ir.37019823403

Posner, M. I., & Barbey, A. K. (2020). General intelligence in the age of neuroimaging. *Trends in Neuroscience and Education, 18*, 100126–100126. DOI: 10.1016/j.tine.2020.100126 PMID: 32085908

Posner, M. I., & Rothbart, M. K. (2007). Research on attention networks as a model for the integration of Psychological Science. *Annual Review of Psychology, 58*(1), 1–23. DOI: 10.1146/annurev.psych.58.110405.085516 PMID: 17029565

Pritchard, P. (2007). Video of Robert Dziekanski's Taser death, *CBC News,* https://www.cbc.ca/player/play/video/1.1808186

R. *v.* Anderson, 2014 SCC 41, [2014] 2 S.C.R. 167, https://decisions.scc-csc.ca/scc-csc/scc-csc/en/item/14222/index.do

Anderson, R. v. [2022] EWCA Crim 1465, https://www.casemine.com/judgement/uk/636bf68fb3d7a21f332b937b

Walcott, R. v. (K.L.), [2008] O.T.C. 97 (SupCt), https://ca.vlex.com/vid/r-v-walcott-k-680633937

Rabinovich-Einy, O. (2003). The Ford-Firestones of the future: Resolving offline disputes in an online society. In A. Lodder et al, (Eds.). *Essays on legal and technical aspects of Online Dispute Resolution,* June 28, Edinburgh, UK, http://odrworkshop.info/odrworkshopproceedings2003.pdf

Reigeluth, C. M. (Ed.). (1999). *Instructional-design theories and models: A new paradigm of instructional theory* (Vol. 2). Lawrence Erlbaum Associates Publishers.

Ronell, A. (2005). ArtForum, The Rodney G. King "event, https://www.artforum.com/features/avital-ronell-227724/

Smaldino, S. E., & Lowther, D. L. (2007). *Instructional technology and media for Learning* (9th ed.). Prentice Hall.

Tweedie, R., & Mengersen, K. (1999). Calculating accuracy rates from multiple assessors with limited information. *The American Statistician, 53*(3), 233–238. DOI: 10.1080/00031305.1999.10474465

Wadhwa, G., Schulz, H., & Mann, B. L. (2006). Effects of anonymity and peer-accountability during online peer assessment. In Mann, B. L. (Ed.), *Selected styles in web-based educational research* (pp. 300–331). Information Science Publishing., https://www.cdli.ca/~bmann/0_StylesBook/20_Wadhwa_Peer_06.pdf DOI: 10.4018/978-1-59140-732-4.ch020

WIPO. (2008) Expert determination, https://www.wipo.int/portal/en/index.html

Wissler, R., & Rak, R. (2004). Assessing mediator performance: The usefulness of participant questionnaires. *Journal of Dispute Resolution*, 229.

ENDNOTES

1 A verbal promise made that a contract will *not* be enforced, preventing subsequent proceedings to enforce the contract against the person who relied on the promise.

2 Political points of view, in Mann, 2008, p.1166.

3 Used in Baddeley (2013) to explain his "episodic buffer"; and what O'Reilly (2010) called "the output buffer for episodic information"

4 The substance or meaning of a context, in Mann 2008, p.1167.

5 Giving or expecting something in exchange for something else of equal value.

6 Through my fault.

7 Windrunner is a non-player character in the *World of Warcraft* MMORPG, as described in White (2012).

8 A fallacious argument whereby genuine discussion of the topic is avoided by attacking the character, motive, or other attribute of the person making the argument.

Section 2
Intellectual Property Law in Educational Technology

Chapter 10
Copyright Distinctions: The Lone Ranger and The Posse

ABSTRACT

Copyright is the world's most recognizable form of intellectual property, yet perhaps the most misunderstood form of intellectual property in Educational Technology. What isn't always clear is that "copyright" constitutes an economic right, distinct from droits d'auteur or "the moral rights of the author," meaning the right to be acknowledged for one's work. Copyright laws differ from country to country. The differences depend on the jurisdiction and the type of law practiced (i.e., common or civil), the economic interests of the copyright holders, the interests of the users in the protected work, and sometimes conflicts with other laws, such as privacy and free speech. This chapter discusses ownership of online course materials and methods by a solo faculty member, often referred to as a "Lone Ranger," who handles everything, and that of several committee members, or a "Posse," who contribute to an online course in various ways. This chapter also separates the lawful protections for interface and database expressions within a Learning Management System.

COPYRIGHT: A NATURAL RIGHT?

In 1690, English Philosopher and Physician John Locke set down a natural rights argument of copyright, sometimes called "Labour Theory" (Carrier & Lastowka, 2007). Locke's *Labour Theory of Property* states that people are entitled to the fruits of their labour. This can be extended to intellectual property, which can be seen as the product of an individual's mental labour. Locke merged two critical aspects of property: industry and labour of thought (Locke, 1690). According to Locke, the labour supplied by an author provided the necessary justification to exclude others from copying the work, even when the author was working with materials that were freely available (Murray & Trosow, 2013). In this way, Locke's approach to

DOI: 10.4018/979-8-3373-3126-3.ch010

property was consistent with the concept of intellectual property as a commercial entity within a market-driven economy.

Nearly a century later, Thomas Jefferson, a primary author of the *American Declaration of Independence (July 4, 1776)*, was inspired by the sanctity of the individual in the writings of John Locke (Bowers, 1945). Locke's ideas about natural rights, such as the rights to life, liberty, and property, influenced the American Revolution and modern liberalism. He also originated much of the ideological impetus behind Western liberal constitutions. More recently, John Willinsky (2006) extended *Locke's Theory of Property* into the *Commonwealth of Learning* by holding that the improvement of ideas is what warrants all claims of having created intellectual property.

THE FIRST COPYRIGHT LAW

Six years after Locke died in 1704, an important event occurred in the history of intellectual property law - the passing of the *Statute of Anne* to rein in book publishers, book printers, and booksellers from reprinting and selling books without the author's consent. The *Statute of Anne* (1710) was the first copyright law in the U.K. designed as an Act for the encouragement of learning by vesting the copies of printed books in the authors or purchasers of such copies for a particular duration of time. The statute was intended to encourage public learning and to regulate the book trade. However, any benefits for authors in the statute were incidental. Whereas the statute established the author as legal owner, it also provided a 21-year copyright term to books already in print. At the end of the 21st year, the literary property reverted to the bookseller rather than the author, as most authors continued to sell their works outright to booksellers.

THE BERNE CONVENTION

Personal right is the inspiration of the mainstream of international law as expressed in the *Berne Convention (1971)*. This right must be asserted before it applies. So, in teaching materials and on contract with a publisher, an author must state that they assert their right to be identified as the author of their work. The *Berne Convention for the Protection of Literary and Artistic Works (1886/1979)* made an explicit exemption for teaching. So quotations from a work which has already been lawfully made available to the public, and the use of literary or artistic works through illustration in publications, broadcasts, or visual recordings for teaching, provided such utilization is compatible with fair practice were exempted (WIPO 1886/1979, Article 10).

"Authorship" is usually straightforward for print technology (i.e., books, articles, photographs, or works of fine art). For a film, there is some dispute. What, for example, are the relative degrees of authorship of scriptwriters, specialist dialogue writers, and directors? Many multimedia and new media works are already collaborative works, and this trend is expected to intensify. The Berne Convention makes special provisions for collaborative works, as described in Section 2.2. The special provision reduces the stress on film directors, for example, when scriptwriters withhold their film scripts because their integrity has not been honoured. However, a clearer definition of "moral rights" will soon be needed in future multimedia works relative to both the Director's input, and contributions from individual authors, and purveyors of AI-generated scripts.

Before the Berne Convention, national copyright laws only applied to works created within each country. Consequently, a work published in France by a French national would be copyright-protected there but could be copied and sold by anyone in the U.K. or Germany. Today, under the Berne Convention, French copyright law applies to anything published or performed in France, regardless of where it was created. The Berne Convention requires its signatories to recognize the copyright of works of authors from other participating countries in the same way that it recognizes the copyright of its nationals.

THE WIPO

The *World Intellectual Property Organization (WIPO)* was created in 1967 to harmonize the protection of intellectual property mostly in first-world countries. In 1974, WIPO became an agency of the United Nations to promote creative activity and facilitate technology transfer to developing countries to accelerate economic, social and cultural development. In 2004, the General Assembly of WIPO agreed to adopt a proposal offered by Argentina and Brazil to establish a Development Agenda for WIPO to reduce the inequality of access to education that undermined development and social cohesion (Geneva Declaration, 2004).

The WCT

The *WIPO Copyright Treaty,* or WCT (1996), has inadvertently permitted the entertainment industry to dictate the terms of how business is to be conducted to stakeholders in online distance education. Under WCT, signatories could grant exceptions for uses deemed in the public interest, such as for non-profit educational and research purposes. The WCT could not grant these rights directly but instead required member WIPO countries to grant certain rights to ensure that right-holders could effectively use technology to protect their rights and license their works online.

Anti-Circumvention

The first, known as the "anti-circumvention" provision, was meant to confront "hacking" of technological measures (such as encryption). The second was information that accompanied any protected material available online and identified the work, its creator, performer, or owner, and the terms and conditions for its use. Therefore, the net effect of WCT in online distance education has been a climate of digital rights management that applies more to online music file sharing than online teaching and learning.

Copyfraud

"Copyfraud" is a form of copyright fraud, involving false copyright claims aimed at controlling works outside one's legal rights. Copyfraud includes falsely claiming copyright in a work in the public domain, such as when universities pay licensing fees for almost everything they reproduce and distribute to their students, whether supported by copyright law or not (Mazzone, 2006). Copyfraud has serious consequences. Besides enriching publishers who make false copyright claims at the expense of legitimate users, it suppresses legitimate reproduction and creativity and undermines free speech.

SLAPP

Another form of fraud is the *Strategic Lawsuit Against Public Participation,* or SLAPP, which aims to shut down critics and satirists who parody by intimidating them with threats of legal action, draining their resources and, wherever possible, undermining their active public engagement (Verza, 2018). A key feature in a SLAPP is the power disparity between the plaintiff and the defendant. News journalists in Europe working in the public interest have become particular targets of intimidation. See Guardian News & Media (2019) for more on SLAPP against journalists in the U.K. and abroad.

Anti-SLAPP laws are more developed in Australia, Canada, and in the U.S. In Europe, SLAPPs remain primarily unrecognized, with little consideration for their use and impact. According to some scholars, this difference is grounded on the different considerations of the right to freedom of expression in the countries' constitutional systems. While "freedom of speech" is protected as an almost absolute right by the U.S. First Amendment, there is a necessary balance between this fundamental right and other interests, such as reputation rights, which is provided in the European domestic and regional systems (e.g. by Article 10 (2) of the *European Convention on Human Rights.*

THE TRIPS

The *Trade-Related Aspects of Intellectual Property Rights,* or TRIPS, introduced intellectual property law into the international trading system and remains the most comprehensive global agreement on intellectual property. TRIPS was negotiated at the end of the Uruguay Round of the *General Agreement on Tariffs and Trade* or GATT in 1994. Many of the TRIPS provisions on copyright were imported from the Berne Convention. TRIPS requires the member states to provide strong protection for intellectual property rights. For example, under TRIPS, Copyright terms must extend to 50 years after the death of the author, must be granted automatically, and not be based upon any "formality." Computer programs must be regarded as "literary works" under copyright law and receive the exact terms of protection.

JURISDICTIONS

Copyright laws differ from country to country. The differences depend on jurisdiction and the type of law practiced (i.e., common or civil), economic interests of the copyright holders, interests of the users in the protected work, and sometimes conflicts with other laws such as privacy or free speech. More than whether the owner's name was cited correctly, copyright is more about whether the owner was paid for the use of his or her work – a "licensing fee."

Copyright in the United States

Copyright Law in the United States resides in Title 17 (United States Code, 2022), which includes the *Copyright Act* (1976), which was amended by the *Digital Millennium Copyright Act* (DMCA, 1998). The DMCA came into force in 2000. The DMCA was written as part of the United States' commitment to comply with two treaties passed by the *World Intellectual Property Organization (WIPO)* in 1996 that dealt with the nature of copyright with modern information systems such as the

Internet. The DMCA also includes a process called a DMCA takedown, which allows the content owner to request that a website or internet platform remove content.

The *Technology, Education, and Copyright Harmonization or TEACH Act* (17 U.S.C. § 110(2) came into force in 2002. The TEACH Act allows for the use of copyrighted material in online and distance learning if the organization is an accredited nonprofit institution, the use is part of a class session and directly related to teaching, access is restricted to enrolled students, and the institution applies technological measures to prevent unauthorized distribution. Institutions often subscribe to digital libraries that provide licensed access to books, articles, and videos. Educators can request permission from publishers to use copyrighted materials.

Educational Materials

Educational materials, including textbooks, online courses, syllabi, lecture slides, and exams, are protected by copyright as soon as they are created and fixed in a tangible medium (e.g., hardcopy, webpage, podcast, video demo or lecture). The copyright owner is usually the author, such as a professor or teacher (i.e., the Lone Ranger), unless the work was created as part of a work for hire or under a contract that assigns rights elsewhere (i.e., the Posse). Copyright typically lasts for the life of the author plus 70 years. For works made for hire, it lasts 95 years from publication or 120 years from creation, whichever is shorter.

Fair Use Exception (17 U.S.C. § 107)

Educators and students can use copyrighted material without permission under fair use if the purpose is nonprofit educational use, which favours fair use, especially if used for teaching, scholarship, or research. Factual or published works qualify in non-substantive portions (e.g., an excerpt rather than a full textbook). So, small excerpts of classroom handouts may be used under fair use, but full books require permission. Professors and teachers may retain copyright of their recorded lectures, but institutions may claim ownership depending on employment agreements. Students retain copyright over their work unless they sign a release.

Some educational materials, known as Open Educational Resources (OER), are licensed under a Creative Commons licence, allowing free use and modification. Older works, typically published before 1929, become part of the public domain, are no longer under copyright, and can be freely used.

In 2010, the *U.S. Copyright Office* made a new exemption covering educational uses by college and university professors and by college and university film and media studies students, as well as noncommercial videos. In 2018, the Copyright Office made a new exemption covering short portions of motion pictures for criticism or comment, for supervised educational purposes, or to accommodate for accessibility for disabled students in educational institutions. In 2021, the *U.S. Copyright Office* made an exemption covering literary works distributed electronically that are protected by technological measures that either prevent the enabling of read-aloud functionality from interfering with screen readers or other applications or assistive technologies or for research purposes at educational institutions.

The exemptions covering literary works don't (yet) apply to AI. U.S. news publishers *Dow Jones & Co* and *NYP Holdings* have sued AI search engine startup Perplexity for scraping their content without paying for it (Thomson, 2024). The plaintiffs accuse the AI biz of two counts of copyright infringement to feed the data requirements of its training models. News Corp's CEO Robert Thomson claimed this could be the first of many such lawsuits against AI developers.

Copyright has also been used as a tool to silence critics (Stoltz & Noble, 2024). Yet copyright's fair use doctrine protects free expression against the threat of ruinous lawsuits. For example, in a recent court case, *LifeWise Inc.*, a private organization that markets religious instruction for public school students, produced controversial religious education programs for public elementary school students during school hours. After encountering the program at his daughter's public school, Mr. Parrish co-founded *Parents Against LifeWise*, a group that strives to warn others about the harm they believe LifeWise's programs caused. To help other parents make fully informed decisions about signing their children up for a LifeWise program, Mr. Parrish obtained a copy of LifeWise's elementary school curriculum, which the organization kept secret from everyone except instructors and enrolled students and posted it to the *Parents Against LifeWise* website. LifeWise sent a copyright takedown to the website's hosting provider to get the curriculum taken down and followed up with an infringement lawsuit against Mr. Parrish. The Electronic Frontier Foundation filed a motion to dismiss LifeWise's baseless attempt to silence Mr. Parrish.

Copyright in the United Kingdom

Copyright in the United Kingdom is automatic, meaning it applies from the moment of creative expression of text, painting, or music. There's no need for registration. The relevant legislation is called the *Copyright Designs and Patents Act 1988,* updated by the *Copyright and Related Right Regulations 2003,* implementing international and EU rules on copyright to digital environments (Tate Legal and Copyright Department, 2007). Copyright gives the owner of the original work exclusive rights to collect rental fees from it for a certain period, including its publication, distribution and adaptation.

Educational Materials

In the U.K, copyright law protects educational materials similarly to other forms of creative works. However, certain exceptions exist to allow for educational use under specific conditions. Below is an overview of how copyright applies to educational materials in Britain. Copyright automatically applies to original works, including textbooks, lecture notes, online courses, teaching materials, and research papers. Again, here too, the author - teacher, lecturer, researcher (i.e., a Lone Ranger) is typically the copyright owner unless the work was created as part of employment (i.e., the Posse) in which case the employer, such as a university or school, may own the copyright, commissioned or published under contract, which might assign copyright to a publisher. U.K. copyright lasts for 70 years after the death of the author. If the work is owned by an institution (e.g., a school or university), it may last 70 years from publication.

Educational Exceptions

The *Copyright, Designs and Patents Act 1988* (CDPA) includes specific exceptions for education. These allow limited use of copyrighted material in teaching without the need for permission.

Fair Dealing for Education (Section 32, CDPA 1988)

Teachers and students may use limited parts of copyrighted works for non-commercial instruction, examination, and study, provided the use is for educational purposes only, does not involve copying a significant portion of the work, and is not distributed beyond the educational setting. Teachers can use excerpts from copyrighted works for illustrative purposes in lectures or teaching materials. This includes quotations, images, or short clips, if they are relevant to teaching and not excessive. Schools, colleges, and universities can make copies of copyrighted works for teaching, but only limited portions, not entire books (Section 36, CDPA 1988).

Educational Licensing

Educational institutions must hold a license from the Copyright Licensing Agency (CLA) to copy beyond fair dealing limits. Educational institutions often rely on licensing to legally use copyrighted materials beyond fair dealing. The CLA License allows schools and universities to copy and share sections of books, journals, and digital materials for teaching.

Many educational resources are released under Creative Commons (CC) licenses, allowing teachers and students to use, modify, and distribute materials freely. Works where copyright has expired and published before 1954 can be freely used. Linking to copyrighted content is allowed, but uploading copyrighted content (e.g., full PDFs of books) to online learning platforms without permission is not. YouTube and online videos can be used in teaching if they are legally uploaded and not restricted by licensing. Digital copies of copyrighted works (e.g., scanned textbooks) often require an educational license.

Students retain copyright over their work (essays, dissertations, projects) unless they sign an agreement transferring rights. Universities may request permission to use student work for teaching or promotional purposes.

Copyrighted materials can be used in exams and assessments without permission, including text excerpts, images, and audio clips, provided they are relevant to the exam.

Copyright in Europe

In Europe, *EC Directive 2001* permits exceptions or limitations in the public interest for education and teaching. Member states are encouraged to provide exceptions or limitations for cases such as educational purposes, including distance education. The Post-92 National Contract includes sections on copyright and academic freedom that improve on the statutory position in that staff can retain copyright over some kinds of work they produce as part of their scholarly activity.

16.4 The copyright in any material produced by you for your personal use and reference, including as an aid to teaching, shall belong to you.

16.5 However, the copyright in course materials produced by you in the course of your employment for the curriculum of a course run by (the institution) and produced, used or disseminated by (the institution) shall belong to (the institution), as well as the outcomes from research specifically funded and supported by (the institution).

In 2012, the U.K. Government expanded the copyright exceptions to enable distance learners to access educational materials over secure networks (Hargreaves, 2011). The Government wished to ensure that acts permitted under the education exceptions were permitted to the same extent over secure distance learning networks controlled by educational establishments as they were within those educational establishments.

The Association of University Teachers, before it merged with *University and College Union (UCU)* in 2006, maintained that materials created by staff members for distance education courses should be treated in the same fashion as materials created for traditional courses. The *UCU* is a British trade union in higher education representing over 120,000 academics, instructors, trainers, researchers, managers, administrators, computer staff, librarians and postgraduates in universities, colleges, prisons, adult education, and training organizations (UCU, 2020). Authors should seek to retain the copyright of this material, whether it is in print or electronic form while allowing for its free use by the institution for legitimate teaching purposes. Where the institution chooses to exploit such material commercially, the revenues should be distributed in line with negotiated arrangements (AUC, 2002).

In the European Union, the United Kingdom, and the United States, that period is Life plus 70 years. In Canada, it's Life plus 50 years. In India, the duration is Life plus 60 years. In the UK, the test of copyright, according to the *Copyright Designs and Patents Act 1988,* is an *original expression in* a literary work on a web page or in a web database. Copyright of original works in the common law tradition emphasizes the economic role of copyright, "a means by which socially beneficial activities can be made financially worthwhile for those engaging in them. Civil Law sees copyright as springing from the personality rights of the individual creator of the subject matter" (MacQueen, Waelde, Laurie & Brown, 2010, p.41-42).

The concern expressed in this paper and elsewhere in higher education is that the UCU has advised its members to be aware of the potential for university administrators who want to develop cheaper alternatives to the high cost of low-enrollment distance courses (UCU, 2019). Of greater, or at least equal importance to the instructor, is that the integrity and attribution of the original work are maintained in all its forms.

Copyright in Canada

Copyright law in Canada protects educational materials under the Copyright Act (R.S.C., 1985, c. C-42), but there are also specific exceptions for education. Copyright applies automatically to original works, including textbooks, lecture notes, slides, exams, and online courses, created by a teacher, lecturer, or researcher (i.e., a Lone Ranger) who is the copyright owner. That is unless the material was created by several individuals (i.e., the Posse). Copyright lasts for 70 years after the author's death, changed from 50 years in 2022. In Canada, the test of copyright is the author's exercise of skill and judgment. Copyright purports to protect author rights, comprising both the economic value of a work, that is, the traditional Anglo–American copyright, and the moral rights of attribution, integrity, and the first publication of the work, akin to *droit d'auteur* in Continental Europe (Lametti, 2005).

Fair Dealing for Education (Copyright Act, Section 29)

In 2004, the Supreme Court of Canada in *CCH* recognized that fair dealing is part of copyright law and not merely an exception to it (*CCH Canadian Ltd. v. Law Society, 2004*) which allows limited use of copyrighted works without permission for educational purposes. To qualify as fair dealing, the use must be used for education, research, private study, criticism, review, or news reporting. Fair Dealing permits short excerpts of books, journal articles, or reports, as well as showing films, TV programs, images and short video clips in presentations and online videos for educational purposes. Copying an entire textbook or large portions of a book are not permitted.

Educational Exceptions Under the Copyright Act

The Copyright Act includes several special exceptions that allow broader use of copyrighted materials in education. Teachers can make copies of copyrighted material for students in class under fair dealing (Section 30.02). However, full books and commercial educational materials require a license. Teachers and students can display copyrighted works (e.g., books, PowerPoint slides, maps, images) in class without permission (Section 29.4). This applies to in-person and online learning, as long as the material is legally obtained.

In 2012, the Copyright Modernization Act introduced an unprecedented exception into Canadian copyright law, that is, the noncommercial user-generated content exception (Turnbull, 2014). Users can use existing works to create new works without infringing copyright as long as they do so for solely non-commercial purposes (Section 30.01). Online courses can use copyrighted material under fair dealing, but access must be restricted (e.g., only registered students can view it). Also, streaming videos and playing music is allowed if it's legally obtained (e.g., from YouTube or licensed sources). However, the provision does not exempt users from infringing the author's moral rights. So, while user-generated content is now protected in Canada from copyright infringement claims, copyright owners and authors may still use moral rights as a continuing restraint on this form of expression and limit the effectiveness of the exception.

Educational Licensing System

Canadian educational institutions rely on licenses to copy and share copyrighted materials beyond fair dealing. The *Access Copyright License* provides rights to copy and distribute portions of books, articles, and journals. Universities often negotiate institution-wide licenses for using educational materials.

Open Educational Resources (OER)

Canadian universities and educators use open educational resources (OER), which can be freely used, modified, and shared. Works enter the public domain 70 years after the author's death and can be used freely. Students own the copyright to their essays, research papers, and projects. Universities may require permission to publish student work in journals or promotional materials. Excerpts of copyrighted works can be used in exams without permission. This includes text passages, images, or audio clips, as long as they are relevant to the assessment.

MORAL RIGHTS OF THE AUTHOR

Moral Rights in the U.S.

In the United States, moral rights for authors, including those who create educational materials, are very limited compared to countries like Canada or the UK. Unlike in many other jurisdictions, U.S. copyright law primarily protects economic rights (i.e., the right to reproduce, distribute, and adapt a work) rather than moral rights. In the United States, the *Copyright Act* of 1976 and amendments, including the 1998 *Digital Millennium Copyright Act (DMCA),* don't allow authors to launch lawsuits over their "moral rights", except for some works of visual art covered by the *Visual Artists Rights' Act* (Sheehan & Walsh, 2017).

For educational material, moral rights protections are weak, but some protections exist under other laws. *Right of Attribution* (the right to be credited as the author) is not explicitly protected under U.S. copyright law, but it can sometimes be enforced through contractual agreements (e.g., publishing contracts). *Right of Integrity* (preventing distortion or modification of work) is not broadly recognized except for visual artists under VARA. The fight over moral rights, particularly the right of Integrity, is ultimately one about who gets to control the meaning of a particular work (Sheehan & Walsh, 2017). If an author can prevent a use they perceive as a "prejudicial distortion" of their work, that author has the power to veto others' attempts to contest, reinterpret, criticize, or draw new meanings from those works.

Since the U.S. lacks strong moral rights laws, authors of educational materials often rely on contracts and institutional policies to protect their moral interests. Many universities have policies that determine the ownership and use of faculty-created materials. If a professor creates a textbook or course material, they may need a written agreement to ensure they retain authorship credit. Authors of textbooks and academic articles often sign contracts specifying attribution and how their work may be modified. Although copyright law does not explicitly protect the right of attribution, academic institutions enforce it through plagiarism policies and academic integrity standards. Under U.S. copyright law, if a work is created as part of employment, the employer typically owns the copyright. Many educational materials (e.g., course content created by professors for universities) fall under "work-for-hire," meaning the institution owns the rights. Professors and educators might not even retain the right to be credited unless their contract specifies it.

Moral rights in the U.S. are mostly recognized only for visual artists under the *Visual Artists Rights Act (VARA, 1990, 17 U.S.C. § 106A).* These rights apply mainly to paintings, sculptures, drawings, and some photography but not to educational materials like textbooks, research papers, or lecture slides.

Mash-Up, Remixing

By limiting authors' abilities to control how their works are used, U.S. copyright law creates space for downstream creators and users to adapt and remix existing works to create new interpretations and meanings without facing a veto from the original author. It also allows those who own physical copies of copyrighted works to use those copies in the ways that make the most sense for them – they can annotate them, take them apart and reassemble them into new creations, give them away, or even destroy them.

Moral Rights in the U.K.

Unlike copyright, moral rights cannot be transferred from the author. In the UK, *droit d'auteur* or the moral rights of the author comprise: i) The *right of attribution:* to be identified as the author of the work when a work is copied or communicated; ii) The *right to object to false attribution* (being named in respect of a work not created by the author); iii.) The *right to control the form of the work* (right of integrity/to object to derogatory treatment.

Although most of us already know about copyright infringement, what isn't so well known is that the Copyright Act also has a provision for moral rights to enhance and protect the reputation of authors. Moral rights are personal and must be declared on the expression to be "in effect," using a statement such as "moral rights are in force" and the date. The moral rights of the author of the Web material or Internet program last as long as the copyrighted work itself and can only be vested in the author, regardless of who owns the copyright. Furthermore:

- The author's work cannot be distorted or mutilated to harm the author's reputation.

- The author's work should not be associated with any product, service, cause or institution where such association would hurt the author's reputation.
- Even where copyright has been contracted away from them, the author has the right to be associated with a work by name or by pseudonym or the right to remain anonymous at the author's option.

Although notable exceptions for intellectual property infringement have been made for educational institutions (Copyright, Designs and Patents Act, 1988), Internet-based educational materials are covered by EU directives (2003).

Moral Rights in Canada

In Canada, the moral rights of the author including those who create educational materials (i.e., Lone Ranger or Posse), are protected under the *Copyright Act (R.S.C., 1985, c. C-42, Section 14.1-14.2)*. The original author automatically holds the moral rights. When a Professor or Teacher creates lecture materials, textbooks, or research papers, they retain moral rights unless they waive them. If an institution modifies or republishes an educator's work without permission, the author may have a legal claim. If educational content is reused or altered in a way that damages the author's reputation, they can assert their right of integrity.

Moral rights last as long as copyright exists (typically 70 years after the author's death). After that, the work enters the public domain, and moral rights no longer apply. Moral rights cannot be transferred (unlike economic copyright), but they can be waived in writing. Authors can choose to waive their moral rights in a contract. For example, a university may require faculty to waive moral rights over course materials they develop as part of their employment. These rights exist independently of economic rights (such as reproduction and distribution rights) and remain with the author even if they sell or transfer their copyright. Moral rights protect the personal connection between an author and their work. There are three key moral rights:

Right of Paternity (Attribution)

The author has the right to be identified as the creator of the work. They can demand that their name be included or removed when the work is used. For example, A professor who writes a textbook must be credited as the author unless they waive this right.

Right of Integrity

The author has the right to prevent distortions, modifications, or misuse of their work that could harm their reputation. This applies even if the author no longer owns the copyright. For example, a university cannot modify a professor's lecture slides in a way that misrepresents their views.

Right of Association

The author can prevent their work from being associated with products, services, or causes that harm their reputation. For example, if a company uses a researcher's paper in an ad campaign without consent, the author can object.

THE LONE RANGER

During the 1990s and early 2000s, as Internet learning technologies were being developed and understood, a course author, audio-visual developer, content provider, and rights-holder of an online course were typically the same person—an early adopter, *a Lone Ranger*. This individual was often a full-time university or college faculty member working independently, creating and maintaining educational media and methods for students.

In the past, these Lone Rangers faced challenges in deciding which Learning Management System to implement and how to use them effectively. Consultants were engaged, and funds were allocated to compare these systems directly. The developers of these systems asserted that their products required minimal technical skill, allowing instructors to apply the most suitable methods they considered necessary and sufficient for managing their web courses. However, the developers' claims were not substantiated (Mann, 2006a).

An intrinsic case study examined the assertion that distance instructors with some knowledge of instructional design but limited technical expertise could, without human support, utilize course management tools to create sophisticated online educational environments (Mann, 2006b). The results of the study indicated that these participants required more assistance in both technical and design aspects of web course management than is currently provided by the tools and help in the web management systems. Even those with some background in course design found that well-known models of instructional design could not adequately dictate interactive learning in all web-based learning situations. Then again, during COVID in 2020, school teachers were hard pressed to accommodate students working from home.

THE POSSE

Since that time, colleges and universities committed to distance education—whether launching new initiatives or transitioning established programs into a digital environment—have invested considerable time, effort, and resources in supporting course development. Their non-academic university staff, known as *the Posse,* began taking on more roles previously held by the Lone Ranger (see Table 1). In doing so, colleges and universities have disassembled the faculties' jobs, distributing various tasks among different members of a casualized academic workforce, which has distanced the owners from their product.

Today, universities not only hold the copyright for online courses completed under several employment contracts but have also established *a full-time Posse* to assert some control over the creative process of developing online courses, thereby removing certain creative decisions from academic staff.

Table 1. Description of ownership of the Posse in online courses

Content Provider	Provides original subject matter that is saved to the hard drive and back-up drives, to be used by the backend of the system, for database development, information summaries, research annotations, and document editing.
Developer	Decides on a particular arrangement of multimedia capabilities, tools, files and develops instruction, writes directions, or provides unique feedback for an online course, and designs the system inputs at the front-end of the system, including instructional design, interface design, graphic art, video, and audio cues.
Author	The Author is the main content writer or experienced technical expert. The Author is usually a regular academic staff member, teaching assistant, or visiting faculty.
ISP	Internet Service Provider (ISP) provides online services, as defined by the E-commerce Directive, that transmits or stores content that has been provided by a third party (European Commission, 2015).
Rights-Holder	The Rights-Holder is someone paid by a collection society which has been collected money from the university for use of the used in the online course. The Rights-Holder may different from the Author or Content-Provider.
End-Users	The end-users are the registered students with their passwords.
Public	The public are private citizens who patronize college and universities through their taxes and donations to support higher education.

(Mann, 2008)

FORMS OF LAWFUL PROTECTION

Learning management systems typically provide instructors with design tools to manage their courses online. Since these tools are usually grouped under a course name and protected by a password, they can be regarded as a closed system—a *learning management system*. Today, learning management systems are classified as "open source," such as *Canvas* (Instructure, 2020) and *Moodle* (Moodle, 2020), "cloud-based," such as *Google Classroom* (Google Inc., 2020), or "proprietary," such as *Edmodo* (Edmodo, 2020) or *Brightspace* (Desire2Learn, 2020). Table 2 illustrates forms of lawful protection in a Learning Management System, one for the interface or front end and another for the database or back end.

Table 2. Forms of lawful protection in a learning management system, one for the interface or front-end, another for the database or back-end

The User Interface: Design Copyright & Moral Rights	**Database of Coursework: User Data Protection**
IP Law: Database copyright vs. the public interest and the fair dealing exceptions.	IP Law: Sui generis database right vs. the public interest (Sims, 2006), the public interest defense and breach of confidence.
Criterion for Protection: Author's own intellectual creation Genuine intellectual creation in selection or arrangement for a database (Waelde, 2007).	Criterion for Protection: Substantial investment of money, time, effort in obtaining verification and presentation of the contents of the database
Exceptions: Article 2 European Court of Human Rights (2003) & Article 2 in the Human Rights Act (1998)	Exceptions: Article 6 extraction for private purposes, illustration, teaching or scientific research
Cases & Reports: For some (Yurkowski, 2001) the human right of freedom of expression (public interest defence) is a necessary part of copyright law (original expression of an idea). Not in Hyde Park Copyright of screen captures of video tapes taken by Princess Diana before her death. Excessive reselling can render fair dealing, unfair. In Ashdown, the court held that the newspaper should not profit from the use of Mr Ashdown's copyright without paying compensation.	Cases & Reports: Whether substantial part of a database was used. BHB v Hill (2004) held intrinsic value of the database was irrelevant when deciding whether or not a substantial part of a database is used.

(Mann, 2009a, p.10)

User Interface

Either active teaching faculty (i.e., the Lone Rangers) or university staff (i.e., the Posse) develop an online course based on a preferred method or guideline. This is because online course development holds different meanings for different people. The guideline can be linked to a specific definition of multimedia learning. There are at least eight distinct guidelines for designing online courses (see Table 3).

Table 3. Summary of design guidelines and supporting rationale

Design Guideline	Supporting Rationale
Favorite Feature	We design with our new AI technology, which is better than older technologies (Stansberry, Anderson & Rainie, 2019).
Favorite Method	We design with our teaching methods, that are better than any other. E.g. Direct instruction method is better than discovery method (Kirschner, Sweller & Clark, 2006)
Balance-the-Input	We design for separate working memories imagens for images, and logogens for printed or spoken language, based on dual coding theory (Paivio, 1986; Sadoski, Paivio & Goetz, 1991)
Maximum Impact	We design for sensory impressions on working memory: a visuo-spatial sketchpad and a phonological loop an episodic buffer and a central executive, based on a working memory model (Baddeley, 1986; Penney, 1989)
Cognitive Load	We design to reduce cognitive load by changing intrinsic and extrinsic loads into germane load (Chandler & Sweller, 1991; Sweller, 2005)
Design-By-Type	We choose our design from the taxonomy of instructional software - drill & practice, tutorial, simulation, or game (Hannafin & Peck, 1988)
Structure a Sound	We design sound cues to focus attention on visuals and orient attention in the brain (Mann, 1992, 1995a, 1997a, Mann, 2008, 2009b, Mann, Schulz & Cui, 2012; Mann & Schulz, 2004; Mann, Newhouse, Pagram, Campbell & Schulz, 2002)
Whatever Works	Whatever worked last time will work this time. Methods over results. One size fits all, based on the intuition of the developers. (Abrahamsson, Salo, Ronkainen & Warsta, 2002; Kupersmith, 2011).

(Mann, 2009b, p.3)

Coursework Protection

Database copyright is usually a *sui generis* right. *Sui generis* rights are intended to accommodate emerging technologies such as AI in online courses. In Europe, compilations of data can receive protection as databases in two distinct ways (MacQueen, Waelde, Laurie & Brown, 2010). The first way in which compilations of data can gain protection under database copyright is when the structure of the compilation is original. The second way that material can be protected by database copyright is through sufficient investment in its compilation. 'Investment' is defined as encompassing both time and financial expenditures, including a ranking of student post-test scores, a profile of entry behaviours, or even course evaluations that assess attitudes toward a course. In this way, these composites may be deemed eligible for database copyright protection. This material is safeguarded by a database right, entitling the compiler to prevent others from extracting the whole or a significant portion of the database without permission.

Several lingering copyright and privacy concerns come to mind: Where is the old online course data being stored? Is personal privacy still assured in previous online distance courses (i.e., discussion board postings and chat room texts)? What about archived discussion board postings or recorded chat sessions with students? What about original student projects submitted for credit? Are those data archived? If so, why? Was permission ever sought to retain private personal information? Are there policies in place for protection or a timeline for the destruction of this data?

Phase Theory

Uploading original content into a course shell on the Internet involves a commitment to a specific teaching and learning behaviour, referred to as *a phase* (Mann, 2000). Each phase of online teaching and learning behaviours reflects the creator's intuition at the time, personal preferences, and prior educational experiences with online tools and resources. Each phase requires new teaching materials or learning resources developed by the instructor or course manager, sourced from a repository. Unlike more didactic methods of online instruction, phase theory encourages instructors to monitor their evolving perceptions of their efforts as well as those of their students while progressing through the course and transitioning into a different phase at the appropriate time (Mann, 2000). The phases are:

1. Lesson Enhancement
2. Resource-Based Learning
3. Online Learning Environment

Phase 1: Lesson Enhancement

Typically, with help from a resident technologist, the instructor will choose to introduce the Web-supported material as an extracurricular activity to enrich a lesson. For this phase, three types of lesson enhancement are identified: (1) immersive collaborative environment, (2) online self-expression, and (3) online lesson assessment.

Immersive Collaborative Environment

Immersive collaborative environments (ICEs) are among the most popular venues for conducting Web-based educational research. They aim to increase the quantity and quality of interaction between students on bulletin boards or chat rooms. More recently, an ICE has been any combination of threaded bulletin boards, real-time audio chat, and instant messaging.

Online Self-Expression

Similar to creative writing for a magazine, online self-expression serves as a student's introduction to the Web as an author. The instructor supplies the Web tools and support throughout the authoring process. Research can be conducted on the products or on the learning process itself.

Online Lesson Assessment

Online lesson assessment is an enhancement of lessons that uses the Web to evaluate students, groups of students, or the web course itself. In educational research, this can refer to student assessment, peer assessment, self-assessment, formative evaluation, summative evaluation, course evaluation, or program evaluation. Lesson assessment may also include feedback gathered from the maintenance of discussion topics in a computer conference or chat room.

Lesson enhancement describes the instructor's initiation into Web-course management. Instructors, after working on lesson enhancement, said they should not have used so many features. The process was overbearing and, at times, difficult to manage. With many students and too many student postings, there can be too much variety to handle for one instructor. Terms such as "sharing opinions," "interacting with students," "socializing," "socialization," and perhaps even "social learning" adequately define the linguistic framework of this phase.

Phase 2: Online Resource-Based Learning

Resource-based learning is the second phase of web course management. "Resources" can be of any form, namely text, pictures, video clips, and any knowledge-type declarative, procedural and/or strategic knowledge for subsequent retrieval by students. The mindset for resource-based teaching is similar to that of storing and retrieving materials in a media repository or school library:

Resources that provide content (i.e., online notes, online reader, or an online resource pack).

Figure 1. UNESCO's global open educational resources that provide content in education, arts, sciences and culture (UNESCO)

Resources that support a learning activity (i.e., an online manual, online lab guide, seminar guide, fieldwork guide, online project facts guide, or an online work placement guide).

Figure 2. Learning exercises that support a learning activity in undergraduate and graduate courses in the MIT OpenCourseWare repository, free to anyone, anywhere (MIT)

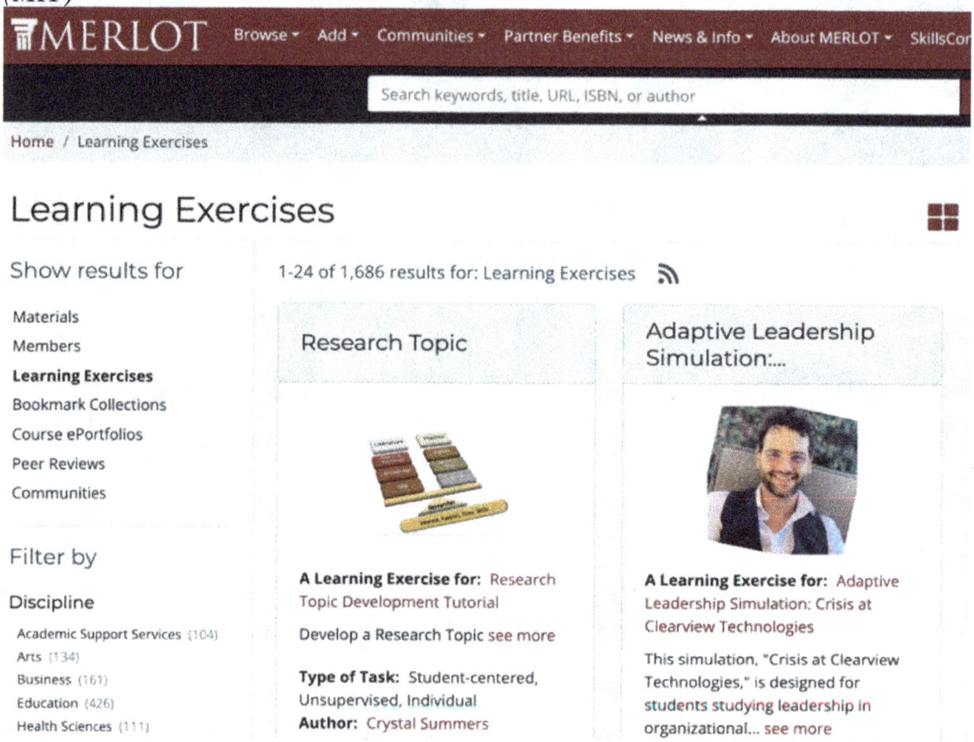

Resources that support a learning process (i.e., online skills guide, skills profile, or an online student log).

Figure 3. Harvard Business School's skills that support the learning process for guiding an organization successfully (Harvard University)

Resources that build on other resources (i.e., online textbook study guide, online readings guide, or an online lesson outline). Resource-based Learning may require a redefinition of pedagogical goals, restructuring of curricular offerings, provision for instructor training and support material, and sufficient online tools for the collection of student data. Terms like "stockpiling," "massing," "stacking," "accessing," and "accumulating" might well define the linguistic framework of the resource-based teaching phase.

Phase 3: Online Learning Environment

An "online learning environment" is the third phase of Web course management. An online learning environment can be classified as either augmented reality, virtual reality, or mixed reality (Franklin Institute, 2019).

Augmented Reality

Augmented Reality (AR) technology superimposes new data (e.g., audio, animation, graphics, text, video) onto the 2-dimensional physical world we experience with the naked eye by adding layers of digital information. Augmented Reality technology can be incorporated into most subjects in a curriculum (Fourtané, 2019).

Figure 4. Augmented Reality: A person showing his forearm on camera, with a graphic of a radius and a text-bubble describing the radius super-imposed over the person's image (Magyari, 2016)

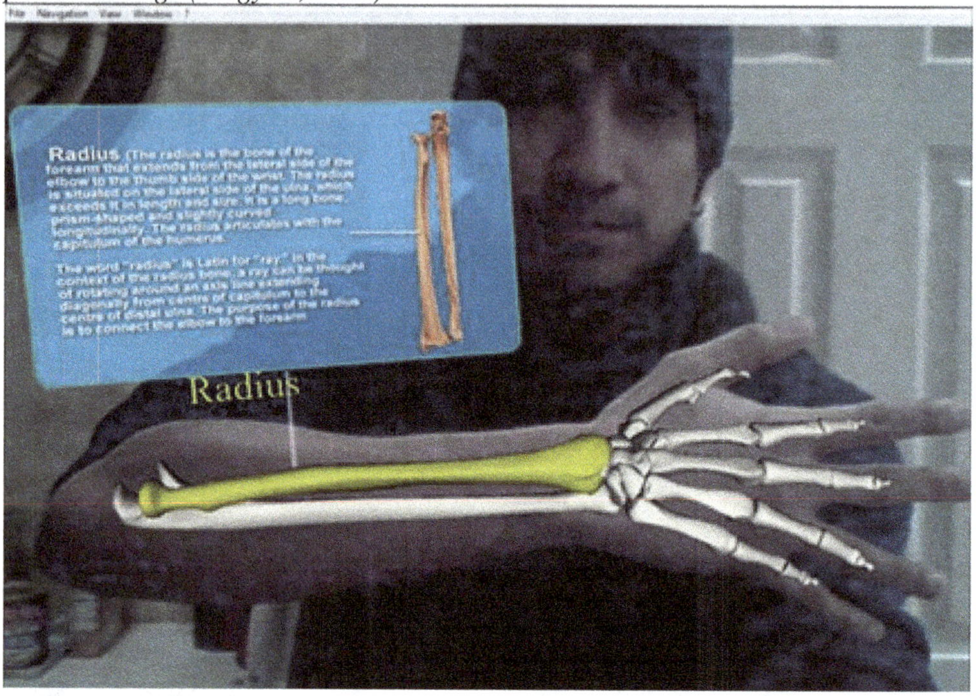

Augmented reality (AR) adds digital elements to a live view, often by using the camera on a smartphone. Examples of augmented reality experiences include:

- At historical sites like Pompeii in Italy, AR can project views of ancient civilizations over today's ruins, bringing the past to life.
- Military fighter pilots see an AR projection of their altitude, speed, and other data on their helmet visors, which means they don't need to waste focus by glancing down to see them.
- Neurosurgeons sometimes use an AR projection of a 3-D brain to aid them in surgeries.
- Ground crew at Singapore's airport wear AR glasses to see information about cargo containers, speeding up loading times
- Enhanced navigation systems use augmented reality to superimpose a route over the live view of the road.
- In sports, broadcasters use AR to draw lines on the field to illustrate and analyze plays.

- Furniture and housewares giant IKEA offers an AR app (called IKEA Place) that lets you see how a piece of furniture will look and fit in your space.

Table 4. Positive and negative effects of augmented reality on learners

Positive Effects of Augmented Reality on Learners	**Negative Effects of Augmented Reality on Learners**
• Increased content understanding • Learning spatial structure and function • Learning language associations • Long-term memory retention • Improved physical task performance • Improved collaboration • Increased student motivation	• Attention tunneling • Usability difficulties • Ineffective classroom integration • Learner differences

(Radu, 2014)

Virtual Reality

Virtual reality (VR) implies a complete immersion experience that shuts out the physical world. Using VR devices such as HTC Vive (HTC Corporation, 2020), which has a head-mounted display with a camera, two wireless handheld controllers, and two Lighthouse base stations. Users can be transported into several real-world and imagined environments (Gupton & Kiper, 2020).

Figure 5. Virtual reality (VR) describes a complete immersion experience that shuts out the physical world (Dolan, 2019)

Virtual reality experiences in education should have the following properties (Babich, 2018):

- ***Immersive.*** Designers should strive to create the feeling that users are in an experience. For example, if you develop a history app, make history come alive for students.
- ***Easy to use.*** Eliminate the need to have special skills to interact with a VR app.
- ***Meaningful.*** Meaning is really important for students. You can't create a good VR learning experience without a good story. That's why it is so important to advance the art of storytelling. Stories quite simply provide the best vehicle for delivering messages that are not only heard and understood but that also inspire and elicit action.
- ***Adaptable.*** VR experiences should allow students to explore at their own pace. The app should provide complete control over the level of difficulty. Designers should establish how students learn and then use this knowledge to design VR products that allow effective learning.
- ***Measurable.*** Each educational tool should provide a measured impact. Teachers should be able to track the metrics of education so they can measure

the resulting knowledge of a subject. When designing VR experiences, it's essential to choose appropriate metrics and make it clear what criterion will be used to measure success and failure.

Mixed Reality

In a mixed reality (MR) experience, which combines elements of both AR and VR, real-world and digital objects interact. Mixed reality technology is just now starting to take off with Microsoft's *HoloLens,* one of the most notable early mixed reality apparatuses.

MOVING FORWARD

This chapter deconstructed the typical kinds of distance education technology products into copyright and moral rights related to front-end design and user protection of back-end data storage. During course development, online course instructors, students, and stakeholders aim to manage the variety within that substantial public domain of knowledge. The public domain encompasses our shared human experience, knowledge, and culture, which is available for everyone to enjoy. Some intellectual property rights are awarded within the public domain for specific purposes. School and college courses are developed either by the one person responsible for delivering the course (i.e., a Lone Ranger) or produced by several members of university staff (i.e., a Posse). The Lone Ranger is usually a full-time university or college faculty member working alone, creating and maintaining educational media and methods for their students.

REFERENCES

American Declaration of Independence (July 4, 1776), Declaration of Independence: A Transcription, U.S. National Archives and Records Administration, https://www.archives.gov/founding-docs/declaration-transcript

Ashdown v Telegraph Group Ltd [2002], http://www.bailii.org/ew/cases/EWCA/Civ/2001/1142.html

Association of University Teachers (AUC). (2002). Online distance education: An AUT statement, letter to its membership, http://www.ucu.org.uk/media/html/9/b/ucu_autla7134_elearning_1.html

Babich, N. (2018). How Virtual Reality Will Change How We Learn and How We Teach, *Adobe Blog,* https://theblog.adobe.com/virtual-reality-will-change-learn-teach/

Berne Convention for the Protection of Literary and Artistic Works (1971). https://global.oup.com/booksites/content/9780198259466/15550001

Bowers, C. (1945). *The Young Jefferson 1743–1789.* Houghton Mifflin Company.

British Horseracing Board Ltd & Ors v William Hill Organization Ltd [2001] EWCA Civ 1268, http://www.bailii.org/ew/cases/EWCA/Civ/2001/1268.html

Carrier, M.A. & Lastowka, G. (2007). Against Cyberproperty, Berkeley Technology Law Journal, 22, 1483

CCH Canadian Ltd. v. Law Society of Upper Canada (2004). SCC 13, www.canlii.org/ca/cas/scc/2004/2004scc13.html

Copyright Act (R.S.C., 1985, c. C-42) Justice Laws Website, https://laws-lois.justice.gc.ca/eng/acts/C-42/Index.html

Copyright Modernization Act (2012). Justice Laws Website, https://laws-lois.justice.gc.ca/eng/annualstatutes/2012_20/fulltext.html

Desire2Learn (2020). Brightspace, https://www.d2l.com/

Dolan, D. (2019). Using VR for Experiential Learning, *Veative Labs,* https://www.veative.com/blog/using-vr-experiential-learning

Edmodo (2020). Edmodo global education network, https://new.edmodo.com/?go2url=%2Fhome'

EU Directives (2003). Ensuring environmental information is systematically available and distributed to the public. European Parliament and of the Council, EU Monitor, https://www.eumonitor.eu/9353000/1/j4nvk6yhcbpeywk_j9vvik7m1c3gyxp/vitgbgid9hzk

European Commission. (2015). Public consultation on the regulatory environment for platforms, online intermediaries, data and cloud computing and the collaborative economy, https://www.politico.eu/wp-content/uploads/2015/09/Platforms-consultation.pdf

Fourtané, S. (2019). Augmented reality: The future of education. Interesting Engineering, 1–6, https://interestingengineering.com/augmented-reality-the-future-of-education

Google. (2020). Google Classroom, https://edu.google.com/products/classroom/?modal_active=none

Google Cardboard. (2020). https://arvr.google.com/cardboard/

Gupton, N., & Kiper, P. J. (2020). What is the difference between AR, VR, and MR? *The Franklin Institute,* https://www.fi.edu/difference-between-ar-vr-and-mr

Hargreaves, I. (2011). Digital opportunity: A review of intellectual property and growth, Report, https://assets.publishing.service.gov.uk/government/uploads/system/uploads/attachment_data/file/32563/ipreview-finalreport.pdf

Hyde Park Residence Ltd v Yelland [1999] RPC 655; [2000] RPC 604 (CA), http://www.bailii.org/ew/cases/EWCA/Civ/2000/37.html

Lametti, D. (2005). Coming to terms with copyright, in (ed.) Michael Geist, *In the public interest: The future of Canadian copyright law.* Toronto: Irwin Law, pp. 480–516, and at http://www.irwinlaw.com/PublicInterest/three_3_lametti.htm

MacQueen, H., Waelde, C., Laurie, G., & Brown, A. (2010). *Contemporary intellectual property: Law and Policy.* Oxford University Press.

Magyari, D. (2016). Getting a glimpse of virtual and augmented reality in healthcare, Health Data Management, https://www.healthdatamanagement.com/articles/getting-a-glimpse-of-virtual-and-augmented-reality-in-healthcare

Mann, B. L. (2000). Phase Theory: A Teleological Taxonomy of Web Course Management. In Mann, B. L. (Ed.), *Perspectives in Web Course Management* (pp. 3–25). Scholar's Press.

Mann, B. L. (2006a). Action research with Internet database tools. In Mann, B. L. (Ed.), *Selected styles in web-based educational research* (pp. 179–187). Idea Group Publishing. DOI: 10.4018/978-1-59140-732-4.ch012

Mann, B. L. (2006b). An intrinsic quantitative case study of WebCT developers. In Mann, B. L. (Ed.), *Selected styles in web-based educational research* (pp. 80–89). Information Science Publishing. DOI: 10.4018/978-1-59140-732-4.ch006

Mann, B. L. (2009a). Action research with Internet database tools. In Halpin, T. (Ed.), *Readings on Database Technologies & Applications*. Information Science Reference.

Mann, B.L. (2009a). Intellectual property laws confer rights in respect of online distance education, yet most learning resources are still free - Truth or fiction? *i-manager's Journal of Educational Technology, 6*(3), 1-13

Mann, B. L. (2009b). Computer-aided instruction. In Wah, B. W. (Ed.), *Wiley Encyclopedia of Computer Science & Engineering* (Vol. 1, pp. 583–592). John Wiley & Sons, Inc. DOI: 10.1002/9780470050118.ecse935

Mazzone, J. (2006). Copyfraud, New York University Law Review, 10(13), 1026-1100, https://www.nyulawreview.org/wp-content/uploads/2018/08/NYULawReview-81-3-Mazzone.pdf

Moodle (2020). Moodle 3.8 Learning Management System, https://moodle.org/

Radu, J. (2014). Augmented reality in education: A meta-review and cross-media analysis. *Personal and Ubiquitous Computing, 18*(6), 1533–1543. https://romisatriawahono.net/lecture/rm/survey/computer%20vision/Radu%20-%20Augmented%20reality%20in%20education%20-%202014.pdf. DOI: 10.1007/s00779-013-0747-y

Scholl, T. (2012). Augmented Reality & Education, Teacher Cadet Technology: *Blogspot,* http://teachercadettechnology.blogspot.com/2012/09/augmented-reality-education.html

Sheehan, K., & Walsh, K. (March 30, 2017). EFF Says No to So-Called "Moral Rights" Copyright Expansion, *Electronic Frontier Foundation,* https://www.eff.org/deeplinks/2017/03/eff-says-no-so-called-moral-rights-copyright-expansion

Sims, A. (2006). The public interest defence in copyright law: myth or reality? E.I.P.R., 28(6), 335-343

Statute of Anne (1710). The first copyright act, U.K. Parliament, 8 Anne c.21 1709, Jeremy Norman's History of Information, https://www.historyofinformation.com/detail.php?entryid=3389

Stoltz, M., & Noble, T. (August 28, 2024). Copyright is not a tool to silence critics of religious education, *Electronic Frontier Foundation,* https://www.eff.org/deeplinks/2024/08/copyright-not-tool-silence-critics-religious-education

Tate Legal and Copyright Department. (2007). Digitization and Conservation: Overview of Copyright and Moral Rights in UK Law, in *Tate Papers*, no.8, https://www.tate.org.uk/research/publications/tate-papers/08/digitisation-and-conservation-overview-of-copyright-and-moral-rights-in-uk-law

TEACH Act (2002). Technology, Education, and Copyright Harmonization, An act to amend chapter 1 of title 17, United States Code, https://web.archive.org/web/20070404164532/http://www.ala.org/washoff/teach.html

Thomson, I. (October 22, 2024). Major publishers sue Perplexity AI for scraping without paying, *The Register,* https://www.theregister.com/2024/10/22/publishers_sue_perplexity_ai/

Turnbull, F. (2014). The morality of mash-ups: Moral rights and Canada's non-commercial user-generated content exception. *Intellectual Property Journal.*

University and College Union. (2019), UCU Brexit Update, https://www.ucu.org.uk/

VARA (1990).Visual Artists Rights Act 17 U.S. Code § 106A, Rights of certain authors to attribution and integrity, Cornell Law School, https://www.law.cornell.edu/uscode/text/17/106A

Verza, S. (2018). SLAPP: the background of Strategic Lawsuits Against Public Participation, European Centre for Press and Media Freedom, https://www.ecpmf.eu/slapp-the-background-of-strategic-lawsuits-against-public-participation/

Waelde, C. (2007). Database copyright: the story of *BHB*. In Torremans, P. (Ed.), *Copyright Law: A Handbook of Contemporary Research*. Edward Elgar Publishing.

Willinsky, J. (2006). The properties of Locke's common-wealth of learning, Policy Futures in Education, 4(4), 348-364.

WCT (1996). WIPO Copyright Treaty, https://www.wipo.int/treaties/en/ip/wct/summary_wct.html#:~:text=The%20WIPO%20Copyright%20Treaty%20(WCT)%20is%20a%20special%20agreement%20under,authors%20in%20the%20digital%20environment

WIPO (1967, 1979). Article 10, Convention Establishing the World Intellectual Property Organization, https://www.wipo.int/wipolex/en/text/283854

Yurkowski, R. A. (2001). Is *Hyde Park* hiding the truth? An analysis of the public interest defence to copyright infringement. *Victoria University of Wellington Law Review*, *32*(4), 1053–1086. https://www.victoria.ac.nz/__data/assets/pdf_file/0004/838309/Yurkowski.pdf. DOI: 10.26686/vuwlr.v32i4.5857

Chapter 11
Trademarks:
The Badges of Origin

ABSTRACT

Students often display their university loyalty by wearing school-branded clothing like t-shirts, sweatshirts, or hats, either as a sign of pride or sometimes as social commentary. A school's trademark, whether a visual symbol or a sound, signifies an official educational identity. It serves not just as a revenue source but also as a badge of origin. Trademarks evoke feelings of familiarity, adaptation, or even reconciliation. They can also represent endorsement, identity, or serve as a means for individuals to comment on, criticize, or satirize the trademark owner. While courts may recognize a parody defence, its boundaries are complex and difficult to define precisely. Additionally, negative comments, criticism, or satirical parodies can lead to a SLAPP, or Strategic Lawsuit Against Public Participation. A SLAPP aims to silence critics by threatening legal action. Journalists are particularly susceptible to SLAPPs.

SCHOOL SWAG

Whereas most students live on a limited disposable income, university gift shops nevertheless tend to sell their merchandise at high prices. As a result, students will browse third-party websites for less expensive school-branded apparel that they are not licensed to sell (Klein, 2021). One of the recent battles in the trademark war between universities and online retailers is *Purdue University v. Vintage Brand, LLC*. Purdue University in West Lafayette, Indiana, alleged that Vintage Brand violated trademark law by manufacturing and selling apparel that displayed the words and logos associated with Purdue University, e.g., Figure 1. In addition to the Purdue University lawsuit, Penn State University and Washington State University, joined

DOI: 10.4018/979-8-3373-3126-3.ch011

with nine other West Coast universities, also suing Vintage Brand for trademark infringement.

Figure 1. Screenshot of a t-shirt with the words and logo associated with Purdue University, trademarks allegedly violated by Vintage Brand, LLC

(CobbleStore Vintage, 2024)

Trademark Parody

Parodies of trademarks or artistic expressions of marks are prevalent worldwide, adopted to make fun of, comment on, or criticize famous brands (Masood, 2016). Parody of the marks gives the parodist an advantage of capitalizing at the expense of the parodied brand and attracting consumers. Concerning parody of university's trademarks, when the mark is used, it is not meant as a source identifier or even an identifier of an endorsement. Instead it is intended to further the expression of the user, to comment or criticize the trademark owner, and to satirize broader social issues through the juxtaposition of the trademark (Garon, 2018). There are numerous other examples of parody in the history of intellectual property. Surprisingly, even prestigious institutions of higher education are susceptible to legal disputes over their badges of origin.

THE SHOPKEEPER'S EXPERTISE

In the nineteenth century, when consumers wanted to purchase something, they had to rely on the expertise of the shopkeeper for advice as to the origin of the goods and their quality. The traditional enforcement of intellectual property rights was a matter of civil law, which proved inadequate to handle the increase of deliberate counterfeiting of famous-name goods, often manufactured or imported in secret, stored at concealed locations and sold from non-fixed premises. It was not until 1875 that a register was first introduced in the UK, partly in response to the growth in international trade where an increasing variety of goods were being traded under marks usually associated with British manufacturers.

Perhaps new to trade-mark historical development is the idea that a trademark, whether seen or heard, is an orienting cue. More than a badge of origin, a trademark, whether seen or heard, orients public attention to a particular university brand represented by the trademark. Cueing to orient attention with a trademark evokes a psychological state of familiarity, acclimatization, adaptation, alignment, acculturation, or reconciliation. Orienting cues like trademark logos or unique sounds can signal particular behaviours (Mann, 2025).

U.S. TRADEMARKS

U.S. trademark law protects names, logos, and branding of educational materials, not the content itself. Academic institutions, publishers, and platforms frequently trademark course names and digital products. Registering a trademark requires applying through USPTO and proving commercial use. Trademark infringement can lead to legal action if another entity creates confusion.

Trademark law in the United States applies to educational materials primarily when they are used for branding, commercial purposes, or to prevent consumer confusion. Universities frequently trademark their name and logo (e.g., Harvard or Stanford), course names, sports team names and mascots (e.g., Alabama Crimson Tide). Professors and educators may need permission to use university trademarks in books, courses, or research published under their name. Unlike copyright (which protects original content), trademark law protects names, logos, slogans, and distinctive identifiers associated with educational content.

What Can Be Trademarked in the U.S?

Trademark protection applies to distinctive elements used to identify and distinguish educational materials from others in the marketplace. This includes names of textbooks & courses – If a book or course has a unique title, it may qualify for trademark protection (e.g., Khan Academy or McGraw-Hill Math Series). Universities, publishers, and e-learning platforms often trademark their logos (e.g., the Harvard University logo). If a phrase is associated with a particular educational brand, it may be trademarked (e.g., Hooked on Phonics). Names of learning management systems (LMS), apps, and digital products (e.g., Blackboard or Duolingo) can be trademarked.

How to Get a U.S. Trademark

1. ***Ensure Uniqueness*** – Check the *United States Patent and Trademark Office (USPTO)* database to confirm there are no existing trademarks. Example: Rosetta Stone (a language learning program) is a registered trademark, meaning others cannot use the name for similar services.
2. ***File an Application*** – Submit a trademark application through the USPTO website.
3. ***Use in Commerce*** – A trademark must be used in commerce (e.g., a published book, an online course platform, or a branded test).
4. ***Maintain & Renew*** – Trademarks must be renewed periodically (first after 5-6 years, then every 10 years).

Limits & Fair Use in the U.S.

Trademarks cannot prevent others from descriptively using a term (e.g., SAT preparation is allowed, but SAT Study Guide in a title may not be). Educational content that critiques or parodies a trademarked course or product (e.g., a blog reviewing Common Core) is generally protected. Universities and publishers often license their trademarks for use in third-party educational materials. Example: If a company wants to publish "A Student's Guide to Harvard Business School", it may need permission to use Harvard in the title.

U.S. Trademark Infringement

Trademark owners can sue for infringement if someone uses a confusingly similar name or logo for educational materials. To win a case, they must show that a new course or book could be mistaken for an existing one (i.e., likelihood of confusion), that an educational brand's reputation is weakened (e.g., low-quality courses using a well-known name) (i.e., dilution), or that a competitor misleads consumers by using a similar brand name (i.e., unfair competition). Example: The College Board has taken legal action against test prep companies that use SAT in a way that suggests an official connection.

Both federal and state laws protect trademarks, but federal protection has expanded over the last century, preempting much of state common law. The primary law related to trademarks is federal: *the Lanham Act.* U.S. trademarks can be words, phrases, symbols, designs, or combinations. A consumer can quickly look at a shoe and, rather than carefully read a product sheet to figure out who produced the shoes, see a swoosh symbol and understand this to mean that Nike, not one of its competitors, made the shoe.

U.S. Trademark Parody

In the U.S., defendants in a trademark infringement or dilution claim can assert one of two types of affirmative defence: fair use or parody. The exception called fair use authorizes the use of a parodied trademark if it is for purposes of criticism, news reporting, teaching or research, even if it would otherwise be considered an infringement (Mazurek, 2023). Although the courts recognize a parody defence, the precise contours of such a defence are complex and cannot be outlined with any precision (Fisher, 2019). Twitter provides guidelines on how to manage parody accounts (Jacques, 2014). Several requirements have to be met:

(a) 'The avatar should not be the exact trademark or logo of the account subject'
(b) 'The name should not be the exact name of the account subject without some other distinguishing word, such as not, fake, or fan.'
(c) 'The bio should include a statement to distinguish it from the account subject, such as This is a parody, This is a fan page, Parody Account, Fan Account, Role-playing Account, or This is not affiliated with…'

Figure 2. Two different parodies of the registered marks for Harvard University in the United States: The LOL School (LookHuman Designs, 2019) and the BDSM Club

(Prylake Designs, 2019)

CANADIAN TRADEMARKS

In Canada, trademark law protects names, logos, slogans, and other distinctive identifiers used in connection with educational materials. Unlike copyright, which protects the content of academic works (e.g., textbooks, courses, research papers), trademark law protects the branding of those materials to prevent consumer confusion and unauthorized use. Canadian universities, exam boards, and publishers frequently register trademarks.

What Can Be Trademarked in Canada?

Educational systems and educational materials can be trademarked in Canada. If the name is distinctive, Course & Exam Name may qualify for trademark protection (e.g., Bureau du Québec Exam). Universities, schools, and educational publishers in Canada frequently trademark their logos (e.g., McGill University). SAT is a registered trademark of the College Board, meaning Canadian test prep companies cannot use SAT in their branding without permission. Unique phrases associated with educational products or services (e.g., Success for Every Student). Also, the names of learning management systems (e.g., Desire2Learn, Kumon, Brightspace). Trademarks in Canada are valid for 10 years from the registration date and can be renewed indefinitely as long as they continue to be used.

How to Register a Trademark in Canada

To register a trademark in Canada, an application must be filed with the *Canadian Intellectual Property Office (CIPO).* Check the CIPO database to ensure the name/logo is not already registered. Apply online through the CIPO website with details about the mark and its intended use. CIPO will review the application and may request modifications. If no challenges are filed and no objections arise, the mark will proceed to approval and will be published in the Trademarks Journal for public review. Example: Nelson Education Ltd., a Canadian educational publisher, registered a trademark to protect its branding.

Fair Use of Trademarks in Canada

Common educational phrases like "Math Workbook" or "Science for Kids" cannot be trademarked. A name that is too similar to an existing trademark may be rejected. A trademarked name can be used descriptively (e.g., Preparing for the IELTS Exam). Discussions or critiques of trademarked educational products (e.g., Pros and Cons of Pearson Textbooks) are generally allowed. Educational institutions often license their trademarks for use by publishers and e-learning platforms. Example: A company selling "McGill University Test Prep" might need permission from McGill to use its name in a commercial context.

Trademark Infringement in Canada

Trademark owners in Canada can enforce their rights by filing an infringement claim when someone uses a similar name or logo misleadingly, creates confusion about the source of educational material, or dilutes or damages the reputation of a brand.

Can a University Own a Trademark on Educational Material?

Canadian universities and educational publishers can register trademarks with the university name and logo (e.g., University of Toronto), educational qualifications and courses (e.g., Canadian Securities Course), or the publishing house brand (e.g.,

Scholastic Canada). Professors and educators may need permission to use these trademarks in books, courses, or promotional materials.

U.K. TRADEMARKS

Trademark law in the United Kingdom applies to names, logos, slogans, and other distinctive identifiers used in connection with educational materials. Unlike copyright, which protects the content of academic works (e.g., textbooks, courses, lecture slides), trademark law protects the branding of those materials to prevent consumer confusion (e.g., "Oxford English Dictionary").

U.K. trademark law protects brand identifiers, not educational content. Educational publishers, universities, and exam boards often trademark their logos and branding (e.g., "Cambridge University Press"). Unique phrases associated with educational brands may qualify for trademark protection (e.g., "Edexcel" for exams). Learning management systems (LMS), apps, and online courses can also be trademarked (e.g., "BBC Bitesize"). GCSE and A-Levels are registered trademarks in the UK, meaning that only authorized organizations, like exam boards, can use them for official materials. The Pearson educational publisher and "Ofqual Exam Regulator" are also registered U.K. trademarks. However, common educational terms such as "Maths Tutoring" or "Science Guide" cannot be trademarked. Also, if a name is similar to an existing trademark, it may be rejected.

How to Register a U.K. Trademark

U.K. trademark applications must declare a class before they can be examined. Of the 45 goods and services eligible for trademark registration, Class 41 includes education services. That said, although Class 41 mentions education, the language is not educational but administrative. As written, the educational provisions for Class 41 are idiosyncratic and stochastic.

Trademark registration involves submitting an application to the *UK Intellectual Property Office (UKIPO)*. The use of trademarked terms in educational contexts is permissible under fair use; however, misleading use may result in legal consequences. Here are the steps to register a trademark in the UK:

1. Search the *U.K. Intellectual Property Office (UKIPO)*trademark database to ensure the name or logo isn't already registered. Check for conflicts.
2. File an application via the UKIPO website with details about the mark and the goods or services it covers.
3. The UKIPO reviews the application and publishes it for objections.

4. If there are no objections, the trademark will be officially registered.

Fair Use of U.K. Trademarks

Using a trademarked name to describe something factual (e.g., "A Guide to the GCSE Exams") is allowed. Discussing or reviewing a trademarked course, book, or exam is also allowed (e.g., "Comparison of Pearson's GCSE Books"). Educational institutions often license trademarks to publishers or e-learning platforms. Example: A company selling "Oxford University Preparation Courses" might need permission from Oxford University to use its trademark.

Figure 3. This Edutec mark was registered under class 41 at the UK's Intellectual Property Office in February 1996 and renewed in February 2006, specifically for consultancy in the field of education, training, and the supply of educational materials and equipment

EduteC

Education & Training Technology

Consultancy • Manpower • Equipment

U.K. Trademark Infringement

The U.K.'s *Intellectual Property Office (IPO)* is the official government body responsible for intellectual property (IP) rights comprising copyrights, patents, industrial designs, and trademarks. In 2017, the IPO increased their contingent of Trade Mark Examiners to 90 to manage the 55,000 trademark applications (Townley, 2017).

Figure 4. This Edutec mark was registered at the UK's Intellectual Property Office in August 2000 under several classes. The priority country was Germany. The date of protection of the international registration in UK was April 2002.

Notably, the Class 41 "EduTec" mark in Figure 4 *is not limited to* training, education and teaching, also using telecommunications media, in particular professional training, continuous training and retraining, including vocational training for young people and management training for company executive staff… (Gov.UK, 2017). Class 42 is also included *but not limited to* the development of computer software and computer programming, in particular information and training programs… (Gov.UK, 2017). The other services registered within Class 41 are non-educational.

Trademark owners can take legal action when someone uses a similar name or logo that could confuse or create misleading educational content under a known brand or dilute or damage the reputation of a brand. As long as a teacher's memo doesn't mislead students into thinking it's an official guide, "How to Pass A-Levels" is allowed. However, a company selling "Unofficial A-Level Exams" without permission from the exam board is not.

Many universities and educational institutions register their university names and logos (e.g., "University of Cambridge", exam board names (e.g., "Edexcel", "AQA"), and course and qualification titles (e.g., "International Baccalaureate"). Professors and educators may need permission to use these trademarks in books, courses, or online content.

EUROPEAN UNION TRADEMARKS

The *European Union Intellectual Property Office (EUIPO),* formerly known as OHIM, manages the European Union trademark and the registered Community design. They also work with the IP offices of the EU Member States and international partners to offer a similar registration experience for trademarks and designs across Europe and the world. In Europe, EUIPO can provide applicants with exclusive rights for their trademarks throughout the European Union with just a single application. For unregistered trademarks, like domain names, for example, there is protection in common law countries under the law of passing off. Passing off inhibits one trader from misrepresenting goods or services as being the goods and services of another.

Figure 5. This MU DE TEC mark was filed at the European Union Intellectual Property Office in Bologna, Italy in July 2019

The "MU DE TEC" mark, in figure 4, filed under Class 41at the *European Union Intellectual Property Office*, again includes, *but is not limited to*, training car drivers, training for automobile competitions, instruction in automotive repair, driving instruction, training courses in engine design and engine repair, and racing driver training. The other services registered within Class 41 are all non-educational.

MOOC TRADEMARKS

A Massive Open Online Course, or MOOC, is aimed at maximum open access and participation. It's massive because enrollments are unlimited and can run into hundreds of thousands of enrollments (Online Course Report, 2019). It's open because anyone can enrol. It's online because course content is accessed and discussions facilitated over the Internet. It's called a course because their goal is to teach a specific subject. Figure 6 shows three different Class 41 marks denoting three of the world's top MOOC providers: "Coursera", "Udacity" and "edX" (MyLeanMBA, 2017).

Figure 6. Three different badges of origin denote three of the top MOOC providers: Coursera, Udacity & edX

(MyLeanMBA, 2017)

Approximately 120 MOOC providers are worldwide (Online Course Report, 2019). Coursera offers over 800 MOOC courses, most certified, some for credit, at the low cost of $30-USD 90. Edx offers 200 MOOC courses, some certified depending on the institution, some for credit, and some with small certification fees. Udacity offers 50 MOOC courses, most focused on Computer Science and Data Science, most certified, some for credit, either free or up to USD 200. Each provider is different, yet as educators, they share the same mission: to offer courses online to the society at large for free or a nominal fee.

U.K. Trademark Duration

Several trademarks have been on the register for over a hundred years. In 1837, Englishman William Procter and Irishman James Gamble started what later became a multinational consumer goods corporation called "Procter & Gamble" and located their business in the United States.

Today, it is the origin of the trademark that sells the product or service rather than the expertise of the shopkeeper. In 2018, Procter & Gamble Inc., wishing to appeal to younger customers, filed for trademarks incorporating several Internet slang abbreviations, including OMG, LOL, and WTF, for use in four categories of their cleaning products (Orlowski, 2018). However, the *European Union Intellectual Property Office* was already showing 177 records for word marks containing the abbreviation OMG, and the *United States Patent and Trademark Office* database had some 483 records. So, they were denied.

UNREGISTERED TRADEMARKS

Unregistered trademarks in common law countries such as the U.S., the UK, Australia, Canada, and New Zealand all rely on the law of passing off, wherein one party's goods or services are presented in a way that causes confusion between them and the goods or services of another party. Passing off prevents one trader from misrepresenting goods or services as being the goods and services of another. Also, it prevents a trader from holding out their goods or services as having some association or connection with another when this is not true.

Earlier Trademark

The *Trade Marks Act of 1994* defines an earlier trademark as:

(a) A registered trademark, international trademark (UK) or Community trade-mark that has a date of application for registration earlier than that of the trademark in question, taking into account (where appropriate) of the priorities claimed in respect of the trademarks

(b) A Community trade mark which has a valid claim to seniority from an earlier registered trade mark or international trademark (UK)

(c) A trademark which, at the date of application for registration of the trademark in question or (where appropriate) of the priority claimed in respect of the application, was entitled to protection under the Paris Convention as a well-known trademark

The *UK Trade Marks Registry* has the power to reject applications if there are any pre-existing trademarks which conflict with the new application.

TRADEMARK ROUTES IN EUROPE

Figure 7 shows the organizations and countries comprising the system open to the applicant to register a trademark: National, Community, or International.

Figure 7. The organizations and countries comprising the system open to the applicant to register a trademark

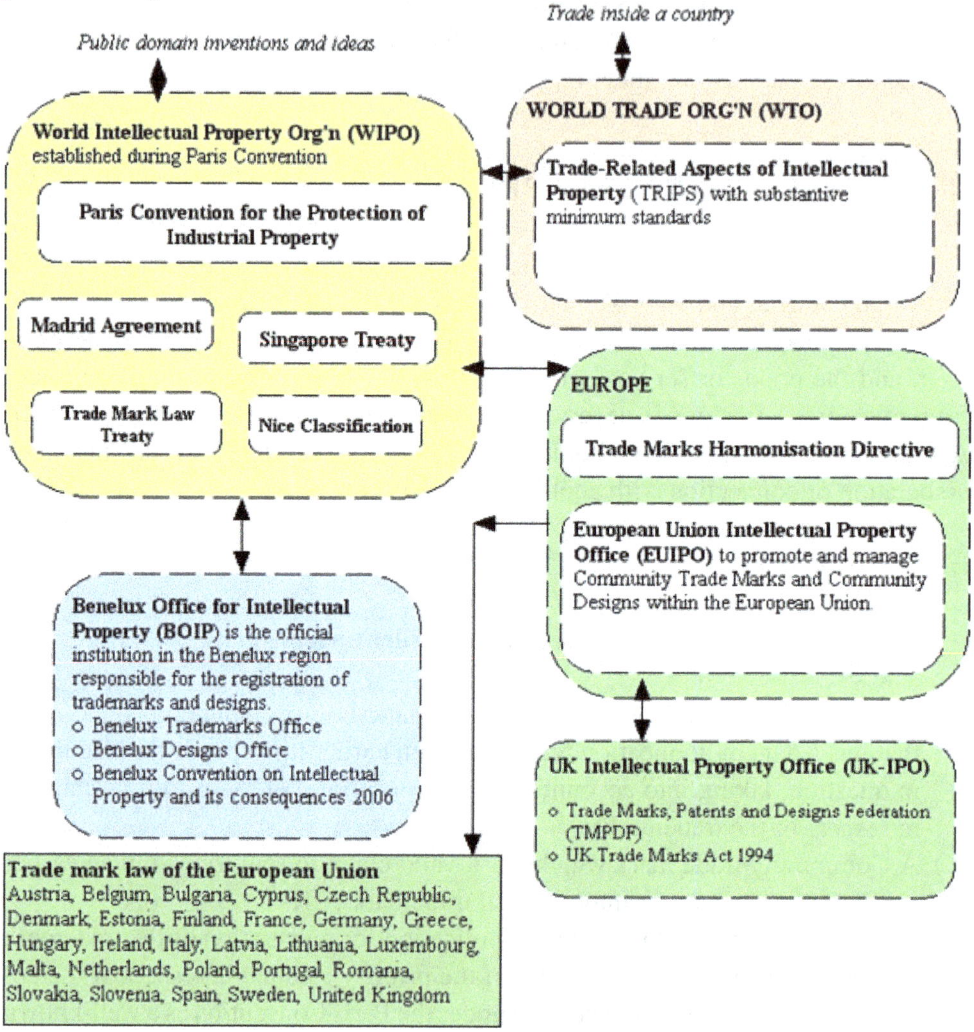

(Mann, 2008)

TRADEMARK COUNTERFEITING

Trademark counterfeiting was first introduced as a criminal offence in 1988 under the *Copyright, Designs and Patents Act* (Todd, 1995), where an offence was committed only if a person intended that the goods in question should be accepted as connected in the course of trade with a person entitled to use the mark in question, in other words, that the public was led to believe that the goods were genuine. The provision, therefore, did not apply to the case where a trader admitted to the public that the goods were fakes.

Trademark owners tend to overreach, however, making broad claims for their marks, and trying to control simple shapes, words, or even letters regardless of context or whether trademark law gives any right over those things (Lemley 2019, p.2). They often threaten to sue people they have no business suing, including satirists, parodists, non-commercial users, and gripe sites. Plaintiffs aim to exhaust resources and morale, making exorbitant claims for damages and allegations designed to smear, harass and overwhelm activists or civil society organizations. But they shouldn't. Parody, criticism, and being part of the cultural conversation come with the territory of fame.

Trade Mark SLAPP

Strategic Lawsuit Against Public Participation, or SLAPP, aims to shut down critics and satirists who parody by intimidating them with threats of legal action, draining their resources and, wherever possible, undermining their active public engagement (Verza, 2018). A key feature in a SLAPP is the power disparity between the plaintiff and the defendant. In Europe, news journalists working in the public interest have become particular targets of intimidation.

Student Union Lettings v. Essex Student Lets

In March 2018, the Claimant *Student Union Lettings Ltd* sued the Defendant *Essex Student Lets Ltd* at the Royal Courts of Justice in London. Both parties provided accommodation for university students. A dispute arose from the re-branding of SU LETS, a name which the Claimant says infringed on its registered UK trademark, SULETS, and passed off the Defendant's business as connected with the Claimant.

Figure 8. Trademarks of two student union accommodation services, one trading on the reputation of the other

University icons are visual self-representations and symbolic forms of their organizational identity (Drori, Delmestro & Oberg, 2016). In this case, the claimant was incorporated in July 2012 and carried on business as a lettings agency for university students at the University of Leicester and De Montfort University in Leicester. It provided accommodation in private halls of residence and had charitable status. It was owned by the Student Unions of both universities. The Claimant was the proprietor of UK registered of the word mark SULETS in respect of various accommodation letting agency services. There was no challenge to the validity of the trademark, despite the Defendant's contention that it was broadly descriptive of student letting services. The Mark had been used as a word mark, as well as in the form of the logo (figure 6), with or without the strapline 'Better student living.

The judge did not doubt that the use of the Defendant's name, SU LETS, whether as a name or in the form of the Defendant's logo, would have amounted to a misrepresentation. There would have been no direct loss of sales caused by such misrepresentation because of the different geographical areas in which the parties have, to date, provided their services. However, that is not to say that the misrepresentation would not cause damage or have the potential to cause damage to the Claimant through the erosion of the distinctiveness of the SULETS name, the potential harm caused by any inadequacies in the Defendant's services, or the potential restriction of the Claimant's intended expansion of its activities.

Regent University v Regent's College

In 2005, Regent University, located in Virginia Beach in the United States, applied for registration of a trademark with the *European Union Intellectual Property Office (EUIPO)*. The services sought were Educational services, namely, developing, arranging for, and providing courses of instruction and training at undergraduate and graduate students via a global computer network *(Regent University v. Regent's College, 2017).*

Figure 9. The earlier mark claims the Earlier Right (Regent University, U.S. v Regent's College, U.K., 2017)

In 2013, Regent's College, located in Regent's Park in London, UK, applied for a declaration of invalidity. In 2014, the European Intellectual Property Office declared the mark invalid on the grounds of similarity of signs and the identity of the services covered by the two marks at issue - that there would likely be confusion on the part of the relevant public *(Regent University v Regent's College 2017).* The application for a declaration of invalidity was based on the United Kingdom figurative mark, filed in 1993 in Figure 8. The *Trade Marks Act* refers to someone entitled to prevent the use of a trademark as the trademark proprietor of an *Earlier Right.*

Later that year, Regent University appealed, contending that this decision was based on an incorrect comparison of the signs being a word mark and a composite figurative mark containing word elements. However, the court rejected this appeal and made several observations about assessing the similarity between two marks of this nature. *Priority* is the time granted to a mark owner who has made an application in the home country and is busy making applications in other member states. These filers gain priority for that filing over and above other pending applications from a third party. This may be important for entities attempting to protect trademarks in several countries: it ensures that they may do so ahead of other pre-emptive applications. *Seniority* allows a mark owner to claim the seniority of earlier national registrations in the Member States of the same mark when applying for a Community trademark. To apply for seniority, an applicant must be able to show that the earlier national mark is for the same sign, the same goods and services, and has the same proprietor as the Community trademark.

European Trademark Parody

European countries, such as Portugal, have long embraced the notion of parody and accepted satire and irony in the arts (Figueiredo, 2016). In Europe, a parody-exception regulation is expected in the future. For the time being, however, trademark parody will continue to be considered based on fair dealing between the rights holders' interests and the rights of those who intend to use the protected works, taking into account all the circumstances of the case, among other things.

Figure 10. On the left, the registered marks of the University of Oxford, U.K: (Cambridge University Souvenirs, 2019). On the right, a parody of the same marks

(Zazzle Cambridge College T-Shirts, 2019

UNIVERSITY ICONOGRAPHY

What identity is conveyed through the iconography of universities? Drori, Delmestri and Oberg (2016) attempted to answer this question by examining the Internet home pages of 826 universities in 22 countries to identify four distinguishing identity characteristics:

- The Guild-Like Classic Identity,
- The Professional Scientific Identity,
- The Localized identity, and
- The Organizational Identity.

The authors characterized universities with a *Guild-Like Classic Identity* as institutions that derived their legitimacy from an age-old existence wherein the academic profession should be granted the autonomy to persist in their civilizing project. Universities with the *Professional Scientific Identity* are conceived of in vocational and educational terms: that is, training sites for certain professions, while also serving as sites for professional scholars, and places for individuals to live the values of the Enlightenment. Universities with a *Localized Identity* were conceived of as particularistic institutions, often national, that carried local pride and exhibited local uniqueness. Finally, universities with the *Organization Identity* conceived of themselves as universalistic which was considered embedded as a ''brand society''.

MOVING FORWARD

Whereas copyright law gives broad rights of control over an original expression, including manuscripts, periodicals, and logos, trademark law protects students and other consumers from confusion about the source of the word, letter, or sound.

Table 1. Trademark vs. copyright in educational materials

Aspect	Copyright	Trademark
Protection	Content (text, graphics, lectures, videos)	Brand identifiers (names, logos, slogans)
Duration	Life of author + 70 years	Indefinitely (if renewed)
Application	Books, research papers, presentations, videos	Course titles, logos, publishing brands
Registration	Automatic	Requires application with USPTO

USPTO, 2025

Orienting cues like a trademark logo or unique sound can instantly signal a specific behaviour in the viewer or listener, such as familiarity, acclimatization, adaptation, alignment, acculturation, or reconciliation (Mann, 2025). A trademark is simultaneously an indication of origin and quality, a means of advertising, and an investment vehicle (Lemley, 2019, p.2). In short, a good trademark can effectively balance the interests and expectations of the trademark owner, competitors, and consumers.

REFERENCES

CIPO. (2025). Canadian Intellectual Property Office, https://ised-isde.canada.ca/site/canadian-intellectual-property-office/en

CobbleStore Vintage. (2024). Purdue University t-shirt, https://cobblestore.com/?srsltid=AfmBOorY_5QAw8Wgj-qFREpCQ4528rLFleqrJy2RNQ8BrBBIwn2DUQ2v

Designs, P. (2019). Harvard Law Just Kidding Full-Time Mom Ladies' Scoopneck T-Shirt, https://www.prylake.com/products/harvard-law-just-kidding-full-time-mom-ladies-scoopneck-t-shirt

Drori, G. S., Delmestro, G., & Oberg, A. (2016). The iconography of universities as institutional narratives. *Higher Education*, *71*(2), 163–180. DOI: 10.1007/s10734-015-9894-6

EUIPO. (2025). European Union Intellectual Property Office, Trademarks, https://www.euipo.europa.eu/en/trade-marks/before-applying/availability

Figueiredo, J. L. (2016). Trademark Parody: a trademark infringement? Kluwer Trademark Blog, https://trademarkblog.kluweriplaw.com/2016/07/13/trade-mark-parody-a-trade-mark-infringement/

Fisher, W. (2019). Overview of Trademark Law, Berkman Klein Center for Internet & Society at Harvard University, https://cyber.harvard.edu/metaschool/fisher/domain/tm.htm

Garon, J. (2018). Ownership of university intellectual property, *Cardozo Arts & Entertainment Law Journal, 36*(3), 635, 673.

Gov.UK. (27 June 2017). General indication of goods and services, Intellectual Property Office, https://www.gov.uk/government/publications/how-to-classify-trade-marks/trade-mark-classification-list-of-goods-and-services

Guardian News & Media. (2019). Letter: Press freedom campaigners call for action on vexatious lawsuits, *The Guardian,* 20 July, https://www.theguardian.com/world/2019/jul/20/letter-press-freedom-campaigners-call-for-action-on-vexatious-lawsuits

Highland Games, at http://www.highlandgames.net/

Jacques, S. (2014). Has UK IP lost all its sense of humour? Another parody tale, EU Law Analysis: Expert insight into EU law developments, School of Law, University of Nottingham (UK), https://eulawanalysis.blogspot.com/2014/12/has-ukip-lost-all-sense-of-humour.html

Klein, D. (December 14, 2021). Trademark Infringement: Universities v. Online Retailers, Klein Moynihan Turco LLP., https://kleinmoynihan.com/trademark-law-infringement-universities-v-online-retailers/?utm_source=mondaq&utm_medium=syndication&utm_content=articleoriginal&utm_campaign=article

Lemley, M. A. (2019). Fame, Parody, and Policing in Trademark Law. *Detroit College of Law at Michigan State University Law Review*, *1*, 1–21.

LookHuman Design. (2019). Harvard LOL School, Fake Harvard T-Shirts, https://www.lookhuman.com/design/15091-harvard-lol-school/3600-athletic_gray-md

Mann, B. L. (2008). *Routes open to the trademark applicant, Computer Program.* University of Edinburgh, School of Law.

Mann, B. L. (2025). Speech cueing curricular multimedia: Instructional design that activates the orienting attention network. *Journal of Interactive Learning Research*, *36*(1), 191–214. DOI: 10.70725/115195dejbne

Masood, A. (2016). Sattar Buksh - Parody or the dilution of trademark? IP Nexus, November, https://secure.ipnexus.com/en/articles/46#_ftnref1

Mazurek, S. V. (April 10, 2023). Laugh it off: A guide to parody under U.S. Trademark Law, Faegre Drinker Biddle & Reath LLP, https://www.tcamtoday.com/2023/laugh-it-off-a-guide-to-parody-under-us-trademark-law/

MyLeanMBA. (2017). Breaking down the top 3 MOOC platforms: Coursera, Udacity & edX, Medium, April, https://medium.com/@MyLeanMBA/breaking-down-the-top-3-mooc-platforms-coursera-udacity-edx-13e5ed481337

National Telecommunications and Information Administration, U.S. Department of Commerce. (April 2008). ICANN. A statement on the Mid-Term Review of the Joint Project Agreement (JPA) Between NTIA and ICANN, Washington, DC, http://www.ntia.doc.gov/ntiahome/domainname/ICANN_JPA_080402.html

Orlowski, A. (24 Aug 2018). OMG! Battle looms over WTF! Trademarks: P&G wakes up to Internet abbreviations, LOL, *The Register*, https://www.theregister.co.uk/2018/08/24/omg_battle_looms_over_wtf_trademarks/

Paris Convention for the Protection of Industrial Property, (March 20, 1883). https://www.wipo.int/treaties/en/ip/paris/index.html

Regent University v Regent's College [2017] EUECJ T-538/15 (28 March 2017), http://www.bailii.org/eu/cases/EUECJ/2017/T53815.html

Regulation (EC) No 733/2002 Of The European Parliament And Of The Council, April 22, 2002, on the implementation of the.EU Top Level Domain, https://www.eurid.eu/files/733_2002_EN_1.pdf

Report, O. C. (2019). A Comprehensive Guide to MOOC Providers, https://www.onlinecoursereport.com/a-comprehensive-guide-to-mooc-providers/

Souvenirs, C. (2019). University of Oxford, https://graces-accessories-uk.myshopify.com/collections/cambridge-souvineers/souvenir

Staff. (March 2008). ICANN CEO welcomes concerns as NTIA weighs role, *Telecommunications Reports, 74*(6), 6-7.

Student Union Lettings Limited v Essex Student Lets Limited [2018] EWHC 419 (IPEC) (07 March 2018), http://www.bailii.org/ew/cases/EWHC/IPEC/2018/419.html

Todd, M. (1995). The new United Kingdom trademarks law. *World Patent Information, 17*(1), 24–28.

Townley, G. (2017). What's in a name? Trade marks explained. Podcast by the UK Intellectual Property Office on SoundCloud, https://soundcloud.com/user-24788401

USPTO. (2025). United States Patent and Trademark Office, https://www.uspto.gov/

UK Copyright Service. (2000). UK Copyright Law, Factsheet No. P-01, https://www.copyrightservice.co.uk/ukcs/docs/edupack.pdf

UKIPO. (2025). UK Intellectual Property Office, Trademarks, https://www.gov.uk/government/collections/intellectual-property-trade-marks

Verza, S. (2018). SLAPP: The background of 'Strategic Lawsuits Against Public Participation,' *European Centre for Press and Media Freedom,* 18 July, https://www.ecpmf.eu/news/legal/slapp-the-background-of-strategic-lawsuits-against-public-participation

WIPO. (2019). Summary of the Nice Agreement Concerning the International Classification of Goods and Services for the Registration of Marks (1957), https://www.wipo.int/treaties/en/classification/nice/summary_nice.html

Zazzle Cambridge College T-Shirts. (2019). Oxfart University, https://www.zazzle.ca/oxfart_university_crest_t_shirt-235174744088935669

Chapter 12
Academic Domain Names

ABSTRACT

Domain names are part of a system. The Domain Name System electronically translates text-based names into a corresponding binary IP address that moves data packets around the Internet. The first stakeholders in the Domain Name System are called "Root Node Owners". An academic domain name is not only an address in a web browser, like a postal address, but also a distinctive badge of origin that denotes a unique set of educational services. Protection of the badge may be required against fraudsters who hope to trade on an institution's good name. Schools and educational platforms can register trademarks for their names and programs to prevent cybersquatting. Cybersquatters are speculators who register misspelled trade name lookalikes to dupe consumers into thinking they are loading the websites of well-known trademark owners. Cybersquatters use a university or school name without affiliation with the actual institution. The Anticybersquatting Consumer Protection Act can protect school names against bad-faith domain name registration.

DOMAIN NAME SYSTEM

The Domain Name System was created in 1983. The World Wide Web was invented in 1989. The first Internet Service Providers emerged in 1992. By the end of 1994, the Web had 10,000 servers and 10 million users. Netscape was the most popular browser (CERN, 2025). This was a time before spam, phishing, cyberbullying, music downloading, e-commerce, and multiplayer games.

A *Domain Name System (DNS)* electronically translates text-based names into the corresponding binary IP address that moves the data packets around the Internet. The first stakeholders in the Domain Name System are the Root Node Owners. Figure 1 illustrates the hierarchical structure of the Domain Name System.

DOI: 10.4018/979-8-3373-3126-3.ch012

Figure 1. Hierarchical structure of the domain name system

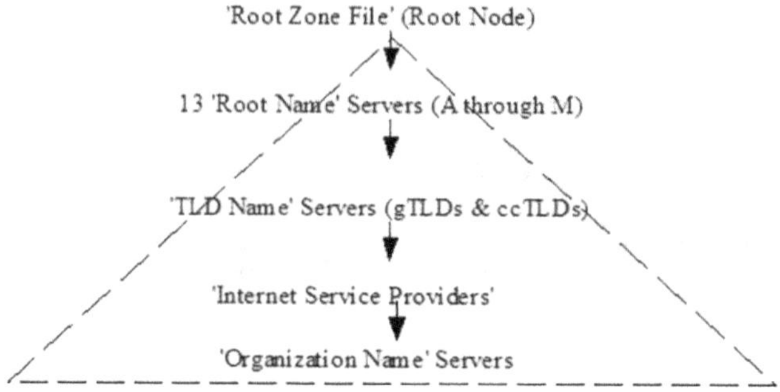

Domain Name Registrars

Domain names can only be registered by an accredited Domain Name Registrar (DNR), of which not all are created equal. At this level of the system, *Registrars Network Solutions, LLC* is a technology company and a domain name registrar in the United States. Their size, founding status, and longevity have made them one of the most important corporations affecting domain name price and policy.

In Scotland, the Registrar's 'Easyspace,' for example, is located in Glasgow. Easyspace is long on promotion and may have served Registrants better than some others, but it seems to be short on information about their registration fees (Easyspace, 2019).

Nominet UK is the .uk domain name registry in the United Kingdom. Nominet manages the registry of the following top-level domains: .uk is the top-level domain for the United Kingdom, .cymru is the top-level domain for Wales, and .wales is the top-level domain for Wales. Nominet manages the following second-level domains:

Figure 2. A sample of second-level domains managed by NominetUK

.co.uk	Unrestricted, intended for businesses.
.org.uk	Unrestricted, intended for non-profit organizations.
.net.uk	Reserved exclusively for UK internet service providers.
.ltd.uk	Reserved exclusively for UK limited liability companies; subdomain must correspond to the company's registered name.
.plc.uk	Reserved exclusively for UK public limited companies; subdomain that must correspond to the company's registered name.
.sch.uk	Reserved exclusively for primary and secondary schools.
.me.uk	Unrestricted, intended for personal use.

EuroDNS is a domain name registrar with over 800 domain extensions. EuroDNS offers several suggestions for education domain names, including .college, .university, .school, .academy, and .institute (EuroDNS, 2019). A .college or .university domain name is an unambiguous way to attract staff to advertised positions and students to academic programs. Furthermore, SCHOOL domain names are generic enough that they can work for eLearning programmes initiated by lecturers, student organizations, and administrators, as well as textbook publishers, testing services, and parent-teacher associations. The .school domain extension creates a broad and dynamic digital space for all things school-related.

Internet Service Providers

An Internet Service Provider (ISP) is a business that pays the Domain Name Registrar for the privilege to provide individuals and businesses with a technical connection to the Internet and some basic communication services. Originally, ISPs were owned by telephone companies. Today, anyone with the equipment can rent time from the owner of the telephone poles and underground fibre-optic cable to start an ISP.

Generally speaking, ISPs can not be held liable for the content of their service, though it's not for the lack of trying. According to *EC Directive Article 12(1)*. 'Where an information society service is provided that consists of the transmission in a communication network of information provided by a recipient of the service, or the provision of access to a communication network, Member States shall ensure that the service provider is not liable for the information transmitted, on condition that the provider: (a) does not initiate the transmission; (b) does not select the receiver of the transmission; and (c) does not select or modify the information contained in the transmission.'

This protection extends to any manner of services the 'service provider' *provides*. The key here is 'service provider'. Article 13 on "Caching" states that 'Member States shall ensure that the service provider is not liable for the automatic, intermediate and temporary storage of that information, performed for the sole purpose of making more efficient, the information's onward transmission to other recipients of the service upon their request, on condition that:

(a) The provider does not modify the information
(b) The provider complies with conditions on access to the information
(c) The provider complies with rules regarding the updating of the information, specified in a manner widely recognized and used by the industry
(d) The provider does not interfere with the lawful use of technology, widely recognized and used by industry, to obtain data on the use of the information
(e) The provider acts expeditiously to remove or to disable access to the information it has stored upon obtaining actual knowledge of the fact that the information at the initial source of the transmission has been removed from the network, or access to it has been disabled, or that a court or an administrative authority has ordered such removal or disablement

In general, the 'limited liability/notify and takedown approach' is the preferred approach to regulating ISP liability in most jurisdictions (Edwards, 2005; Waelde & Edwards, 2005). However, these criteria may be a tall order to meet given that many ISPs today are more than providers of tools, blogs, wikis, podcasts, etc. – they are also trademark owners and Domain Name Registrars, like 'Easyspace' for example.

ICANN: JUST THE ONE INTERNET?

At present, there is only one Internet, one root zone file, and therefore one Root Node Owner – the *Internet Corporation for Assigned Names and Numbers* (ICANN), operated in the United States and administered by the *U.S. Department of Commerce* (USDoC). A statement from the USDoC in April 2008 clarified their monitoring duties of ICANN,

Although views during the midterm review represented diverse perspectives, there was consensus on the need to preserve the security and stability of the

DNS and the recognition that ICANN is the appropriate technical coordinator of the Internet DNS (U.S. Dept of Commerce, 2008).

When will there be equitable sharing of power of the root zone file? In 2005, it looked for a while that some of the authority of ICANN over the DNS might be shared among other nations. The U.S. government retains ultimate control over the DNS. Then, in 2006, the media announced that the Chinese had initiated the process of creating a new, separate root node physically located in China. Ostensibly, China could, within several minutes, completely disconnect itself from the ICANN system and route all internal Internet traffic through their domain servers. Oxford Professor Jonathan Zittrain noted, "It'll be fascinating to see whether global companies feel compelled to register Chinese-language counterparts to existing .com names" (Bray, 2006). For millions of Internet consumers and creators, this means that their work and leisure time will be even more susceptible to censorship by the government than it already is. In 2007, ICANN launched a blog, ostensibly to address criticism over its openness and transparency. The postings read like a newsletter to the public, with comments devoid of criticism (ICANN Blog, 2007).

ICANN Issues

Even within the hierarchy of the Domain Name System (DNS) itself, the phrase 'absolute power corrupts absolutely' (Phrase Finder, 2008) is not lost on critics of ICANN. The root zone file (figure 3) is at the apex of a hierarchical distributed database called the Domain Name System. Control over the root server means substantial economic and political power since whoever controls the DNS decides what new suffixes will be added to the root server and how names and essential routing numbers will be assigned to websites and other Internet sources (Schiavetta & Komaitis, 2003). Until 1999, Network Solutions had sole control over the .com, .net, and .org top-level domains, for which it gouged the public with the permission and support of the ICANN (Gibbs, 2008). The US Dept of Commerce oversees the work at ICANN.

Arbitration Providers

ICANN initially accredited three Arbitration Providers: WIPO, NAF and eResolution. Arbitration Providers offer conflict resolution services, frequently through online dispute resolution (ODR). See Chapter 6 for an overview of the three different emphases prevalent in online dispute resolution: Structured argument, ODR technology, and presentation design.

CYBERSQUATTERS

Cybersquatters are speculators that register misspelled trade name look-alikes to dupe consumers into thinking they are loading the websites of well-known trademark owners. In the education sector, cybersquatters typically exploit the reputation of schools, universities, or educational platforms by misleading students, faculty, and the public. A common type of cybersquatting in education is a university or school name without affiliation with the actual institution, such as HarvardOnlineCourses.com or MIT-Scholarships.org, to sell the domain back to the school or to mislead students for financial gain.

A second type of cybersquatting in education is the scholarship or financial aid scam to trick students into providing personal information or paying fees. For example, websites like Federal-StudentAid.com or FAFSAGrants.org. It's often used for phishing or collecting money.

A third type of cybersquatting in education is online learning fraud, which entails registering a domain like KhanAcademyFree.com or CourseraCertificates.org to mislead learners. The purpose of these sites is either to distribute malware, collect user data, or charge fees for free courses.

A fourth type of cybersquatting in education is the impersonation of a teacher. For example, when someone registers MrSmithsOnlineClassroom.com to impersonate and discredit a real teacher to trick students. This type of cybersquatting can be used for scams, misinformation, or even fraudulently collecting payments.

Cybersquatters infringe on existing trademarks for personal gain or diluting an established brand's image (UDRP, 2019). Cybersquatting is illegal, and trademark violators can be reported through the UDRP process. Trademark owners may neglect to reregister their domain names, and by forgetting this important update, cybersquatters can easily steal domain names. Cybersquatting also includes advertisers who mimic domain names that are similar to popular, highly trafficked websites. Cybersquatting is one of several types of cybercrimes.

WIPO reported that in 2007, a record 2,156 complaints alleging cybersquatting were filed with the *WIPO Arbitration and Mediation Center*, representing an 18% increase over 2006 and a 48% increase over 2005 in the number of generic and country code Top Level Domain (gTLDs and ccTLDs) disputes' (WIPO, 2008). It is, after all, in WIPO's interest to protect trademark owners from cybersquatters. WIPO advocates strong intellectual property rights with five strategic goals: to promote an IP culture, integrate IP into national development policies and programs, develop international IP laws and standards, deliver quality services in global IP protection systems, and increase the efficiency of WIPO's management and support processes.

Cases of cybersquatting have become so rampant that the U.S. government has begun a crackdown, with courts listening sympathetically to organizations and individuals claiming their names have been misappropriated in Web addresses (Gutierrez, 2001). In 2015, the University of Cambridge lost a cybersquatting dispute against the owner of Cambridge.com (Allemann, 2015). Kirkland Holdings LLC, located in Boston, Massachusetts, had already bought the Cambridge.com domain name in 2010 for $85,000 and created a website for Cambridge, U.S. and another for Cambridge, U.K., on the domain name with two pending trademarks for the site. The panel found that Cambridge University and its lawyers, Stobbs IP Limited located in Cambridge Research Park, "seriously misdescribed" contents of the domain name owner's website, alleging it was a front to steal web traffic rather than a bona fide site (Alwakeel, 2015).

Similarly, the University of Oxford was in a dispute in 2000 with "Mr University," aka Doc Seagle, an Australian cybersquatter, over domain name ownership. At the time, the University of Oxford owned several domain names, comprising ox.ac.uk, oxforduniversity.com, oxforduniversity.co.uk, oxford-university.co.uk, oxford-university.net, and oxforduniversity.net.

Typosquatting

Typosquatting targets Internet users who incorrectly type a website address into their Web browser, for example, "Carnbridge.org" instead of "Cambridge.org." When users make such a typographical error, they may be led to an alternative website owned by a hacker that is usually designed for malicious purposes (McAfee, 2013). In 2008, the University of Cambridge started a UDRP proceeding against Sunny Legend under the auspices of the WIPO's Arbitration and Mediation Center to obtain the transfer of the unsettling domain name carnbridge.org. In this case, two issues lie at the heart of the decision: typosquatting and identity theft. In 2024, Blefari, Furfaro, Ianni, and Viscomi designed TypoAlert, a dedicated extension for detecting typosquatted sites.

Domain Name Tasting

When a domain name is registered, the registrant is given five days to cancel for a full refund. While the purpose of this grace period is to protect those who innocently err in the registration process, speculators have taken advantage of the "Add Grace Period" or AGP, through a process called ***"domain tasting"*** (Healey, 2007). These "domain tasters" register hundreds of thousands of domain names and cancel the vast majority of them within the five-day grace period, keeping only those that may be valuable as placeholder advertising websites or to holders of trademark rights.

Domain Name Kiting

Domain name kiting is a form of fraud involving the moving of theoretical funds between two bank checking accounts. Unlike domain tasters, domain kiters never pay the registration fee for any of their websites (Healey, 2007). Instead, they continually cancel each registration within the five-day grace period and then renew the same name repeatedly, thus running a more or less continuous website that always falls within the Add Grace Period (AGP).

Domain kiting is similar to the illegal practice of check kiting (Parsons, 2006), a form of fraud involving the sloshing of theoretical funds between two bank checking accounts. A check written to the criminal from one bank is deposited and, more importantly, credited to an account at a second bank. Because that second bank now shows a positive balance, the criminal can withdraw enough money to deposit back into the first bank before the check bounces for lack of funds (Pollick, 2008). Unlike check kiting, however, domain kiting is not illegal.

'Domain kiting takes millions of good names off the system and makes them unavailable for the purposes for which those names were originally intended. It places an unnecessary burden on every registry' (Parsons, 2006). US Registrar Bob Parsons reported that 32 million of the 35 million domain names that were registered with his ICANN-accredited domain name registrar, GoDaddy' were part of a domain kiting scheme. 32.7 million names were used – most again and again – but never permanently registered. These 32.7 million names were part of a scheme – a growing abuse of the domain system. Similarly, in February 2007, 55.1 million domain names were registered. Of those, 51.5 million were cancelled and refunded just before the 5-day grace period expired, and only 3.6 million domain names were kept. Except for just a few names, 93.5% of those names were registered simply to see how much advertising revenue – paid by big search firms like our "do no evil" friends at Google – will generate when they are associated with a one-page Web site and related links.

Domain Name Front-Running

ICANN issued an advisory on a process in 2007 known as 'Domain Name Front Running,' the practice of stealing a person's domain name search queries and registering the domain name before the original person can register it. Access is obtained using any one of several methods (DomainTools Blog, 2007).

The *One in a Million* case was exactly that - a win for the identities of several large corporate entities but not for the wider Internet community (Elmslie, 1998). In that case, the Court of Appeal upheld a decision of the High Court granting summary judgment on behalf of six major U.K. brand owners. Despite the proliferation of domain registration and use, the *One in a Million* case continues to be one of the most cited cases to describe this activity *(BT and others v One in a Million Ltd, 1998)*. The decision in *One in a Million* is useful for trade-mark holders to prevent a cybersquatter from maintaining ownership over a domain name based on the possibility of passing off in future. This opening of a 'new branch' of passing off shows us how the courts responded to the threat of cybersquatting, taking an accepted principle, passing off, and extending its remit to provide an equitable and pragmatic solution to the problem caused by cybersquatting (Hutchinson, 2001).

It appears, however, that the judgment was seen to be little more than a policy decision, not a straightforward application of the law of passing off (Bennett & Thorne, 1998). A necessary distinction was missed, it seems, between the consequences of registering a domain name and intending to use it to trade. At the time of litigation, none of the domain names had been used as active sites. The defendant planned to block registrations to sell the name. The well-known companies were objecting, therefore, to the mere registration of domain names without any active use.

Anyone can become a stakeholder in the Domain System by owning a Domain Name. However, finding a suitable domain name that hasn't been taken is due in large part to domain *tasting* and *kiting*. Domain tasting involves the registration of domains and cancellation of them within five days. Registrants of .com, .net, .org, .biz, .info and .pro names are entitled to a full refund when they delete a domain within that period (OUT-LAW News, 2007).

In *Diamonique Corporation v. Maison Tropicale S.A.* (2007), the respondent engaged in a practice known as "domain kiting" and "domain tasting," wherein they took advantage of the pay-per-click keyword programs of a search engine, and ICANN's 5-day domain name trial period, by registering a multitude of domain names that were misspellings of well-known trademarks, and then delisting those that were not generating sufficient traffic to justify the expense of linking them to a parked page.

THE UDRP

The *Uniform Dispute Resolution Procedure (UDRP)* is intended to resolve disputes between domain name owners, though it is not a panacea for all disputes (Deveci, 2003). There has been disagreement. Although ICANN's domain name dispute resolution is a fast, inexpensive process for victims of cybersquatters to vindicate their rights more easily than it would be possible through the courts, UDRP sacrifices the interests of domain name registrants in favour of trademark registrants for the communal good (Komaitis, 2003). The consensus of knowledgeable stakeholders is that the U.S. government, through ICANN, has controlled Internet use since 1999 through its management of the domain name system (ICANN, 2008). ICANN controls Internet information through the mandatory character of the UDRP, decisions taken in cases heard under the UDRP regarding freedom of speech, and the operation of the WHOIS database (Schiavetta & Komaitis, 2003).

NATIONAL SECURITY

Another big issue for ICANN is national security. Since the increase in terrorist attacks around the world, surveillance and national security have been major factors in all manner of Internet communications. This is the main reason they are reluctant to change the WHOIS database configuration from its current setting, collecting personal data from each Registrant.

Perhaps in the coming years, there will be several loosely connected Root Nodes, one for Scandinavia, Russia and the European Union, another for the African continent, India and Australasia, and another for North and South America (ICANN, 2020). The idea seems outrageous now but is analogous to the email systems from the 1980s, where to contact someone in the U.S. from the U.K., you would first have to contact the country code email server, say JNet in the U.K., then type a permission code to the U.S. BitNet system and wait for a reply and distinctive prompt, and then you could begin sending your email message. Back then, batch processing was the faster alternative, as it was done overnight. Perhaps once again, we will be saving our emails and attachments and batch processing them all at once, between separate systems, and maybe relying more on cloud and mobile phone technologies.

IANA: DNS MANAGEMENT

IANA, or *Internet Assigned Numbers Authority*, is the overall authority for the IP Addresses and Domain Names used by the Internet. IANA is responsible for the management of the DNS root zone (IANA, 2019). This role involves assigning operators for top-level domains, such as .uk, .com, and .ca, and managing their technical and administrative details. Servers of the DNS root zone are called "root servers." Root servers comprise a network of hundreds of servers in many countries around the world. As of 21 October 2019, the root server system consisted of 1,015 instances, of which 13 root name servers are operated by 12 independent organizations.

Figure 3. DNS root servers

(Skeptics Stack Exchange, 2012)

Root Name Server Operators (A Through M)

DNS Root Name Servers publish the contents of one small file, called the root zone file, to the Internet. According to the structure of the Domain Name System, thirteen root DNS Root Name Servers (A through M) operate as a public service to the Internet (Root Servers, 2019). These root servers are operated by twelve organizations known as 'Root Server Operators" (Karrenberg, 2007). VeriSign is a Root Server Operator responsible for 2 of the 13 (A and J) Root Name Servers. As a Root Server Operator, Verisign manages relationships with the Domain Name Registrars, who submit over 100 million domain name transactions daily. COM NET Registry is VeriSign's registry for .com and .net generic Top-Level Domains (gTLDs). Originally, the gTLD was used for commercial organizations but is now unrestricted. The country code Top-Level Domain (ccTLD) is generally reserved for a country or a dependent territory (IANA, 2008). The ccTLD for the European Union, for example, is ".eu".

The ccTLD for the United Kingdom is ".uk". The ccTLDs are ultimately sanctioned in the US by the *Internet Assigned Numbers Authority (IANA).*

Over the past few years, the high demand for ".com" and ".net" top-level domain names has led people and organizations to ccTLDs to fill the need. Puerto Rico, for example, has been marketing its domain name ".pr" to public relations companies. The domain name ".dj" for the African country of Djibouti appeals to specific music sites (Heater, 2007). In the EU, the *European Registry of Internet Domain Names (EURid)* manages the .eu top-level Internet domain under contract to the European Commission. In April 2006, the .eu domain was made accessible to the general public within the European Union. It quickly became one of Europe's most extensive top-level domains. Today, there are more than 2.8 million registered .eu domain names, and approximately 2500 new .eu domain names are registered each business day (EURid, 2008).

Reverse Domain-Hijacking

Reverse domain hijacking is when a trademark owner attempts to acquire a domain name from a legitimate private registrant by asserting their expansive trademark rights. The UDRP resolves disputes between trademark holders and domain name owners. Since they advocate substantial IP rights, it is no surprise that WIPO documents offer little information on 'reverse domain-hijacking.' The process of reverse domain hijacking runs as follows (Lewis, 2006):

1) A small company registers a dictionary word domain name.
2) A big company wants the domain name. So, the big company files with the UDRP, hoping to intimidate and outspend the domain name away from the small company.
3) Panellist awards the domain name to a big company, often without opposition from the small company—the small company fumes about the unfairness of the domain name dispute resolution process.

The case *Veolia Environnement v Tom Baert* was filed with the WIPO Arbitration and Mediation Center in January 2007. The disputed domain name <veolia.mobi> was registered with GoDaddy Software in the U.S. The Respondent stated that the case was filed in bad faith and that the Complainant had abused the administrative proceedings in an attempt to reverse domain hijack the Respondent's domain name. The Panel disagreed and ordered the domain name veolia.com be transferred to the Complainant. The results were not surprising since reverse domain hijacking is difficult to prove, and the WIPO Centre has a mandate to protect IP rights, which begs the question, who protects the rights of private registrants from greedy trademark owners? Not WIPO in this case.

Domain Name Speculating

Speculators engage in registering and selling domain names. They, or their proxies, register numerous variations of domain names as quickly as possible to prevent others from using them. The practice of registering a domain name similar to a well-known brand with the intent of selling it to that brand owner has been described using inflammatory terms such as 'domain name piracy,' 'domain name grabbing,' and 'cybersquatting' (United States Patent and Trademark Office, 2008). 'The law should resist the tendency to support the creation of corporate domain name monopolies' (Scanlan, 2007).

Online Game Trademark Law

As of August 2019, the MMO game (Massively Multiplayer Online Game) population had attracted 114 of the highest subscribers (Industry Six, 2019). *World of Warcraft* (WoW) was number one, with a total population of 61,404,181 and an average number of daily players of 5,833,397. *World of Warcraft* takes place within the Warcraft world of Azeroth. *World of Warcraft* (WoW) was released in 2004 by Blizzard Entertainment and is the fourth game set in the Warcraft fantasy universe.

The potential for trademark disputes exists in any Massively Multiplayer Online Game (aka MMO) that permits users to create in-world brands, counterfeits, and even in-world parodies. Unlike Internet service providers who exercise little or no control over the content transmitted through their systems, MMORPG providers exercise substantial control over what users can bring into their worlds (Varas, 2008).

Uneven Bargaining

In 1994, American Journalist Josh Quittner registered the domain name "mcdonalds.com" for his writing piece. Initially, McDonald's Corporation did not respond to his inquiries. However, they eventually complained to InterNIC about granting Quittner the domain name. Subsequently, Quittner and McDonald settled the dispute, and Quittner assigned the domain name back to McDonald (Quittner, 1994).

In 2006, the *WIPO Arbitration and Mediation Center favoured* the complainant 'McDonald's Corporation.' The Respondent 'Easy Property' of Beijing, China, had registered the disputed domain name 'mcdonalds.biz' in June 2004 (WIPO, 2006). The McDonald's Corporation has plenty of trademarks on its Terms of Service site to generate ideas for more domain names (McDonald's, 2019). At the registration level, the reputation of the trader, rather than the trader's reputation *in the product,* sets a dangerous precedent (Deveci, 2003).

The balance of stakeholder interests at the domain registration level is usually tipped in favour of those with power and influence (i.e., trademark owners). The domain name 'mcdonalds.com' located in the Scottish Highlands, for example, is not owned by 'The MacDonald's B&B' nor 'McDonald's Electrical' situated in Florida, but instead owned by 'The McDonald's Corporation' with its head office in Oak Brook, Illinois (MacQueen, Waelde & Laurie, 2008, p. 676).

ACADEMIC DOMAIN NAMES

An academic domain name is a text-based Internet address used in the address bar of a Web browser to denote the physical location of a particular host server, such as the address "https://www.law.ed.ac.uk/" which has a physical location on the campus of the Law School at the University of Edinburgh. An 'IP address' is the binary value of the Internet address of the form "172.16.3.52".

Figure 4. Internet address of the Law School at the University of Edinburgh

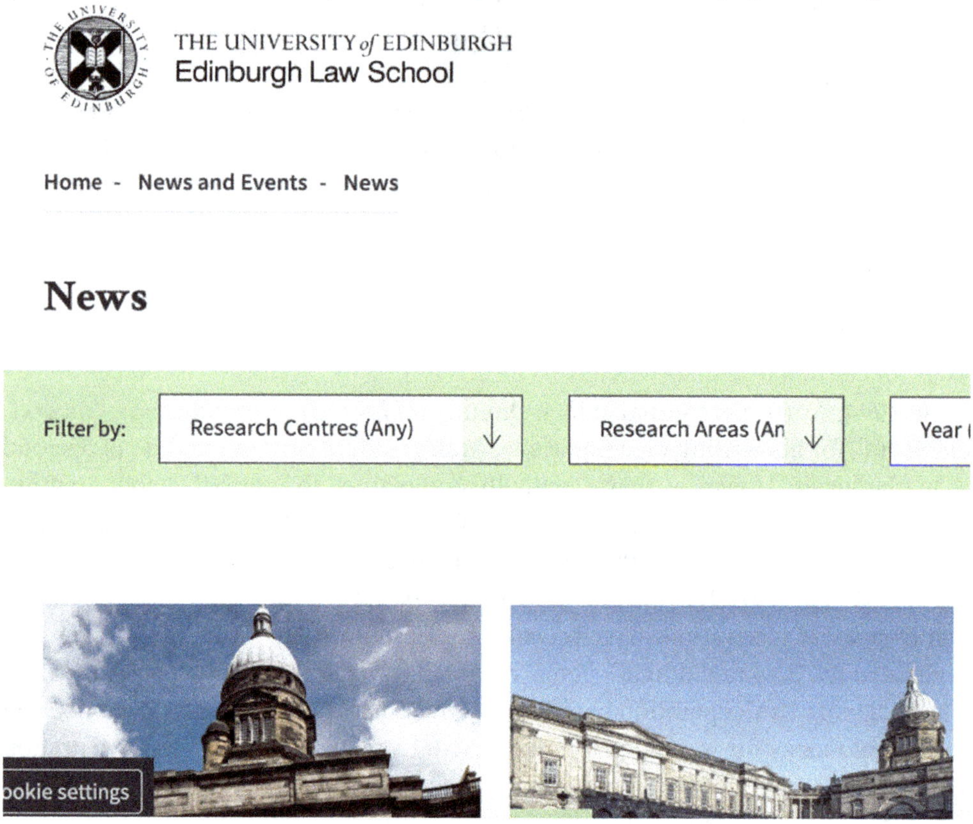

(University of Edinburgh, 2025)

DOMAIN NAMES AS STUDENT RESEARCH

In some universities, students doing domain name research will find many issues to write about, such as intellectual property, personal property, or a unique institutional identity. As a Registrar recently lamented (Bluehost, 2019),

> *You have unique things to offer that set you apart from others. That's why it's smart to establish yourself online through a portfolio, blog, or NextBigThing.com that projects your message to the world. It's creating your very own marketable brand—something future employers, editors, admissions committees and in-laws can check out.*

Student Organizations

Student organizations can request to have their domain name hosted directly by the University on the Student Council Server if the domain name is not in violation of any policies or procedures (University of Virginia Student Council, 2019). Even Fraternities and Sororities may request a group name domain name for their organization, such as groupname.berkeley.edu. Students may also purchase a domain name through a variety of third-party vendors (University of California at Berkeley, 2019). Several domain name registrars offer students "education bundles." Bluehost, for example, has education plans that "include everything you need to be bundled into one low price for as long as you keep the account active" (Bluehost, 2019).

MY DOMAIN NAME

In 2004, a 17-year-old Grade 12 student at Vancouver Island High School was locked in a battle with Microsoft Corp. over his Internet domain name, www.mikerowesoft.com, which had the software giant claiming copyright infringement. After Mike Rowe's plight became public, however, Microsoft softened." We do take our trademark seriously, but maybe in this case a little too seriously," said Jim Desler of Microsoft's corporate communications department (BBC News, 2004).

DOMAIN NAME SYSTEM IN THE U.S.

The United States has played a crucial role in Domain Name System (DNS) development and governance since the Internet's inception in 1983, influencing global policies on domain name administration. In the United States, the DNS is part of a global infrastructure that translates human-friendly domain names (e.g., example.com) into IP addresses (e.g., 192.0.2.1) that computers use to locate and communicate with each other on the internet. The DNS is managed globally, but in the U.S., it is primarily overseen by the *Internet Corporation for Assigned Names and Numbers (ICANN),* a nonprofit organization responsible for coordinating domain names and IP addresses. Before ICANN became fully independent in 2016, the *National Telecommunications and Information Administration (NTIA)*, a branch of the U.S. Department of Commerce, had oversight over certain aspects of DNS management.

Generic TLDs (gTLDs) are common worldwide, such as .com, .org, .net, .edu for accredited U.S. educational institutions, and .gov which is restricted for U.S. government use. The U.S. has its own ccTLD, .us, which is managed by GoDaddy Registry, under NTIA oversight.

Domain names are registered through ICANN-accredited registrars such as GoDaddy, Namecheap, or Google Domains. The registrant must provide valid contact information, which is stored in the WHOIS database, though privacy protection services can hide personal details.

There are security measures. *Domain Name System Security Extensions (DNSSEC)* helps prevent DNS spoofing by ensuring domain name queries come from legitimate sources. Through agencies like the FBI and the *Department of Homeland Security (DHS),* the U.S. government monitors domain-related fraud, including cybersquatting, phishing, and domain hijacking.

DOMAIN NAME SYSTEM IN CANADA

Canada's Domain Name System is part of the global DNS infrastructure. Canada has its own country-code top-level domain (ccTLD), .ca, managed by the *Canadian Internet Registration Authority (CIRA),* which is responsible for managing the .ca domain. The CIRA ensures fair registration, security, and dispute resolution. Canadians also use .com, .org, and .net, which are not country-specific. Canadians can register .ca domains through CIRA-accredited registrars, such as GoDaddy, Tucows, and Rebel.com. Personal information of .ca domain registrants is automatically protected under CIRA's WHOIS policy, unlike some other TLDs where data is publicly visible.

Unlike some other countries, Canada does not require second-level domain categorizations like .co.uk in the U.K. The Canadian Radio-television and Telecommunications Commission (CRTC) plays a role in Internet regulation and security oversight. ICANN governs global DNS policies, overseeing generic TLDs like .com, .org, and .net, which are also used in Canada.

The Domain Name System Security Extensions (DNSSEC) protects .ca domains from cyber threats like DNS spoofing and cache poisoning. Also CIRA's Canadian Shield is a free DNS security service offering malware protection and privacy for individuals and businesses. The *Canadian Centre for Cyber Security (CCCS)* and RCMP work to combat domain-related fraud, phishing, and cybersquatting. Finally, the CIRA has a *Canadian Dispute Resolution Policy (CDRP)* to handle domain disputes, particularly cases involving cybersquatting.

DOMAIN NAME SYSTEM IN THE U.K.

After the Brexit passed on January 31st, 2020, in favour of leaving the European Union (EU), all .eu domain names registered by U.K. citizens or businesses without a presence in the European Union (EU) were revoked or transferred to eligible EU entities. U.K. companies now need a legal EU presence to register or maintain a .eu domain.

The UK's Domain Name System (DNS) operates similarly to the US system but is overseen by different regulatory bodies. The primary organization responsible for the .uk country-code top-level domain (ccTLD) is Nominet, a nonprofit company that manages and regulates .uk domain registrations. ICANN still oversees the broader global DNS, including generic domains like .com, .org, and .net, which are also used in the UK. However, the UK government and law enforcement agencies can monitor and take action against illegal activities involving domains.

The official country-code Top-Level Domain (TLD) in the U.K. is .uk. Second-Level Domains (SLDs) under .uk, include .sch.uk for schools in the U.K, ac.uk for higher education and research institutions, .gov.uk for U.K. government entities, .nhs.uk used by the National Health Service (NHS), .co.uk for businesses, .org.uk for non-profit organizations, and .me.uk for personal use.

Individuals and businesses can register .uk domains through Nominet-accredited registrars such as GoDaddy, 123 Reg, and Names.co.uk. A WHOIS lookup is available through *Nominet* for checking domain ownership, though GDPR have restricted publicly visible personal data.

Domain Name System Security Extensions (DNSSEC) helps protect against DNS spoofing and domain hijacking. U.K. authorities, such as the *National Cyber Security Centre* (NCSC) and *Action Fraud,* monitor and act against domain-related fraud, including phishing, cybersquatting, and fake websites. Nominet provides a Dispute Resolution Service (DRS) to help resolve domain name disputes, especially cases of cybersquatting.

Unregistered Trade-Marks in the U.K

As an unregistered trademark, an academic domain name is a sign that can distinguish the programs and services of one university from those of another. A trade-mark may, in particular, consist of words (including personal names), designs, letters, numerals or the shape of goods or their packaging (Trade Marks Act 1994, s.1). So a trade-mark can be a name, such as "Aberystwyth.ac.uk", and a trade mark for "Aberystwyth University. "The registrant would have to show that the domain name is not merely functioning as an address for communication, like a postal address or phone number, but rather as a distinctive badge of origin, of a particular level of service. Surprisingly, at this writing, less than 10% of the 4,100 higher education institutions in the UK with domain names use it as a badge of origin (FOI.wiki.com, 2018).

WRAPPING-UP

A domain name is a person-friendly form of an Internet address. A domain consists of three elements: the hostname or server, the domain name, and the top-level domains or TLDs (Gutierrez, 2001). The Internet is divided into several top-level domains or TLDs, organized according to a hierarchy. Increasing use of the Internet has meant more people are creating personal websites and are expecting to use their first name or surname in the domain name. Existing international and national legal regulations are insufficient to protect personal names effectively (Anisimov, Ryzhenkov & Kozhemyakin, 2015). Current approaches in this area are scattered and not systematic.

REFERENCES

Allemann, A. (2015). The University of Cambridge loses case against Cambridge.com, *Domain Name Wire,* https://domainnamewire.com/2015/10/12/university-of-cambridge-loses-case-against-cambridge-com/

Alwakeel, R. (2015). Cambridge University loses legal fight to get rival cambridge.com website shut down, *Evening Standard,* https://www.standard.co.uk/news/uk/cambridge-university-loses-legal-fight-to-get-rival-cambridgecom-website-shut-down-a3090086.html

Anisimov, A. P., Ryzhenkov, A. J., & Kozhemyakin, D. V. (2015). Theory and practice of protection of personal names in the domain space or "renewed" cybersquatting. *Information & Communications Technology Law, 24*(1), 104–117. DOI: 10.1080/13600834.2015.1012393

BBC News. (2004). Boy swaps MikeRoweSoft for Xbox, http://news.bbc.co.uk/2/hi/technology/3429485.stm

Blefari, F., Furfaro, A., Ianni, G. & Viscomi, A. (2024). Combining anti-typosquatting techniques, Conference paper, Web Engineering, https://link-springer-com.qe2a-proxy.mun.ca/content/pdf/10.1007/978-3-031-62362-2_17

Bennett, S., & Thorne, C. (1998). Domain names - Internet warehousing: Has protecting well-known names on the Internet gone too far? Case Comment. *European Intellectual Property Review, 20*(12), 468–470.

Bluehost Inc. (2019). Special Offer for Students & Faculty, https://www.bluehost.com/hosting/education

Bray, H. (March 2006). China creates own Net domains: Bypass of US control stirs fear of censorship, Boston Globe, https://www.boston.com/news/world/asia/articles/2006/03/01/china_creates_own_net_domains/

British Telecommunications Plc & Ors v One In A Million Ltd & Ors [1998] EWCA Civ 1272 (23 July 1998), http://www.bailii.org/ew/cases/EWCA/Civ/1998/1272.html

CERN. (2025). A short history of the Web, *CERN Accelerating Science,* https://home.cern/science/computing/birth-web/short-history-web#:~:text=Where%20the%20Web%20was%20born,and%20institutes%20around%20the%20world

Deveci, H. (2003). Domain names: Has trade-mark law strayed from its path? *International Journal of Law and Information Technology, 11*(3), 203–225. DOI: 10.1093/ijlit/11.3.203

Diamonique Corp v. Maison Tropicale S.A., WIPO Arbitration and Mediation Center, https://www.wipo.int/amc/en/domains/decisions/html/2007/d2007-1093.html

DomainTools Blog. (October 2007). ICANN's Security and Stability Advisory Committee, http://blog.domaintools.com/2007/10/domain-name-front-running/

Easyspace Ltd. (2019). https://www.easyspace.com/index.html

Edwards, L. (2005). Article 12-15 ECD: ISP liability - The problem of Intermediate Service Provider liability. In Edwards, L. (Ed.), *The New Legal Framework for E-Commerce in Europe* (pp. 93–136). Hart Publishing.

EURid. (March 2008). *The European Registry of Domain Names,* http://www.eurid.eu/

EuroDNS. (2019). Great education domain name ideas for eLearning websites: https://www.eurodns.com/

FOI.wiki.com (2018). List of .ac.UK domain names,

Gutierrez, O. R. (2001). Get Off My URL: Congress outlaws cybersquatting in the Wild West of the Internet. *Santa Clara High-Technology Law Journal*, *17*, 139. https://digitalcommons.law.scu.edu/chtlj/vol17/iss1/5

Healey, C. (2007). Due to ICANN's "Add Grace Period," *Duke Law & Technology Review, 9, domain tasting is taking over the Internet.*

Heater, B. (September 2007). Eminent Domains, *PC Magazine.*

Hutchinson, J. P. (2001). Can trade-mark protection respond to the international threat of cybersquatting? *Journal of Information, Law and Technology*, http://elj.warwick.ac.uk/jilt/01-1/hutchinson.html

IANA. (2008). Country-code Top-level Domains, http://www.iana.org/domains/root/cctld/

IANA. (2019). Root Zone Management, Overview, https://www.iana.org/domains/root

IANA. (2019). Root Server Website, 2019, https://root-servers.org/

ICANN. (2008, March). ICANN CEO welcomes concerns as NTIA weighs role. *Telecommunications Reports*, *74*(6), 6–7.

ICANN blog (January 2007), https://blog.icann.org/

Industry Six. (2019). MMO Population, https://mmo-population.com/top/2019

Karrenberg, D. (September 2007). DNS Root Name Servers Explained For Non-Experts, https://www.isoc.org/briefings/019/

Komaitis, K. (2003). ICANN: Guilty as charged? Journal of Information, Law & Technology, 1.

Lewis, B. (2006). Reverse Domain Hijacking: Extreme Makeover, DNJournal, https://www.dnjournal.com/legal/extreme-makeover.htm

MacQueen, H., Waelde, C., & Laurie, G. (2008). *Contemporary Intellectual Property: Law and Policy*. Oxford University Press.

Masnick, M. (July 27th 2010). The University of Texas discovers it does not get to control the words 'Texas' & 'Sports' when used together, https://www.techdirt.com/2010/07/27/university-of-texas-discovers-it-doesnt-get-to-control-the-words-texas-sports-when-used-together/

McAfee, L. L. C. (2013). What is Typosquatting? https://securingtomorrow.mcafee.com/consumer/family-safety/what-is-typosquatting/

McDonald's. (2019). Internet Site Terms and Conditions, http://mcdonalds.com/terms.html

Outlaw News. (March 2007). Domain tasting makes WIPO sick, *OUT-LAW News*, https://www.out-law.com/default.aspx?page=7878

Parsons, B. (May 2006). Domain Kiting: A serious problem gets worse, *Go Daddy Group, Inc.*, Blog, http://www.bobparsons.com/DomainKiting.html

Pollick, M. (2008). What is Check Kiting? *WiseGeek*, https://www.wisegeek.com/what-is-check-kiting.htm

Quittner, J. (October 1994). Billions Registered, *Wired*, https://www.wired.com/wired/archive/2.10/mcdonalds.html

Rooksby, J. H. (2015). Defining Domain: Higher education's battles for cyberspace. *Brooklyn Law Review*, *80*(3). https://brooklynworks.brooklaw.edu/blr/vol80/iss3/5

Schiavetta, S., & Komaitis, K. (2003). ICANN's role in controlling information on the Internet. *International Review of Law Computers & Technology*, *17*(3), 267–284. DOI: 10.1080/1360086032000174379

Trade Marks Act. 1994, s.1 Legislation.gov.uk, https://www.legislation.gov.uk/ukpga/1994/26/contents

United States Patent and Trademark Office (April 2008) Anticybersquatting Consumer Protection Act of 1999, s 3006, https://www.uspto.gov/web/offices/dcom/olia/tmcybpiracy/repcongress.pdf

University of California at Berkeley. (2019). Student Organization Domain Name Guidelines, https://lead.berkeley.edu/wp-content/uploads/2014/12/student-org-domain-guidelines.pdf

University of Virginia Student Council. (2019). FAQs about Domain Names, http://www.student.virginia.edu/domains.php#6

U.S. Department of Commerce (April 2008). National Telecommunications and Information Administration, ICANN. A statement on the Mid-Term Review of the Joint Project Agreement (JPA) Between NTIA and ICANN, Washington, DC,

Varas, C. (2008). Virtual protection: Applying trade-mark law within virtual worlds such as Second Life, *Entertainment. Law Review, 19*(1), 5–11.

Waelde, C., & Edwards, L. (April 2005). Online intermediaries and liability for copyright infringement, A report to the WIPO Seminar on Copyright and Internet Intermediaries.

WIPO. (March 2008). DNS Developments Feed Growing Cybersquatting Concerns, The WIPO Press Room, https://www.wipo.int/pressroom/en/articles/2008/article_0015.html

WIPO Arbitration and Mediation Center (2006). *McDonald's Corporation v. Easy Property*, Case D2006-1142, https://www.wipo.int/amc/en/domains/decisions/html/2006/d2006-1142.html

Chapter 13
Patent Law and the Entrepreneurial University

ABSTRACT

This chapter is an introduction to the use of patent law in educational technology in the U.K., Europe, Canada, and the U.S., focusing on faculty and student innovations within the entrepreneurial university and the potential rewards of protecting intellectual property. University researchers in several countries who previously enjoyed full patent rights to their innovations, upon policy reform, have been moved toward a version of the U.S. model, where the university holds majority rights. However, initiating entrepreneurial activities does not automatically transform a university into an entrepreneurial university. Challenges emerge from promising rewards to university researchers to innovate. Common terms used in discussing patents include "purposive construction of the patent specification", "priority date", "enabling disclosure", and in the U.S., "the doctrine of equivalents". There are also recent proposals in the patent-granting process to include outsiders as judges and a democratic process for judging the validity of those judgments.

WHAT IS A PATENT?

A patent is the exclusive right granted by a government to protect an invention (British Library, 2019). A patent makes it illegal for anyone, except the owner, or someone with the owner's permission, to make, use, import or sell the invention in the country where the patent was granted (Machlup & Penrose, 1950).

A patent is not a brick, a piece of metal, or anything else tangible; its existence and value are determined simply by the rights it gives to restrain unlicensed users (Laddie, 2001, p.14).

Patent claims define the scope of patent protection. Whether a claim covers a product accused of infringement frequently determines whether a patent holder will

DOI: 10.4018/979-8-3373-3126-3.ch013

be rewarded or left with nothing (Walsh & DiPietrantonio, 2011). A good patent attorney contributes to the value of a patent by identifying features that characterize the invention, as it will be put into practice now and in the future when the patent might be enforced. This task, while on its face seems straightforward, often proves to be quite challenging.

British Patents

In the U.K., a patent is the exclusive right granted by a government to protect an invention. A patent makes it illegal for anyone, except the owner or someone with the owner's permission, to make, use, import or sell the invention in the country where the patent was granted. A U.K. patent has a life of 20 years and protects the U.K. so long as renewal fees are paid every year.

Table 1. Historical timeline of patent law in Britain

Period	Key Event	Impact
Pre-1600	Crown-issued monopolies	Arbitrary privileges for trade
1624	Statute of Monopolies	First formal limit on monopolies, patent system born
1852	Patent Law Amendment Act	First UK Patent Office, a simpler system
1883	Further reforms	Allowed patent attorneys, improved transparency
1977	Patents Act 1977	Aligned with European Patent Convention
2000s	Digital reforms, Brexit	Online filing, non-EU patent cooperation continues

For a patent to be granted, the invention must be novel, inventive, and have industrial applicability. To be patentable, the invention must be new, that is to say, never made public in any way, anywhere in the world, before the date on which the application for a patent is filed. The invention must involve an *inventive step,* which means that it is different from others of its type and not obvious to someone with knowledge of the subject. The invention must also have an industrial application, a practical form, such as an apparatus or device or an industrial process or method of operation.

Most writers on the origins of the patent system discuss the development of patent grants under the reigns of Elizabeth and James I in England in 1623, when the Crown granted privileges of monopoly under the *Statute of Monopolies.* That said, the patent system is not chiefly a British creation (Machlup & Penrose, 1950).

European Patents

Almost everywhere in Europe, privileges were granted to inventors. A rather well-developed patent system has existed in Venice since the fifteenth century, and in many parts of western and central Europe in the sixteenth and seventeenth centuries (Machlup & Penrose, 1950). Today, European patents are granted by the *European Patent Office (EPO)* under the *1973 European Patent Convention.* Thirty-eight countries are parties to the Convention. The EPO applies a uniform system. An applicant can go to the EPO and, through one application, request a bundle of national patents for any of the countries party to the Eur*opean Patent Convention*, including all the European Union Member States except Finland (Vinje, 1995).

Table 2. Historical timeline of patent law in Europe

Year	Event	Significance
1474	Venice Patent Statute	First patent law in Europe
1624	UK Statute of Monopolies	Basis for modern patent concepts
1883	Paris Convention	International priority rights
1973	European Patent Convention (EPC) signed	Created European Patent Organization (EPO)
1977	EPO is operational	Unified filing system begins
2000	EPC is revised	Modernized European patent framework
2023	Unified Patent Court is launched	Centralized patent litigation in the European Union

In deciding to grant a European patent, the EPO applies a single set of rules on patentability. If granted, the holder of the European patent then has the option to 'localize' the European patent in any or all EPC member countries by asking the *European Patent Office* to register the patent (and pay the relevant fees to each country). Yet a good patent lasts a very long time, and for new technologies, the longevity of that protection may either be pointless or act as a brake on further innovation. The call has been for shorter rights or different ones (Brimelow, 2001). Figure 1 shows the organizations and countries comprising the system open to the applicant to register a patent: National, community, or international.

Figure 1. European routes open to the patent applicant

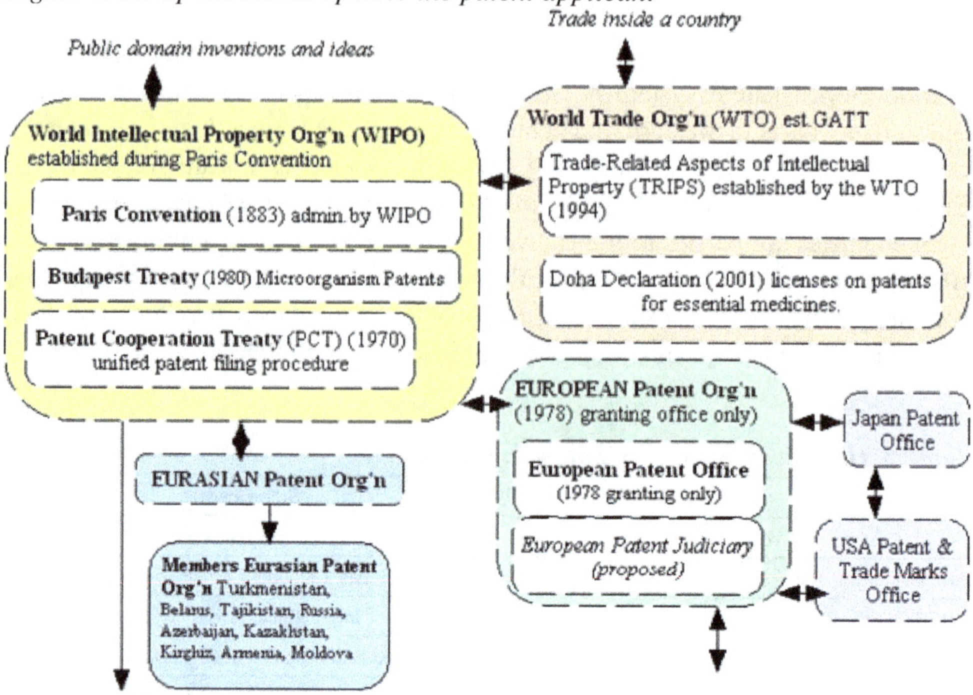

(Mann, 2008)

An invention developed at a university in Sweden, with the professor's privilege (aka a teacher's exemption from prosecution), is owned by the researcher. The option to commercialize also belongs to the researcher (Berggren, 2017). Researchers holding patents or making use of research results in other ways have no duty to inform their university. Research is too narrowly measured in patents, licensing and spin-off companies. Not only policy but also research about "the entrepreneurial university" has mainly focused on comparably easily measurable interactions such as researchers' patenting, licensing and USOs.

Canadian Patents

The first Canadian patent was granted in 1824 in Upper Canada (now Ontario). The first patent in Canada was granted by the legislature of Quebec in 1791. No official patent act followed until about 30 years later, when Upper and Lower Canada enacted patent acts in the 1820s. The provinces held the responsibility for patents within their boundaries.

Table 3. Historical timeline of patent law in Canada

Period	Key Milestone	Notable Changes
Pre-1867	Colonial systems	British-influenced laws in each colony
1869	First federal Patent Act	Unified Canadian patent system
1900s–1980s	Periodic amendments	Compulsory licensing, patent office reform
1989–1995	Global integration	Joined PCT, NAFTA, TRIPS compliance
2000s–Today	Modernization	Digital, biotech, streamlined procedures

The *British North America Act* established that patents were a federal responsibility. The first federal Patent Act was passed in 1869, creating a *Patent Office* in Ottawa and a unified system across all provinces. The act granted patents for a term of 15 years, divided into three five-year periods, and allowed any new and useful art, process, machine, manufacture, or composition of matter to be patented.

The second federal Patent Act was passed in 1872, allowing foreigners to register patents. In the 1880s and 1890s, the Patent Act was amended to extend patent terms from 15 to 18 years, divided into three six-year periods. The *Patent Office* and *Commissionaire of Patents* were established by statute between 1900 and 1919. In 1923, the third federal Patent Act provided for inventions created by public servants. The fourth federal *Patent Act* was passed in 1935, which set provisions for the procedure of obtaining patents on inventions related to national defence and atomic energy. The Patent Office and the position of *Commissionaire of Patents* were incorporated into the new *Canadian Intellectual Property Office* in 1991. In 1993, the requirement that an invention could not be obvious was added to the Patent Act. In 1996, the *TRIPS Implementation Act* was passed. In 2001, patents were extended from 18 to 20 years as a result of a WTO ruling that 18-year patents violated TRIPS requirements.

The *Patent Act (1985)* is one of the main pieces of Canadian legislation governing patent law in Canada. It sets out the criteria for patentability, what can or cannot be patented in Canada, the process for obtaining a Canadian patent, and provides for the enforcement of Canadian patent rights. Before Canada became a country, patents were issued under British colonial rule. Each colony (e.g., Upper Canada, Lower Canada, Nova Scotia) had its own patent legislation based on British models.

American Patents

In 1980, the Bayh-Dole Act granted $8 billion to American universities for their original academic research. Before then, no simple mechanism existed to take the innovations of academic research out of the university and put them in the marketplace (Senator Birch Bayh, April 23, 1980).

Table 4. Historical timeline of patent law in the United States

Year	Event
1790	First Patent Act; patent board created
1793	Simplified process; no examination
1836	Modern patent office and examination introduced
1870	Codification and stricter standards
1952	Comprehensive Patent Act with "non-obviousness"
1980	Bayh-Dole Act on university patents
1982	Federal Circuit Court is created
2011	America Invents Act is passed

Unlike copyrights, which are registered with the *Library of Congress throug*h the *U.S. Copyright Office,* patents and trademarks are registered at the *United States Patent and Trademark Office (USPTO, 2007*). To obtain a patent in the U.S., an invention must be deemed useful, novel, and non-obvious. For instance, on November 12, 2024, the *USPTO* granted a patent to Bilac Jugoslav and eight others from D2L Corporation in Kitchener, Ontario, Canada, for a learning management system designed to administer, document, track, report, automate, and deliver educational courses, training programs, and learning materials.

Figure 2. A United States patent showing a schematic for a learning management system and the administration, documentation, tracking, reporting, automation, and delivery of educational courses, training programs, materials or learning and development programs

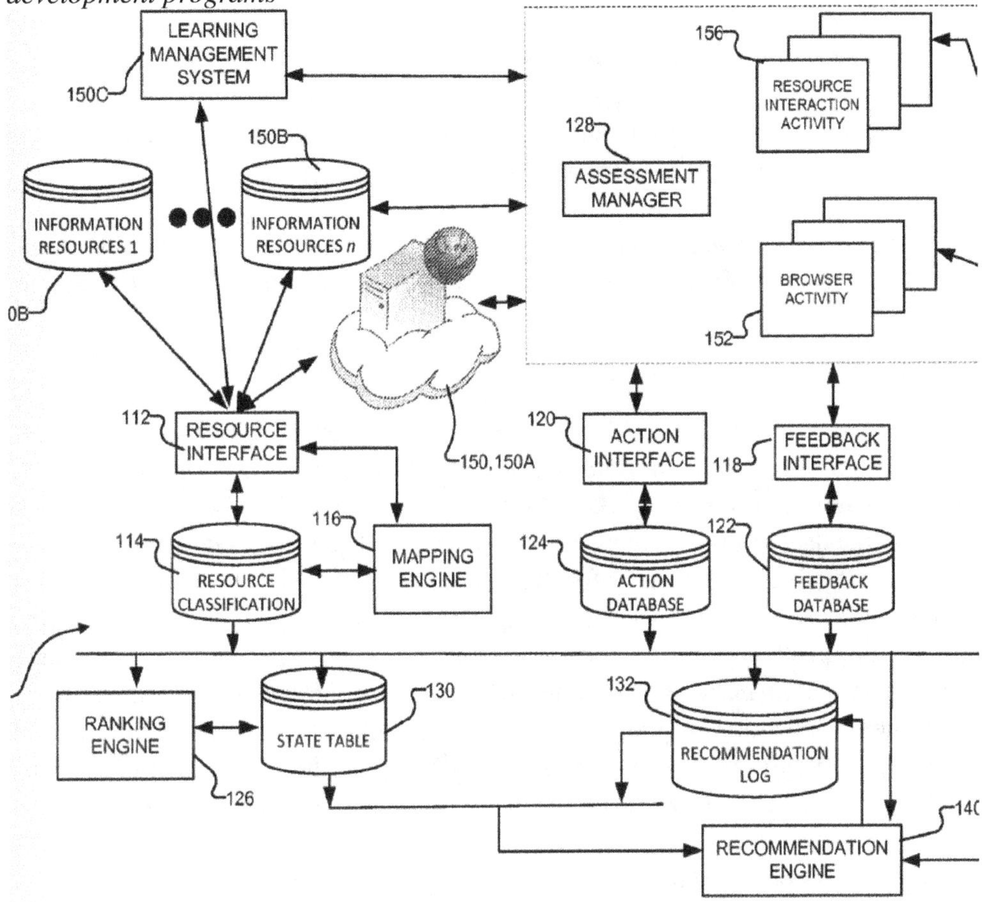

(Bilac Jugoslav et al., 2024)

Purposive Interpretation of Claims

A patent specification should be given *a purposive construction* rather than a purely literal one. The language of the claim should be construed purposively to extract from it the essence or the essential elements of the invention. Cullet has remarked that a *purposive construction* suggests that 'use' is limited by the subject matter of the invention and that any acts for a purpose, whether foreseen or not by the inventor, may constitute an infringing use (Cullet, 2005). The problem with defining ‘use’ as in commercial use is that the inventor is not obliged to describe the utility of the invention; the inventor must merely describe the invention to produce it. An invention is *not* patentable if it is:

- A discovery
- A scientific theory or mathematical method
- An aesthetic creation, literary, dramatic or artistic work
- A method for performing a mental act, playing a game or doing business
- The presentation of information or a computer program

If the invention involves more than these abstract aspects so that it has physical features (such as a special apparatus to play a new game), then it may be patentable.

Priority Date

Priority date, in patent law, is the date of filing of the first application. Whereas in the United Kingdom, some decisions refer to 'the day of publication,' in Germany, the courts refer to the priority date. In the Netherlands and France, court practice refers to 'the date of infringement' (Tilmann, 2006). The p*riority date* is considered to be the effective date of filing for the examination of novelty and inventive steps or non-obviousness for the subsequent application claiming the priority of the first application. In other words, the *prior art* which is taken into account for examining the novelty and *inventive step* or non-obviousness of the invention claimed in the subsequent application, would not be everything made available to the public before the filing date (of the subsequent application) but everything made available to the public before the *priority date,* i.e. the date of filing of the first application.

Enabling Disclosure

An *enabling disclosure* is a sufficiently written description within the patent to enable a *Person Having Ordinary Skill in the Art* (PHOSITA) to make and use the full breadth of the invention. The person, then, to whom the invention must be taught is a 'person skilled in the art.' Such a person is competent and already well-trained in the common practices of the art. Exactly what such a person knows is a question of fact to be determined, where necessary, by evidence in each particular case. It will vary according to the art and naturally according to the date of the invention (Roberts, 2006).

An *enabling disclosure* is a description of the substance of the patent that someone skilled in the subject could reproduce the work about to be patented. This requirement, which is one of the most crucial ones in patent law, is capable of having a considerable amount of influence on the scope of protection of the patent claimed. If, as Bostyn (2003) has suggested, the requirement is applied in a lenient manner, i.e., vague and generalizing, despite the complexity of the invention, even if the disclosure in the application is rather, then it is facilitated to obtain broad patent protection without the necessity to provide detailed disclosure of all the embodiments which are claimed to fall under the scope of the patent (Bostyn, 2003). If, on the other hand, the requirement is applied strictly, i.e., a detailed disclosure of the invention, then the scope of the patent could be narrower than originally claimed by the applicant.

In the United States, *public disclosure* must impact patent rights. To do this, the description of the invention must be detailed enough to enable a person skilled in the art to duplicate or use it or make the invention obvious to the person. Tips to avoid public disclosure of an invention (Technology Transfer, 2007):

- Publish only broad generalities
- Avoid the disclosure of detailed information that might be enabling (e.g., descriptions of structures, gene names or sequences, exact compositions, sources of origin, graphs or figures that show the novel features of the invention, the ultimate use of the invention as part of a larger or more complex novel device)

Doctrine of Equivalents

In the U.S., the *doctrine of equivalents* arises in the context of an infringement action. The essential question is: "Does the accused product or process contain elements identical or equivalent to each claimed element of the patented invention?" The goal of the *doctrine of equivalents* is to provide patent owners with fair protection for their patents.

The U.K. has never employed a *doctrine of equivalents* approach. Instead, the U.K. follows the Protocol on the Interpretation of Article 69 of the European Patent (EPC), which requires member states to draw a balance between interpreting patent claims with strict literalism (with the description and drawings only helping resolve ambiguity) and regarding the claims as a mere guideline only. Garde (2005) suggests that the *doctrine of equivalents* inherently adds uncertainty to the scope of a patent. When evaluating the *doctrine of equivalents* to provide further certainty to the scope of protection, the courts have effected an unintended yet opposite result; namely, they have only succeeded in increasing legal uncertainty as to the availability of the doctrine.

U.S. Peer-To-Patent

One of the most promising conditions under which patent law is applied in educational technology is the Peer-To-Patent, initially introduced in the U.S. As a means of democratizing the patenting process, the U.S. Patent Office initiated a peer-to-patent process. Peer-To-Patent was developed as a community-based pilot study to improve the quality of information available to patent examiners deciding on whether a patent should be granted. As part of the efforts to implement its Strategic Plan, Commissioner of U.S. Patents John J. Doll announced a pilot project to determine the extent to which the organized submission of documents and comments by the public would provide helpful prior art for examiners (USPTO, 2007).

Advances in Internet-based collaboration methods have produced both technological and business models that have significantly increased productivity in the American economy. A group of academic and business professionals proposed a collaborative, online process in which members of the public pool together their knowledge and locate potential prior art. This pilot would test whether such collaboration could effectively locate *prior art* that the Office might not otherwise locate during the typical examination process.

U.K. Peer-To-Patent

In June 2011, the Minister for Intellectual Property in Britain, Baroness Wilcox, launched the Peer to Patent website. This website allowed experts in science and technology to view and comment on patent applications (Gov. U.K., 2011). Baroness Wilcox was Parliamentary Under Secretary for Business, Innovation and Skills. Baroness Wilcox wrote,

Patent applications granted after using the Peer to Patent website review will be potentially more substantial, giving businesses better protection to grow their innovative ideas. This will give the IPO access to a broader body of knowledge when deciding whether a patent should be granted. The pilot will allow experts to comment on patent applications and share their vital expertise before patents are granted. It will also mean that inventions already known on the broader community will be filtered out more readily (Gov. U.K., 2011).

During the six-month pilot, over 200 applications in the computing field were uploaded for review on the website. These included a range of inventions, from computer mice to complex processor operations. The benefits of Peer to Patent:

- Opens the patent examination process.
- Improves the current system by helping to avoid the granting of overly broad patents

- Demonstrates the role that non-governmental experts can play in improving the patenting process.
- Makes public participation relevant to actual decision-making.
- Provides the opportunity for scientific and technical communities to research and discuss a patent application and share their knowledge with the IPO.

Despite gaining governmental, national, and international notoriety, the USPTO chose not to extend the project beyond its second year (Heise Media, 2009). Similarly, the U.K. Peer to Patent website closed. The Peer-to-Patent blog, which provided the latest news, views and updates, is also closed. The Peer-to-Patent Australia website cannot be reached. Philip Leith (2012) accurately predicted that participatory projects can demonstrate involvement and are undoubtedly educational. However, online peer-to-patent projects are likely incapable of achieving the goals set by their more optimistic advocates. Professor Leith suggests we learn from the peer-to-patent pilot studies. The primary point is that the technocratic view is always overly optimistic.

Peer-Assessment

Weatherall (2009) proposed including outsiders in the patent-granting process. First, it can provide a second pair of eyes. Having a motivated, interested party do their search can improve the quality of patent office decision-making by introducing additional information, such as prior art not found in the initial examination, or by highlighting any possible overbreadth or lack of clarity in the claims. Second, it may provide an inexpensive mechanism for resolving differences between competitors or other affected companies.

Validity of the judgments can be enhanced by applying Expert-Peer Assessment (Mann, 2009). The method includes the option to collect both inter-rater and intra-rater consistency data to weigh the assessments of each peer, arbitrator and expert. The Expert-Peer Assessment formula shown in Figure 3 is recommended as a method of judging how the assessments of experts and peers should be used to judge patent applications (Mann, 2009). Two tests of the validity of the process and formula were conducted with pre-service teachers (Mann, 2005). Validity was determined by calculating a Pearson product-moment correlation and corresponding coefficient of determination that compared the average grade assigned by the teachers with the grade assigned independently by a course instructor. Results of both studies showed that the method and formula were valid with these groups (Mann, 2009). Findings from these studies may apply to expert-peer assessments of patent applications.

Figure 3. Expert-peer assessment formula adapted to patent granting

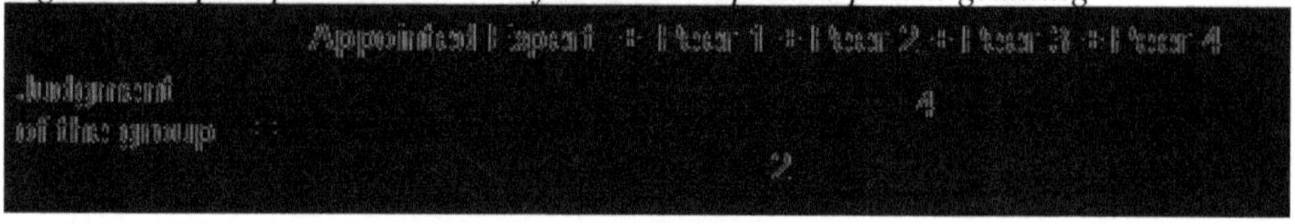

(Mann, 2009)

THE ENTREPRENEURIAL UNIVERSITY

Universities like to engage in entrepreneurial activities to keep pace with the evolving demands of a knowledge-based economy, to address the massification of education, to offset decreased public funding, and to compete globally (Etzkowitz, 2013; Sam & van der Sijde, 2014). Therefore, universities have increased their emphasis on commercializing original research partly for economic benefit and partly for the social development of their region (Saiz-Santos, Araujo-De la Mata & Hoyos-Iruarrizaga, 2017). "Commercializing" in this context includes applying for patents (Harmon, 2016b; Philpott, Dooley, O'Reilly & Lupton, 2011). The transformation of a traditional university into an entrepreneurial university can play an important role in the global knowledge-based economy (Sidrata & Frikhab, 2018). However, initiating entrepreneurial activities does not automatically transform a university into an entrepreneurial university; it only happens when these activities create added value in higher education and research.

Reward Theory

A university is incentivized to create start-ups if it owns the rights, but the problem first arises in how to encourage the research faculty. It does not appear that allocating intellectual property rights to the university is sufficient to increase the rate of startups, and a need to *incentivize* researchers to do so (Saiz-Santos *et al.*, 2017). The *Reward Theory of Intellectual Property* aims to promote innovation by engendering a cyclical pattern of incentives whereby those who innovate are rewarded through the granting of property rights, which, in turn, acts as an incentive to others to innovate, who are rewarded in their turn, and so on (MacQueen, Waelde, Laurie & Brown, 2010). According to this point of view, inventors are incentivized to invest their labour and capital into their ideas, thereby accelerating society's technological and economic progress.

Reward theory provides the oldest description of the intended impacts of patents on inventions. This type of theory treats patents as a method of influencing the production of new advances. The special rewards of patent rights are attached to non-obvious advances that are intellectual outliers in their respective technical fields to encourage more such advances and diversify the technological approaches used in various fields. A recent study (Åstebro et al., 2018) reported that entrepreneurship is more prevalent for those with a doctorate in medicine or engineering than for those with a doctorate in the natural sciences. Having a Ph.D. in medicine and in engineering are good predictors of the probability of becoming an entrepreneur when originating from the non-university sector, but predict little when originating from academia.

Reward theory, more commonly known as *reinforcement theory* (Adams, 2000; Skinner, 1953, 1968), describes behaviours followed by a reinforcing stimulus that increases the probability of that behaviour occurring in the future. Like Thorndike's *Law of Effect* (Thorndike, 1901) and Skinner's *Operant Conditioning* (Skinner, 1953, 1968), *reward theory* is a simple and widely applied method of influence that lawyers, psychologists, business leaders, and educators have learned to apply to measurable effect. For maximum effect with academic staff, reinforcers include money, influence, and, for patenting students, high grades, which should always be delivered to the researchers or students in the same conditions. To ensure the theory works properly, the lawyer, psychologist, business leader, or educator should be trained in the theory and practice of reinforcement.

Disillusioned Faculty & Students

Not everyone on campus is infatuated with an incentivized university. The push toward becoming an entrepreneurial university has had the effect that some academic staff in universities are increasingly dissatisfied and disillusioned, even voicing their despair. Some academic staff are frustrated and feel powerless to resist, not least because teaching, research, and administrative responsibilities leave them chronically overstretched and unable to mount a coherent opposition (Ginsberg, 2011). Challenges can emerge in motivating university researchers to innovate (Saiz-Santos *et al.*, 2017). Fewer inventions were patented in Germany after the abolition of the professor's privilege (van Dongen, Yergos, Tijssen & Claassen, 2017). Martin (2016) has outlined five reasons for this state of affairs.

1. The first reason is the emphasis on economic efficiency, measured in economic terms.

2. A second reason why some academic staff are dissatisfied is a sense of creeping accountability and performance targets designed to encourage changes in everyone's behaviour toward maximizing one's score according to the designated metric (Burrows, 2012).
3. Martin's third reason why some academic staff are dissatisfied is the perceived concern by senior administrators with globalization and increasing competition among academic staff and students. Over the last 30 years of globalization and growing competitive pressure, there has been increasing emphasis on the ability of organizations to generate and successfully implement innovation, both technological and organizational (Martin, 2016).
4. Martin's fourth reason why some academic staff are dissatisfied is their belief that there seems to be a dramatic rise in the number of senior university administrators and support staff, and
5. The first reason is the growing use of headhunters to fill senior university posts.

In the view of some (Gill, 2009; Ginsberg, 2011; Burrows, 2012; Haack, 2013), institutions of higher education are now mainly controlled by administrators and staffers who make the rules and set more and more of the priorities of academic life.

Boiled Frog

This begs the question, why have most academics so meekly accepted these developments? Are some too timid to voice their concerns publicly, particularly if they are on performance-related pay? An analogy can be drawn with the boiled frog (Tichy & Ulrich, 1984, p.60). Experiments by physiologists in the 1870s showed that a frog dropped into a saucepan of very hot water immediately jumps out, but a frog placed in a saucepan of cold water, which is then gradually brought to a boil, will not jump out but remains until it is eventually boiled (Sedgwick, 1882).

PROFESSOR'S PRIVILEGE VS. THE BAYH-DOLE ACT

Who are the rightful owners of scientific discoveries at the university – the researcher, or the university? "Professor's Privilege" meant that a patent generated by academic research belonged to the researcher, not the university. This interpretation of the Professor's Privilege has been closely associated with the notion of academic freedom (Pettersson, 2018). Then, in 1980, the United States Congress passed the Bayh-Dole Act, which allowed universities to retain title to inventions funded by government research money. As a result, university research has become less about scientific inquiry and more about business (Welch, 2008). Since 2000, several European countries, following the U.S., have changed their legislation on university patents. Denmark, Germany, Austria, Norway and Finland have cancelled the Professor's Privilege to own patents, and transferred the majority of the patent rights to the universities (Tichý & Rehák, 2025). At the same time, the universities have created an administrative system to ensure better protection of intellectual property and improve the commercial use of academic research. Notably, replacing the Professor's Privilege with Bayh-Dole–type regimes in Germany, Finland, Norway, and Denmark has been associated with significant decreases in patenting rates and start-up businesses by academics (Åstebro, Braguinsky, Braunerhjelm & Brostro, 2019). Universities in Italy and Sweden, however, still implement The Professor's Privilege, allowing the inventor to become the patentee (van Dongen, Yergos, Tijssen & Claassen, 2017).

Before the Bayh-Dole Act of 1980, the U.S. government retained ownership of inventions developed with federal funding, even if the research was conducted at universities or other non-profit institutions. This often led to a lack of commercialization for these inventions because the government lacked the resources and incentives to develop and market them. Universities, as key research institutions, faced challenges in translating their discoveries into tangible benefits for the public and their institutions due to the government's ownership of intellectual property. The Bayh-Dole Act aimed to address these issues by allowing universities, small businesses, and non-profit research institutions to elect to own the inventions they developed with federal funding. This policy change aimed to incentivize commercialization and accelerate the transfer of federally funded research into the marketplace. In the U.S., *the Bayh–Dole Act or Patent and Trademark Law Amendments Act, 1980* fundamentally changed the nation's system of technology transfer by enabling universities to retain title to inventions and take the lead in patenting and licensing groundbreaking discoveries.

In 2011, the U.S. Supreme Court clarified in *Stanford v Roche* that the original ownership of patents always vests with their inventor first, even if the inventor is a researcher at a federally funded lab subject to the 1980 Bayh–Dole Act. The judges affirmed the common understanding of U.S. constitutional law that inventors originally own inventions they make, and contractual obligations to assign those rights to third parties are secondary. So, the inventors' employers can own patents only when the inventors explicitly assign their patents to their employers. In this way, the patent provides exclusive rights to the inventor to create and utilize an original invention or method for a specified duration.

HOW DID WE GET HERE?

Historically, there have been four models of higher education. Table 5 is an overview of the higher education models from the perspective of understanding the concept of the entrepreneurial university (Sam & van der Sijde, 2014).

Table 5. Models of higher education, their basic features, and impact on transformation in higher education

Higher Education Model	Basic features	Impacts
Humboldtian Model	Research-based learning Academic freedom of research and learning Centralized system of governance	Research becoming a central area of study in modern higher education
Napoleonic Model	High-level vocational training Professional education Centralized system of governance	Vocational and technical training becoming crucial to prepare students for the rapidly-changing labor markets
Anglo-Saxon Model	Personality development through liberal education Professionalism Institutional autonomy or self-governing institutions	Soft skills being emphasized in modern higher education to enable students to act flexibly and intelligently in a changing and challenging environment
Anglo-American Model	All the basic features of the European models integrated	Research, technical training and professionalism being incorporated in contemporary higher education worldwide
	Decentralized system of governance Massification of higher education	Entrepreneurialism model of higher education institutions becoming critical for the competitive academic market place

Sam & van der Sijde, 2014, p.896

VON HUMBOLDT'S MODEL

Improvisation remains one of the few things equally valued by the Humboldtian university and the neo-liberal academy. Indeed, only closeted authoritarians fear and loathe improvisation (Fuller, 2023, p.151). The core Humboldtian principle was the unity of research and teaching in the person of the 'academic', understood as a free inquirer who served as an exemplar for students to emulate in their own way as part of their *Bildung,* the German tradition of self-cultivation, wherein philosophy and education are linked to a process of both personal and cultural maturation (Fuller, 2023). Unlike prior and subsequent conceptions of the university, the Humboldtian one was not about 'credentialing' people as 'experts' but about giving a focus and direction to their humanity.

According to the von Humboldtian model, professors are not there for the students but rather for the science (Gellert, 1993). von Humboldt (1810) considered the university as the observable form of an idea, spirit or reason that could not be grasped by the senses: *Wissenschaft,* which can be translated as "science as a unit." Its main characteristics can be found in Von Humboldt's (1810) recommendations for the University of Berlin.

Certain knowledges must be universal, and even more so, a certain formation of attitudes and character that no one should be without. Everyone is only a good craftsman, merchant, soldier, and businessman if, in themselves and without regard to their particular profession, they are a good, decent, enlightened person and citizen. If schooling provides them with what is necessary for this, they will subsequently acquire the specific skills of their profession very easily and will always retain the freedom, as so often happens in life, to move from one to the other. (von Humboldt, quoted in Ellwein, 1985, p.116).

Books, Articles and Patents

In the Germanized world, such a work was necessary simply to qualify for a regular professorship. Von Humboldt's first recommendation concerned the conception. Science should only deal with concepts in their general and universal dimension, detached from any immediate or direct application. His second recommendation concerned the unity of teaching and research. Von Humboldt considered teaching as the anticipation and purpose of every investigation, as well as the natural destiny of achievements. Masters were expected to convey the spirit of fundamental research, develop a passion for knowledge production and contribute to the organization and transformation of human experience (Schleiermacher, 1808).

Von Humboldt's third recommendation concerned the autonomy of reason and the principle of 'solitude and freedom.' Von Humboldt tried to divorce the university from the Church. For him, the university, as an autonomous institution, had to be a self-governing community. Hence, corporate autonomy was conceived of as an adaptation of its Medieval University meaning. While the latter meant to be autonomous from the King, Pope, Emperor and/or Feudal Lord, the former pursued its autonomy from nation-states.

NAPOLEONIC MODEL

The Napoleonic model of higher education was a centralized, state-controlled system in France initiated by Napoleon Bonaparte, influencing European higher education after 1815. It focused on professional training and specialized institutions like the Grandes Écoles, while relegating general education to secondary schools, both located in Paris. Les "Grandes Écoles" were elite schools, established alongside regular universities, offering specialized training in fields like science and engineering (Sam & van der Sijde, 2014). Unlike the Anglo-Saxon model, universities were not self-governing institutions. The Napoleonic model focused on practical training, while the Von Humboldtian model (which emerged around the same time) emphasized the integration of research and teaching.

ANGLO-SAXON MODEL

The Anglo-Saxon model, which emerged in the nineteenth century with Oxford and Cambridge University, has the basic feature of personality development through "liberal education" in which there is a close relationship between teachers and students (Gellert, 1993). Unlike the above two models, the Anglo-Saxon model of higher education is a less well-developed system of vocational training and higher education because it provides, instead, a broad educational base with less emphasis on subject-specific and skill-related content (Little, 2001) and is not intended to prepare students for a specific profession after graduation (Sam & van der Sijde, 2014). Notably, one of the key factors in encouraging the creation of entrepreneurial activities is to own intellectual property. Patents and the strategic way they can be applied, namely as a means to acquire competitive advantage, are an important element of business that justifies the development of courses dedicated to these subjects. A general grounding in intellectual property law would already be desirable for business students at the undergraduate level (Gubby, 2015). Business students must become familiar with the concept of having a patent strategy as part of that overall business strategy. If business schools are not to be out of step with business practice, it is time to reassess the curricula.

ANGLO-AMERICAN MODEL

The Anglo-American model of higher education was derived from the European models and has been imported back into European countries. At the undergraduate level, the Anglo-American model of higher education emphasizes the liberal arts and multi-disciplinary curricula, following the Anglo-Saxon model (Sam & van der Sijde, 2014). At the postgraduate level, the Anglo-American model emphasizes research, following the Von Humboldt model. Compared to the European-style higher education system, the Anglo-American system has a more structured approach to teaching and learning, which helps students plan their studies and allocate a period to complete their academic programs (Buchori & Malik, 2004). The Anglo-American model has influenced higher education around the world. Other higher education institutions have adopted the US credit-based system to increase the flexibility in the design and organization of their academic programs (Salmi, 2001).

STUDENTS AND PATENTS

The patent is a legal concept, an idea originated and developed by lawyers.

What relevance does patent law have for the university student? One purpose is to learn to use patents in their student design projects. Another is as a strategic learning resource to understand the rightful place of their invention in the marketplace of new inventions. Enterprising business students should be familiar with the concept of using a patentable invention as part of their overall business strategy. Included as part of that strategy, however, is that students should know there is no single rationale for the patent system; some believe it makes little sense at all. When business education becomes out of step with business practice, it is time to reassess the curricula and include patent law at the undergraduate level (Gubby, 2015).

In the student context, a patent is more valuable when viewed as a learning resource than as a list of *prior art* to be considered for infringement. As a learning resource, it's a practical approach to patent searching, clustering, and using creatively in student design projects summarised (Maclachlan, Wodehouse and Vasantha. 2018). After practicing search strategies on sample design problems and a prototype morphological patent gallery, trialled within a student workshop, participants found they could quickly understand abbreviated visual and text representations of the patents and were able to synthesize concepts from multiple patent clusters. Patents and the strategic ways they can be applied for competitive advantage are important elements of business that justify the development of courses dedicated to these subjects (MacLachlan *et al.*, 2018).

There is a support structure in the form of a boot, a primary lever being pivotally mounted adjacent to the heel of the boot, the primary lever extending downward below the sole of the boot so that downward movement of the boot, being resiliently deformed, the stored energy will assist the motion of the boot in the upward direction Furthermore interchangeable components, for example, secondary levers, may be provided to adapt the article of footwear for different terrains.

Most patent applications are for a utility. A utility patent protects any new process, machine, manufactured article, new chemical compound, or any new improvement to an existing invention. In this case, KHS claimed that he was entitled to the invention covered by the application because he had made the invention as part of an A-level course before enrolment at Coventry University. He subsequently included the invention as part of his coursework while studying at the University. KHS, therefore, claimed that the invention was not covered by the University Regulations, and in the absence of any other assignment of the invention to the University, the application should proceed in his name. The University, as proprietor of the application, did not file a counterstatement, which led to the case being treated as undefended and each fact set out in the referrer's statement as being conceded. The referrer, therefore, succeeded in showing that he was entitled to the application in question, and an order was made for it to proceed solely in his name.

Student Inventor vs University

The Intellectual Property Office in the U.K. granted a U.K. Patent for the boot design to student K. Howard Seymour, who invented it, but not without a fight. Coventry University challenged a student's U.K. patent application, which proceeded under the university name because their regulations specified that intellectual property rights arising from work forming part of a student's coursework belonged to the university. In *K. Howard Seymour v Coventry University, 2000,* a patent application was filed by K. Howard Seymour, for original footwear (Google Patents, 2019). The court held that the U.K. Patent for the boot design (figure 4) was to be granted to student K. Howard Seymour instead of the name of Coventry University.

Figure 4. Illustration of the student's patent application showing downward movement of the boot, being resiliently deformed, the stored energy assists motion of the boot in the upward direction

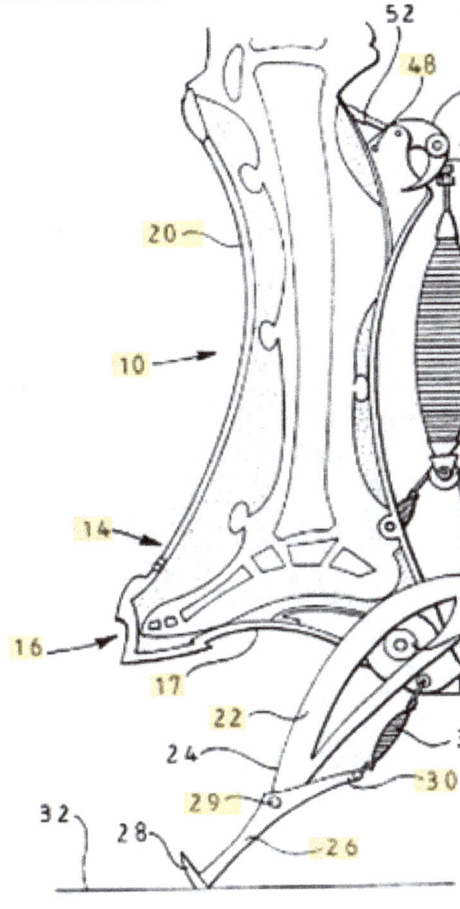

(U.K. Patent Office, 2000)

Sports Glove and the University of Ghent

In 2017, Ashkan Joshghani, a third-year master's student in Veterinary Medicine at Ghent University, designed a sports glove to solve the problem wherein fingers are prone to injury as the joints consistently endure significant force and impact (Figure 5). The majority of hand injuries, depending on this type of injured tissue, may require a long time to heal, e.g. particularly in the case of torn or ruptured ligaments. Ashkan had determined that some sports have a higher frequency of wrist and finger injuries, such as wrestling, as well as combat sports that require a gi or training uniform, such as Judo, JiuJitsu, and Budokai-do. In practicing combat sports, an injury can easily result from a wrong grip. Other sports activities with a high risk of hand injuries may include, for example, basketball and American football. He classified the injuries into two main categories: traumatic (acute) and overuse (chronic).

Figure 5. A device for protecting the proximal inter-phalangeal and distal inter-phalangeal joints in the human finger

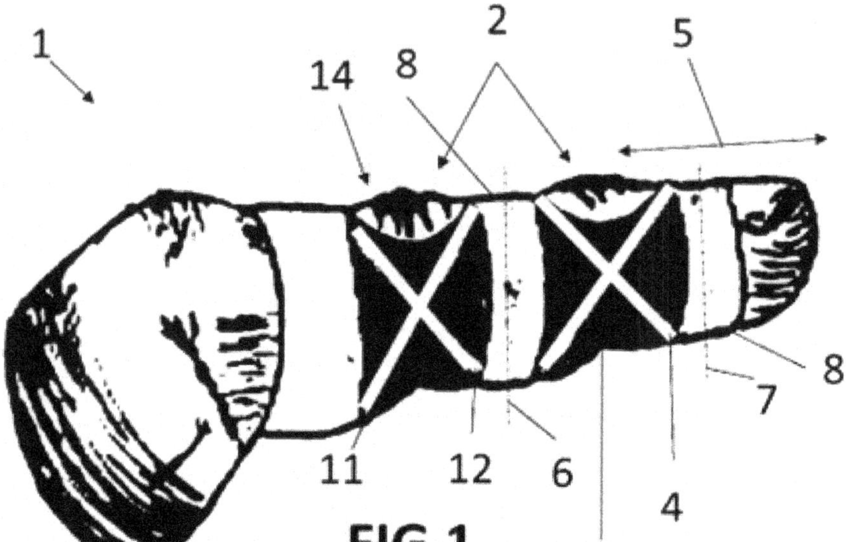

FIG 1

(Joshghani, A. & The University of Ghent, 2018)

Ashkan also had arranged meetings with professors and researchers at Ghent University to present his idea. He also approached the appropriate business developer, Kristof De Mey (2017) and the central Tech Transfer (TT) office for legal and intellectual property (IP) support.

PATENT TROLLS

When universities patent inventions, they should benefit everyone. Patent law is modelled on a utilitarian framework (Merges, Menell & Lemley, 2012). Utilitarianism is an ethical theory that determines the rightness or wrongness of actions based on their consequences, aiming to maximize overall happiness or well-being for the greatest number of people. It's a form of consequentialism, meaning the morality of an action is judged on its outcomes, not on the action itself or its intent (Boschert, 2014). While it does have societal utility, some believe (Cameron & Berger, 2004; Laddie, 2001) that patenting has been allowed to run rampant and become uncontained (Harmon, 2016a). "A patent demands fidelity onto itself in ways that do not always find justification in the originating conception" (Cameron & Berger, 2004, p. 543).

Unfortunately, they sometimes end up in the hands of patent trolls, companies that serve no purpose but to amass patents and demand money from other innovators and inventors. As university research ideas become accessible to a wider public, some of those ideas are falling into the hands of patent trolls who serve no purpose but to amass patents and sue innovators who independently created similar inventions. When universities file patents on scientific research and then sell those patents to trolls, it puts a strain on innovation. *Electronic Frontier Foundation (EFF)* has fought patent trolls in the courts and advocated for laws that bring fairness to the patent system. EFF wants to stop the flow of university inventions into the hands of bad actors. In 2017, EFF, along with our partner organizations, launched "Reclaim Invention", a campaign to encourage universities across the country to commit to adopting patent policies that advance the public good. Reclaim Invention asks universities to focus on bringing their inventions to the public rather than selling or licensing them to patent assertion entities whose sole business model is threatening other innovators with patent lawsuits (Sheehan, 2017).

The origin of the term "patent troll" has been attributed to American inventor George Selden, who is frequently cited as an early example of a patent troll. From 1903 to 1911, Selden, who never built a car, used his patent on the automobile to collect royalties from other automobile companies (Burke, 2023). A series of rulings in American courts on technology innovations in the 1990s made it easier to patent software and computing methods. Those rulings were followed by an increasing number of patents, some of which were criticized as overly broad and thus were easily abused by patent trolls.

A patent troll, then, is an organization or person who buys a patent, rather than invent a new product or create a new idea, with the sole intent of collecting licensing fees or settlements from other individuals or companies. Organizations of any size can be affected, but smaller companies are particularly vulnerable because of the associated costs (Burke, 2023). Today, "patent troll" is a pejorative term for an organization or person, usually in the IT sector, that uses a portfolio of patents to collect licensing fees or settlements on patent infringements from other individuals or companies.

University support for patent trolls has been especially disappointing because many of the innovations that come from academia are funded by public tax dollars (Glaser, 2014). University research is often made possible by grants from the *National*

Science Foundation and other federal programs that support important academic innovation. While the law allows for universities to patent and license federally funded inventions, universities don't always take care in ensuring that their deals align with the interests of the public whose funds they are using.

MOVING FORWARD

Burton Clark (2004) predicted that a large number of globally dispersed universities, perhaps a majority, will not venture very far down the road of self-induced major change. Should a university want to increase academic entrepreneurship in the U.S., it might allocate a greater share of ownership of the IP to its creators in academia (Åstebro et al., 2018), i.e., back to The Professor's Privilege system. Any suggestion of a wholesale changeover from the Bayh-Dole regulation to the Professor's Privilege, however, would impart only a 4.5% increase in academic entrepreneurship relative to the base rate of nonacademic entrepreneurship. "As many as 80 percent of software engineers say the patent system actually hinders innovation" (NAT'L PUB. RADIO, 2011). And entrepreneurial earnings are associated with significantly higher income risk than wages.

Paradoxically, those who make significant advances to benefit humanity and even spend considerable sums in the process are less likely to be rewarded by the grant of a patent in recognition of their endeavors. Unlike copyright, a patent can be a substantial investment for an individual. Costs can include patent filing fees, search fees, examination fees, and any patent attorney fees (Gubby, 2015). Critics have questioned whether patents are beneficial, reporting that weak patent systems can mildly increase innovation with limited side effects. Still, strong patent systems can retard innovation with many negative side effects. The best solution is to abolish patents entirely. (Boldrin & Levine, 2012). And while the 400-year history of patents indicates that they must serve a useful purpose, copyright plays much the same role as the much slower, expensive, and registration-based patent system (Laddie, 2001).

REFERENCES

Adams, M. A. (2000). Reinforcement theory and behaviour analysis. *Behavioral Development Bulletin, 9*(1), 3–6. DOI: 10.1037/h0100529

Ashkan Joshghani and Ghent University (2017). Exoligamentz: Sports Glove.

Åstebro, T., Braguinsky, S., Braunerhjelm, P., & Broström, A. (2018). Academic entrepreneurship: Bayh-Dole versus the 'Professor's Privilege'. *Industrial & Labor Relations Review, 72*(5), 1094–1122. DOI: 10.1177/0019793918819809

Bayh–Dole Act or Patent and Trademark Law Amendments Act (December 12, 1980), https://research.wisc.edu/bayhdole/

Berggren, E. (2017). Researchers are enablers of commercialization at an entrepreneurial university. *Journal of Management Development, 36*(2), 217–232. DOI: 10.1108/JMD-06-2016-0117

Boldrin, M., & Levine, D. K. (2012). The case against patents, *Fed. Reserve Bank of St. Louis*, Working Paper, http://research.stlouisfed.org/wp/2012/2012-035.pdf

Boschert, T. J. (2014). Would utility models improve American Innovation? Evidence From Brazil, Germany, and the United States. *Journal on Telecommunications & High Technology Law*, 12.

Bostyn, S. J. R. (2003). The prodigal son: The relationship between patent law and health care. *Medical Law Review, 11*(1), 67–120. DOI: 10.1093/medlaw/11.1.67 PMID: 14606473

Brimelow, A. (2001). Does intellectual property need a new set of wheels? *European Intellectual Property Review, 23*(1), 44–48.

Buchori, M., & Malik, A. (2004). The evolution of higher education in Indonesia. In Altbach, P. G., & Umakoshi, T. (Eds.), *Asian universities: Historical perspectives and contemporary challenges* (pp. 249–277). The Johns Hopkins University.

Burke, T. (2023). The chilling effect of patent trolls, *Rotman Insights Hub,* University of Toronto, https://www-2.rotman.utoronto.ca/insightshub/finance-investing-accounting/patent-trolls-effect

Burrows, R. (2012). Living with the h-index?: Metric assemblages in the contemporary academy. *The Sociological Review, 60*(2), 355–372. DOI: 10.1111/j.1467-954X.2012.02077.x

Cameron, E., & Berger, J. (2004). *Patents and Public Health: Principle, Politics and Paradox and Public Health Paradox*. Lecture at Edinburgh University.

Canadian Intellectual Property Office. (2004). Patents Main Page: About priority dates, https://www.ic.gc.ca/sc_mrksv/cipo/patents/e-filing/proc5-31.htm

Clark, B. R. (2004). Delineating the character of the entrepreneurial university. *Higher Education Policy*, *17*(4), 355–370. DOI: 10.1057/palgrave.hep.8300062

Cullet, P. (2005). Monsanto v Schmeiser: a landmark decision concerning farmer liability and transgenic contamination, *Journal of Environmental Law, 17*(1), 83-108.

De Mey, K. (2017). Exoligamentz: From student idea to funded R&D, Victoris – Ghent University and Ashkan Joshghani, https://www.victoris.be/exoligamentz-from-student-idea-to-funded-rd/

Etzkowitz, H. (2013). Anatomy of the entrepreneurial university. *Social Sciences Information. Information Sur les Sciences Sociales*, *52*(3), 486–511. DOI: 10.1177/0539018413485832

Fuller, S. (2023). Back to the University's Future: The Second Coming of Humboldt, Springer International Publishing, https://link-springer-com.qe2a-proxy.mun.ca/book/10.1007/978-3-031-36327-6

Garde, T. (2005). Legal certainty, stare decisis and the doctrine of equivalents. *European Intellectual Property Review*, *27*(10), 365–370.

Gellert, C. (1993). Structural and functional differentiation: Remarks on changing paradigms of higher education in Europe. In Gellert, C. (Ed.), *Higher education in Europe*. Jessica Kingsley Publications.

Gill, R. (2009). 'Secrecy, silence, toxic shame and the hidden injuries of the neo-liberal university' in R. Gill and R. Ryan-Flood (eds.). Secrecy and Silence in the Research Process: Feminist Reflections, Routledge, London

Ginsberg, B. (2011). *The Fall of the Faculty: The rise of the all-administrative university and why it matters*. Oxford University Press. DOI: 10.1093/oso/9780199782444.001.0001

Glaser, A. (2014). Students and researchers: Take a stand against patent trolls, *Electronic Frontier Foundation,* https://www.eff.org/deeplinks/2014/05/students-and-researchers-take-stand-against-patent-trolls

Google Patents. (2019). Article of footwear, https://patents.google.com/patent/US6397496B1/en

Gov, U. K. (2011). The benefits of Peer to Patent, Peer to Patent launches in the UK, https://www.gov.uk/government/news/peer-to-patent-launches-in-the-uk

Gruner, R. S. (2012). Why we need a strong patent system and when: Filling the void left by the Bilski case. *Santa Clara High-Technology Law Journal*, *499*, •••. https://digitalcommons.law.scu.edu/chtlj/vol28/iss3/2

Gubby, H. (2015). Universities need to teach business students about patents: A suggested approach. *European Journal of Law and Technology*, *6*(3), 1–22.

Haack, S. (2013). Out of Step: Academic ethics in a preposterous environment, https://papers.ssrn.com/sol3/papers.cfm?abstract_id=2135732

Harmon, E. (October 28, 2016a). Patent trolls undermine open access, *Electronic Frontier Foundation,* https://www.eff.org/deeplinks/2016/10/patent-trolls-undermine-open-access

Harmon, E. (October 28, 2016b). Inside Intellectual Ventures' portfolio: Nearly 500 university patents, *Electronic Frontier Foundation,* https://www.eff.org/deeplinks/2016/10/inside-intellectual-ventures-portfolio-nearly-500-university-patents

Heise Media, U. K. Ltd (July 2009). U.S. Peer-To-Patent Program closed, http://www.h-online.com/open/news/item/Peer-To-Patent-Program-Closed-742445.html

Hvide, H. K., & Jones, B. F. (2018). University Innovation and the Professor's Privilege. *The American Economic Review*, *108*(7), 1860–1898. DOI: 10.1257/aer.20160284

Joshghani, A., & the The University of Ghent. (2018). Protective device for human joint, *WIPO International Application Published Under The Patent Cooperation Treaty*, International Publication Number: WO 2018/154062 Al, https://patentimages.storage.googleapis.com/ad/d4/6a/32a0b025e87d89/WO2018154062A1.pdf

K. Howard Seymour v Coventry University (Patent) [2000] U.K.IntelP (29 June 2000), http://www.bailii.org/U.K./cases/U.K.IntelP/2000/o22300.html

Laddie, H. (2001). National I.P. rights: A moribund anachronism. *European Intellectual Property Review*, *23*(9), 402–408.

Leith, P. (2012). E-participation and e-participants: Solving the patent 'crisis'. *International Review of Law Computers & Technology*, *26*(1), 7–24. DOI: 10.1080/13600869.2012.646783

Little, B. (2001). Reading between the lines for graduate employment. *Quality in Higher Education*, *7*(2), 121–129. DOI: 10.1080/13538320120060015

Machlup, F., & Penrose, E. (1950). The patent controversy in the nineteenth century. *The Journal of Economic History, 10*(1), 1–29. DOI: 10.1017/S0022050700055893

MacLachlan, R., Wodehouse, A., & Vasantha, G. (2018). A new approach for patent use in student design engineering projects, In *Proceedings of the 20th International Conference on Engineering and Product Design Education, E&PDE 2018* (pp. 288-293). Glasgow.

MacQueen, H., Waelde, C., Laurie, G., & Brown, A. (2010). *Contemporary intellectual property: Law and Policy*. Oxford University Press.

Mann, B. L. (2005). Testing the validity of Post and Vote Web-based peer assessment, in David Williams. Scott Howell and Mary Hricko (Eds.). *Online Assessment, Measurement & Evaluation: Emerging Practices* (pp. 132-153). Hershey, PA: Information Science Publishing.

Mann, B. L. (2008). *Routes open to the patent applicant in Europe, Computer Program*. University of Edinburgh, School of Law.

Mann, B. L. (2009). Smoothing some wrinkles in online dispute resolution. *International Journal of Law and Information Technology, 17*(1), 83–112. DOI: 10.1093/ijlit/ean017

Martin, B. R. (2016). What is happening to our universities? *Prometheus, 34*(1), 7–24. DOI: 10.1080/08109028.2016.1222123

Merges, R. P., Menell, P. S., & Lemley, M. A. (2012). *Intellectual Property in the New Technological Age* (6th ed.), 29.

National Public Radio. (July 22, 2011). When Patents Attack, http://www.npr.org/templates/transcript/transcript.php?storyId=138576167

Pettersson, I. (2018). The nomos of the university: Introducing the Professor's Privilege in 1940s Sweden. *Minerva, 56*(3), 381–403. DOI: 10.1007/s11024-018-9348-2 PMID: 30147148

Philpott, K., Dooley, L., O'Reilly, C., & Lupton, G. (2011). The entrepreneurial university: Examining the underlying academic tensions. *Technovation, 31*(4), 161–170. DOI: 10.1016/j.technovation.2010.12.003

Roberts, T. (2006). *Sufficiency of disclosure Council Member*. Chartered Institute of Patent Agents., www.wipo.int/meetings/en/2006/scp_of_ge_06/presentations/scp_of_ge_06_roberts.pdf

Saiz-Santos, M., Araujo-De la Mata, A., & Hoyos-Iruarrizaga, J. (2017). Entrepreneurial University: Educational Innovation and Technology Transfer, In (eds.) Marta Peris-Ortiz, Jaime Alonso GómezJosé, M. Merigó-Lindahl-Carlos, and Rueda-Armengot, (pp. 105-121), *Entrepreneurial Universities Exploring the Academic and Innovative Dimensions of Entrepreneurship in Higher Education,* Springer

Salmi, J. (2001). Tertiary education in the 21st century: Challenges and opportunities. *Higher Education, 13*(2), 105–125.

Sam, C., & van der Sijde, P. (2014). Understanding the concept of the entrepreneurial university from the perspective of higher education models. *Higher Education, 68*(6), 891–908. https://www.jstor.org/stable/43648761. DOI: 10.1007/s10734-014-9750-0

Schleiermacher, F. (1808). Gelegentliche Gedanken iiber Universitaten im deutschen Sinn, in: E.Anrich (1956) Die Idee der deutschen Universitdt (Darmstadt, Hermann Gentner), 219-308.

Sedgwick, W. T. (1882). On variations of reflex-excitability in the frog, induced by changes in temperature in studies from the biological laboratory, ed. pp.385-410. Newell, Martin, Johns Hopkins University, Baltimore.

Sheehan, K. (March 17, 2017). One step closer to reclaiming university innovation from trolls, *Electronic Frontier Foundation*, https://www.eff.org/deeplinks/2017/03/were-one-step-closer-reclaiming-university-innovation-trolls

Sidrata, S., & Frikhab, M. A. (2018). Impact of the manager's qualities and type of university on the development of the entrepreneurial university. *The Journal of High Technology Management Research, 29*(1), 27–34. DOI: 10.1016/j.hitech.2018.04.003

Skinner, B. (1953). *Science and human behaviour*. MacMillan.

Skinner, B. (1968). *The technology of teaching*. Appleton-Crofts.

Skinner, B. F. (1938). *The Behavior of Organisms*. Appleton-Century-Crofts.

Stanford University v. Roche Molecular Systems, Inc., 563 U.S. 776 (2011), https://supreme.justia.com/cases/federal/us/563/776/

Technology Transfer. What you need to know about protecting patent rights (2007). WIPO, www.lbl.gov/tech-transfer/researchers/NEO_Patent_RPC_20071220.pdf

Thorndike, E. L. (1901). Animal intelligence: An experimental study of the associative processes in animals. *Psychological Review Monograph*, (Supplement, 2), 1–109.

Tichý, J. & Rehák, S. (2025). Abolishment of the professor's privilege and its impact on the university patent quality, *Ekonomika a spoločnosť, 26*(1), 142-152.

Tichy, N. M., & Ulrich, D. O. (1984). The leadership challenge: A call for the transformational leader, *MIT Sloan Management Review,* https://sloanreview.mit.edu/article/the-leadership-challenge-a-call-for-the-transformational-leader/

Tilmann, W. (2006). Harmonization of invalidity and scope-of-protection practice of national courts of EPC Member States. *European Intellectual Property Review, 28*(3), 169–173.

USPTO. (2007). Pilot concerning public submission of peer-reviewed prior art, Commissioner for Patents John J. Doll, United States Patent and Trademark Office, https://www.uspto.gov/web/offices/com/sol/og/2007/week26/patsuba.htm

van Dongen, P., Yergos, A., Tijssen, R., & Claassen, E. (2017). The relationships between university IP regimes, scientists' motivations and their engagement with research commercialization in Europe. *European Journal of Law and Technology, 8*(2).

Vinje, T. (1995). Harmonizing intellectual property laws in the European Union: Past, present and future. *European Intellectual Property Review, 17*(8), 361–377.

von Humboldt, W. (1810). On the internal and external organization of the higher scientific institutions in Berlin, *German History in Documents and Images,* https://ghdi.ghi-dc.org/sub_document.cfm?document_id=3642

Walsh, E.J. & DiPietrantonio, H.J. (2011). Getting the most value from patent claims, *Intellectual Property & Technology Law Journal, 23*(7).

Weatherall, K. (2009). It is not just competitors: Acknowledging and accommodating 'interfering busybodies' and their challenges to patent validity. *The Journal of World Intellectual Property, 12*(5, 5z), 500–523. DOI: 10.1111/j.1747-1796.2009.00372.x

Welch, H. L. (2008). The experimental use exception and undergraduate engineering projects. *Marquette Intellectual Property Law Review, 12*(2), 409–436.

Wikipedia. World Trade Organization, https://en.wikipedia.org/wiki/World_Trade_Organization

Wikipedia. Priority date, WIPO, https://en.wikipedia.org/wiki/Priority_right

WIPO. https://www.wipo.int/portal/index.html.en

WIPO Guide to Intellectual Property Worldwide. WIPO, https://www.wipo.int/about-ip/en/ipworldwide/treaties.htm

World Trade Organization. WIPO, http://www.wto.org:80/

Compilation of References

Aakhus, M. (August 2001). Constituting deliberation as "buy-in" through GDSS design and implementation. *SIGGROUP 22,* (2).

ABC7 Eyewitness News. (2025). Teen charged after laptop fire at New Jersey high school believed to be part of TikTok challenge, https://abc7chicago.com/post/chromebook-challenge-teen-charged-laptop-fire-new-jersey-high-school-believed-part-tiktok-trend/16417860/

Abrahamsson, P., Salo, O., Ronkainen, J., & Warsta, J. (2002). Agile Software Development Methods: Review and Analysis, VTT Publications. 478.

Acton, B. & Koum, J. (2009). WhatsApp. Computer program.

Adams, M. A. (2000). Reinforcement theory and behaviour analysis. *Behavioral Development Bulletin*, *9*(1), 3–6. DOI: 10.1037/h0100529

Aftab, P. (2016). Put down the mouse and step away from the computer…and no one will get hurt! Stop Cyberbullying, *WiredSafety.org*, http://www.stopcyberbullying.org/teens/index.html

Agence nationale de la sécurité des systèmes d'information (April 2019). Raising awareness on cyber-security through cartoons, https://www.ssi.gouv.fr/en/actualite/raising-awareness-on-cybersecurity-through-cartoons/

Albors, J. (January 2017). Fast Flux networks: What are they and how do they work? WeLiveSecurity, https://www.welivesecurity.com/2017/01/12/fast-flux-networks-work/

Allemann, A. (2015). The University of Cambridge loses case against Cambridge.com, *Domain Name Wire,* https://domainnamewire.com/2015/10/12/university-of-cambridge-loses-case-against-cambridge-com/

Alphonso, C. (2024). Five more Canadian school boards sue social media giants, alleging harm to students' mental health, *The Globe and Mail Inc.,* https://www.theglobeandmail.com/canada/article-school-boards-sue-byte-dance-meta-snap/

Alwakeel, R. (2015). Cambridge University loses legal fight to get rival cambridge.com website shut down, *Evening Standard,* https://www.standard.co.uk/news/uk/cambridge-university-loses-legal-fight-to-get-rival-cambridgecom-website-shut-down-a3090086.html

AMA. (2025). American Psychiatric Association, https://rarediseases.org/organizations/american-psychiatric-association/

American Arbitration Association. (2006). Arbitration & ADR Services, https://www.adr.org/

American Declaration of Independence (July 4, 1776), Declaration of Independence: A Transcription, U.S. National Archives and Records Administration, https://www.archives.gov/founding-docs/declaration-transcript

American Swiss Foundation. (2016). https://www.americanswiss.org/switzerland-and-the-european-union/

Amnesty International. (2016). Poland: Counter-terrorism bill would give security service unchecked power, https://www.amnesty.org/download/Documents/EUR3742632016ENGLISH.pdf

Anderson, R. v. [2022] EWCA Crim 1465, https://www.casemine.com/judgement/uk/636bf68fb3d7a21f332b937b

Andrews v. Law Society of British Columbia, 1989 CanLII 2 (SCC), [1989] 1 S.C.R. 143, at para. 19.

Anisimov, A. P., Ryzhenkov, A. J., & Kozhemyakin, D. V. (2015). Theory and practice of protection of personal names in the domain space or "renewed" cybersquatting. *Information & Communications Technology Law, 24*(1), 104–117. DOI: 10.1080/13600834.2015.1012393

Anns v Merton London Borough Council [1977] UKHL 4, [1978] AC 728, https://www.bailii.org/uk/cases/UKHL/1977/4.html

APA. (2025). Technology Addictions: Social Media, Online Gaming, and More, *American Psychiatric Association,* https://www.psychiatry.org/Patients-Families/Technology-Addictions-Social-Media-and-more/Expert-Q-A-Technology-Addiction

Aqsacom (2005). Lawful interception for IP networks. White Paper. Washington, DC, Layers 1 and 2, http://www.aqsacomna.com/us/articles/LIIPWhitePaperv21.pdf

Aristotle. (350 B.C.) Rhetoric. Translated by W. Rhys Roberts. In Lee Honeycutt (ed.). Aristotle's Rhetoric: A hyper-textual resource, http://classics.mit.edu/Aristotle/rhetoric.html

Arkansas State Legislature. (2023). Social Media Safety Act 689, https://arkleg.state.ar.us/Bills/Detail?id=sb396&ddBienniumSession=2023%2F2023R

Arntfield, M. (2015). Toward a Cybervictimology: Cyberbullying, routine activities theory, and the anti-sociality of social media, Canadian Journal of Communication 40(3)

Arzt, N., & Abulhosn, R. (7 July 2023). TikTok addiction: Causes, signs, & how to stop, choosing therapy, https://www.choosingtherapy.com/tiktok-addiction/

Ashdown v Telegraph Group Ltd [2002], http://www.bailii.org/ew/cases/EWCA/Civ/2001/1142.html

Ashkan Joshghani and Ghent University (2017). Exoligamentz: Sports Glove.

Associated Press. (2024). Zuckerberg apologizes to families at heated U.S. Senate hearing on social media child safety, CBC News, https://www.cbc.ca/news/world/social-media-senate-hearing-child-safety-exploitation-1.7100952

Associated Press. (December 5, 2002). Teacher Praised for Heroism at Columbine, *L.A. Times Archives,* https://www.latimes.com/archives/la-xpm-2002-dec-05-me-miller5-story.html

Association of University Teachers (AUC). (2002). Online distance education: An AUT statement, letter to its membership, http://www.ucu.org.uk/media/html/9/b/ucu_autla7134_elearning_1.html

Åstebro, T., Braguinsky, S., Braunerhjelm, P., & Broström, A. (2018). Academic entrepreneurship: Bayh-Dole versus the 'Professor's Privilege'. *Industrial & Labor Relations Review*, *72*(5), 1094–1122. DOI: 10.1177/0019793918819809

Ayer, L., Boudreaux, B., Paige, J., Holmes, P., Blagg, T., & Mendon-Plasek, C. (December 5, 2023). Artificial intelligence–based student activity monitoring for suicide risk considerations for K–12 schools, caregivers, government, and technology developers, *RAND Research Report,* https://www.rand.org/pubs/research_reports/RRA2910-1.html

Babich, N. (2018). How Virtual Reality Will Change How We Learn and How We Teach, *Adobe Blog,* https://theblog.adobe.com/virtual-reality-will-change-learn-teach/

Baddeley, A. (1986). *Working memory. Clarendon Press.* University Press.

Baddeley, A. (2013). On applying cognitive psychology. *British Journal of Psychology, 104*(4), 443–456. DOI: 10.1111/bjop.12049 PMID: 24094277

Bailey, , J. (2014). Time to unpack the juggernaut? Reflections on the Canadian federal parliamentary debates on cyberbullying. *SSRN, 37*(2), 662–707. doi:10.2139/ssrn.2448480DOI: 10.2139/ssrn.2448480

Baker, E.-R. (July 19, 2017). People are dying and injuring themselves for the perfect Insta snap, *Vice Magazine,* https://www.vice.com/en/article/people-are-literally-dying-and-injuring-themselves-for-the-perfect-insta-snap/

Baker, K. (2023). The Zeus Trojan Malware: Definition and Prevention, CrowdStrike, https://www.crowdstrike.com/en-us/cybersecurity-101/malware/zeus-malware/

Barrett, B. (2019). The US Air Force will let hackers try to hijack an orbiting satellite: At the Defcon Hacking Conference next year, the US Air Force will bring a satellite for fun and glory, *Wired, 09/17/2019,* https://www.wired.com/story/air-force-defcon-satellite-hacking/

Barron, A., & Kysilka, M. (1993). The effectiveness of digital audio in computer-based training. *Journal of Research on Computing in Education, 25*(3), 277–289. DOI: 10.1080/08886504.1993.10782051

Bates, L. (June 2011). The law as it affects older adults, The Law Commission of Ontario, www.lco-cdo.org

Bayh–Dole Act or Patent and Trademark Law Amendments Act (December 12, 1980), https://research.wisc.edu/bayhdole/

BBC News. (2004). Boy swaps MikeRoweSoft for Xbox, http://news.bbc.co.uk/2/hi/technology/3429485.stm

BBC News. (2019). French 'cyber cops' dismantle pirate computer network, https://www.bbc.com/news/world-europe-49494927

BC Aware Campaign. (2021). Reboot Communications, https://www.rebootcommunications.com/bcaware/

BC Teachers' Federation. (2023). Kids matter, Teachers care, https://www.bctf.ca/

Bedi, R. v. (2016) BCSC 1930, https://www.canlii.org/en/bc/bcsc/doc/2016/2016bcsc1930/2016bcsc1930.html?resultId=0c46ec9329ed414c86a04f4f3ba3b0a1&searchId=2025-07-24T01:30:37:999/10cdd435aa6d41bdbe7277d9b6a17b15

Beek, C. (2017). Emotet Downloader Trojan Returns in Force, McAfee, https://securingtomorrow.mcafee.com/other-blogs/mcafee-labs/emotet-downloader-trojan-returns-in-force/

Beever, S. (September 30, 2022). Social media content contributed to the tragic teenager Molly Russell, HullLive, https://www.hulldailymail.co.uk/news/uk-world-news/social-media-content-contributed-tragic-7648709

Bennett, S., & Thorne, C. (1998). Domain names - Internet warehousing: Has protecting well-known names on the Internet gone too far? Case Comment. *European Intellectual Property Review*, *20*(12), 468–470.

Berggren, E. (2017). Researchers are enablers of commercialization at an entrepreneurial university. *Journal of Management Development*, *36*(2), 217–232. DOI: 10.1108/JMD-06-2016-0117

Bergstrom, I. (2008). Facebook can ruin your life. And so can MySpace, Bebo... *The Independent,* https://www.independent.co.uk/life-style/gadgets-and-tech/news/facebook-can-ruin-your-life-and-socan-myspace-bebo-780521.html

Berne Convention for the Protection of Literary and Artistic Works (1971). https://global.oup.com/booksites/content/9780198259466/15550001

Bishop, M. J. (2013). Reconceptualizing instructional message design: Toward the development of a new guiding framework. In Hokanson, B., & Gibbons, A. (Eds.), *Design In Educational Technology: Design Thinking, Design Process, and the Design Studio*. Springer.

Bishop, M. J. (2014). Reconceptualizing instructional message design: Toward the development of a new guiding framework. In Hokanson, B., & Gibbons, A. (Eds.), *Design in Educational Technology, Educational Communications and Technology: Issues and Innovations* (Vol. 1)., DOI: 10.1007/978-3-319-00927-8_9

Bishop, M. J., Amankwatia, T. B., & Cates, W. M. (2008). Sound's use in instructional software to enhance learning: A theory-to-practice content analysis. *Educational Technology Research and Development*, *56*(4), 467–486. DOI: 10.1007/s11423-006-9032-3

Black Duck. (2025). Penetration testing, *Black Duck Software, Inc.,* https://www.blackduck.com/glossary/what-is-penetration-testing.html#:~:text=Definition,of%20weaknesses%20in%20a%20system

Blefari, F., Furfaro, A., Ianni, G. & Viscomi, A. (2024). Combining anti-typosquatting techniques, Conference paper, Web Engineering, https://link-springer-com.qe2a-proxy.mun.ca/content/pdf/10.1007/978-3-031-62362-2_17

Blodgett, S. L., Green, L., & O'Connor, B. (2016). Demographic dialectal variation in social media: A case study of African-American English, *Proceedings of the 2016 Conference on Empirical Methods in Natural Language Processing,* pgs. 1119–1130, Austin, Texas, November 1-5. DOI: 10.18653/v1/D16-1120

Bluehost Inc. (2019). Special Offer for Students & Faculty, https://www.bluehost.com/hosting/education

Blumenthal, R. (September 13, 2024). New Polling Shows Massive Public Support for the Kids Online Safety Act, *U.S. Senator,* https://www.blumenthal.senate.gov/newsroom/press/release/icymi_new-polling-shows-massive-public-support-for-the-kids-online-safety-act Richard Blumenthal

Boesveld, S. (2012). RCMP launch probe into Facebook post after man brags of tormenting teens who committed suicide, *National Post,* https://nationalpost.com/news/canada/n-s-rcmp-launch-probe-into-facebook-post-after-man-brags-of-tormenting-teens-who-committed-suicide

Boldrin, M., & Levine, D. K. (2012). The case against patents, *Fed. Reserve Bank of St. Louis*, Working Paper, http://research.stlouisfed.org/wp/2012/2012-035.pdf

Bonesteel, A., & Greer, E. (2024). This Bill purports to protect kids from big tech. For LGBTQ+ Youth, It's a Grave Danger, *Them,* https://www.them.us/story/kids-online-safety-act-kosa-youth-lgbtq-content?utm_source=chatgpt.com

Boschert, T. J. (2014). Would utility models improve American Innovation? Evidence From Brazil, Germany, and the United States. *Journal on Telecommunications & High Technology Law*, 12.

Bostyn, S. J. R. (2003). The prodigal son: The relationship between patent law and health care. *Medical Law Review*, *11*(1), 67–120. DOI: 10.1093/medlaw/11.1.67 PMID: 14606473

Bowers, C. (1945). *The Young Jefferson 1743–1789*. Houghton Mifflin Company.

Boyd, D. (2010). Risk Reduction Strategies on Facebook Apophenia: making connections where none previously existed, online, https://www.zephoria.org/thoughts/archives/2010/11/08/risk-reduction-strategies-on-facebook.html

Boyd, D. (September 2006). Facebook's privacy trainwreck: Exposure, invasion, and drama, *Apophenia Blog,* https://www.danah.org/papers/FacebookAndPrivacy.html

Bray, H. (March 2006). China creates own Net domains: Bypass of US control stirs fear of censorship, Boston Globe, https://www.boston.com/news/world/asia/articles/2006/03/01/china_creates_own_net_domains/

Brimelow, A. (2001). Does intellectual property need a new set of wheels? *European Intellectual Property Review*, *23*(1), 44–48.

British Columbia Workers Compensation Act, RSBC (1996) c 492, https://www.canlii.org/en/bc/laws/stat/rsbc-1996-c-492/latest/rsbc-1996-c-492.html

British Horseracing Board Ltd & Ors v William Hill Organization Ltd [2001] EWCA Civ 1268, http://www.bailii.org/ew/cases/EWCA/Civ/2001/1268.html

British Telecommunications Plc & Ors v One In A Million Ltd & Ors [1998] EWCA Civ 1272 (23 July 1998), http://www.bailii.org/ew/cases/EWCA/Civ/1998/1272.html

Brodsky, G., Cox, R., Day, S., & Stephenson, K. (2006). Gosselin v. Quebec (Attorney General). *Canadian Journal of Women and the Law*, *18*, 189. http://www.thecourt.ca/the-womens-court-of-canada-gosselin-v-quebec-attorney-general-2006-1-w-c-r-193/

Brown, R. (2019). Security Breach Update, https://tct.com.au/security-breach-update-15-march-2019/

Buchori, M., & Malik, A. (2004). The evolution of higher education in Indonesia. In Altbach, P. G., & Umakoshi, T. (Eds.), *Asian universities: Historical perspectives and contemporary challenges* (pp. 249–277). The Johns Hopkins University.

Burack, C. (2018). German federal police use Trojan virus to evade phone encryption, *Deutsche Welle,* https://www.dw.com/en/german-federal-police-use-trojan-virus-to-evade-phone-encryption/a-42328466

Burke, T. (2023). The chilling effect of patent trolls, *Rotman Insights Hub,* University of Toronto, https://www-2.rotman.utoronto.ca/insightshub/finance-investing-accounting/patent-trolls-effect

Burrows, R. (2012). Living with the h-index?: Metric assemblages in the contemporary academy. *The Sociological Review*, *60*(2), 355–372. DOI: 10.1111/j.1467-954X.2012.02077.x

Butler, J. (2004). *Precarious life: The power of mourning and violence.* Verso.

Buxton, W. (1987). The audio channel. In Baecker, R. M., & Buxton, W. A. S. (Eds.), *Readings in Human-Computer Interaction: A Multidisciplinary Approach* (pp. 393–399). Morgan Kaufman Associates.

Cameron, E., & Berger, J. (2004). *Patents and Public Health: Principle, Politics and Paradox and Public Health Paradox.* Lecture at Edinburgh University.

Camp, J. S., & DeBloois, P. B. (2007). [IT issues *Educause Review,* May/June.]. *Top (Madrid)*, 10.

Canada Pension Plan, R.S.C. 1985, c. C-8, https://laws-lois.justice.gc.ca/eng/acts/c-8/index.html

Canadian Charter of Rights and Freedoms. (1982). Part I of the Constitution Act, c 11, Justice Laws Website, https://laws-lois.justice.gc.ca/eng/const/page-15.html

Canadian Intellectual Property Office. (2004). Patents Main Page: About priority dates, https://www.ic.gc.ca/sc_mrksv/cipo/patents/e-filing/proc5-31.htm

Capoot, A., & Vanian, J. (2025). Meta scraps fact-checking, brings back political content in latest Trump-friendly move, *CNBC,* https://www.cnbc.com/2025/01/07/meta-eliminates-third-party-fact-checking-moves-to-community-notes.html

Card v. Ontario (Ministry of Training, Colleges and Universities), 2017 HRTO 35 (CanLII), https://canlii.ca/t/gwwtb

Carnevale, D. (2007). Supreme Court's patent ruling could spell trouble for Blackboard and others [May.]. *The Chronicle of Higher Education*, *53*, 37.

Carrier, M.A. & Lastowka, G. (2007). Against Cyberproperty, Berkeley Technology Law Journal, 22, 1483

Casey, E. (2004). *Digital evidence and computer crime: Forensic science, computers and the Internet* (2nd ed.). Academic Press.

Cassidy, T. (October 2014), "Regina man's identity used in online romance scamming," *CBC News,* [Podcast], https://www.cbc.ca/news/canada/saskatchewan/regina-man-s-identity-used-in-online-romance-scamming-1.2800046

CBC News. (2007). https://www.cbc.ca/news

CBC News. (28 March 2011), Bullied teen's death sparks campaign, https://www.cbc.ca/news/canada/nova-scotia/bullied-teen-s-death-sparks-campaign-1.996424

CBC News. (Dec 04, 2018) RCMP release name of youth charged in connection with threats to Selkirk-area schools, https://www.cbc.ca/news/canada/manitoba/selkirk-school-threats-students-return-1.4931490

CBC News. (Jan 23, 2019). Children, ages 12 and 13, charged for allegedly threatening Winnipeg schools: Incredibly complex investigation had police working with overseas social media company to identify anonymous users, https://www.cbc.ca/news/canada/manitoba/winnipeg-school-threats-arrests-1.4989564

CBC News. (May 03, 2002) Sharpe sentenced in B.C. child pornography case, https://www.cbc.ca/news/canada/sharpe-sentenced-in-b-c-child-pornography-case-1.315991

CBC. (2023). Cybersecurity issue affecting Grenfell Campus of Memorial University, CBC, https://www.cbc.ca/news/canada/newfoundland-labrador/grenfell-cybersecurity-issue-12-31-1.7071898

CBS News Staff. (November 27, 2001). Most Columbine Lawsuits Dismissed, *CBSNews.com,* https://www.cbsnews.com/news/most-columbine-lawsuits-dismissed/

CCH Canadian Ltd. v. Law Society of Upper Canada (2004). SCC 13, www.canlii.org/ca/cas/scc/2004/2004scc13.html

CERN. (2025). A short history of the Web, *CERN Accelerating Science,* https://home.cern/science/computing/birth-web/short-history-web#:~:text=Where%20the%20Web%20was%20born,and%20institutes%20around%20the%20world

Cerulus, L. (February 2019). Europe hopes to fend off election hackers with 'cyber sanctions, POLITICO, https://www.politico.eu/article/europe-cyber-sanctions-hoped-to-fend-off-election-hackers/

Chandler, P., & Sweller, J. (1991). Cognitive load theory and the format of instruction. *Cognition and Instruction*, *8*(4), 293–332. DOI: 10.1207/s1532690xci0804_2

Charter of Fundamental Rights of the European Union (2000). Official Journal of the European Communities, C 364/01, Article 8, https://www.europarl.europa.eu/charter/pdf/text_en.pdf

Charter of Fundamental Rights of the European Union. (2016), https://www.refworld.org/legal/agreements/eu/2007/en/13901

Chatterjee, A. (2019). Five phases of hacking, *GeeksforGeeks, A Computer Science Portal for Geeks,* https://www.geeksforgeeks.org/5-phases-hacking/

Chen, S., Hurley, C. & Karim, J. (2005). YouTube, a computer program.

CIPO. (2025). Canadian Intellectual Property Office, https://ised-isde.canada.ca/site/canadian-intellectual-property-office/en

Civici e Innovatori. (2017). Rules governing government Trojan use with respect to individual rights, https://issuu.com/civicieinnovatori/docs/sintesi_pdl_captatori_en

Claburn, T. (2023). *Secret Service, ICE break the law over and over with fake cell tower spying*. Security.

Clark, B. R. (2004). Delineating the character of the entrepreneurial university. *Higher Education Policy, 17*(4), 355–370. DOI: 10.1057/palgrave.hep.8300062

CobbleStore Vintage. (2024). Purdue University t-shirt, https://cobblestore.com/?srsltid=AfmBOorY_5QAw8Wgj-qFREpCQ4528rLFleqrJy2RNQ8BrBBIwn2DUQ2v

Cole, D. (June 23, 2021). The Supreme Court teaches students an important lesson on free speech, *Washington Post,* https://www.washingtonpost.com/opinions/2021/06/23/cheer-case-supreme-court-speech/

College of Policing. (November 2017). Coventry, UK, video, https://www.college.police.uk/About/Pages/Conference_-_Everyday-innovation.aspx

Congress.gov. (2000). Children's Online Privacy Protection Act (COPPA), https://www.govinfo.gov/content/pkg/PLAW-105publ277/pdf/PLAW-105publ277.pdf

Congress.gov. (2023). Children and Teens' Online Privacy Protection Act (CTOPPA), https://www.congress.gov/bill/118th-congress/senate-bill/1418/text

Constantin, L. (2012). Citadel banking malware is evolving and spreading rapidly, Researchers Warn, *PCWorld,* https://www.pcworld.com/article/474333/citadel_banking_malware_is_evolving_and_spreading_rapidly_researchers_warn.html

Constitution of the United States. (March 4, 1789). First Amendment, https://constitution.congress.gov/constitution/amendment-1/

Cooper, A. (December 15, 2024). Schools face a new threat: "nudify" sites that use AI to create realistic, revealing images of classmates, 60 Minutes, *CBS News,* https://www.cbsnews.com/news/schools-face-new-threat-nudify-sites-use-ai-create-realistic-revealing-images-60-minutes-transcript/

Copyright Act (R.S.C., 1985, c. C-42) Justice Laws Website, https://laws-lois.justice.gc.ca/eng/acts/C-42/Index.html

Copyright Modernization Act (2012). Justice Laws Website, https://laws-lois.justice.gc.ca/eng/annualstatutes/2012_20/fulltext.html

Correll, S., Benard, S., & Paik, I. (2007). Getting a job: Is there a motherhood penalty? *American Journal of Sociology, 112*(5), 1297–1339. DOI: 10.1086/511799

Cortés, P. (2008, February). Effective disputes. *The New Law Journal, 158,* 7306.

Council of Europe (1950). *Convention for the Protection of Human Rights and Fundamental Freedoms,* Council of Europe Treaty Series 005,

Council of Europe. (2016). Poland: On the Act of 15 January 2016 amending the Police Act and certain other Acts, Opinion No. 839/ 2016, Adopted by the Venice Commission at its 107th Plenary Session, Strasbourg, https://www.venice.coe.int/webforms/documents/default.aspx?pdffile=CDL-REF(2016)036-e

Couros, A. (October 2015). Romance Scams Continue, and I Need Your Help, [Blog], https://educationaltechnology.ca/couros/2627

Coyle, S. (2014). Social media and suicide prevention, *Social Work Today, 14,* 1, https://www.socialworktoday.com/archive/012014p8.shtml

Criminal Code *(R.S.C., 1985, c. C-46),* https://laws-lois.justice.gc.ca/PDF/C-46.pdf

Cross, G. (2025). What is the Chromebook Challenge? The trend that has students destroying school laptops, *USA Today,* https://www.usatoday.com/story/tech/2025/05/20/chromebook-challenge-tiktok-trend/83730941007/

Crowe, K. C. (2012). Troy will turn off Shotspotter, *Times Union,* https://perma.cc/Y4MSSNSP

Crown Prosecution Service. (2024). Cybercrime definitions: Doxing, https://www.cps.gov.uk/legal-guidance/cybercrime-prosecution-guidance

Cullen, D. (2009). Columbine. Hachette Book Group, https://en.wikipedia.org/wiki/

Cullet, P. (2005). Monsanto v Schmeiser: a landmark decision concerning farmer liability and transgenic contamination, *Journal of Environmental Law, 17*(1), 83-108.

Culture Magazine. (2025). Students Intentionally Setting Laptops on Fire for TikTok Sparks Safety Concerns in Canadian Classrooms, *Asian-English Culture Magazine*, https://culturemagazin.com/students-intentionally-setting-laptops-on-fire-for-tiktok-sparks-safety-concerns-in-canadian-classrooms/

Currie, , R. J. (2004). Of neighbours and netizens, or, duty of care in the tech age: A comment on Cooper v. Hobart. *Canadian Journal of Learning and Technology, 3*(2). https://digitalcommons.schulichlaw.dal.ca/cjlt/vol3/iss2/2/

Cybersecurity Guide. (2024). Cybersecurity degree programs, https://cybersecurityguide.org/programs/

Cybersettle (2025). https://www.cybersettle.com/

Cybertip.ca. (2025). Canadian Centre for Child Protection Inc., https://cybertip.ca/en/

Das, M. (July 28, 2024). As 'killfie' threat mounts, no-selfie zones planned in 2016 a non-starter, *The Times of India,* https://timesofindia.indiatimes.com/city/mumbai/as-killfie-threat-mounts-no-selfie-zones-planned-in-2016-a-non-starter/articleshow/112074139.cms

De Mey, K. (2017). Exoligamentz: From student idea to funded R&D, Victoris – Ghent University and Ashkan Joshghani, https://www.victoris.be/exoligamentz-from-student-idea-to-funded-rd/

DeBrosse, J. (March 2008). UD Law Prof using the innovative website to teach mediation skills. Cox Ohio Publishing, Dayton, Ohio, USA.

DEF CON Training. (2025). DEF CON Training Las Vegas, https://defcon.org/

Delcker, J., Honal, A., & Ifenthaler, D. (2018). Mobile device usage in higher education, *International Conference on Cognition and Exploratory Learning in the Digital Age,* https://files.eric.ed.gov/fulltext/ED571401.pdf

Dempsey, C. (2025). Connecticut students arrested for TikTok 'Chromebook Challenge' fire, *Journal Inquirer,* https://www.firerescue1.com/arson-investigation/conn-students-arrested-for-tiktok-chromebook-challenge-fire

Department for Education. (2024) Keeping children safe in education 2024: statutory guidance for schools and colleges, London, U.K: Department for Education, https://assets.publishing.service.gov.uk/media/66d7301b9084b18b95709f75/Keeping_children_safe_in_education_2024.pdf

Department of Environment, Labour and Justice (2025). Taking Stock of Cyberbullying: A Scan of the PEI Context, https://www.princeedwardisland.ca/sites/default/files/publications/taking_stock_of_cyberbullying.pdf

Department of Justice Canada (2017). Cyberbullying and the non-consensual distribution of intimate images, https://www.justice.gc.ca/eng/rp-pr/other-autre/cndii-cdncii/p4.html

Designs, P. (2019). Harvard Law Just Kidding Full-Time Mom Ladies' Scoopneck T-Shirt, https://www.prylake.com/products/harvard-law-just-kidding-full-time-mom-ladies-scoopneck-t-shirt

Desire2Learn (2020). Brightspace, https://www.d2l.com/

Deveci, H. (2003). Domain names: Has trade-mark law strayed from its path? *International Journal of Law and Information Technology, 11*(3), 203–225. DOI: 10.1093/ijlit/11.3.203

Dhaliwal, R. v. 2019 ONCA 398 (CanLII), https://www.canlii.org/en/on/onca/doc/2019/2019onca398/2019onca398.html?resultId=15530ec8d6d0428a98184741dde73502&searchId=2025-07-24T01:32:49:499/e990f65ad42849be8e553e09fa1863aa

Diamonique Corp v. Maison Tropicale S.A., WIPO Arbitration and Mediation Center, https://www.wipo.int/amc/en/domains/decisions/html/2007/d2007-1093.html

Dieguez, J. (2008). Does the proposed European procedure enhance the resolution of small claims? *Civil Justice Quarterly*, *27*(1), 83–97.

Directive (EU) 2016/680 of the European Parliament and of the Council of 27 April 2016, EUR-LEX, https://eur-lex.europa.eu/eli/dir/2016/680/oj/eng

Doctorow, C. (February 17, 2010). “School used student laptop webcams to spy on them at school and home.” *Boing Boing,* https://boingboing.net/2010/02/17/school-used-student.html

Dodge, , ASpencer, , D. C. (2018). Online sexual violence, child pornography or something else entirely? Police responses to non-consensual intimate image sharing among youth. *Social & Legal Studies*, *27*(5), 636–657. doi:10.1177/0964663917724866DOI: 10.1177/0964663917724866

Dokur, M., Petekkaya, E., & Karadağ, M. (2018). Media-based clinical research on selfie-related injuries and deaths. *Ulusal Travma ve Acil Cerrahi Dergisi = Turkish Journal of Trauma & Emergency Surgery : TJTES*, *24*(2), 129–135. DOI: 10.5505/tjtes.2017.83103 PMID: 29569684

Dolan, D. (2019). Using VR for Experiential Learning, *Veative Labs,* https://www.veative.com/blog/using-vr-experiential-learning

DomainTools Blog. (October 2007). ICANN’s Security and Stability Advisory Committee, http://blog.domaintools.com/2007/10/domain-name-front-running/

Donoghue v Stevenson. (1932) A.C. 562. Legal Case Summary, *LawTeacher,* https://www.lawteacher.net/cases/donoghue-v-stevenson.php

Drew, D. (September 2017). The 'hack back' is not a defence strategy, IDG Contributor Network, https://www.csoonline.com/article/3228118/the-hack-back-is-not-a-defense-strategy.html

Drori, G. S., Delmestro, G., & Oberg, A. (2016). The iconography of universities as institutional narratives. *Higher Education*, *71*(2), 163–180. DOI: 10.1007/s10734-015-9894-6

DSM-5 (2013). Diagnostic and Statistical Manual of Mental Disorders, https://psychiatryonline.org/doi/book/10.1176/appi.books.9780890425787

Dyzenhaus, D., Moreau, S. R., & Ripstein, A. (2007). *Law and Morality: Readings in Legal Philosophy* (3rd ed.). University of Toronto Press.

Easyspace Ltd. (2019). https://www.easyspace.com/index.html

EC-Council iClass (2019). EC-Council Academic Credits Program: Turn Certification into Education with Academic Credits, https://iclass.eccouncil.org/ec-council-academic-credits-program/

EC-Council. (2019). Certified Ethical Hacker, https://www.eccouncil.org/programs/certified-ethical-hacker-ceh/

ECODIR. (2001). Electronic Consumer Dispute Resolution (ECODIR), https://www.arbitration-adr.org/resources/?p=serviceproviders&a=show&id=40

Edmodo (2020). Edmodo global education network, https://new.edmodo.com/?go2url=%2Fhome'

éducaloi (2025). la loi expliquée en un seul endroit, https://educaloi.qc.ca/

Éducaloi. (2019). Cyberbullying, https://www.educaloi.qc.ca/en/youth/capsules/cyberbullying

Edwards, B. (2011). 'I wish I could be happy,' *Ottawa East News,* https://www.insideottawavalley.com/news-story/3800605--i-wish-i-could-be-happy-/

Edwards, L. (2005). Article 12-15 ECD: ISP liability - The problem of Intermediate Service Provider liability. In Edwards, L. (Ed.), *The New Legal Framework for E-Commerce in Europe* (pp. 93–136). Hart Publishing.

Eerste Kamer der Staten Generaal. (2016). Artikel 126nba, Gewijzigd Voorstel van Wet – *Computercriminaliteit III,* https://www.eerstekamer.nl/wetsvoorstel/34372_computercriminaliteit_iii

EFF. (2025). Tools to Address Known Exploitation by Immobilizing Technological Deepfakes on Websites and Networks, *Electronic Frontier Foundation,* https://www.eff.org/document/take-it-down-act-one-pager

Eldridge, A. (2019). The ZeroAccess Rootkit Trojan, Nerds On Call, https://callnerds.com/the-zeroaccess-rootkit-trojan/

Elgan, M. (2019). People are falling off buildings in search of the perfect Instagram shot, *Fast Company,* https://www.fastcompany.com/90287323/people-are-falling-off-buildings-in-search-of-the-perfect-instagram-shot

Eros LLC v. Leatherwood, https://virtuallyblind.com/files/eros_default.pdf

Etzkowitz, H. (2013). Anatomy of the entrepreneurial university. *Social Sciences Information. Information Sur les Sciences Sociales, 52*(3), 486–511. DOI: 10.1177/0539018413485832

EU Directives (2003). Ensuring environmental information is systematically available and distributed to the public. European Parliament and of the Council, EU Monitor, https://www.eumonitor.eu/9353000/1/j4nvk6yhcbpeywk_j9vvik7m1c3gyxp/vitgbgid9hzk

EUIPO. (2025). European Union Intellectual Property Office, Trademarks, https://www.euipo.europa.eu/en/trade-marks/before-applying/availability

EURid. (March 2008). *The European Registry of Domain Names,* http://www.eurid.eu/

EuroDNS. (2019). Great education domain name ideas for eLearning websites: https://www.eurodns.com/

Eurojust (April 2017). Operation Avalanche: A closer look, The Hague, Netherlands, https://www.eurojust.europa.eu/doclibrary/Eurojust-framework/Casework/Operation%20Avalanche%20-%20A%20closer%20look%20(April%202017)/2017-04_Avalanche-Case_EN.pdf

European Commission. (2015). Public consultation on the regulatory environment for platforms, online intermediaries, data and cloud computing and the collaborative economy, https://www.politico.eu/wp-content/uploads/2015/09/Platforms-consultation.pdf

European Convention for the Protection of Human Rights and Fundamental Freedoms, Article 8, https://www.echr.coe.int/documents/d/echr/convention_ENG

European Court of Human Rights. (1950). Convention for the Protection of Human Rights and Fundamental Freedoms, https://www.echr.coe.int/european-convention-on-human-rights

European Telecommunications Standards Institute. (2015). Critical Security Controls for Effective Cyber Defence, Technical Report, https://www.etsi.org/deliver/etsi_tr/103300_103399/103305/01.01.01_60/tr_103305v010101p.pdf

European Union Agency for Cybersecurity. (2019). National Cybersecurity Strategy 2015 – 2020, Czech Republic, https://www.enisa.europa.eu/about-enisa/structure-organization/national-liaison-office/news-from-the-member-states/czech-republic-national-cyber-security-strategy-2015-2020

Europol (December 2016). 'Avalanche' network dismantled in international cyber operation, https://www.europol.europa.eu/newsroom/news/%E2%80%98avalanche%E2%80%99-network-dismantled-in-international-cyber-operation

EvalCommunity. (2024a). Understanding Effectiveness Evaluation: Definition, Benefits, and Best Practices, https://www.evalcommunity.com/career-center/effectiveness-evaluation/

Eysenck, M. W., & Keane, M. T. (2020). *Cognitive Psychology: A Student's Handbook* (8th ed.). Psychology Press. DOI: 10.4324/9781351058513

Farah, C. (2005). Critical analysis of online dispute resolution: The optimist, the realist and the bewildered. *Computer and Telecommunications Law Review*, *11*(4), 123–128.

Faruqi & Faruqi, LLP (2022). Faruqi & Faruqi, LLP, New York office.

FATF. (2018). Recommendations, https://www.fatf-gafi.org/media/fatf/documents/recommendations/pdfs/FATF%20Recommendations%202012.pdf

Federal Bureau of Investigation. (2020). $3M Bounty for ZeuS Trojan Author, U.S. Department of Justice, https://www.fbi.gov/wanted/cyber/evgeniy-mikhailovich-bogachev

Federal Bureau of Investigation. (2025). Most Wanted, Evgeniy Mikhaylovich Bogachev, https://www.fbi.gov/wanted/cyber/evgeniy-mikhailovich-bogachev

Feinstein, R., & Shack, J. (2024). Making ODR more accessible to self-represented parties: Focus group perspectives, Resolution Systems Institute, https://s3.amazonaws.com/aboutrsi/591e30fc6e181e166ffd2eb0/Final-Report-OPEN-16April2024-R.pdf

Felner, L. (July 30, 2024). Senate passes the Kids Online Safety Act, *The Verge,* https://www.theverge.com/2024/7/30/24205718/senate-passes-kids-online-safety-act-kosa-content-moderation

Figueiredo, J. L. (2016). Trademark Parody: a trademark infringement? Kluwer Trademark Blog, https://trademarkblog.kluweriplaw.com/2016/07/13/trade-mark-parody-a-trade-mark-infringement/

Firewalls.com. (2025). https://www.firewalls.com/blog/security-terms/backdoor-trojan/?srsltid=AfmBOoqgA-oDEMZAjzTSdwTOf-wTGxleAyJ3tVmSEUcFlEbttGoQKoWj

Fisher, W. (2019). Overview of Trademark Law, Berkman Klein Center for Internet & Society at Harvard University, https://cyber.harvard.edu/metaschool/fisher/domain/tm.htm

Flanagan, R. (2019). Police in U.K. issue warning about 'Momo Challenge' urging kids to self-harm, *CTV News,* https://www.ctvnews.ca/sci-tech/police-in-u-k-issue-warning-about-momo-challenge-urging-kids-to-self-harm-1.4313148

Fodor, J. (1980). Methodological Solipsism Considered as a Research Strategy in Cognitive Science. *Behavioral and Brain Sciences, 3*(1), 63–73. DOI: 10.1017/S0140525X00001771

FOI.wiki.com (2018). List of .ac.UK domain names,

Foody, M., & Samara, M. (2018). Considering mindfulness techniques in school-based anti-bullying programmes. *Journal of New Approaches in Educational Research, 7*(1), 3–9. DOI: 10.7821/naer.2018.1.253

Fortinet (2025). Swatting: The danger of false emergency calls, https://www.fortinet.com/resources/cyberglossary/swatting

Fortinet (2025). Trojan Horse Virus, *Fortinet, Inc.,* https://www.fortinet.com/resources/cyberglossary/trojan-horse-virus

Fourtané, S. (2019). Augmented reality: The future of education. Interesting Engineering, 1–6, https://interestingengineering.com/augmented-reality-the-future-of-education

Fowler, G. A. (2022). Shadowbanning is real: Here's how you end up muted by social media, *The Washington Post,* https://www.washingtonpost.com/technology/2022/12/27/shadowban/

F-Secure. (2025). Trojan:W32/PFV-Exploit, https://www.f-secure.com/v-descs/pfv-exploit.shtml

Fuller, L. (1969). *The Morality of Law*. Yale University Press.

Fuller, S. (2023). Back to the University's Future: The Second Coming of Humboldt, Springer International Publishing, https://link-springer-com.qe2a-proxy.mun.ca/book/10.1007/978-3-031-36327-6

Gagvani, N. (2008). Introduction to video analytics, *EE Times,* https://www.eetimes.com/Introduction-to-video-analytics/?pageNumber=1/

Garde, T. (2005). Legal certainty, stare decisis and the doctrine of equivalents. *European Intellectual Property Review, 27*(10), 365–370.

Garon, J. (2018). Ownership of university intellectual property, *Cardozo Arts & Entertainment Law Journal, 36*(3), 635, 673.

Gavois, S. (20245). Cyberattack underway against the University of Reims Champagne-Ardenne, *Next Media*, https://next.ink/brief_article/cyberattaque-en-cours-contre-luniversite-de-reims-champagne-ardenne/

Gellert, C. (1993). Structural and functional differentiation: Remarks on changing paradigms of higher education in Europe. In Gellert, C. (Ed.), *Higher education in Europe*. Jessica Kingsley Publications.

Gibson, C., Olszewski, D., Brigham, N.G., Crowder, A., Butler, K.R.B., Traynor, P., Redmiles, E.M., & Kohno, T. (November 14, 2024). Analyzing the AI nudification application ecosystem, arXiv.org; Ithaca, NY.

Gilbert, K. (2024). How shadow banning can silently shift opinion online, *Yale Insights,* https://insights.som.yale.edu/insights/how-shadow-banning-can-silently-shift-opinion-online

Gile, N. (2025). Long Beach teenager arrested for arson after viral "Chromebook Challenge" prank sparks fire, *KCAL News*, https://www.cbsnews.com/losangeles/news/long-beach-teenager-arrested-for-arson-after-viral-chromebook-challenge-prank-sparks-fire/

Giles, M. (2017). Hacking Back Makes a Comeback—But It is Still a Bad Idea, *MIT Technology Review,* https://www.technologyreview.com/s/609555/hacking-back-makes-a-comeback-but-its-still-a-really-bad-idea/

Gill, R. (2009). 'Secrecy, silence, toxic shame and the hidden injuries of the neo-liberal university' in R. Gill and R. Ryan-Flood (eds.). Secrecy and Silence in the Research Process: Feminist Reflections, Routledge, London

Gilmour, M. (2018). West Island high school targeted by Instagram cyberbully, https://www.cjad800.com/news/west-island-high-school-targeted-by-instagram-cyber-bully-1.8575283.html

Gilmour, M. (2025). Dawson College teachers say government probe into tensions on campus creating climate of fear, *CTV News,* https://www.ctvnews.ca/montreal/article/dawson-college-teachers-say-government-probe-into-tensions-on-campus-creating-climate-of-fear/

Ginsberg, B. (2011). *The Fall of the Faculty: The rise of the all-administrative university and why it matters*. Oxford University Press. DOI: 10.1093/oso/9780199782444.001.0001

Glaser, A. (2014). Students and researchers: Take a stand against patent trolls, *Electronic Frontier Foundation,* https://www.eff.org/deeplinks/2014/05/students-and-researchers-take-stand-against-patent-trolls

Glastra, J. L. (2020). The legality of hacking back under international law, Masters Thesis, *Faculty of Law, University of Oslo,* https://www.duo.uio.no/bitstream/handle/10852/79232/ICTL-Master-Thesis-candidate-9015.pdf?sequence=1&isAllowed=y

Goode, E., & Ben-Yehuda, N. (2013). *Moral panics: The social construction of deviance* (2nd ed.). Wiley-Blackwell.

Goodman, J. (2003). The pros and cons of online dispute resolution: An assessment of cyber-mediation websites. *Duke L. & Tech. Rev. 0004.*

Google Cardboard. (2020). https://arvr.google.com/cardboard/

Google Patents. (2019). Article of footwear, https://patents.google.com/patent/US6397496B1/en

Google. (2020). Google Classroom, https://edu.google.com/products/classroom/?modal_active=none

Gosselin v. Quebec (Attorney General), [2002] 4 S.C.R. 429, 2002 SCC 84, https://scc-csc.lexum.com/scc-csc/scc-csc/en/item/2027/index.do

Goswami, U. (2004). Neuroscience, education and special education. *British Journal of Special Education, 31*(4), 175–183. DOI: 10.1111/j.0952-3383.2004.00352.x

Gov, U. K. (2011). The benefits of Peer to Patent, Peer to Patent launches in the UK, https://www.gov.uk/government/news/peer-to-patent-launches-in-the-uk

Gov, U. K. (2025). What does the Online Safety Act do? Department for Science, Innovation & Technology, https://www.gov.uk/government/publications/online-safety-act-explainer/online-safety-act-explainer#:~:text=The%20Act%20requires%20social%20media,are%20shielded%20from%20harmful%20content

Gov.UK. (27 June 2017). General indication of goods and services, Intellectual Property Office, https://www.gov.uk/government/publications/how-to-classify-trade-marks/trade-mark-classification-list-of-goods-and-services

Government of Newfoundland and Labrador. (2025). Bullying: Awareness and Prevention, https://www.gov.nl.ca/education/k12/bullying/

Government of Nunavut. (2025). Connecting Nunavummiut: How to Protect Children Online, https://www.gov.nu.ca/en/connecting-nunavummiut/how-protect-children-online

Government of the Northwest Territories. (2025). Education, Culture and Employment, Digital Literacy - Teacher Resource, https://www.ece.gov.nt.ca/en/services/resources-current-education-staff/digital-literacy-teacher-resource

Grant, K. (2020). ShotSpotter sensors send SDPD Officers to false alarms more often than advertised, *Voice of San Diego*, https://perma.cc/NRY8-JU3G

Greig, J. (2025). The University of Oklahoma isolates systems after 'unusual activity' on IT network, *The Record*, https://therecord.media/university-of-oklahoma-isolates-systems-unusual-activity

Gropper, G. L. (1983). A behavioral approach to instructional prescription. In Reigeluth, C. M. (Ed.), *Instructional-design theories and models: An Overview of Their Current Status*. Lawrence Erlbaum Associates.

Grother, P., Ngan, M., & Hanaoka, K. (December 2019). Face RecognitionVendor Test (FRVT) Part 3: Demographic Effects, *U.S. Department of Commerce, National Institute of Standards and Technology,* https://nvlpubs.nist.gov/nistpubs/ir/2019/NIST.IR.8280.pdf

Grover, S. (2005). The Equality and Liberty Rights of the Destitute: A Canadian Charter Case Example. *International Journal on Minority and Group Rights*, *12*(1), 43–61. DOI: 10.1163/1571811053890416

Gruner, R. S. (2012). Why we need a strong patent system and when: Filling the void left by the Bilski case. *Santa Clara High-Technology Law Journal*, *499*, •••. https://digitalcommons.law.scu.edu/chtlj/vol28/iss3/2

Guardian News & Media. (2019). Letter: Press freedom campaigners call for action on vexatious lawsuits, *The Guardian,* 20 July, https://www.theguardian.com/world/2019/jul/20/letter-press-freedom-campaigners-call-for-action-on-vexatious-lawsuits

Gubby, H. (2015). Universities need to teach business students about patents: A suggested approach. *European Journal of Law and Technology*, *6*(3), 1–22.

Gupton, N., & Kiper, P. J. (2020). What is the difference between AR, VR, and MR? *The Franklin Institute,* https://www.fi.edu/difference-between-ar-vr-and-mr

Gutierrez, O. R. (2001). Get Off My URL: Congress outlaws cybersquatting in the Wild West of the Internet. *Santa Clara High-Technology Law Journal*, *17*, 139. https://digitalcommons.law.scu.edu/chtlj/vol17/iss1/5

Gyselinck, V., Jamet, E., & Dubois, V. (2008). The role of working memory components in multimedia comprehension. *Applied Cognitive Psychology*, *22*(3), 353–374. DOI: 10.1002/acp.1411

Haack, S. (2013). Out of Step: Academic ethics in a preposterous environment, https://papers.ssrn.com/sol3/papers.cfm?abstract_id=2135732

Haines, L. (2007). Canadian taser death caught on camera: Vancouver Airport amateur footage shocker, *The Register,* https://www.theregister.com/2007/11/15/taser_death_video/#:~:text=Vancouver%20Airport%20amateur%20footage%20shocker,more%20Taser%20shot%20into%20Dziekanski

Hamilton, J. W., & Koshan, J. (2015). Adverse Impact: The Supreme Court's Approach to Adverse Effects Discrimination in Section 15 of the Charter, 19:2. *Review of Constitutional Studies*, 191–235. https://ssrn.com/abstract=2528157

Hammond, A.-M. (2001). The effectiveness of online dispute resolution. Department of Conflict and Management. Masters thesis. Royal Roads University.

Hannafin, M. J., & Peck, K. L. (1988). *The Design, Development and Evaluation of Instructional Software*. MacMillan Publishing Co.

Hargreaves, I. (2011). Digital opportunity: A review of intellectual property and growth, Report, https://assets.publishing.service.gov.uk/government/uploads/system/uploads/attachment_data/file/32563/ipreview-finalreport.pdf

Harmon, E. (October 28, 2016a). Patent trolls undermine open access, *Electronic Frontier Foundation,* https://www.eff.org/deeplinks/2016/10/patent-trolls-undermine-open-access

Harmon, E. (October 28, 2016b). Inside Intellectual Ventures' portfolio: Nearly 500 university patents, *Electronic Frontier Foundation,* https://www.eff.org/deeplinks/2016/10/inside-intellectual-ventures-portfolio-nearly-500-university-patents

Hart, C. (1999). Online dispute resolution and avoidance in electronic commerce. The chapter was presented at the *Uniform Law Conference of Canada.* August.

Hawkins, B. (2007). Letter from Brian Hawkins, President of EDUCAUSE, to Blackboard CEO Michael Chasen, https://www.educause.edu/ir/library/pdf/EPO0711.pdf

Healey, C. (2007). Due to ICANN's "Add Grace Period," *Duke Law & Technology Review, 9, domain tasting is taking over the Internet.*

Heater, B. (September 2007). Eminent Domains, *PC Magazine.*

Heaven v Pender. (1883). *(t/a West India Graving Dock Co)* L.R. 11 Q.B.D. 503, CA.

Heiding, F., Lermen, S., Kao, A., Schneier, B., & Vishwanath, A. (2024). Evaluating Large Language Models' capability to launch fully automated spear phishing campaigns: Validated on human subjects, https://arxiv.org/pdf/2412.00586

Heir, S. (2016). Moral panic, moral regulation, and the civilizing process. *The British Journal of Sociology*, *67*(3), 414–434. DOI: 10.1111/1468-4446.12201 PMID: 27444132

Heise Media, U. K. Ltd (July 2009). U.S. Peer-To-Patent Program closed, http://www.h-online.com/open/news/item/Peer-To-Patent-Program-Closed-742445.html

Hern, A. (2024). What is the UK's Online Safety Act and what powers will it provide? *The Guardian News & Media Ltd.*, https://www.theguardian.com/law/article/2024/aug/08/what-is-uk-online-safety-act-new-legislation-laws

Hernandez, T., & Okutan, E. (2023). 'Doxxing truck' appears on Yale's campus, displays student names and photos, *Yale News*, https://yaledailynews.com/blog/2023/11/17/doxxing-truck-appears-on-yales-campus-displays-student-names-and-photos/

Herrero, O. (2025). Why Macron is obsessed with banning social media for kids, *POLITICO*, https://www.politico.eu/article/emmanuel-macron-france-social-media-ban-minors-big-tech/

Highland Games, at http://www.highlandgames.net/

Hodes, C. (2008). Dignity and the conditions of truth: What equality needs from the law. *Canadian Journal of Women and the Law*, *19*(2). https://www.researchgate.net/publication/254942986_Dignity_and_the_Conditions_of_Truth_What_Equality_Needs_from_Law

Homer v Chief Constable of West Yorkshire Police, [2012] UKSC 15

Hopkins, K. (2021). Neuroscience as a contemporary science domain to contextualize the nature of science instruction. *Science & Education*, *30*(3), 463–500. DOI: 10.1007/s11191-020-00187-7

Hörnle, J. (2002) Online Dispute Resolution in Business-to-Consumer E-commerce Transactions. *Journal of Information, Law and Technology, (2).*

Hutchinson, J. P. (2001). Can trade-mark protection respond to the international threat of cybersquatting? *Journal of Information, Law and Technology*, http://elj.warwick.ac.uk/jilt/01-1/hutchinson.html

Hvide, H. K., & Jones, B. F. (2018). University Innovation and the Professor's Privilege. *The American Economic Review*, *108*(7), 1860–1898. DOI: 10.1257/aer.20160284

Hyde Park Residence Ltd v Yelland [1999] RPC 655; [2000] RPC 604 (CA), http://www.bailii.org/ew/cases/EWCA/Civ/2000/37.html

IANA. (2008). Country-code Top-level Domains, http://www.iana.org/domains/root/cctld/

IANA. (2019). Root Server Website, 2019, https://root-servers.org/

IANA. (2019). Root Zone Management, Overview, https://www.iana.org/domains/root

Iasiello, E. (2014). Hacking back: Not the right solution," The U.S. Army War College Quarterly. *Parameters*, *44*(3). Advance online publication. DOI: 10.55540/0031-1723.2732

ICANN blog (January 2007), https://blog.icann.org/

ICANN. (2008, March). ICANN CEO welcomes concerns as NTIA weighs role. *Telecommunications Reports*, *74*(6), 6–7.

illumio (2025). The global cost of ransomware: Study, https://cdn.prod.website-files.com/63e25fb5e66132e6387676dc/679bc0561e9ed06d78d5d9c0_The-Global-Cost-of-Ransomware-Study.pdf

Industry Six. (2019). MMO Population, https://mmo-population.com/top/2019

Information Security Media Group. (2025). https://ismg.io

Intelligence Services Act. (1994). UK Public General Acts 1994 c. 13, https://www.legislation.gov.uk/ukpga/1994/13/contents

Intimate Images and Cyber-protection Act. SNS 2017, c 7, https://nslegislature.ca/legc/bills/63rd_1st/1st_read/b027.htm

Investigatory Powers Act (2016). U.K. Legislation, https://www.legislation.gov.uk/ukpga/2016/25/contents

Jacobson, S. (2025). Common mistakes with conflict resolution, *The Conover Company,* https://www.conovercompany.com/common-mistakes-with-conflict-resolution/

Jacques, S. (2014). Has UK IP lost all its sense of humour? Another parody tale, EU Law Analysis: Expert insight into EU law developments, School of Law, University of Nottingham (UK), https://eulawanalysis.blogspot.com/2014/12/has-ukip-lost-all-sense-of-humour.html

Jaén, X., Bohigas, X., & Novell, M. (2009). Semi-virtual classroom for physics contents, *EAEEIE Annual Conference*.

Johnson, S. (April 19, 2018). State Supreme Court hears arguments over suspension of Marquette Professor, *Wisconsin Public Radio,* https://www.wpr.org/justice/state-supreme-court-hears-arguments-over-suspension-marquette-professor

Jones, M. (October 5, 2015). "How Columbine Spawned Dozens of Copycats".

Jones, P. (2006). The Blackboard patent: Where's Waldo? Eklektix. Inc. https://lwn.net/Articles/197535/

Joshghani, A., & the The University of Ghent. (2018). Protective device for human joint, *WIPO International Application Published Under The Patent Cooperation Treaty*, International Publication Number: WO 2018/154062 Al, https://patentimages.storage.googleapis.com/ad/d4/6a/32a0b025e87d89/WO2018154062A1.pdf

K. Howard Seymour v Coventry University (Patent) [2000] U.K.IntelP (29 June 2000), http://www.bailii.org/U.K./cases/U.K.IntelP/2000/o22300.html

K12 Security Information eXchange (2023). *The K-12 Cyber Incident Map*, https://www.k12six.org/map

Kaeding, D. (April 12, 2024). Wisconsin tribe sues social media companies over suicide rates among Native youth, *Wisconsin Public Radio,* https://www.wpr.org/news/menominee-indian-spirit-lake-tribe-sues-social-media-suicide-rates-native-youth

Kamer der Staten Generaal. (2016) https://www.tweedekamer.nl/kamerstukken/kamervragen/detail?id=2018D34764&did=2018D34764

Kant, I. (1781). Transcendental Analytic: First Book, The Analytic of Concepts, Section II. On the logical function in Judgments 4, 100, Critique of Pure Reason. Translated and edited by Paul Guyer and Allen W. Wood.

Kant, I. (1993). *[1785]. Groundwork of the Metaphysics of Morals* (3rd ed.). (Ellington, J. W., Trans.). Hackett.

Karrenberg, D. (September 2007). DNS Root Name Servers Explained For Non-Experts, https://www.isoc.org/briefings/019/

Katsh, E. (2002). Online dispute resolution: The next phase. *Lex Electronica, 7*,(2),

Katsh, E., & Rule, C. (2016). What we know and need to know about online dispute resolution, South Carolina Law Review, 67(2), 329-344, https://scholarcommons.sc.edu/sclr/vol67/iss2/10 67(2)

Katsh, E., Osterweil, L., Sondheimer, N., & Rainey, D. (2006). Experimental application of process technology to the creation and adoption of online dispute resolution. Project highlights proceedings. *The National Center for Technology and Dispute Resolution.* http://www.odr.info/nmb/DGo2006%20Project%20Highlights%20proceedings%200303061.pdf

Katsh, E. (2011). ODR: A Look at History – A Few Thoughts About the Present and Some Speculation About the Future. In Abdel Wahab, M. S., Katsh, E., & Rainey, D. (Eds.), *Online Dispute Resolution: Theory and Practice: A Treatise on Technology and Dispute Resolution*. Eleven International Publishing., https://www.ombuds.org/odrbook/Table_of_Contents.htm

KD & AFP. (2024). Paris-Saclay University victim of a cyberattack, *BFM Tech & Co,* https://www.bfmtv.com/tech/cybersecurite/l-universite-paris-saclay-victime-d-une-cyberattaque_AD-202408130311.html

Kelley, J. (January 1, 2025). Kids Online Safety Act continues to threaten our rights online: 2024 in Review, *Electronic Frontier Foundation,* https://www.eff.org/deeplinks/2024/12/kids-online-safety-act-continues-threaten-our-rights-online-year-review-2024

Kenton, W. (2018). Banker Trojan, Laws & Regulations Crime & Fraud, Investopedia, https://www.investopedia.com/terms/b/banker-trojan.asp

Kessler, B., & Martinez, M. (July 12, 2022). Disturbing new footage shows Salvador Ramos roaming Uvalde school halls, cops running away from gunshots, *U.S. News,* https://nypost.com/2022/07/12/cops-ran-away-from-gunshots-during-uvalde-school-shooting-video/

KFSM-TV. (February 23, 2023). Greenwood Police assure high school is safe after false alarm leads to lockdown, https://www.5newsonline.com/article/news/local/false-alarm-greenwood-high-school-gunshot-detector/527-be4f0e9b-b096-4aee-bdea-25339135f998

Kharpal, A. (August 2, 2023). China floats two-hour daily limit of smartphone screen time for kids, *CNBC,* https://www.cnbc.com/2023/08/02/china-floats-two-hour-daily-limit-of-smartphone-screen-time-for-kids.html#:~:text=Time%20restrictions&text=Children%20under%20the%20age%20of%20eight%20should%20be%20restricted%20to,a%20maximum%20of%20two%20hours

Kids in the Know. (2025). Canadian Centre for Child Protection, https://www.kidsintheknow.ca/app/en/

Kids Online Safety Act (KOSA), H.R. 7891 (2023). https://www.congress.gov/bill/118th-congress/senate-bill/1409/text

Kimery, A. (2025). Congress renews fight over kids online safety with revived KOSA bill, *Biometrics Research Group,* https://www.biometricupdate.com/202505/congress-renews-fight-over-kids-online-safety-with-revived-kosa-bill

Kim, N., & Piper, T. (2003). Gosselin v. Quebec: Back to the Poorhouse. *McGill Law Journal. Revue de Droit de McGill, 48*, 749.

Kirschner, P. A., Sweller, J., & Clark, R. E. (2006). Why minimal guidance during instruction does not work: An analysis of the failure of constructivist, discovery, problem-based, experiential, and inquiry-based teaching. *Educational Psychologist, 41*(2), 75–86. DOI: 10.1207/s15326985ep4102_1

Kiss, J. (2013). Cyber scams take advantage of hope and trust, The Guardian, https://www.theguardian.com/society/2013/aug/16/cyber-scams-take-advantage-hope-trust

Klein, D. (December 14, 2021). Trademark Infringement: Universities v. Online Retailers, Klein Moynihan Turco LLP., https://kleinmoynihan.com/trademark-law-infringement-universities-v-online-retailers/?utm_source=mondaq&utm_medium=syndication&utm_content=articleoriginal&utm_campaign=article

Klinger, A., & Klinger, H. (2024). Violent Threats and Incidents in Schools: An Analysis of the 2023-2024 School Year, *The Educator's School Safety Network,* www.eSchoolSafety.org

Komaitis, K. (2003). *ICANN: Guilty as charged?* Journal of Information, Law, &. *Technology (Elmsford, N.Y.)*, 1.

Koon v. United States | 518 U.S. 81 (1996), https://supreme.justia.com/cases/federal/us/518/81/

Koroghlanian, C., & Klein, J. (2004). The effect of audio and animation in multimedia instruction. *Journal of Educational Multimedia and Hypermedia, 13*(1), 23–46.

Krebs, B. (2014). 'Blackshades' Trojan Users Had It Coming, KrebsonSecurity, https://krebsonsecurity.com/2014/05/blackshades-trojan-users-had-it-coming/

Krebs, B. (2014). Feds to Charge Alleged SpyEye Trojan Author, KrebsonSecurity, https://krebsonsecurity.com/2014/01/feds-to-charge-alleged-spyeye-trojan-author/

Krebs, B. (2016). 'Blackhole' Exploit Kit Author Gets 7 Years, KrebsonSecurity, https://krebsonsecurity.com/2016/04/blackhole-exploit-kit-author-gets-8-years/

Krebs, B. (2020). DDoS Mitigation Firm Founder Admits to DDoS, KrebsonSecurity, https://krebsonsecurity.com/

Kupersmith, K. (2011). Agile is a Fad, The BA Times: Resources for Business Analysts, https://www.batimes.com/articles/agile-is-a-fad/

Kurtz, G. (2025). *CrowdStrike global threat report*. CrowdStrike, Inc.

Laddie, H. (2001). National I.P. rights: A moribund anachronism. *European Intellectual Property Review*, *23*(9), 402–408.

Lamba, H., Bharadhwaj, V., Vachher, M., Agarwal, D., Arora, M., Sachdeva, N., & Kumaraguru, P. (2017). From camera to deathbed: Understanding dangerous selfies on social media, *Proceedings of the Eleventh International AAAI Conference on Web and Social Media, 11*, 1, https://ojs.aaai.org/index.php/ICWSM/article/view/14956

Lametti, D. (2005). Coming to terms with copyright, in (ed.) Michael Geist, *In the public interest: The future of Canadian copyright law.* Toronto: Irwin Law, pp. 480–516, and at http://www.irwinlaw.com/PublicInterest/three_3_lametti.htm

Lanier Law Firm. (2025). Social Media Addiction Statistics, Redefining Legal Care, https://www.lanierlawfirm.com/social-media-addiction/statistics/

Lau, H. (2019). Backdoor Trojan, Security Centre, *Symantec,* https://www.symantec.com/security-center/

Law v. Canada (Minister of Employment and Immigration), [1999] I S.C.R. 497, https://scc-csc.lexum.com/scc-csc/scc-csc/en/item/1691/index.do

Le Monde. (2024). Zuckerberg apologizes in US Congress after tech grilling, https://www.lemonde.fr/en/pixels/article/2024/02/01/zuckerberg-apologizes-in-us-congress-after-tech-grilling_6483502_13.html

Leith, P. (2012). E-participation and e-participants: Solving the patent 'crisis'. *International Review of Law Computers & Technology*, *26*(1), 7–24. DOI: 10.1080/13600869.2012.646783

LeLievre v. Gould, [1893] 1 Q.B. 491 at 497.

Lemley, M. A. (2019). Fame, Parody, and Policing in Trademark Law. *Detroit College of Law at Michigan State University Law Review*, *1*, 1–21.

Lemos, R. (2017). Why the hack-back is still the worst idea in cybersecurity, *TechBeacon,* https://techbeacon.com/security/why-hack-back-still-worst-idea-cybersecurity

Lenoir, A. (2024). The Columbine High School shooting: The massacre that shook America, *Mahanoy Area School Dist. v. B.L., 141 S. Ct. 2038, 2021*, https://www.supremecourt.gov/opinions/20pdf/20-255_g3bi.pdf

Leung, W., & Bascaramurty, D. (12 October 2012). Amanda Todd tragedy highlights how social media makes bullying inescapable, The Globe and Mail Inc, https://www.theglobeandmail.com/news/national/amanda-todd-tragedy-highlights-how-social-media-makes-bullying-inescapable/article4611068/

Levy v Langridge (1838) *150 E.R. 1458,* 4 M. & W. 337

Lewis, B. (2006). Reverse Domain Hijacking: Extreme Makeover, DNJournal, https://www.dnjournal.com/legal/extreme-makeover.htm

Leyden, J. (2007). Germany seeks malware 'specialists' to bug terrorists, *The Register,* http://www.theregister.co.uk/2007/11/21/germany_vxer_hire_plan/

Little, B. (2001). Reading between the lines for graduate employment. *Quality in Higher Education*, *7*(2), 121–129. DOI: 10.1080/13538320120060015

Lodder, A. & Verheij, B. (1999). Computer-mediated legal argument: Towards new opportunities in education. *Journal of Information, Law and Technology, 2.*

Lodder, A., & Zeleznikow, J. (2005). Developing an online dispute resolution environment: Dialogue tools and negotiation support systems in a three-step model. *Harvard Negotiation Law Review*, *10*(287), 302.

Lofton, C. (July 21, 2022). Suicide deaths of 2 area teens subject of lawsuit against social media companies, *Fox 22*, https://abc17news.com/cnn-regional/2022/07/21/suicide-deaths-of-2-area-teens-subject-of-lawsuit-against-social-media-companies/

Longmeid and Wife v Holliday (1851) *155 E.R. 752,* 6 Ex. 761.

LookHuman Design. (2019). Harvard LOL School, Fake Harvard T-Shirts, https://www.lookhuman.com/design/15091-harvard-lol-school/3600-athletic_gray-md

Lucas v Department of Finance (Discrimination - Age) [2022] NIit 17429_19it, https://www.bailii.org/nie/cases/NIIT/2022/17429_19it.html

Maas, D. (March 9, 2021). Scholars Under Surveillance: How Campus Police Use High Tech to Spy on Students, *Electronic Frontier Foundation*, https://www.eff.org/deeplinks/2021/03/scholars-under-surveillance-how-campus-police-use-high-tech-spy-students

MacDonnell, V. A. (2012). Protective function and section 7 of the Canadian Charter of Rights and Freedoms. *Review of Constitutional Studies*, *17*(1).

Machlup, F., & Penrose, E. (1950). The patent controversy in the nineteenth century. *The Journal of Economic History, 10*(1), 1–29. DOI: 10.1017/S0022050700055893

MacLachlan, R., Wodehouse, A., & Vasantha, G. (2018). A new approach for patent use in student design engineering projects, In *Proceedings of the 20th International Conference on Engineering and Product Design Education, E&PDE 2018* (pp. 288-293). Glasgow.

MacLauchlan, W. (2016). Report of the Justice and Public Safety Victims of Crime Act 2015-2016, Minister of Justice and Public Safety and Attorney General, https://www.princeedwardisland.ca/sites/default/files/publications/april_1_2015-march_31_2016_victims_of_crime_annual_report_1.pdf

MacLeod v. Newsquest (Sunday Herald) Ltd | [2007], https://www.casemine.com/judgement/uk/5a8ff84a60d03e7f57ebdf28

MacQueen, H., Waelde, C., & Laurie, G. (2008). *Contemporary Intellectual Property: Law and Policy*. Oxford University Press.

MacQueen, H., Waelde, C., Laurie, G., & Brown, A. (2010). *Contemporary intellectual property: Law and Policy*. Oxford University Press.

Madfisa, E., Hirschfield, P., & Addington, L. A. (2021). School securitization and its alternatives: The social, political, and contextual drivers of school safety policy and practice. *School Psychology Review, 50*(2-3), 191–205. DOI: 10.1080/2372966X.2020.1855063

Magyari, D. (2016). Getting a glimpse of virtual and augmented reality in healthcare, Health Data Management, https://www.healthdatamanagement.com/articles/getting-a-glimpse-of-virtual-and-augmented-reality-in-healthcare

Mahanoy Area School District v. B.L., (2021). https://www.oyez.org/cases/2020/20-255

Maher, R. C., & Routh, T. K. (September 2016). Wideband audio recordings of gunshots: Waveforms and repeatability, 141ST *Audio Eng'g Soc'y Convention*, at 3, https://perma.cc/TRZ3-SJ3K

MalwareBytes. (2025). Android banking trojans: How they steal passwords and drain bank accounts, *MalwareBytes,* https://www.malwarebytes.com/search/mobile%20banking%20trojan%20

Manitoba (2013). Bill 214. Cyberbullying Prevention Act, https://web2.gov.mb.ca/bills/40-2/b214e.php

Mann, B. L. (2005). Testing the validity of Post and Vote Web-based peer assessment, in David Williams. Scott Howell and Mary Hricko (Eds.). *Online Assessment, Measurement & Evaluation: Emerging Practices* (pp. 132-153). Hershey, PA: Information Science Publishing.

Mann, B. L. (2015). Social networking websites, in Philip Leith (Ed.). *Privacy in the Information Society* (pp. 493–503), Part VI Social Networks, Volume II of 3-volume series, The Library of Essays on Law and Privacy, London, U.K: Ashgate Publishing. January.

Mann, B. L. (2015). Social networking websites: A concatenation of impersonation, denigration, sexual and aggressive solicitation, cyber-bullying and happy slapping videos, in Philip Leith (Ed.). *Privacy in the Information Society* (pp. 493–503), Part VI. Social Networks, Volume II of a 3-volume series. The Library of Essays on Law and Privacy. London, U.K.: Ashgate Publishing. January.

Mann, B. L. (2015). Social networking websites: A concatenation of impersonation, denigration, sexual and aggressive solicitation, cyber-bullying and happy slapping videos. In Philip Leith (Ed.). *Privacy in the Information Society* (pp. 493–503), Part VI. Social Networks, Volume II of a 3-volume series. The Library of Essays on Law and Privacy. London, U.K.: Ashgate Publishing. January

Mann, B.L. (1994). Computing then and now. *New Morning Watch: Educational & Social Analysis, 22* (1-2).

Mann, B.L. (2009a). Intellectual property laws confer rights in respect of online distance education, yet most learning resources are still free - Truth or fiction? *i-manager's Journal of Educational Technology, 6*(3), 1-13

Mann, B. L. (1993). Technology orientation for educators: Learning from the industrial subculture. *New Morning Watch: Educational & Social Analysis, 20*(3), 18–25.

Mann, B. L. (2000). Phase Theory: A Teleological Taxonomy of Web Course Management. In Mann, B. L. (Ed.), *Perspectives in Web Course Management* (pp. 3–25). Scholar's Press.

Mann, B. L. (2006). Conducting formative evaluations of online instructional material. In Mann, B. L. (Ed.), *Selected styles in web-based educational research* (pp. 232–242). Information Science Publishing. DOI: 10.4018/978-1-59140-732-4.ch016

Mann, B. L. (2006). Making your own educational materials, part II: Multimedia design for learning. *International Journal of Instructional Technology & Distance Learning, 3*(10).

Mann, B. L. (2008). Computer-aided presentations. In Wah, B. W. (Ed.), *Encyclopedia of Computer Science and Engineering*. John Wiley & Sons Inc., https://www.cdli.ca/~bmann/0_ARTICLES/Mann_CAI_Wiley.pdf

Mann, B. L. (2008). Copyright protection and the new stakeholders in online distance education. *First Monday*, *13*(7). http://www.uic.edu/htbin/cgiwrap/bin/ojs/index.php/fm/article/viewArticle/2095/1997. DOI: 10.5210/fm.v13i7.2095

Mann, B. L. (2008). *Routes open to the patent applicant in Europe, Computer Program*. University of Edinburgh, School of Law.

Mann, B. L. (2008). *Routes open to the trademark applicant, Computer Program*. University of Edinburgh, School of Law.

Mann, B. L. (2009). Computer-aided instruction. In Wah, B. W. (Ed.), *Wiley Encyclopedia of Computer Science & Engineering* (Vol. 1, pp. 583–592). John Wiley & Sons, Inc. DOI: 10.1002/9780470050118.ecse935

Mann, B. L. (2009). Smoothing some wrinkles in online dispute resolution. *International Journal of Law and Information Technology*, *17*(1), 83–112. DOI: 10.1093/ijlit/ean017

Mann, B. L. (2009). Social networking websites: A concatenation of impersonation, denigration, sexual and aggressive solicitation, cyber-bullying and happy slapping videos. *International Journal of Law and Information Technology*, *17*(3), 252–267. DOI: 10.1093/ijlit/ean008

Mann, B. L. (2009a). Action research with Internet database tools. In Halpin, T. (Ed.), *Readings on Database Technologies & Applications*. Information Science Reference.

Mann, B. L. (2020). *Applying Internet Laws and Regulations to Educational Technology, Public Policy and Administration Book Series*. IGI Global.

Mann, B. L. (2025). Speech cueing curricular multimedia: Instructional design that activates the orienting attention network. *Journal of Interactive Learning Research*, *36*(2), 191–214. DOI: 10.70725/115195dejbne

Marlow, C., Greytak, E., Duarte, K., & Sun, S. (October 2, 2023). Digital dystopia: The danger in buying what the edtech surveillance industry is selling, report, *American Civil Liberties Union,* https://www.aclu.org/publications/digital-dystopia-the-danger-in-buying-what-the-edtech-surveillance-industry-is-selling

Martin, A. (2024). Attack on IT infrastructure of the Vocational Training Center (BBZ) Schaffhausen, *The Record: Recorded Future News*, https://therecord.media/ransomware-attack-german-speaking-school-switzerland-bbz-schaffhausen

Martin, J. P. (April 16, 2015). "Lower Merion schools". *The Philadelphia Inquirer.*

Martin, B. R. (2016). What is happening to our universities? *Prometheus*, *34*(1), 7–24. DOI: 10.1080/08109028.2016.1222123

Masnick, M. (July 27th 2010). The University of Texas discovers it does not get to control the words 'Texas' & 'Sports' when used together, https://www.techdirt.com/2010/07/27/university-of-texas-discovers-it-doesnt-get-to-control-the-words-texas-sports-when-used-together/

Masood, A. (2016). Sattar Buksh - Parody or the dilution of trademark? IP Nexus, November, https://secure.ipnexus.com/en/articles/46#_ftnref1

Max, B. (2023). SoundThinking's black-box gunshot detection method: Untested and unvetted tech flourishes in the criminal justice system. *Stanford Technology Law Review: STLR: An Online High-Technology Law Journal from Stanford Law School*, *26*, 193.

Mayer, R. E. (2021). *Multimedia learning* (3rd ed.). Cambridge University Press.

Mayer, R. E., & Moreno, R. (1998). A split attention effect in multimedia learning: Evidence for dual processing systems in working memory. *Journal of Educational Psychology*, *90*(2), 312–320. DOI: 10.1037/0022-0663.90.2.312

Mazurek, S. V. (April 10, 2023). Laugh it off: A guide to parody under U.S. Trademark Law, Faegre Drinker Biddle & Reath LLP, https://www.tcamtoday.com/2023/laugh-it-off-a-guide-to-parody-under-us-trademark-law/

Mazzone, J. (2006). Copyfraud, New York University Law Review, 10(13), 1026-1100, https://www.nyulawreview.org/wp-content/uploads/2018/08/NYULawReview-81-3-Mazzone.pdf

McAfee, L. L. C. (2013). What is Typosquatting? https://securingtomorrow.mcafee.com/consumer/family-safety/what-is-typosquatting/

McClellan, M., & Portnoy, E. (October 1, 2024). How to stop advertisers from tracking your teen across the Internet, *Electronic Frontier Foundation,* https://www.eff.org/deeplinks/2024/09/how-stop-advertisers-tracking-your-teen-across-internet

McCoy, D. (May 1, 2018). When studying, doxing gets you doxed, *Huff Post,* https://www.huffpost.com/entry/opinion-mccoy-doxing-study_n_5ae75ec7e4b02baed1bd06cc?utm_source=chatgpt.com

McDonald's. (2019). Internet Site Terms and Conditions, http://mcdonalds.com/terms.html

McKay, K. (February 22, 2023). Doxxing – A 21st Century Crime, *Glasgow Guardian*, https://glasgowguardian.co.uk/2023/02/22/doxxing-a-21st-century-crime/?utm_source=chatgpt.com

McLaughlin, E. C., & Park, M. (2018). Social media paints picture of racist professional school shooter, CNN, https://web.archive.org/web/20180216085130/https://edition.cnn.com/2018/02/14/us/nikolas-cruz-florida-shooting-suspect/index.html

McLuhan, M., & Lapham, L. H. (1994). *Understanding Media: The Extensions of Man*. McGraw-Hill.

McMahon, L., Kleinman, Z., & Subramanian, C. (January 7, 2025). Facebook and Instagram get rid of fact-checkers, *BBC News,* https://www.bbc.com/news/articles/cly74mpy8klo

McSherry, C., Guariglia, M., Gilligan, B., & Crocker, A. (June 6, 2024). Security, surveillance, and government overreach – the United States set the path, but Canada shouldn't follow it, *Electronic Frontier Foundation,* https://www.eff.org/deeplinks/2024/06/security-surveillance-and-government-overreach-united-states-set-path-canada

Meaker, M. (2022). How a British teen's death changed social media, *Wired,* https://www.wired.com/story/how-a-british-teens-death-changed-social-media/

MediaSmarts. (2025). Centre of Digital Media Literacy, https://mediasmarts.ca/

Merges, R. P., Menell, P. S., & Lemley, M. A. (2012). *Intellectual Property in the New Technological Age* (6th ed.), 29.

Merisalo, T. (2020). Five phases of a cyber attack: The attacker's view, F-Secure, blog, https://blog.f-secure.com/5-phases-of-a-cyber-attack-the-attackers-view/

Meyer, D. (June 23, 2017). Police get broad phone and computer hacking powers in Germany, ZDNet CBS Interactive, https://www.zdnet.com/article/police-get-broad-phone-and-computer-hacking-powers-in-germany/

Miller, S. (February 15, 2024). Nevada attorney general's lawsuits against social media companies underscore impact on youth, Las Vegas Weekly, https://lasvegasweekly.com/news/2024/feb/15/nevada-attorney-generals-lawsuits-social-media/

Milt, K., Guteil, M., Liger, Q., Heetman, A., Eager, J., & Crawford, M. (2017). Legal Frameworks for Hacking by Law Enforcement: Identification, Evaluation and Comparison of Practices, The Policy Department for Citizens' Rights and Constitutional Affairs, *European Parliament Committee on Civil Liberties, Justice and Home (LIBE),* https://www.europarl.europa.eu/RegData/etudes/STUD/2017/583137/IPOL_STU(2017)583137_EN.pdf

Ministry for Europe and Foreign Affairs. (2019). France and Cybersecurity, *France Diplomatie*, https://www.diplomatie.gouv.fr/en/french-foreign-policy/defence-security/cyber-security/

Moodle (2020). Moodle 3.8 Learning Management System, https://moodle.org/

Morrison, J. (2021). Cameras are being used to punish students, not stop school shooters, *Forbes,* https://www.forbes.com/sites/nickmorrison/2021/04/11/cameras-are-being-used-to-punish-students-not-stop-school-shooters/?sh=6d9842f83669

Motion, P. (2003). Internet arbitration clauses: Shock and awe? *The Journal: Magazine of the Law Society of Scotland*, p. 42.

Motion, P. (2005). Article 17: Encouragement of alternative dispute resolution – Online dispute resolution: A view from Scotland. In Edwards, L. (Ed.), *The new legal framework for e-commerce in Europe* (pp. 137–169). Hart Publishing.

Muecke, N., & Stranieri, A. (2007). An argument structure abstraction for Bayesian belief networks: Just outcomes in online dispute resolution. *Proceedings of the APCCM,* 35-40.

Mullin, J. (2025). The Kids Online Safety Act Will Make the Internet Worse for Everyone, *Electronic Frontier Foundation, https*://www.eff.org/deeplinks/2025/05/kids-online-safety-act-will-make-internet-worse-everyone

Multani v. Commission scolaire Marguerite-Bourgeoys, [2006] 1 S.C.R. 256, 2006 SCC 6, https://decisions.scc-csc.ca/scc-csc/scc-csc/en/item/15/index.do

Munson, L. (2019). The 6 Types of Trojans, Security-FAQs, https://www.security-faqs.com/admin-server-dos-log-steal-and-kill-the-6-types-of-trojans.html

Murray, J., & Syal, R. (August 2024). Two men jailed for social media posts that stirred up far-right violence, *Guardian News & Media,* https://www.theguardian.com/politics/article/2024/aug/09/two-men-jailed-for-social-media-posts-that-stirred-up-far-right-violence

MyLeanMBA. (2017). Breaking down the top 3 MOOC platforms: Coursera, Udacity & edX, Medium, April, https://medium.com/@MyLeanMBA/breaking-down-the-top-3-mooc-platforms-coursera-udacity-edx-13e5ed481337

NAAG. (February 21, 2024). A Bipartisan Coalition of 39 State Attorneys General Urge Congressional Action on Pharmacy Benefit Manager Reform, *National Association of Attorneys General,* https://www.naag.org/press-releases/a-bipartisan-coalition-of-39-state-attorneys-general-urge-congressional-action-on-pharmacy-benefit-manager-reform/

Nasaw, D. (2010). U.S. school district spied on students through webcams, court told. *The Guardian,* https://en.wikipedia.org/wiki/Robbins_v._Lower_Merion_School_District#cite_note-guardian1-6

National Cyber and Information Security Agency. (2015). Action Plan for the National Cybersecurity Strategy of the Czech Republic for the Period from 2015 to 2020, https://www.govcert.cz/download/gov-cert/container-nodeid-578/ap-cs-2015-2020-en.pdf

National Public Radio. (July 22, 2011). When Patents Attack, http://www.npr.org/templates/transcript/transcript.php?storyId=138576167

National Telecommunications and Information Administration. (April 2008). ICANN. U.S. Department of Commerce. A statement on the Mid-Term Review of the Joint Project Agreement (JPA) Between NTIA and ICANN, Washington, DC, http://www.ntia.doc.gov/ntiahome/domainname/ICANN_JPA_080402.html

Nicholas, R. (2007). Trouble in the classroom. *Patent World., 190*, 12–13.

Nielson, T., & Staalesen, A. (2024). Norwegian police make an arrest in Russia-related espionage, *The Barents Observer,* https://www.thebarentsobserver.com/security/norwegian-police-makes-arrest-in-russiarelated-espionage/421016

NYC Press Office. (February 14, 2024). Mayor Adams announces lawsuit against social media companies fueling nationwide youth mental health crisis, *City of New York,* https://www.nyc.gov/office-of-the-mayor/news/125-24/mayor-adams-lawsuit-against-social-media-companies-fueling-nationwide-youth-mental-health?ref=upstract.com#/0

Ogletree v. Cleveland State University, 1:21-cv-00500 (Dec. 20, 2022), https://www.govinfo.gov/content/pkg/USCOURTS-ohnd-1_21-cv-00500/pdf/USCOURTS-ohnd-1_21-cv-00500-0.pdf

Okanagan College v Okanagan College Faculty Assoc., 2024 CanLII 88299 (BC LA), https://canlii.ca/t/k6w2z

Okla. Admin. Code tit. 210, ch. 20, subch. 29 - *Standards of Performance and Conduct for Teachers,* https://www.law.cornell.edu/regulations/oklahoma/title-210/chapter-20/subchapter-29

Oklahoma Admin. Code § 210:20-29-5 (Principle III)

Olijnyk, Z. (2022). The 'Paisley snail' again emerges as legal community celebrates Donoghue case of spoiled ginger beer, *Canadian Lawyer,* https://www.canadianlawyermag.com/practice-areas/litigation/the-paisley-snail-again-emerges-as-legal-community-celebrates-donoghue-case-of-spoiled-ginger-beer/366977

Online Ombuds Office. https://ombuds.org/

Ontario Ministry of Education. (2025). Creating safe and accepting schools, https://www.ontario.ca/page/creating-safe-and-accepting-schools

OpenMedia. (2015). Communication Security Establishment is monitoring our private online activities on a massive scale and sharing sensitive data with other governments, https://openmedia.org/press/item/breaking-spy-agency-cse-monitoring-our-private-online-activities-massive-scale-and-sharing

Orlowski, A. (24 Aug 2018). OMG! Battle looms over WTF! Trademarks: P&G wakes up to Internet abbreviations, LOL, *The Register*, https://www.theregister.co.uk/2018/08/24/omg_battle_looms_over_wtf_trademarks/

Ortutay, B. (2025). President Trump signs Take It Down Act, addressing nonconsensual deepfakes. What is it? *Associated Press,* https://apnews.com/article/take-it-down-deepfake-trump-melania-first-amendment-741a6e525e81e5e3d8843aac20de8615

OUT-LAW News. (July 2006). Friendster patents social networking, http://www.outlaw.com/default.aspx?page=7092

Outlaw News. (March 2007). Domain tasting makes WIPO sick, *OUT-LAW News*, https://www.out-law.com/default.aspx?page=7878

Out-Law.com. (2008). *Dispute resolution*. Pinsent Masons LLP.

Paivio, A. (1986). *Mental representations: A dual coding approach.* Oxford University Press.

Papert, S. (1988). *A critique of technocentrism in thinking about the school of the future. Children in the Information Age*. Elsevier.

Paris Convention for the Protection of Industrial Property, (March 20, 1883). https://www.wipo.int/treaties/en/ip/paris/index.html

Parsons, B. (May 2006). Domain Kiting: A serious problem gets worse, *Go Daddy Group, Inc.,* Blog, http://www.bobparsons.com/DomainKiting.html

Patton, M. Q. (1982). Qualitative methods and approaches: What are they? *New Directions for Institutional Research, 1982*(34), 3–15. DOI: 10.1002/ir.37019823403

Pavlich, G. (2011). *Law & Society Redefined.* Oxford University Press.

People v. Reed, No. 16015117 (July 6, 2017) (Cal. Super. Ct. S.F. County)

Pettersson, I. (2018). The nomos of the university: Introducing the Professor's Privilege in 1940s Sweden. *Minerva, 56*(3), 381–403. DOI: 10.1007/s11024-018-9348-2 PMID: 30147148

Philpott, K., Dooley, L., O'Reilly, C., & Lupton, G. (2011). The entrepreneurial university: Examining the underlying academic tensions. *Technovation, 31*(4), 161–170. DOI: 10.1016/j.technovation.2010.12.003

Pietrosanti, F., & Aterno, S. (2017). Italy unveils a legal proposal to regulate government hacking, Boing Boing, http://boingboing.net/2017/02/15/title-italy-unveils-a-law-pro.html

Plato. (380 B.C.). Gorgias. Translated by Benjamin Jowett. In D.C. Stevenson (ed.). *The Internet Classics Archive,* http://classics.mit.edu/Plato/gorgias.html

Plaxton, M. (2008). Foucault, Agamben, and Arbour J.'s dissent in Gosselin. *Canadian Journal of Law and Jurisprudence, 21*(2), 2. DOI: 10.1017/S0841820900004471

Poblet, M., & Casanovas, P. (2007). Emotions in ODR. *International Review of Law Computers & Technology, 21*(2), 145–155. DOI: 10.1080/13600860701492146

Police Service of Northern Ireland in Craigavon. (2018). Momo Image: *Facebook,* https://www.facebook.com/PSNI.Craigavon/photos/a.390441237658321/2097736956928732/?type=3

Pollick, M. (2008). What is Check Kiting? *WiseGeek,* https://www.wisegeek.com/what-is-check-kiting.htm

Posner, M. I., & Barbey, A. K. (2020). General intelligence in the age of neuroimaging. *Trends in Neuroscience and Education, 18,* 100126–100126. DOI: 10.1016/j.tine.2020.100126 PMID: 32085908

Posner, M. I., & Rothbart, M. K. (2007). Research on attention networks as a model for the integration of Psychological Science. *Annual Review of Psychology, 58*(1), 1–23. DOI: 10.1146/annurev.psych.58.110405.085516 PMID: 17029565

PREVNet Inc. (2025). Promoting Relationships & Eliminating Violence Network, https://www.prevnet.ca/

Priest v. Canada (Attorney General), 2022 FC 1598, https://canlii.ca/t/jt41v

Pritchard, P. (2007). Video of Robert Dziekanski's Taser death, *CBC News,* https://www.cbc.ca/player/play/video/1.1808186

ProRat Trojan. (2008), http://www.prorat.net/

Quittner, J. (October 1994). Billions Registered, *Wired*, https://www.wired.com/wired/archive/2.10/mcdonalds.html

R v Gardner. (2018) ONCA 584, https://www.ontariocourts.ca/decisions/2018/2018ONCA0584.pdf

R. c. Morin. (2014) QCCQ 1609, https://www.canlii.org/en/qc/qccq/doc/2014/2014qccq1609/2014qccq1609.html?resultIndex=1

R. v Dragos. (2012) ONCA 538, http://canlii.ca/t/fs9ps

R. v J.M.D. (2018) BCPC 211, http://canlii.ca/t/htm3x

R. v Legare. (2009) 3 SCR 551, 2009 SCC 56, https://www.canlii.org/en/ca/scc/doc/2009/2009scc56/2009scc56.html?resultIndex=1

R. v MacFarlane. (2018) MBCA, https://bcsth.ca/what-to-do-if-someone-has-shared-or-threatened-to-share-your-intimate-image/

R. v Paré. (1987) 2 SCR 618, 1987, https://www.canlii.org/en/ca/scc/doc/1987/1987canlii1/1987canlii1.html?resultIndex=1

R. v Pengelley. (2009) 19936 (ON SC), http://canlii.ca/t/239jh

R. v S. H. (2018) NLSC 218, https://www.canlii.org/en/nl/nlsc/doc/2018/2018nlsc218/2018nlsc218.html?searchUrlHash=AAAAAQAZUi4gdi4gUy5ILiwgMjAxOCBOTFNDIDIxOAAAAAAB&resultIndex=1

R. v Sharpe. (2001) 1 SCR 45, 2001 SCC 2, https://scc-csc.lexum.com/scc-csc/scc-csc/en/item/1837/index.do

R. v Simoes. (2014) ONCA 144, https://www.canlii.org/en/on/onca/doc/2014/2014onca144/2014onca144.html

R. v Spencer. (2014) 2 SCR 212, 2014 SCC 43, https://www.canlii.org/en/ca/scc/doc/2014/2014scc43/2014scc43.html?resultIndex=1

R. v Topham. (2017) BCSC 551 (CanLII), <https://canlii.ca/t/h3cv5>

R. *v.* Anderson, 2014 SCC 41, [2014] 2 S.C.R. 167, https://decisions.scc-csc.ca/scc-csc/scc-csc/en/item/14222/index.do

R.L. v Canada Employment Insurance Commission, 2023 SST 2056 (CanLII), https://canlii.ca/t/k5vh6

Raab, R. (November 27, 2023). Faculty pen letter pledging to defend doxxed students, including 'nonviolent direct action, up to and including arrest,' *Yale Daily News,* https://yaledailynews.com/blog/2023/11/27/faculty-pen-letter-pledging-to-defend-doxxed-students-including-nonviolent-direct-action-up-to-and-including-arrest/?utm_source=chatgpt.com

Rabinovich-Einy, O. (2003). The Ford-Firestones of the future: Resolving offline disputes in an online society. In A. Lodder et al, (Eds.). *Essays on legal and technical aspects of Online Dispute Resolution,* June 28, Edinburgh, UK, http://odrworkshop.info/odrworkshopproceedings2003.pdf

Radio-Canada. (2023). The University of Sherbrooke was the victim of a cyberattack, CBC, https://ici.radio-canada.ca/nouvelle/2033246/cyber-attaque-udes-universite-sherbrooke

Radu, J. (2014). Augmented reality in education: A meta-review and cross-media analysis. *Personal and Ubiquitous Computing*, *18*(6), 1533–1543. https://romisatriawahono.net/lecture/rm/survey/computer%20vision/Radu%20-%20Augmented%20reality%20in%20education%20-%202014.pdf. DOI: 10.1007/s00779-013-0747-y

Rawls, J. (1999). *A Theory of Justice*. Cambridge University Press. DOI: 10.4159/9780674042582

Regehr, C., Kanani, K., McFadden, J., & Saini, M. (2016). *Essential Law for Social Work Practice in Canada* (3rd ed.). Oxford University Press.

Regent University v Regent's College [2017] EUECJ T-538/15 (28 March 2017), http://www.bailii.org/eu/cases/EUECJ/2017/T53815.html

Regulation (EC) No 733/2002 Of The European Parliament And Of The Council, April 22, 2002, on the implementation of the.EU Top Level Domain, https://www.eurid.eu/files/733_2002_EN_1.pdf

Regulation Respecting Social Aid, RRQ (1981) c A-16, r 1

Reigeluth, C. M. (Ed.). (1999). *Instructional-design theories and models: A new paradigm of instructional theory* (Vol. 2). Lawrence Erlbaum Associates Publishers.

Report, O. C. (2019). A Comprehensive Guide to MOOC Providers, https://www.onlinecoursereport.com/a-comprehensive-guide-to-mooc-providers/

Reuters (2024). What countries do to regulate children's social media access, https://www.reuters.com/technology/what-countries-do-regulate-childrens-social-media-access-2024-11-28/

Ritter, K. (January 31, 2024). Nevada AG launches lawsuits against social media firms in state court, Associated Press, Las Vegas Sun, https://lasvegassun.com/news/2024/jan/31/nevada-ag-launches-go-it-alone-lawsuits-against-so/

Robbins v. Lower Merion School District 2016, Pennsylvania Eastern District Court.

Roberts, T. (2006). *Sufficiency of disclosure Council Member.* Chartered Institute of Patent Agents., www.wipo.int/meetings/en/2006/scp_of_ge_06/presentations/scp_of_ge_06_roberts.pdf

Roblyer, M. D. (2015). *Introduction to Systematic Instructional Design for Traditional, Online, and Blended Environments*. Pearson.

Rodriguez, I. (November 22, 2011). Broward Sheriff Dropping Gunshot Detection System, S. FLA. *Sun-Sentinel*, midnight), https://perma.cc/Z473-ZQ3M

Ronell, A. (2005). ArtForum, The Rodney G. King "event, https://www.artforum.com/features/avital-ronell-227724/

Rooksby, J. H. (2015). Defining Domain: Higher education's battles for cyberspace. *Brooklyn Law Review*, *80*(3). https://brooklynworks.brooklaw.edu/blr/vol80/iss3/5

Roos, F. (2003). First Come, Not Served': Domain Name Regulation in Sweden. *International Review of Law Computers & Technology*, *17*(1), 63–72. DOI: 10.1080/1360086032000063129

Rosener, J., & McAveney, S. (2006). Controlling chaos - frameworks for governing virtual relationships: Part II Substantive law issues. *Intellectual Property & Technology Law Journal*, *18*(7), 11–20.

Rule, C. (2002). *Online dispute resolution for business: For e-commerce, B2B, consumer employment, insurance and other commercial conflicts*. Jossey-Bass.

Ruskin, B. (2015). Court strikes down anti-cyberbullying law created after Rehtaeh Parsons's death, CBC News, https://www.cbc.ca/news/canada/nova-scotia/cyberbullying-law-struck-down-1.3360612

Sagduyu, Y. E., Erpek, T., Ulukus, S., & Yener, A. (2022). Vulnerabilities of deep learning-driven semantic communications to backdoor trojan attacks, arXiv:2212.11205v1 [cs.CR]

Saiz-Santos, M., Araujo-De la Mata, A., & Hoyos-Iruarrizaga, J. (2017). Entrepreneurial University: Educational Innovation and Technology Transfer, In (eds.) Marta Peris-Ortiz, Jaime Alonso GómezJosé, M. Merigó-Lindahl-Carlos, and Rueda-Armengot, (pp. 105-121), *Entrepreneurial Universities Exploring the Academic and Innovative Dimensions of Entrepreneurship in Higher Education,* Springer

Salmi, J. (2001). Tertiary education in the 21st century: Challenges and opportunities. *Higher Education, 13*(2), 105–125.

Sam, C., & van der Sijde, P. (2014). Understanding the concept of the entrepreneurial university from the perspective of higher education models. *Higher Education, 68*(6), 891–908. https://www.jstor.org/stable/43648761. DOI: 10.1007/s10734-014-9750-0

Sampson, F. (2006). Gosselin Impact Study, Women's Legal Education and Action Fund, Toronto.

Sancho, D., & Rainer, R. (2019). Sinkholing botnets, A trend micro technical paper, https://www.trendmicro.com.tr/media/misc/sinkholing-botnets-technical-paper-en.pdf

SaskTel. (2025). Be Kind Online, https://bekindonline.com/

Scamwatch (2019). Australian Competition and Consumer Commission, https://www.scamwatch.gov.au/types-of-scams/dating-romance

Schafer, B. (2008). Personal communication. School of Law. UK: University of Edinburgh.

Scherzer, A. (2019). Why is India the world capital for selfie deaths, and what's being done to stop it? ABC News, https://www.abc.net.au/news/2019-03-08/selfie-deaths-india-world-capital-killfies/10874536

Schiavetta, S. (2004). Relationship Between e-ADR and Article 6 of the European Convention of Human Rights under the Case Law of the European Court of Human Rights. *Journal of Information, Law and Technology*, (1).

Schiavetta, S., & Komaitis, K. (2003). ICANN's role in controlling information on the Internet. *International Review of Law Computers & Technology, 17*(3), 267–284. DOI: 10.1080/1360086032000174379

Schleiermacher, F. (1808). Gelegentliche Gedanken iiber Universitaten im deutschen Sinn, in: E.Anrich (1956) Die Idee der deutschen Universitdt (Darmstadt, Hermann Gentner), 219-308.

Schlott, R., & Harris, C. (2025). Hacker claims responsibility for replacing NYU's website with apparent test scores, racial epithets, *AOL*, https://www.aol.com/nyu-website-seemingly-hacked-replaced-163744158.html

Scholl, T. (2012). Augmented Reality & Education, Teacher Cadet Technology: *Blogspot,* http://teachercadettechnology.blogspot.com/2012/09/augmented-reality-education.html

Scott, J. P. (2015). Courtney Brown's suicide and the tragic effects of bullying, Canadian Living, Transcontinental Media, http://www.canadianliving.com/life/community/courtney_browns_suicide_and_the_tragic_effects_of_bullying.php#.UQ12Imtij9g.twitter

Sedgwick, W. T. (1882). On variations of reflex-excitability in the frog, induced by changes in temperature in studies from the biological laboratory, ed. pp.385-410. Newell, Martin, Johns Hopkins University, Baltimore.

Segal, M. (2015). Independent review of the police and prosecution response to the Rehtaeh Parsons case, https://novascotia.ca/segalreport/Parsons-Independent-Review.pdf

Seguin, K. (2025). Students describe a dangerous social media 'challenge' that's made its way to London, Ontario, https://www.cbc.ca/lite/story/1.7555022?feature=random

Shariff, S. & DeMartini, A. (2015). Defining the legal lines: eGirls and intimate images, https://muse.jhu.edu/pub/192/edited_volume/chapter/1579702

Sharma, R. v. 2022 SCC 39, https://canlii.ca/t/jssdp

Shea, C. (2025). The Toronto Catholic District School Board is begging students to stop blowing up their laptops, *Toronto Life,* https://torontolife.com/city/toronto-catholic-district-school-board-students-blowing-up-laptops-chromebook-challenge/

Sheehan, K. (March 17, 2017). One step closer to reclaiming university innovation from trolls, *Electronic Frontier Foundation*, https://www.eff.org/deeplinks/2017/03/were-one-step-closer-reclaiming-university-innovation-trolls

Sheehan, K., & Walsh, K. (March 30, 2017). EFF Says No to So-Called "Moral Rights" Copyright Expansion, *Electronic Frontier Foundation,* https://www.eff.org/deeplinks/2017/03/eff-says-no-so-called-moral-rights-copyright-expansion

Shieh, C. (2007). OSI Model, DoD Model and the TCP/IP Protocol Suite, https://bit.kuas.edu.tw/~csshieh/teach/np/tcpip/index.html

Short, D. (2013). AV v Bragg Communications Law's next steps: Should bullying be a tort... or even a crime? Manitaoba Law Journal, 37(1), 341-352.

Sidrata, S., & Frikhab, M. A. (2018). Impact of the manager's qualities and type of university on the development of the entrepreneurial university. *The Journal of High Technology Management Research, 29*(1), 27–34. DOI: 10.1016/j.hitech.2018.04.003

Sims, A. (2006). The public interest defence in copyright law: myth or reality? E.I.P.R., 28(6), 335-343

Singer, N. (June 26, 2022). Schools are spending billions on high-tech defence for mass shootings," *New York Times,* https://www.nytimes.com/2022/06/26/business/school-safety-technology.html

Skinner, B. (1953). *Science and human behaviour*. MacMillan.

Skinner, B. (1968). *The technology of teaching*. Appleton-Crofts.

Skinner, B. F. (1938). *The Behavior of Organisms*. Appleton-Century-Crofts.

Smaldino, S. E., & Lowther, D. L. (2007). *Instructional technology and media for Learning* (9th ed.). Prentice Hall.

Smale, A. (August 2016). Germany proposes tougher measures to combat terrorism, https://www.nytimes.com/2016/08/12/world/europe/germany-antiterrorism-measures.html

Solomon, A., & Evron, G. (September 2006). The world of botnets. *Virus Bulletin,* http://www.virusbtn.com

Solum, L. B. (2003). Virtue jurisprudence: A virtue-centred theory of judging. *Metaphilosophy, 34*(1-2), 2. DOI: 10.1111/1467-9973.00268

Southall, C., & Foderaro, A. R. (2016). Social media in the educational workplace, *Manitoba Association of School Superintendents*. Fillmore Riley LLP.

Souvenirs, C. (2019). University of Oxford, https://graces-accessories-uk.myshopify.com/collections/cambridge-souvineers/souvenir

SS8 Networks. (December 2007). The ready guide to intercept legislation: Germany, https://www.ss8.com/ready-guide.php

Staff (August 2006). Colin Rule. Workout Business Processes, http://www.ework-out.co.uk/

Staff (March 2006). Canada backs Sikh dagger rights. BBC News, http://news.bbc.co.uk/2/hi/americas/4770744.stm

Staff Outlaw News. (November 2006). Swiss government may tap VoIP calls, OUT-LAW News, https://www.out-law.com/page-7379-theme=print

Staff The Local. (January 2015). Austria's €290m plan to fight terror, *The Local*, https://www.thelocal.at/20150121/austrias-290m-plan-to-fight-terror

Staff. (March 2008). ICANN CEO welcomes concerns as NTIA weighs role, *Telecommunications Reports, 74*(6), 6-7.

Stanford University v. Roche Molecular Systems, Inc., 563 U.S. 776 (2011), https://supreme.justia.com/cases/federal/us/563/776/

Stanley, J. (2012). Video analytics: A brain behind the eye? *ACLU,* https://www.aclu.org/news/national-security/video-analytics-brain-behind-eye

Stansberry, K., Anderson, J., & Rainie, L. (2019). The Internet will continue to make life better, *Pew Research Center,* https://www.pewresearch.org/internet/2019/10/28/4-the-internet-will-continue-to-make-life-better/

Statute of Anne (1710). The first copyright act, U.K. Parliament, 8 Anne c.21 1709, Jeremy Norman's History of Information, https://www.historyofinformation.com/detail.php?entryid=3389

Stoltz, M., & Noble, T. (August 28, 2024). Copyright is not a tool to silence critics of religious education, *Electronic Frontier Foundation,* https://www.eff.org/deeplinks/2024/08/copyright-not-tool-silence-critics-religious-education

StopCyberbullying. (2025). Don't Stand By, Stand Up, http://www.stopcyberbullying.org/index2.html

Student Union Lettings Limited v Essex Student Lets Limited [2018] EWHC 419 (IPEC) (07 March 2018), http://www.bailii.org/ew/cases/EWHC/IPEC/2018/419.html

Studyportals (2025). Master's degrees in Cyber Security in Canada, *Studyportals,* https://www.mastersportal.com/search/master/cyber-security/canada

Sulleyman, A. (2017). Facebook is 'destroying' society and making users feel 'vacant and empty,' former exec says, *The Independent*, https://www.independent.co.uk/life-style/gadgets-and-tech/news/facebook-society-destroy-social-media-network-users-damage-communicate-connect-chamath-palihapitiya-a8105131.html

Sweller, J. (2005). Implications of cognitive load theory for multimedia learning. In Mayer, R. E. (Ed.), *Cambridge Handbook Of Multimedia Learning* (pp. 19–30). Cambridge University Press. DOI: 10.1017/CBO9780511816819.003

Systrom, K., & Krieger, M. (2010). Instagram, https://www.instagram.com/

Tate Legal and Copyright Department. (2007). Digitization and Conservation: Overview of Copyright and Moral Rights in UK Law, in *Tate Papers*, no.8, https://www.tate.org.uk/research/publications/tate-papers/08/digitisation-and-conservation-overview-of-copyright-and-moral-rights-in-uk-law

TEACH Act (2002). Technology, Education, and Copyright Harmonization, An act to amend chapter 1 of title 17, United States Code, https://web.archive.org/web/20070404164532/http://www.ala.org/washoff/teach.html

Technology Transfer. What you need to know about protecting patent rights (2007). WIPO, www.lbl.gov/tech-transfer/researchers/NEO_Patent_RPC_20071220.pdf

The eGirls Project (3 June 2015). https://egirlsproject.ca/the-project/what-we-are/

Thomson, I. (October 22, 2024). Major publishers sue Perplexity AI for scraping without paying, *The Register,* https://www.theregister.com/2024/10/22/publishers_sue_perplexity_ai/

Thorndike, E. L. (1901). Animal intelligence: An experimental study of the associative processes in animals. *Psychological Review Monograph*, (Supplement, 2), 1–109.

Tichý, J. & Rehák, S. (2025). Abolishment of the professor's privilege and its impact on the university patent quality, *Ekonomika a spoločnosť, 26*(1), 142-152.

Tichy, N. M., & Ulrich, D. O. (1984). The leadership challenge: A call for the transformational leader, *MIT Sloan Management Review,* https://sloanreview.mit.edu/article/the-leadership-challenge-a-call-for-the-transformational-leader/

Tilmann, W. (2006). Harmonization of invalidity and scope-of-protection practice of national courts of EPC Member States. *European Intellectual Property Review, 28*(3), 169–173.

Tinker v. Des Moines Independent Community School District (1969). https://www.oyez.org/cases/1968/21

Todd, M. (1995). The new United Kingdom trademarks law. *World Patent Information, 17*(1), 24–28.

Toulmin, S. (1958). *The uses of argument*. Cambridge University Press.

Townley, G. (2017). What's in a name? Trade marks explained. Podcast by the UK Intellectual Property Office on SoundCloud, https://soundcloud.com/user-24788401

Trade Marks Act. 1994, s.1 Legislation.gov.uk, https://www.legislation.gov.uk/ukpga/1994/26/contents

Turnbull, F. (2014). The morality of mash-ups: Moral rights and Canada's non-commercial user-generated content exception. *Intellectual Property Journal.*

Tweedie, R., & Mengersen, K. (1999). Calculating accuracy rates from multiple assessors with limited information. *The American Statistician, 53*(3), 233–238. DOI: 10.1080/00031305.1999.10474465

U.S. Attorney's Office. (2017). Russian Citizen who Helped Develop the "Citadel" Malware Toolkit is Sentenced, U.S. Attorney's Office, Northern District of Georgia, *U.S. Department of Justice,* https://www.justice.gov/usao-ndga/pr/russian-citizen-who-helped-develop-citadel-malware-toolkit-sentenced-0

U.S. Department of Commerce (April 2008). National Telecommunications and Information Administration, ICANN. A statement on the Mid-Term Review of the Joint Project Agreement (JPA) Between NTIA and ICANN, Washington, DC,

U.S. Dept of Education. (April 2022), Institute of Education, National Center for Education Statistics (NCES), https://nces.ed.gov/programs/digest/d21/tables/dt21_214.30.asp?current=yes

U.S. Dept of State. (2016). Country reports on terrorism, https://www.state.gov/j/ct/rls/crt/2016/272231.htm

UK Copyright Service. (2000). UK Copyright Law, Factsheet No. P-01, https://www.copyrightservice.co.uk/ukcs/docs/edupack.pdf

UKIPO. (2025). UK Intellectual Property Office, Trademarks, https://www.gov.uk/government/collections/intellectual-property-trade-marks

UNCITRAL. (2025). United Nations Commission on International Trade Law, https://uncitral.un.org/

United Kingdom's Human Rights Act (1998). https://www.legislation.gov.uk/ukpga/1998/42/contents

United Nations. (2024). Department of Economic and Social Affairs Statistics, *United Nations Statistics Division,* https://unstats.un.org/UNSDWebsite/

United States Constitution, (1789). https://guides.loc.gov/constitution

United States Patent and Trademark Office (April 2008) Anticybersquatting Consumer Protection Act of 1999, s 3006, https://www.uspto.gov/web/offices/dcom/olia/tmcybpiracy/repcongress.pdf

United States Secret Service. (2024). Network Intrusions and Ransomware, Investigations, https://www.secretservice.gov/investigations

United States v Baratov. (2017) ONCA 481, http://canlii.ca/t/h46t7

United States v. Ellis, 206 U.S. 246 (1907), https://supreme.justia.com/cases/federal/us/206/246/

United States v. Lambis, 197 F. Supp. 3d 606, 609 (S.D.N.Y. 2016), https://case-law.vlex.com/vid/united-states-v-lambis-893647076

University and College Union. (2019), UCU Brexit Update, https://www.ucu.org.uk/

University of California at Berkeley. (2019). Student Organization Domain Name Guidelines, https://lead.berkeley.edu/wp-content/uploads/2014/12/student-org-domain-guidelines.pdf

University of Virginia Student Council. (2019). FAQs about Domain Names, http://www.student.virginia.edu/domains.php#6

USPTO. (2007). Pilot concerning public submission of peer-reviewed prior art, Commissioner for Patents John J. Doll, United States Patent and Trademark Office, https://www.uspto.gov/web/offices/com/sol/og/2007/week26/patsuba.htm

USPTO. (2025). United States Patent and Trademark Office, https://www.uspto.gov/

Utah State Legislature. (2023). Utah Social Media Regulation Act, https://le.utah.gov/~2023/bills/static/SB0152.html

v Stevenson, D. [1932] A.C. 562. Legal Case Summary, *LawTeacher,* https://www.lawteacher.net/cases/donoghue-v-stevenson.php

Vaciago, G., & Ramalho, D. (2016). The use of Trojans and other types of malware as means of obtaining evidence in criminal proceedings, *Digital Evidence and Electronic Signature Law Review, 13*, 88-96, https://journals.sas.ac.uk/deeslr/article/viewFile/2299/2252

Van Brunt, A.V. & Anand, E. (2025). Police abuse: Finch v. Rapp, *Roderick & Solange MacArthur Justice Center,* media@macarthurjustice.org

van Dongen, P., Yergos, A., Tijssen, R., & Claassen, E. (2017). The relationships between university IP regimes, scientists' motivations and their engagement with research commercialization in Europe. *European Journal of Law and Technology, 8*(2).

VARA (1990).Visual Artists Rights Act 17 U.S. Code § 106A, Rights of certain authors to attribution and integrity, Cornell Law School, https://www.law.cornell.edu/uscode/text/17/106A

Varas, C. (2008). Virtual protection: Applying trade-mark law within virtual worlds such as Second Life, *Entertainment. Law Review*, *19*(1), 5–11.

Veeam Software. (2024). Building a cyber-resilient data recovery strategy, https://webobjects2.cdw.com/is/content/CDW/cdw/on-domain-cdw/brands/veeam/veeam-nist-security-white-paper-cdw.pdf?ci=8722

Verza, S. (2018). SLAPP: The background of 'Strategic Lawsuits Against Public Participation,' *European Centre for Press and Media Freedom,* 18 July, https://www.ecpmf.eu/news/legal/slapp-the-background-of-strategic-lawsuits-against-public-participation

Vinje, T. (1995). Harmonizing intellectual property laws in the European Union: Past, present and future. *European Intellectual Property Review*, *17*(8), 361–377.

von Humboldt, W. (1810). On the internal and external organization of the higher scientific institutions in Berlin, *German History in Documents and Images,* https://ghdi.ghi-dc.org/sub_document.cfm?document_id=3642

Waelde, C., & Edwards, L. (April 2005). Online intermediaries and liability for copyright infringement, A report to the WIPO Seminar on Copyright and Internet Intermediaries.

Waelde, C. (2007). Database copyright: the story of *BHB*. In Torremans, P. (Ed.), *Copyright Law: A Handbook of Contemporary Research*. Edward Elgar Publishing.

Wagner, J. (July 2007). Second Life Avatar sued for copyright infringement. Giga Omni Media, Inc., http://gigaom.com/2007/07/04/second-life-avatar-sued-for-copyright-infringement/

Walcott, R. v. (K.L.), [2008] O.T.C. 97 (SupCt), https://ca.vlex.com/vid/r-v-walcott-k-680633937

Walsh, E.J. & DiPietrantonio, H.J. (2011). Getting the most value from patent claims, *Intellectual Property & Technology Law Journal, 23*(7).

Walton, D., & Godden, D. (2005). Persuasion dialogue in online dispute resolution. *Artificial Intelligence and Law*, *13*(2), 273–295. DOI: 10.1007/s10506-006-9014-0

Waluchow, W. (2014). "Constitutionalism", *The Stanford Encyclopedia of Philosophy (Spring),* Edward N. Zalta (ed.), https://plato.stanford.edu/archives/spr2014/entries/constitutionalism/

WCT (1996). WIPO Copyright Treaty, https://www.wipo.int/treaties/en/ip/wct/summary_wct.html#:~:text=The%20WIPO%20Copyright%20Treaty%20(WCT)%20is%20a%20special%20agreement%20under,authors%20in%20the%20digital%20environment

Weatherall, K. (2009). It is not just competitors: Acknowledging and accommodating 'interfering busybodies' and their challenges to patent validity. *The Journal of World Intellectual Property*, *12*(5, 5z), 500–523. DOI: 10.1111/j.1747-1796.2009.00372.x

Webroot (March 2019). Types of Trojan Horse software, https://www.webroot.com/us/en/resources/tips-articles/what-is-trojan-virus

Welch, H. L. (2008). The experimental use exception and undergraduate engineering projects. *Marquette Intellectual Property Law Review*, *12*(2), 409–436.

Wendling, M. (December 10, 2014). #BBCtrending: Twitter declares 2014 the year of the 'selfie', BBC News.

Westermann, H., Savelka, J., & Benyekhlef, K. (2023). LLMediator: GPT-4 Assisted Online Dispute Resolution, *Workshop on Artificial Intelligence for Access to Justice,* Braga, Portugal. June 19.

Wikipedia. (2019). Internet protocol suite, TCP/IP, https://en.wikipedia.org/wiki/Internet_protocol_suite

Wikipedia. Priority date, WIPO, https://en.wikipedia.org/wiki/Priority_right

Wikipedia. World Trade Organization, https://en.wikipedia.org/wiki/World_Trade_Organization

Wilburn, C. (2025). Houston-area schools warn parents about Chromebook Challenge damaging school property, *Houston Chronicle,* https://www.houstonchronicle.com/news/houston-texas/trending/article/tiktok-chromebook-challenge-houston-schools-20321671.php

Willinsky, J. (2006). The properties of Locke's common-wealth of learning, Policy Futures in Education, 4(4), 348-364.

Winograd, T., & Flores, F. (1986). *Understanding computers and cognition: A new foundation for design*. Addison-Wesley.

WIPO (1967, 1979). Article 10, Convention Establishing the World Intellectual Property Organization, https://www.wipo.int/wipolex/en/text/283854

WIPO Arbitration and Mediation Center (2006). *McDonald's Corporation v. Easy Property*, Case D2006-1142, https://www.wipo.int/amc/en/domains/decisions/html/2006/d2006-1142.html

WIPO Guide to Intellectual Property Worldwide. WIPO, https://www.wipo.int/about-ip/en/ipworldwide/treaties.htm

WIPO. (2008) Expert determination, https://www.wipo.int/portal/en/index.html

WIPO. (2019). Summary of the Nice Agreement Concerning the International Classification of Goods and Services for the Registration of Marks (1957), https://www.wipo.int/treaties/en/classification/nice/summary_nice.html

WIPO. (June 2008). ADR Procedures, https://www.wipo.int/amc/en/center/wipo-adr.html

WIPO. (March 2008). DNS Developments Feed Growing Cybersquatting Concerns, The WIPO Press Room, https://www.wipo.int/pressroom/en/articles/2008/article_0015.html

WIPO. https://www.wipo.int/portal/index.html.en

Wissler, R., & Rak, R. (2004). Assessing mediator performance: The usefulness of participant questionnaires. *Journal of Dispute Resolution*, 229.

World Trade Organization. WIPO, http://www.wto.org:80/

Ying, T.-M. (2019). The evolution of mobile banking trojans, Symantec, https://medium.com/threat-intel/the-evolution-of-mobile-banking-trojans-608625c79143

Yorke, C. (March 7, 2016). Understanding adverse effect discrimination, MacDonald & Associates, https://macdonaldassociates.ca/2016/03/07/understanding-adverse-effect-discrimination/

Young Offenders Act, R.S.C. (1985), *c. Y-1,* https://laws.justice.gc.ca/PDF/Y-1.pdf

Yurkowski, R. A. (2001). Is *Hyde Park* hiding the truth? An analysis of the public interest defence to copyright infringement. *Victoria University of Wellington Law Review*, *32*(4), 1053–1086. https://www.victoria.ac.nz/__data/assets/pdf_file/0004/838309/Yurkowski.pdf. DOI: 10.26686/vuwlr.v32i4.5857

Zazzle Cambridge College T-Shirts. (2019). Oxfart University, https://www.zazzle.ca/oxfart_university_crest_t_shirt-235174744088935669

Zondag, B., & Lodder, A. (2007). Constructing computer-assisted dispute resolution systems by developing a generic language to analyze information exchange in conflict discourse. *International Review of Law Computers & Technology*, *21*(2), 191–205. DOI: 10.1080/13600860701492203

Zorz, Z. (2012). Cross-platform Wirenet Trojan targets Mac and Linux users, HelpNetSecurity, https://www.helpnetsecurity.com/2012/08/30/cross-platform-wirenet-trojan-targets-mac-and-linux-users/

Zuckerberg, M. (6 March 2021). A privacy-focused vision for social networking, Facebook, https://www.facebook.com/notes/mark-zuckerberg/a-privacy-focused-vision-for-social-networking/10156700570096634/

Zuckerberg, M., Saverin, E., McCollum, A., Moskovitz, D. & Hughes, C. (2004). Facebook, computer platform.

About the Author

Bruce L. Mann is a Professor of Education at Memorial University in Canada. Professor Mann has been a visiting researcher with the Faculty of Science at Memorial, the Department of Educational Psychology at McGill University in Canada, and with the School of Interactive Multimedia at Edith Cowan University in Australia. Professor Mann's studies of web course behavior and learning from multimedia speech prompting have been cited in many textbooks, international journals and conference presentations. His first book Perspectives in Web Course Management has earned him international recognition.

Index

A

Academic domain name 277, 290, 294
Access Control 61
Accuracy in Media 95
ACLU national study 76
Action Plan for Security 43
Active Cyber Defence 25
Adverse discrimination effect 159
Adverse effects discrimination 159, 170, 172
Adverse impact discrimination 159
After-the-Hack 46
Age-based discrimination, yet again 167
Ageism 165
Aggressive Cyber Defence 25
American Civil Liberties Union (ACLU) 80
American Institute in Taiwan 25
American schools cyberattacked 2
Amnesty International 47, 50
An Act to Amend the Education Act, SNB 133
Andrews v. Law Society of British Columbia 166, 172
Anglo-American model 317
Anglo-Saxon model 316, 317
Annotated screen recordings 208
Anns v. Merton London Borough Council 115
Anti-SLAPP 224
Applied Intelligence 45
Arbitration 180, 181, 182, 191, 192, 202, 209, 211, 212, 215, 281, 282, 283, 288, 289, 296, 298
Arbitration providers 281
Association of University Teachers 229, 248
Audio-visual developer 235
Automated negotiation 181, 182
Awareness-raising 14, 36, 38, 43

B

Bad faith 288
Badge of origin 253, 255, 277, 294
Bark 62, 63, 69
BBC News 20, 24, 42, 50, 112, 127, 194, 291, 295
BC Teachers' Federation 132, 152
Be Kind Online 135, 156
Belief-Desire-Intention Model of Reasoning 185
Berne Convention 222, 223, 225, 248
Berufsbildungszentrum 48
Bill C-13, the Protecting Canadians from Online Crime Act 137
Bitly 30
Black Hat USA 34
Boiled Frog 312
Botnet 5, 10, 11, 36, 42
Brexit 251, 293, 300
BT and others v One in a Million Ltd 285

C

Campus Accountability Campaign 95
Canadian Centre for Child Protection 131, 153, 154
Card v. Ontario Ministry of Training, Colleges & Universities 166
CCH Canadian Ltd. v. Law Society 231, 248
Certified Ethical Hacker 35, 51
Charlie Hebdo attacks 48
Charter of Fundamental Rights of the European Union 118, 125
ChatGPT 110, 111, 125, 176
Children's Online Privacy Protection Act (COPPA) 69, 122, 125
Civil law 230, 255
Coalition of the willing 83
Code of Criminal Procedure 41, 45
College of Policing 39, 51
Communications Monitoring 63
Community Work Program 161
Concatenated scores of online presentations 210
Content provider 235, 236
Cooperation Group 38

Coping strategies 137, 150
Copyfraud 224, 250
Copyright 99, 194, 214, 221, 222, 223, 224, 225, 226, 227, 228, 229, 230, 231, 232, 233, 234, 235, 236, 237, 238, 247, 248, 249, 250, 251, 252, 255, 258, 260, 267, 271, 275, 291, 298, 304, 322
Copyright Designs and Patents Act 227, 230
Copyright Modernization Act 231, 248
Council of Europe 46, 51, 125
Council of the European Union 38
Counselling suicide 138, 146
Counter-Cyberterrorism 11, 14, 23, 33, 43
Counterfeiting 255, 267
Counterterrorism 45, 48
Counterterrorism and Applied Intelligence 45
Course author 235
Coursera 264, 274
Covering tracks 31, 149
Criminal Code of Canada 130, 138, 139, 140, 141
Criminal Harassment 138, 141, 142
Cyberattack types 3
Cyberbullying 62, 83, 88, 94, 106, 108, 111, 119, 121, 129, 131, 132, 133, 134, 135, 136, 137, 138, 139, 141, 142, 143, 144, 145, 146, 148, 149, 152, 153, 155, 156, 204, 277
Cyberbullying Legislation 137
Cyberbullying Prevention 132, 155
Cyber Defense Committee 48
Cybergendarmes 42
Cyberspace Administration of China 92
Cybersquatting 277, 282, 283, 285, 289, 292, 293, 295, 296, 298
Cybertip.ca 131, 153

D

Daguerreotype 101
Database copyright 237, 238, 251
Database of coursework 237
Data Protection Regulation in Europe 37
Data Retention and Acquisition Regulations 39
Date of infringement 306
Declaration of Independence 222, 248
Defamatory Libel 138, 148
Design guidelines 15, 238
Diamonique Corporation v. Maison Tropicale S.A 285
Differential treatment 163
Digital Crime-Fighting Centre 42
Digital Millennium Copyright Act (DMCA) 225, 232
Distributed Denial of Service (DDoS) 1, 4, 10
District of Columbia Court of Appeals 66
Doctrine of Equivalents 299, 307, 324
Domain kiting 181, 193, 284, 285, 297
Domain name front-running 284
Domain Name Registrar (DNR) 278, 279, 284
Domain Name Speculating 288
Domain Name System (DNS) 277, 281, 286, 287, 291, 292, 293
Domain tasting 283, 285, 296, 297
Donoghue v Stevenson 114, 115, 124, 153
Doxing 83, 93, 94, 95, 97, 107, 110
droit d'auteur 230, 233

E

EC Directive 229, 279
Education 2, 3, 14, 16, 36, 38, 43, 44, 51, 70, 75, 81, 116, 117, 118, 120, 125, 133, 134, 135, 136, 154, 155, 160, 161, 164, 168, 169, 171, 173, 192, 202, 209, 212, 213, 214, 215, 223, 224, 226, 227, 228, 229, 230, 231, 236, 246, 247, 248, 249, 250, 251, 254, 259, 260, 262, 273, 279, 282, 291, 293, 294, 295, 296, 297, 310, 312, 314, 315, 316, 317, 323, 324, 325, 326, 327
Educational initiatives 113, 137
Education & Early Childhood Development 133
Education Program 161
edX 264, 274
Effectiveness evaluation 191, 206, 212
Electronic Frontier Foundation (EFF) 79,

80, 122, 124, 126, 127, 154, 227, 250, 251, 321, 324, 325, 327
Employment Standards Act 168
Enabling disclosure 299, 306
Endoxa 185, 186
End-Users 236
Entrepreneurial university 299, 302, 310, 311, 314, 323, 324, 326, 327
Equity 159, 170, 171
EuroDNS 279, 296
European Convention on Human Rights (ECHR) 40, 116, 225
European Court of Human Rights 40, 52, 194, 237
European Parliament 21, 35, 38, 51, 53, 249, 275
European standards 32
European Union Agency for Cybersecurity 43, 52
European Union Agency for Network and Information Security (ENISA) 38
European Union Coalition 38
European Union Intellectual Property Office (EUIPO) 262, 263, 265, 268, 273
Executive Attention Network 198, 199, 211
Expert-peer assessment formula 209, 309
Expert-peer online assessment 206, 207, 208

F

Facebook 72, 81, 84, 85, 88, 89, 99, 100, 106, 107, 111, 112, 117, 123, 127, 130, 133, 136, 142, 148, 151, 152, 155
Facial Recognition 60, 61, 63, 75
Fact-checking 123, 125
Fair use 226, 227, 256, 257, 259, 260, 261
Fast Flux network 28
Federal Court of Justice 44
Federal Office for Cybersecurity 49
Financial Action Task Force (FATF) 36
Firewall 8, 48
Flickr 102
Footprinting 35
Forms of lawful protection 236, 237
Four models of higher education 314
French Code of Criminal Procedure 41
Friendster 105, 110
Front-running 284, 296

G

Gaggle 63, 69
Gaining access 30, 149
Gender Inequality 165
General Data Protection Regulation (GDPR) 37
German Constitutional Court 45
Global village 83
GoDaddy 284, 288, 292, 293
Government of the Northwest Territories (GNWT) 136, 154
Government overreach 120, 127, 138
GPT-4 176, 194
Gramm-Leach-Bliley Act (GLBA) 13
Gunshot detection and analytics 74

H

Hack Back 24, 44, 51
Hacker Lab Modules 35
Hacking Back 14, 24, 25, 52, 53
Hacking then and now 23
Harms 69, 75, 105, 122, 123
Hart's categories 180
Hate speech 4, 116, 123
Health Insurance Portability and Accountability Act (HIPAA) 13
hijacking 35, 288, 292, 293, 297
Hörnle's categories 180
HS Swiss Training Security 49
Human Rights Tribunal of Ontario 166
Humboldtian model 315, 316

I

Identity fraud 138, 143, 144
Incentivized university 311
Inciting hatred 138, 141
Injection 24
Instagram 72, 74, 81, 85, 86, 88, 89, 99, 100, 101, 103, 104, 108, 123, 127, 130, 135, 151, 154

Instructional design 19, 49, 200, 215, 235, 236, 274
Intellectual Property Office 259, 260, 261, 262, 263, 265, 268, 269, 273, 275, 303, 318, 324
Intelligence Services Act 40, 52
Internal Security Agency (ISA) 46, 47
Internet Assigned Numbers Authority (IANA) 286, 287
Internet Corporation for Assigned Names and Numbers (ICANN) 37, 280, 292
Internet Service Provider (ISP) 84, 137, 236, 279
Intimate Images & Cyber-Protection Act 133
Intimidation 137, 138, 142, 224, 267
Inventive step 300, 306
Investigatory Powers Act 21, 39, 138, 154
Investigatory Powers Tribunal 40, 55
Italian Criminal Procedure 46

J

Jurisdiction 24, 69, 221, 225

K

Kids in the Know 131, 154
Kids Online Safety Act (KOSA) 113, 121, 122, 125, 126, 127, 153, 154
Killfies 102, 103, 104, 111
Kirpan dispute 203, 207, 210
KOSA Criticism 122

L

Labour theory of property 221
Lanham Act 257
Law Commission of Ontario 168, 172
Law of Effect 311
Law's Test 159, 162
Learning Management System 15, 221, 235, 237, 250, 304
Legal initiatives 113, 118, 129
LeLievre v. Gould 109
Lesson enhancement 239, 240
Liberal education 316
LLMediator 176, 194
Logo 255, 256, 257, 259, 260, 262, 268, 272
Lone Ranger 221, 226, 228, 230, 234, 235, 236, 247
Luring 140, 141

M

MAC address 27, 31
Mahanoy Area School District v. B.L 62, 80
Malware 1, 3, 4, 7, 8, 9, 10, 11, 17, 20, 24, 25, 26, 28, 29, 35, 37, 43, 44, 45, 48, 53, 55, 282, 293
Manitoba Bill 214 Cyberbullying Prevention Act 132
Massive Open Online Course (MOOC) 263
MediaSmarts 131, 155
Mediation 176, 177, 179, 180, 181, 182, 183, 191, 282, 283, 288, 289, 296, 298
Ministry for Europe and Foreign Affairs 41, 53
Monitoring Software 62
Moral panic 57, 76, 79, 121, 126, 154
Moral Rights of the author 221, 232, 233, 234
Motion's categories 181
Mr. Clever 95
Multi-disciplinary curricula 317
MyLeanMBA, 2017 264

N

Napoleonic model 316
National Cybersecurity Strategy of the Czech Republic 19, 43, 55
National Intelligence Center for Counter-Terrorism and Organized Crime (CITCO) 48
National Police and Civil Guard 48
National Police Chiefs' Council 39
National Trojan Registry 46
Negative discrimination 165
Negative law 163
Negative right 116, 164
Negligence 88, 113, 114, 115, 119, 124, 129, 130
Neighbour principle 115

Network 4, 9, 10, 11, 13, 20, 21, 23, 24, 25, 26, 27, 28, 29, 30, 31, 35, 37, 38, 39, 40, 42, 44, 50, 51, 52, 55, 97, 109, 111, 129, 131, 132, 133, 134, 136, 155, 184, 198, 199, 211, 215, 248, 269, 274, 278, 279, 280, 281, 286
Network and Information Security in Society 38, 44
New Brunswick's Education Act 133
Nominet UK 278
No-selfie zones 105, 107
Nudification 101, 108

O

ODR online assessment 206
Oklahoma Admin. Code § 210:20-29-5 119, 127
Online Dispute Resolution (ODR) 175, 176, 177, 178, 179, 180, 181, 187, 188, 191, 192, 193, 194, 197, 203, 207, 210, 211, 213, 214, 215, 216, 281, 326
Online learning environment 239, 243
Online monitoring 69
Ontario Ministry of Education 134, 155
Ontario Works Act 168
Open Systems Interconnection Reference Model (OSI) 26
Operant Conditioning 311
Operational analysis 36
Operation Avalanche 36, 37, 51
Original expression 230, 237, 271
Overlapping terminology 181
Ownership 221, 226, 232, 236, 273, 283, 285, 293, 313, 322

P

Paisley Snail 113, 114, 124, 127
Paris Convention for the Protection of Industrial Property 274
Passing Off 263, 265, 285
Patent 105, 202, 208, 212, 213, 215, 256, 265, 275, 289, 298, 299, 300, 301, 302, 303, 304, 305, 306, 307, 308, 309, 310, 311, 312, 313, 316, 317, 318, 320, 321, 322, 323, 324, 325, 326, 327, 328
Patent troll 321
Peer-To-Patent 308, 309, 325
Penetration testers 30
Pen registers 12, 67
Pen Register Statute 66
Pen test 30, 31
Person Having Ordinary Skill in the Art (PHOSITA) 306
Phase Theory 239, 249
Phishing 4, 14, 23, 25, 26, 28, 29, 52, 94, 97, 277, 282, 292, 293
Placating the listener 185
Posse 221, 226, 228, 230, 234, 236, 237, 247
Preparing Judges and Prosecutors 43
Preparing School-Age Students 43
Preparing University Students 44
Prince Jones v. United States 65, 68
Prior art 202, 306, 308, 309, 317, 328
Priority 265, 269, 299, 301, 306, 324, 328
Priority date 299, 306, 328
Privacy 12, 13, 14, 20, 21, 31, 40, 47, 57, 58, 67, 68, 69, 75, 76, 84, 97, 107, 110, 112, 113, 119, 121, 122, 125, 127, 132, 137, 138, 151, 155, 214, 221, 225, 238, 292, 293
Protecting the global financial system 36
Proximity 115
Purposive construction 299, 305

Q

Quebec's Social Assistance Program 161

R

Ransomware 1, 2, 3, 4, 5, 11, 13, 14, 18, 19, 20, 24, 31, 37, 40, 41, 42, 49, 53, 55
Rater's experience 211
Rater's skill level 211
Reclaim invention 321
Reconnaissance 29, 35, 149
Reddit 102
Regent University v. Regent's College, 2017 269
Registrars Network Solutions, LLC 278
Regulation Respecting Social Aid, RRQ

162, 173
Reinforcement Theory 311, 323
Remote video monitoring 75
Reposting liability 99
Resolution Systems Institute 188, 191
Resource-based learning 239, 240, 243
Reward Theory of Intellectual Property 310
Richards v Investigatory Powers 40, 55
Rights-holder 235, 236
R.L. v Canada Employment Insurance Commission 166, 173
Robbins v. Lower Merion School District 75, 81
Root node owner 280
Root server operator 287
Root zone file 280, 281, 287
Rosener-McAveney's Spectrum 179
R. v. Bedi 64, 65
R. v. Pengelley 134

S

Safe Schools Plan 136
Scanning 23, 30, 33, 35, 149, 198
Schengen Information System 48
Schools for Social Media Change 93, 130
School shootings 58, 59, 70, 72, 73, 76
Science as a unit 315
Screen time 92, 109
Securly 63
Sextortion 144, 145
Shadowbanning 83, 99, 100, 101, 108
Shopkeeper's expertise 255
Sinkholing 36, 54
SLAPP 224, 251, 253, 267, 275
Social engineering 14, 23, 29, 30, 35
Social Media 15, 48, 58, 62, 63, 69, 71, 72, 78, 80, 83, 84, 85, 86, 87, 88, 89, 91, 93, 94, 95, 99, 101, 103, 105, 106, 107, 108, 109, 110, 111, 113, 116, 117, 118, 119, 120, 121, 122, 123, 124, 125, 127, 128, 129, 130, 135, 137, 142, 143, 146, 148, 150, 151, 152, 157, 176, 204
Social media addiction 87, 88, 109
Social sentinel 58, 62, 63
Source code 46
Sovereign power 165
Spanish Criminal Code 48
Spear-phishing 29
Speculating 288
Standard of Care 115, 130
State Trojans 45
Statute of Anne 222, 251
Stingrays 64
Strategic Lawsuit Against Public Participation (SLAPP) 224, 253, 267
Student design projects 317
Sui generis right 238
Supreme Court of Canada 129, 163, 165, 167, 168, 171, 231
Surveillance 1, 6, 39, 44, 46, 49, 57, 58, 59, 60, 61, 63, 67, 70, 74, 75, 76, 79, 80, 120, 127, 138, 286
Surveillance culture in schools 76
Surveillance technology 57, 59, 61, 70, 76
Swatting 83, 97, 98, 108
Swiss Department of the Environment, Transport, Energy and Communications 49
Swiss Surveillance Act 49
Syllogism 185, 187
Synchronous 176, 182, 183, 188, 197

T

Taking Stock of Cyberbullying: A Scan of the PEI Context 134, 153
TCP 21, 27, 28, 54, 55
Telecommunication Act 47
Territorial School Code of Conduct 136
Tinker v. Des Moines Independent Community School District 63, 81
TinyURL 30
Top-level domains (gTLDs) 278, 281, 286, 287, 288, 294, 296
Trademark 105, 181, 253, 254, 255, 256, 257, 258, 259, 260, 261, 262, 264, 265, 266, 267, 268, 269, 270, 271, 272, 273, 274, 275, 277, 280, 282, 283, 285, 288, 289, 291, 294, 298, 304, 313, 323, 328
Trademark counterfeiting 267
Trademark Duration 264

Trademark Parody 254, 257, 270, 273
Trademark Routes 266
Trade Marks Act of 1994 265
Trade-Related Aspects of Intellectual Property Rights (TRIPS) 225
Training Methods 11, 14, 43
Trojan Horse 1, 5, 6, 8, 13, 14, 15, 18, 20, 49, 149
Trojans in the news 5
Twickelerveld Intelligence and Investigations 45
Twitter 85, 100, 111, 112, 135, 257
Typosquatting 283, 295, 297

U

Udacity 264, 274
UDRP 181, 282, 283, 285, 286, 288
U.K. High Court 39
U.K. Trademark Duration 264
Unequal bargaining 198
Unified Patent Court (UPC) 301
Uniform Dispute Resolution Procedure (UDRP) 181, 285
United States v. Ellis 66, 81
University and College Union (UCU) 229, 251
Unregistered trademark 294
U.S. Copyright Office 226, 227, 304
U.S. Electronic Communications Privacy Act 12
User interface 16, 237
User moderation 123
U.S. Immigration and Customs Enforcement (ICE) 66
U.S. legal framework to address cyberattacks 11
U.S. Patent and Trademark Office (USPTO) 105
Utility patent 318
Uttering threats 138, 142

V

Vice Society Ransomware Group 49
Vintage Brand, LLC 253
Vocational Training Center 48, 53

W

Weapon detection 70
Web filtering 69, 70
WhatsApp 106, 123, 151
What's the problem? 84
White Hat attacking 35
WHOIS 286, 292, 293
WIPO Arbitration and Mediation Center 282, 288, 289, 296, 298
WIPO Copyright Treaty (WCT) 223, 251
WIPO's Categories 180
Wissenschaft 315
World Intellectual Property Organization (WIPO) 180, 223, 225, 252

Y

Young Offenders Act 130, 157
YouTube 21, 72, 78, 86, 88, 89, 107, 204, 229, 231

www.ingramcontent.com/pod-product-compliance
Lightning Source LLC
Chambersburg PA
CBHW080511171025
34126CB00005B/18
9798337331263